Seizing Opportunities

Monographs in Baptist History

VOLUME 36

SERIES EDITOR
Michael A. G. Haykin, The Southern Baptist Theological Seminary

EDITORIAL BOARD
Matthew Barrett, Midwestern Baptist Theological Seminary
Peter Beck, Charleston Southern University
Anthony L. Chute, California Baptist University
Jason G. Duesing, Midwestern Baptist Theological Seminary
Nathan A. Finn, North Greenville University
Crawford Gribben, Queen's University, Belfast
Gordon L. Heath, McMaster Divinity College
Barry Howson, Heritage Theological Seminary
Jason K. Lee, Cedarville University
Thomas J. Nettles, The Southern Baptist Theological Seminary, retired
James A. Patterson, Union University
James M. Renihan, Institute of Reformed Baptist Studies
Jeffrey P. Straub, Independent Scholar
Brian R. Talbot, Broughty Ferry Baptist Church, Scotland
Malcolm B. Yarnell III, Southwestern Baptist Theological Seminary

Ours is a day in which not only the gaze of western culture but also increasingly that of Evangelicals is riveted to the present. The past seems to be nowhere in view and hence it is disparagingly dismissed as being of little value for our rapidly changing world. Such historical amnesia is fatal for any culture, but particularly so for Christian communities whose identity is profoundly bound up with their history. The goal of this new series of monographs, Studies in Baptist History, seeks to provide one of these Christian communities, that of evangelical Baptists, with reasons and resources for remembering the past. The editors are deeply convinced that Baptist history contains rich resources of theological reflection, praxis and spirituality that can help Baptists, as well as other Christians, live more Christianly in the present. The monographs in this series will therefore aim at illuminating various aspects of the Baptist tradition and in the process provide Baptists with a usable past.

Seizing Opportunities

Australian Baptist Women 1830s–1945

REBECCA HILTON

Foreword by Ken R. Manley

◆PICKWICK Publications · Eugene, Oregon

SEIZING OPPORTUNITIES
Australian Baptist Women 1830s–1945

Monographs in Baptist History

Copyright © 2025 Rebecca Hilton. All rights reserved. Except for brief quotations in critical publications or reviews, no part of this book may be reproduced in any manner without prior written permission from the publisher. Write: Permissions, Wipf and Stock Publishers, 199 W. 8th Ave., Suite 3, Eugene, OR 97401.

Pickwick Publications
An Imprint of Wipf and Stock Publishers
199 W. 8th Ave., Suite 3
Eugene, OR 97401

www.wipfandstock.com

PAPERBACK ISBN: 979-8-3852-4222-1
HARDCOVER ISBN: 979-8-3852-4223-8
EBOOK ISBN: 979-8-3852-4224-5

Cataloguing-in-Publication data:

Names: Hilton, Rebecca, author. | Manley, Ken R., foreword.

Title: Seizing opportunities : Australian Baptist women 1830s–1945 / Rebecca Hilton ; foreword by Ken R. Manley.

Description: Eugene, OR: Pickwick Publications, 2025. | Monographs in Baptist History. | Includes bibliographical references and index.

Identifiers: ISBN 979-8-3852-4222-1 (paperback). | ISBN 979-8-3852-4223-8 (hardcover). | ISBN 979-8-3852-4224-5 (ebook).

Subjects: LCSH: Baptist women—Australia. | Baptists—Australia—History.

Classification: BX6493 H55 2025 (print). | BX6493 (ebook).

VERSION NUMBER 08/25/25

To my parents, Helen and Gary, for supporting and inspiring me.
To my husband, Ian, for your love and laughter.
To Samantha, Natasha, Rachel, and Ruby,
giving me hope for the future.

Contents

List of Tables and Illustrations | ix

Foreword by Ken R. Manley | xi

Acknowledgments | xiii

Abbreviations | xv

1	Introduction	1
2	Women in Congregations	19
3	Women in Mission Outside Australia	60
4	Women's State and National Baptist Organizations	111
5	Women's Ordination, Leadership, and Writing	154
6	Women's Social Work and Activities Outside the Denomination	200
7	Conclusion	234

Appendix: Some Australian Baptist Women | 245

Bibliography | 271

Index | 289

List of Tables and Illustrations

Table. Baptist Women's State and National Organizations

1. *Mary Ware*, c. 1854
2. The North Adelaide Baptist Young Women's Bible Class, c. 1914
3. Stanmore Baptist Minister's Wife and Deacons' Wives, 1906
4. The Ten North Adelaide Baptist Deaconesses, 1905
5. Stella and Thomas Churchward Kelly, 1916
6. Alice Mead with Her Daughter Dorothy, 1902
7. Gwenyth Crofts with Her Daughter Ruth, 1928
8. The South Australia Senior Girls' Missionary Union Easter Camp, 1927
9. Some Women at the New South Wales Senior Girls' Missionary Union Easter Camp, c. 1941
10. Lily Higlett, Isabel Church, Dorothea Burnett (Lily's Niece), and William Higlett, c. 1935
11. Lorna Lloyd, c. 1940
12. Some Baptist Women in Canberra Baptist Church, 2025

Foreword

THE CONVENTIONAL VISION OF the role of women believers in Australia was summarized in 1927 by Melbourne Baptist poet Marion Downes (1864–1926):

> To follow daily in the path
> The pure have trod;
> To lead a sinning, suffering world
> Upward to God;
> This, this is woman's work.[1]

But whilst her contemporaries would have agreed with Downes, there was much more to the role of women in Baptist life, even in those days, as this comprehensive study of Australian Baptist women from the 1830s until the end of World War 2 explores. The piety of Downes's poem was certainly a constant, but as Rebecca Hilton details, there is much more to be learned about the identity and roles of women during these decades.

One of the undoubted strengths of this study is the wide range of sources that have been combed to construct the narrative. The details recovered by Dr. Hilton are extraordinary, and the story is told with both academic rigor and a persuasive style. Whilst some of the story has been told by earlier writers, the extent and character of this research is groundbreaking and deeply significant. Informed by painstaking examination of the surprising riches of primary sources, Dr. Hilton's book will be welcomed by all students of Australian Baptist life. Whilst Baptists are a relatively small group in Australia, this analysis is part of a growing body of work on global Baptist women. All who are interested in both feminist and denominational history will welcome this significant addition to our knowledge.

This study complements earlier studies of Australian religious life. The detailed listing of Baptist women is itself a rich resource for further study,

1. M. Downes, "Woman's Work" in Downes, *Wayside Songs* (London: Simpkin, Marshall, Hamilton, Kent, 1927), 97.

and one would hope that Dr. Hilton will be tempted to extend her story to include subsequent generations. Whilst the extension of the role of women as pastors and teachers in ordination by their denominational bodies has been partly recorded, there is, as Dr. Hilton has demonstrated, much more to be explored.

Here is a clear demonstration, then, that modern research methods can shows us how much more we are yet to learn about the place and role of women in Baptist life. Undoubtedly, readers from other denominational traditions will be encouraged by this study.

I most warmly commend this history of Australian Baptist women from the 1830s until 1945 and keenly anticipate further contributions from Dr. Hilton, already a gifted contributor to our small but growing community of Australian Baptist historians.

Ken R. Manley
Melbourne

Acknowledgments

I NEED TO THANK so many people! Ros Gooden provided ongoing support and insights. Ken Manley offered encouragement, and his work provided a sound base for my research. John Walker always responded to my emails about SA Baptist history. Barbara Coe shared in my enthusiasm about Baptist women—we both know there is more to do. Staff and volunteers at various libraries and Baptist archives were generous with their time and access to material. People at St Marks and the Australian Centre for Christianity and Culture, Charles Sturt University were encouraging, particularly Michael Gladwin and Jeanette Mathews, but also Jane, Amy, Felicity, Tracey, Sarah, Sally, and Wayne. I am very appreciative of the support given to me by other historians and academics. My PhD was supported by an Australian Government Research Training Program Scholarship, which was fantastic.

At a personal level, many friends put up with me and my regular moments of outrage—usually related to women being overlooked in historical accounts. Thanks to Anneke, Belinda, Belinda, Beth, Cecelia, Edna, Ella, Felicity, Frances, Jennifer, John, Jolene, Leontine, Libby, Linda, Liz, Lucy, Michele, Monica, Simone, Stefanie, Steve, Sue, Tracey, and many others.

My husband Ian provided so much support. Our daughters Samantha, Natasha, and Rachel have enriched my life. I hope they read this book one day! Lois and Ruth, my sisters, are wonderful: thanks for the love. Meryl, Kathy, and Keith, Ian's siblings, were always enthusiastic: I thank them for sharing their Baptist heritage with me. Our wider family are wonderful, particularly Martin, Roger, Glenn, Ryan, and Lachlan. We are truly blessed.

Finally, I have amazing parents, Helen and Gary. I feel so lucky to have their love, encouragement, and support, and I greatly appreciate all their assistance.

And to those who helped me with editing: a big thank you (especially Dad, but also Sally, Simone, and Ryan). I am sure I've forgotten someone—including some of the Baptist women in Australian history that I have come to know, and my wonderful congregation at Canberra Baptist. I am very grateful.

I feel like—despite the seemingly large amount of women's history—every history book examining women begins with a statement that women have been overlooked, and this book is no different. I've written this book for *all* the active Australian Baptist women, who "came Ministering."[1] This book presents just a sample of the many Australian Baptist women whose faith inspired them to do whatever they could, wherever they were situated. There is more to be said, but these women have most definitely inspired me: "They walk with God. God will understand."[2]

---

1. VBWA, "There Came Women Ministering."
2. Adapted from Alice Skeels's death notice, "Family Notices: Deaths," 1.

Abbreviations

ABFM	Australian Baptist Foreign Mission (1913–1959)
ABFMVC	Australian Baptist Foreign Mission Victorian Committee
ABMS	Australian Baptist Missionary Service (1959–2002)
ABS	Australian Bureau of Statistics
ABW Database	Australian Baptist Women Database
ABWB	Australian Baptist Women's Board
AIF	Australian Imperial Force
AIM	Aborigines [sic] Inland Mission
ALA	Angus Library and Archive, Regent's Park College, Oxford.
APSC	Australian Public Service Commission
AWAS	Australian Women's Army Service
AWRS	The Australian White Ribbon Signal
BMA	Baptist Mission Australia (from 2022)
BMAA	Baptist Mission Australia Archives
BMS	Baptist Missionary Society (United Kingdom)
BR	The Baptist Record (Adelaide)
BUA	Baptist Union of Australia (1926–2009), now Australian Baptist Ministries
BUNSW	Baptist Union of New South Wales
BUQ	Baptist Union of Queensland
BUQA	Baptist Union of Queensland Archives
BUSA	Baptist Union of South Australia
BUTAS	Baptist Union of Tasmania
BUV	Baptist Union of Victoria
BUVA	Baptist Union of Victoria Archives

Abbreviations

BUWA	Baptist Union of Western Australia
BUWAA	Baptist Union of Western Australia Archives
BWGAM	Baptist Women's Goalundo Auxiliary Minutes of Meeting
BWL	Baptist Women's League (SA)
BWMU	Baptist Women's Missionary Union (in several states)
BZM	Baptist Zenana Mission (United Kingdom)
CE	Christian Endeavor
DSBSBM	Dorcas Society Bathurst Street Baptist Church Minutes of Meetings
HPBLASM	Hurlstone Park Baptist Ladies Aid Society Minutes of Meetings
JQBWUM	Jireh Branch QBW Union Minutes of Meetings
LZMS	Ladies' Zenana Missionary Society (NSW)
MM	Minutes of Meetings
NABDM	North Adelaide Baptist Deaconesses Minutes of Meetings
NSW	New South Wales
NSWBA	Baptist Union of New South Wales Archives
NZBMS	New Zealand Baptist Missionary Society
OB	*Our Bond* (Calcutta)
OIF	*Our Indian Field* (Sydney)
"OWTA"	"One Woman to Another" (Adelaide Bamford articles)
PIVM	Poona and Indian Village Mission
QBWU	Queensland Baptist Women's Union
SA	South Australia
SABA	South Australian Baptist Union Archives (held in SA State Library)
SBC	Southern Baptist Convention (USA)
SGMU	Senior Girls' Missionary Union
SLNSW	State Library of New South Wales
SMH	*The Sydney Morning Herald* (Sydney)
TAB	*The Australian Baptist* (Sydney)
TGL	*The Golden Link* (Melbourne)
TP	*Truth and Progress* (Adelaide)
TQB	*The Queensland Baptist* (Brisbane)
TQF	*The Queensland Freeman* (Brisbane)

TRC	*The Roll Call* (Sydney)
TSB	*The Southern Baptist* (Melbourne)
TVB	*The Victorian Baptist* (Melbourne)
TWA	*The West Australian* (Perth)
UAM	United Aborigines [sic] Mission
UK	United Kingdom
USA	United States of America
VBWA	Victorian Baptist Women's Association
WA	Western Australia
WCTU	Woman's Christian Temperance Union
"WVP"	"With the Victorian President" (George Doery articles)
YWCA	Young Women's Christian Association

1

Introduction

I knew her in the home, the Sunday school, and the church, and I never knew her to refuse any request for service. She was among those gracious souls who do not wait for the request, but give the service promptly, and you could always rely upon it being thoroughly done. The outstanding characteristic of our friend in those days was service, unselfish service. "Not to be ministered unto but to minister" might be said to have been her motto.[1]

—EDITH SIMPSON, 1932
(from an obituary written for Annie Gilmour)

BACKGROUND

MANY AUSTRALIAN BAPTIST WOMEN like Annie Gilmour and Edith Simpson spent their lives ministering faithfully within the Australian Baptist community, but Australian Baptists rarely honored their activities. Few individual women have been exalted for their ministry, nor has the combined activities of women been collated and adequately depicted to provide a detailed historical account of Australian Baptist women exploring their roles, experiences, and motivations. Most studies focus on male leaders and the formation of denominational institutions and largely ignore the presence and experiences of women.[2]

1. Edith Simpson, "The Late Mrs. W. Gilmour: A Triumphant Passing," *TAB*, 14 June 1932, 9.

2. Breward, *History of the Churches in Australasia*, 141. See, for example, Rowland, *Century of the English Church in NSW*, 8–10.

From evangelists to providers of afternoon teas, this book seeks to redress women's absence in the historiography through examining the roles Baptist women undertook within their congregations, in broader Baptist and Protestant activities, and how they enhanced Australian religious life. Many Australian Baptist women found roles that were meaningful for their own faith and aspirations. This book documents their successes and analyzes the ways in which women expanded their work outside traditional roles. The book fills in the gaps where women's work has been ignored, overlooked, or dismissed, and discusses some of the restrictions placed upon women, which sometimes gave rise to ministries beyond the scope and structures of Baptist activities.

For many Australian Baptist women their Baptist beliefs defined their identity. They sought opportunities to impart their beliefs to others. Many would have related to the words written by Marion Tranter, a Victorian Baptist woman, in her 1919 poem entitled "Opportunities":

> Each day fresh opportunities are;
> Be eager then to seize them whilst you may
> For though they come, they also pass away,
> And 'tis not sloth that wins a worthy prize.[3]

WOMEN IN AUSTRALIAN SOCIETY AND THE "INTERMEDIATE SPHERE"

From 1788 Australian settlers copied the United Kingdom's social, economic, and political structures in Australia, effectively the patriarchal society migrated with them.[4] Australian Baptists worked in congregations within this setting from the 1830s. A shift transpired from the late nineteenth century when Australian women, following the examples of women in Europe, the United Kingdom (UK), and the United States of America (USA), sought to re-shape their place in society. Many of the new opportunities for women occurred through coordinated activities by groups of women, including organizations which sought womanhood suffrage. From the 1880s colonial universities opened enrolments to women and they increasingly accessed these educational opportunities.[5] Women undertook advocacy for social reform and equality in working conditions, health care, and political and legal

---

3. Tranter, *Call of the Bush and Other Poems*, 28.
4. Grimshaw et al., *Creating a Nation*, 55.
5. Mackinnon, *New Women*, 24.

rights, particularly marriage and property law.⁶ Additionally women gradually increased their paid workforce participation. Until the early twentieth century most Australian women worked within their homes or lived in the home of their employer. In 1911 only 17 percent of Australian women over the age of fifteen were in paid employment outside of their homes. However from this time onwards the proportion of women working in various occupations grew, such as shop assistants, nurses, teachers, and factory workers, especially during the two world wars.⁷

Yet despite increasing political advocacy, in the period to 1945 Australian women were largely excluded from public policy considerations and decision-making within society, often referred to as civil society or the public sphere.⁸ The public sphere was generally the domain of men, the private sphere was generally for women and children, and effectively women were excluded from engaging in public life.⁹ Until 1945 women remained limited in their involvement and influence in civil society.

Given that Baptist women were not full participants in the broader public sphere, their work in congregations and the denomination occurred in what has been labeled the third or intermediate sphere—between the public and private spheres.¹⁰ Although there was not an agreed or consistent approach to women's roles in Baptist congregations or other Baptist activities, women had the opportunity to work in the intermediate sphere through the—mainly—volunteer work they undertook in the Baptist denomination.¹¹

WHAT IS A BAPTIST?

Briefly describing the history of Baptists and what they believed provides context for why Australian Baptist women were confident in their actions but did not push the boundaries of their work.¹² Baptists emerged in the early 1600s during the Reformation period through religious and political events in western Europe and England. Baptists were one of the nonconforming or dissenting denominations that formed by the mid-seventeenth

---

6. O'Brien, *God's Willing Workers*, 64, 152.

7. Abjorensen and Docherty, *Historical Dictionary of Australia*, 396.

8. Hagemann and Michel, "Civil Society"; Harris, "Civil Society in British History."

9. Habermas, "Further Reflections on the Public Sphere," 428; Hagemann and Michel, "Civil Society."

10. Wilson, *Constrained by Zeal*, 11, 175.

11. See Hilton, "Women in the Australian Baptist Denomination."

12. More fulsome Baptist histories are available. See, for example, Bebbington, *Baptists Through the Centuries*; Manley, *From Woolloomooloo*.

century—others being Congregationalists, Unitarians, Quakers, English Presbyterians, and in the eighteenth century Methodists.[13] In England due to the power of the Church of England, nonconforming adherents suffered hardships because of their faith through various official means such as being barred from access to government employment, public office, and graduation from Oxford and Cambridge universities, and restrictions on the size of congregations.[14]

Australian Baptists experienced no legal impediments to their religious liberty as Australia did not have the same sense, or legal reality, of a national, established church, such as existed in England.[15] Possibly there were some small social and cultural impediments for Australian Baptist adherents, however many Baptists believed the denomination was adversely impacted by their intentional dissent such as Ellen Cordiner, who in 1913 wrote that Margaret Ashworth "suffered for her [Baptist] principles."[16] Likewise in 1930 Alice Lane wrote about early Australian Baptists: "It is a fine thing to recognise the debt we owe to these pioneers who stood loyal to their principles."[17] Whether such opinions made Baptist more insular or more determined to succeed is unknown. Certainly any perceived persecution was largely affected by the way Baptists interpreted legal impediments in England from the seventeenth century.

The history of the Baptist denomination is intertwined with the history of Evangelicalism. Evangelicalism is not a separate denomination, but rather a global, pan-denominational, Protestant, Christian movement. It emerged in the 1730s and expanded exponentially over the next two centuries. It emphasized the adoption of a personal and inward "heart-oriented" and experiential faith where a Christian's everyday life reflected their Christian faith—a living faith.[18] Evangelicalism was linked to spiritual awakenings throughout Europe and North America in the eighteenth century, and various holiness movements of the nineteenth century.[19] By the early nineteenth century evangelicals wielded significant social and cultural influence. Many evangelicals believed that voluntary organizations improved individuals and transformed

---

13. Bebbington, *Baptists Through the Centuries*, 13, 16, 19, 44.

14. Bebbington, *Baptists Through the Centuries*, 65.

15. Pickard, "'Home Away From Home,'" 209.

16. See, for example, Ellen M. Cordiner, "Personal: The Late Mrs. Ashworth, of Mosman, NSW," *TAB*, 11 March 1913, 4.

17. Alice Lane, "Our Baptist Veterans," *TAB*, 21 October 1930, 2.

18. McGrath, *Christianity*, 161, 492.

19. Bebbington, *Baptists Through the Centuries*, 16, 71.

society.[20] During the nineteenth century they established and maintained key religious, voluntary, and philanthropic organizations, including the British and Foreign Bible Society, the Young Men's Christian Association, the Young Women's Christian Association (YWCA), and Christian Endeavor (CE).[21] To 1945 almost all Australian Baptists were evangelical.

AUSTRALIAN BAPTIST CORE BELIEFS

Baptist Distinctives or Principles

Baptist historians—from Samuel Carey and William Whitley in the early twentieth century, to Ken Manley and David Bebbington in the late twentieth and early twenty-first centuries—agree that Baptist adherents possessed a wide range of Christian views. There were four broad Baptist distinctives, or principles, which in combination set Baptist adherents apart from other Protestant denominations. These were: religious liberty, or freedom of religion; civil liberty, or separation of the church from the state; the priesthood of all believers; and personal conversion accompanied by believers' baptism.[22]

Religious and civil liberty drove the creation of independent Baptist congregations with internal management and discipline. Individual Baptists sought membership of a congregation, which enabled adherents to gather and meet as a community.[23] Baptists took membership in their congregations seriously and most Baptist congregations examined their membership rolls regularly to remove members for non-attendance. Members were "disciplined" or removed from membership if their behaviour was deemed inappropriate. In 1885 Flinders Street Baptist, Adelaide, removed a woman from the membership list "under discipline."[24] In 1934 Knightsbridge Baptist, SA, "decided that Miss [name removed] be summonsed to attend before officers and requested not to interfere with decorum of church services."[25] The members of Baptist congregations made decisions with respect to the

20. Piggin and Linder, *Fountain of Public Prosperity*, 124.

21. Treloar, *Disruption of Evangelicalism*, 4.

22. Carey, "What Baptists Stand For," 4–7; Whitley, *History of British Baptists*, 53, 281; Manley, *From Woolloomooloo*, 1:221–23; Bebbington, *Baptists Through the Centuries*, 307.

23. Thompson, "Baptist Theology," 101; Hayward, "Gathered Community," 195. Congregations fulfilled the statement by Jesus in Matthew 18:20: "For where two or three are gathered in my name, I am there among them."

24. Flinders Street Baptist Church, Meeting Minutes (MM), SRG465, South Australian Baptist Union, South Australia State Library, Adelaide (SABA).

25. Helm, *Baptists of Burnside*, 125.

congregation's policies. These Baptist distinctives, and the controversies surrounding them, shaped Baptists in Australia.

The doctrine of the priesthood of all believers also directly impacted individuals and was a key principle of the Reformation. In the Baptist denomination this meant that women and men were equally close to God, and women did not need a mediator or "third party"—often male—to connect to God. It also enabled participation of all adherents in the denomination's administration and ministry because there was not a centralized hierarchy. In theory women could be active and equal participants in the congregation's activities because of the Baptist application of the priesthood of all believers, although this was rarely the case in practice.

While all the distinctives were important most Baptists, irrespective of their location or situation, described themselves as Baptist because of their belief in believers' baptism, as opposed to infant baptism practiced by Catholic and other Protestant denominations. Believers' baptism through full immersion was experienced by women and men as a public acknowledgement of Christian commitment or as a conscious decision to become a Baptist. For example, the families of Elizabeth Lister and Elizabeth Wood were Methodist and Anglican respectively but both are described as believing that baptism was a "duty and privilege" that led to them choosing believers' baptism and joining a Baptist congregation.[26] Baptism occurred from about the age of ten, which was deemed the age that an individual could made their own decision about their faith. The average age of baptism for Australian women was nineteen, and the most common age was sixteen.[27] Believers' baptism was an independent decision, marking an individual's intentional Christian commitment.[28]

Evangelicalism

Evangelical beliefs were overlaid on Baptist distinctives. Bebbington provides the most widely accepted definition for evangelicals, and Australian Baptists were characterized by his four defining marks of *conversionism*, *activism*, *biblicism*, and *crucicentrism*.[29]

---

26. R. W. T., "Mrs Elizabeth Lister: St Kilda," *TSB*, 12 February 1907, 47; Harry Wood, "Leaves from My Life Story," *TAB*, 5 October 1926, 2.

27. Bebbington, *Baptists Through the Centuries*, 54. Hilton, "ABW Database." The youngest age known of a woman being baptized was eight and the eldest was seventy-nine.

28. Randall, *What a Friend We Have in Jesus*, 2, 15, 22.

29. Bebbington, *Evangelicalism in Modern Britain*, 4.

Conversionism was the process through which individuals' lives changed when they had a personal experience of God and decisively accepted Christ as their personal saviour.[30] In 1913 one of Australia's best known Baptist ministers and writers, the Rev. Frank Boreham, wrote: "Conversion was a soul-stirring and sensational experience."[31] The first "finding" of the South Australian (SA) Baptist Women's League's 1944 Conference was: "There must be Spiritual re-birth [a conversion] before Church membership."[32] The personal conversion of a Baptist was usually followed by baptism and membership of a congregation, and so the conversion experience was embedded in membership of Baptist congregations.[33]

Activism was the desire to work for the extension of the Kingdom of God, as Bebbington observes, "the expression of the gospel in effort."[34] Activism occurred through the many roles that women undertook within and outside the denomination.

Biblicism was a belief in the supreme authority of the Bible as the word of God with respect to doctrine and practice. *Biblicism* was apparent through the many references women made to the importance of the Bible, which they believed spoke to them in their own context and became an authoritative basis for their doctrine and practice.[35] Teacher Sarah Sharp, for example, always engaged in Bible studies at the various congregations she attended, as "she felt most drawn [to] Bible exposition."[36] At the age of ninety-two Mary Playford said, "I begin the day with my Bible."[37] Florence Benskin wrote: "We must make a real study of [the Bible], we must get our roots deep in, and as the pages unfold to us, new life will spring to the glory of His name."[38]

Crucicentrism emphasized belief in Christ's sacrificial, substitutionary, and atoning death for the sins of humanity.[39] *Crucicentrism* was less explicit than the other marks but was still evident, particularly in writing by

---

30. Bebbington, *Evangelicalism in Modern Britain*, 3, 6.
31. F. W. Boreham, "The Poppies in the Corn," *TAB*, 17 June 1913, 2.
32. Baptist Women's League (BWL), Baptist Women's League MM, SABA.
33. See, for example, Holdsworth et al., *Baptists and Baptism*, 7.
34. Bebbington, *Evangelicalism in Modern Britain*, 3.
35. See, for example, Collins, *Christ's Ambassador*, 9; Bean, *Studies in Romans*.
36. "In Memoriam: Mrs Stephen Sharp," *TAB*, 31 August 1926, 4.
37. "When the Heart is Young," *Observer* (Adelaide), 28 May 1927, 47.
38. Florence Benskin, "Through a Woman's Window: Stunted," *BR*, 15 January 1925, 7.
39. Bebbington, *Evangelicalism in Modern Britain*, 15.

missionary women.⁴⁰ In 1897 Ellen Arnold wrote that in her work "I talked of sin, man's helpless condition, Christ's spotless life, His sacrifice for sin, and His resurrection."⁴¹ The obituary of Rebecca Field observed that she was in "her eternal inheritance" as she had experienced the "welcome Home to all who pass by way of His cross."⁴²

In 1903 Margaret Bean introduced her *Studies in Romans* by writing: "To the young convert (speaking from personal experience) the Epistle to the Romans is of vital importance. When the first joy of the converted life is waning, to know the sureties of Atonement and justification by faith . . . the soul is steadied, rooted and grounded for time and eternity."⁴³ Her statement and work exemplify features of all four marks of Evangelicalism: conversionism by her explicit reference to a conversion experience; activism through writing, and involvement in city mission activities in Melbourne; biblicism in her focus on a study of Romans; and crucicentrism in using the atonement to exemplify Christian faith.

"Contested Concepts"

The term evangelical is a "contested concept" along with other descriptions of Christian beliefs and theology, such as conservative or liberal.⁴⁴ Australian Baptists were often described as conservative, leading to a view that they restricted women's participation in leadership, church management, and participation in worship.⁴⁵ Similarly in the early twentieth century some Baptist adherents and congregations were described as theologically liberal. Describing theological beliefs of Baptists as evangelical, conservative, or liberal is difficult because the terms have shifted in meaning over time.⁴⁶

In 1914 the Rev. Robert Ings provided a light-hearted assessment of conservative views in that: "The ideal man [or woman] is neither a conservative nor a radical, but a judicious mixture of both—one third conservative should be enough for practical purposes!"⁴⁷ Perhaps this is a useful means

---

40. Alice G. Pappin, "Furreedpore [sic]," *Our Bond* (Calcutta) (*OB*), January 1895, 2; Crofts, *Glimpses into the Life of a Missionary Wife*; Lienemann-Perrin et al., *Putting Names with Faces*, 363.

41. Ellen Arnold, "Pubna [sic]," *OB*, February 1897, 5.

42. W. C. B., "The Late Mrs. A. E. [Rebecca] Field," *TAB*, 29 August 1922, 4.

43. Bean, *Studies in Romans*, n.p.

44. Olsen, *How to Be Evangelical*, 18.

45. Murphy and Starling, *Gender Conversation*, 109–10.

46. Olsen, *How to Be Evangelical*, 18; Green, "Whither the Conference," 1.

47. R. [Robert] Ings, "'BMA' Opinions: Please Correct Me if I'm Wrong," *TAB*, 14

of indicating how Baptist adherents held a variety of theological views, and that these were steeped in a conservative structure that also stemmed from radical non-conformist Reformation roots.

Most Australian Baptist women's beliefs—where they are extant and can be discerned—were based on evangelical and Baptist distinctives. Australian Baptist women can be viewed as evangelical as the term applied in that period, rather than being evangelical in the context of, for example, twenty-first-century Evangelicalism in the USA. That is, most Australian Baptist women were "of [their] date, Evangelical."[48] That is not to say that even "of their date" all evangelicals had the same theological views. Evangelicalism had different strands, particularly significant was the Keswick, or holiness movement and fundamentalism, or a belief in the inerrancy of the Bible.[49] Yet throughout this book Baptist women's views, actions, and spiritual practices can be understood through the lens of evangelical principles.

However this book will not use the terms conservative or liberal to describe women's views—or the views of Baptists more generally—given their contested nature. There is no evidence, as this book will show, that the application of conservative or liberal theology reduced or enlarged women's roles in Baptist congregations. Women's participation was more dependent on social conditions.[50] As will become evident in subsequent accounts, women undertook leadership positions within their congregations and in broader Baptist activities across all Australian states.

A BRIEF HISTORY OF AUSTRALIAN BAPTISTS

Baptists have never represented more than 4 percent of the Australian population.[51] Australian Baptists were generally immigrants from the United Kingdom (UK) and congregations mirrored the structure used by Baptists in the UK. The denomination's slow development, commencing in the 1830s, was characterized and entrenched by the lack of funding provided by the Baptist denomination in the UK and the reluctance of Australian Baptists to take up opportunities for government funding.[52]

July 1914, 13.

48. Thomas Hardy, *Jude the Obscure* [1896], as quoted in Bebbington, *Evangelicalism in Modern Britain*, 105.

49. See, for example, Treloar, *Disruption of Evangelicalism*, 7.

50. See, for example, Toit, "Gender," 163; Webb, *Why We're Equal*, 103.

51. Manley, *From Woolloomooloo*, 1:7.

52. Parker, *Pressing on with the Gospel*, 11.

Several requests for funding made by Australian Baptists were rejected by Baptists in the UK. Instead, assistance from the UK was mainly evident in the supply of trained Baptist ministers, as prior to 1945 many ministers were trained in the UK, including some men who had been born in Australia.[53] Several Baptist ministers from the UK considered they were undertaking a form of mission work through migrating to Australia to take up roles in ministry, resulting in the view of Australia as a pseudo-mission field.[54] Up until the mid-twentieth century the relationship between Australian and English Baptists remained important, though increasingly Australian Baptists relied on Baptist resources and people from the USA.[55]

As dissenters, Baptists could have benefited from colonial legislation from the 1830s that provided for greater religious freedom in Australia than in the UK.[56] In New South Wales (NSW) the *Church Building Act 1836* was intended to create a level playing field for the larger Christian denominations, whereby government assistance was provided relative to membership.[57] In the 1830s and 1840s Church Acts were passed throughout Australian colonies to provide support for major denominations. Many Baptist congregations rigidly adhered to Baptist doctrine regarding separation of state and church and did not seek or accept government assistance, which limited their financial capacity to acquire land, build substantial church buildings, or adequately remunerate ministers.[58] In 1938 the Rev. Frederick Wilkin wrote that early Australian Baptists believed that "State aid meant State control of worship and dictation of belief."[59] By the early twentieth century key figures in the Australian Baptist denomination, including Frederick Wilkin, expressed the view that Baptists should accept relevant government assistance.[60] Reluctance to accept government assistance in the nineteenth century was likely a factor that kept the Baptist denomination small in Australia compared to other dissenting denominations, which did accept government funding. Perhaps the ongoing financial stress was one of

---

53. Hilton, "ABW Database"; Wilkin, *Baptists in Victoria*, 33. Prior to 1910 at least seven Australian-born men went to Spurgeon's College.

54. See, for example, "Religious Notes," *Register* (Adelaide), 19 December 1925, 14.

55. Manley, *From Woolloomooloo*, 2:500.

56. Breward, *History of the Churches in Australasia*, 75. For further information on dissenting denominations, see Michael Watts's series, *Dissenters*.

57. Piggin and Linder, *Fountain of Public Prosperity*, 251–53.

58. Wilkin, *Baptists in Victoria*, 23–24; Manley, "Our Own Church," 286.

59. Wilkin, *Baptists in Victoria*, 23.

60. "Baptists in West Australia," *Advertiser* (Adelaide), 13 April 1903, 6; Wilkin, *Baptists in Victoria*, 23; Piggin and Linder, *Fountain of Public Prosperity*, 252; Manley, "Our Own Church," 286–87.

the reasons Australian Baptists retained the notion that Baptist adherents "suffered" because of their Baptist beliefs.

Like Baptists in the UK, Australian Baptists were not a single, unified group, as adherents were Particular Baptists, General Baptists, Scotch Baptists, or Reformed Baptists, each with different origins.[61] The small number of Baptists in Australia meant that some congregations consisted of adherents who had been members of different types of Baptist congregations in the UK. Members forged a mix of various doctrinal beliefs in their Australian Baptist congregations, which sometimes resulted in tension.[62] Arguably ongoing doctrinal differences between individuals within Australian congregations, particularly with respect to membership, also slowed the growth of the denomination. In 1937 the Rev. Escourt Hughes wrote that "a divided church is never attractive."[63]

Congregations were established when a group of people—on average seventeen—agreed to form a Baptist congregation. These members agreed on initial policies regarding requirements for membership, which generally was either open to all believers (open membership) or restricted to those who had evidence of believers' baptism (closed membership). More than half of the foundation members of Australian Baptist congregations were women. This carried over to membership of Baptist congregations, and up to 1945 women represented around two-thirds of congregations' membership.[64]

Baptist congregations met together weekly for one or two Sunday worship services. A worship service contained prayers, Bible readings, singing, and a sermon delivered by the—male—minister that focused on a scriptural, moral, or theological subject. Worship services usually followed the same format each week. Most congregations had a separate Sunday School for children and, from the mid-1890s, CE meetings for young people. Generally Baptist congregations held a communion service monthly as part of, or at the end of, the Sunday worship service. Again, the members decided whether communion was open to all who professed a Christian faith and were converted (open communion) or only offered to baptized believers

---

61. Bebbington, *Evangelicalism in Modern Britain*, 17; *Baptists Through the Centuries*, 31, 45; Manley, "Our Own Church," 285.

62. Manley, "Our Own Church," 286.

63. Hughes, *Our First Hundred Years*, 34.

64. Hilton, "ABW Database"; Bebbington, *Baptists Through the Centuries*, 157; Watts, *Dissenters*, 3:171. Bebbington and Watts also conclude that more women attended worship services than men. For Australian examples, see *Petersham Baptist Church*; Benskin, "Through a Woman's Window: Pull Together," *BR*, 16 March 1925, 10; Otzen, "Calling the Roll," 46.

(closed communion).⁶⁵ Groups of people within the congregation met during the week for specific purposes including prayer, Bible study, social activities, and mission support. Members' meetings were usually held quarterly.

Members appointed unpaid deacons—men in almost all instances—to provide leadership and manage policies, finances, and assets.⁶⁶ Some deacons provided spiritual leadership and conducted worship services, including leading communion in worship services, although in most congregations these tasks were undertaken by a paid minister. Until 1978 all permanent Australian Baptist ministers were men. The process by which a congregation "called" a minister differed, but generally a committee within the congregation, often but not always the deacons' committee, used their Baptist connections to identify a suitable minister and recommend them to the membership, who then "called" that minister. If the minister did not accept the call, the process recommenced. Hence some regional congregations struggled to find ministers, especially if unable to guarantee ongoing funding for the minister's wage, and the task of preaching fell on lay members of the congregation. Once employed by a congregation, a minister's main duties were to develop and care for the spiritual life of members and others connected to the congregation, particularly through conducting weekly Sunday worship services. The minister was accountable to the members of the congregation, and the congregation supported the minister through providing a wage and assisting in other tasks as required.⁶⁷

Between 1862 and 1896 Baptist unions were formed in Victoria, SA, NSW, Queensland, Tasmania, and Western Australia (WA) to allow for joint fellowship and other activities. Due to the independence of Baptist congregations and ongoing differences among congregations, especially General and Particular Baptist congregations, not all chose to join the state Baptist Unions.⁶⁸ While Australian Baptist Congresses were held semi-regularly from 1908, it was not until 1926 that the Baptist Union of Australia was formed. This Union is a symbolic "umbrella" organization that has no power over state unions or Baptist congregations. The establishment of the Union did not bring together all Baptists in a single united denomination.⁶⁹

65. Manley, *From Woolloomooloo*, 1:279.

66. See, for example, Ashfield Baptist Church, Deacons MM, 1895–1907, Baptist Association of New South Wales Baptist Archives, Morling College, Sydney (NSWBA); Canberra Baptist Church, Deacons' MM, 1927, Canberra Baptist Church Records, Australian Capital Territory Heritage Library, Canberra.

67. See, for example, *Mitcham Baptist Church*.

68. For example, Hawthorn Particular Baptist, established in 1880 in Melbourne, has always been an independent congregation and not a member of the BUV. Likewise Ryde Particular Baptist, established in 1862 in Sydney, is not a member of the BUNSW.

69. See https://www.baptist.org.au.

These unions did not have canons or sets of rules that were binding on individuals or congregations, nor did they interfere in congregational management or doctrinal beliefs. The unions established guidelines regarding Baptist ministers but did not appoint, ordain, or move ministers. Often the state unions assisted a congregation in finding a minister or contributing to ministers' salaries where a congregation was too small to support a minister.[70] While the minister and deacons made day-to-day decisions at monthly meetings, all substantive issues were discussed and agreed at members' meetings, which were held every three months or as required.[71]

Throughout the nineteenth and twentieth centuries—and into the twenty-first century—Baptists considered that mission was a key component of their shared beliefs. Australian Baptists, like evangelicals worldwide, justified and promoted mission as a means of expanding the church as well as creating or maintaining a Christian social order: referring to these concepts as extending the Kingdom of God.[72] The missionary zeal permeated many Baptist women's actions. They considered that mission work encompassed a range of activities—including support of mission—undertaken in congregations, in Australian cities, rural and remote regions, and in non-Christian countries.[73] The Australian Baptist denomination was not—and probably never will be—a cohesive and homogenous unit, but all Baptists agreed that mission was essential.[74]

Traditionally evangelical Baptists saw ministry and mission as work undertaken by men. Yet all work undertaken by women within the Christian church is a form of ministry or mission.[75] This book highlights how many Australian Baptist women between the 1830s and 1945, with a strong commitment to evangelical marks of conversionism and activism, undertook activities that fitted within a broad definition of ministry and mission.

---

70. See, for example, Mount Barker Baptist Church MM, SABA.

71. See, for example, Ballarat Baptist Church, Church MM, Baptist Union of Victoria Archives, Camberwell, Victoria (BUVA); Flinders Street Baptist Church MM, SABA; Ashfield Baptist Church, Deacons MM, NSWBA; Petersham Baptist MM, NSWBA; Mount Barker Baptist Church Officers MM, SABA.

72. Bebbington, "Introduction," 2; *Baptists Through the Centuries*, 121; Robert, *Christian Mission*, 59; ABFM, *Extending the Kingdom in Bengal*; Benskin, "Through a Woman's Window: Pull Together," *BR*, 16 March 1925, 10; Hilton, "For the Extension of Christ's Kingdom."

73. Porterfield, *Modern Christianity*, 3.

74. Manley, "Our Own Church," 292.

75. Dzubinski and Stasson, *Women in the Mission of the Church*, ix.

SOURCES

This book draws on an extensive range of primary sources by and about Australian Baptist women that were located in various public and private archives and libraries, as well as held in private hands, including books, letters, notes, speeches, and minutes of meetings. The most numerous sources are the more than 300 articles written by Australian Baptist women in various Baptist papers including the national denominational paper, *The Australian Baptist*, state papers, and mission papers.[76] Papers from non-denominational missions and other religious organizations are also used, especially those of the WCTU and CE.[77] Articles by Baptist men writing *about* Australian Baptist women are another important source, recognising that men wrote most of the published documents, although they described actions and activities from their own perspective. Obituaries of Australian Baptist women, which often included descriptions of their roles, have been used extensively. While there were many Baptist women who worked as missionaries to First Nations people, very little information about First Nations' Baptist women themselves is extant, and accordingly they are not able to be included.

There are few sources on Baptist women prior to the 1870s. The small number of Australian Baptists in the mid-nineteenth century naturally leads to a small number of sources. Prior to 1880 Australian colonial Baptist papers were only published for a total of 22 years. Many of the papers and other sources that would be relevant are not extant.[78] Also, only three women's group's minutes written prior to 1880 are extant—all from SA: Flinders Street Baptist Deaconesses, Flinders Street Dorcas Society, and Norwood Deaconesses.

---

76. Australian Baptist denominational papers include: Baptist Union of Australia, *The Australian Baptist* (Sydney), 1912–1945; Baptist Union of South Australia, *Baptist Record* (Adelaide), 1923–1945; Baptist Union of New South Wales (BUNSW), *Baptist* (Sydney), 1877–1912; Baptist Union of Victoria, *The Southern Baptist* (Melbourne) (*TSB*), 1895–1912; *Truth and Progress* (Adelaide) (*TP*) 1868–1894; The Queensland Baptist Association/The Queensland Baptist Union, *The Queensland Baptist* (Brisbane) (*TQB*), 1890–1913, 1923–1945; and Baptist Union of Western Australia, *Western Australia Baptist* (Perth), 1902–1945. Mission papers include *Our Bond* (Calcutta) 1893–1941; *Our Indian Field* (Sydney) (*OIF*) 1915–1949; and *Vision* (Sydney) 1950–1973.

77. Woman's Christian Temperance Union of Victoria (later of Australia), *Australian White Ribbon Signal* (Melbourne) (*AWRS*), 1931–1939; *The Roll Call* (Sydney) (*TRC*), 1897–1946; and *The Golden Link* (Melbourne) (*TGL*), 1894–1910.

78. Papers published prior to 1880 were: *Australasian Baptist Magazine* (1858–1859), Victoria; *Australian Christian Messenger* (1870–71), NSW; *Banner of Truth* (1877–1885), NSW; *Queensland Freeman* (1881–1888), Queensland; *Truth and Progress* (1868–1894) SA; and *Victorian Freeman* (1876–1889), Victoria. See Burn, "Australian Baptist Heritage Collection," 233–47.

To balance the dearth of sources prior to 1880 this book uses the technique of prosopography to obtain information about Australian Baptist women. Prosopography is the analysis of a group of people to determine broad social characteristics and can yield important insights and historical knowledge of groups of people.[79] The information is based on quantitative data rather than impressionistic generalisations. Prosopography focuses on groups for whom there is little information known, and the prosopography of Baptist women created for this book—referred to hereafter as the Australian Baptist Women's Database (ABW Database)—contains many women for whom little information is available about their lives, yet their inclusion in the aggregate data demonstrates trends and patterns. The ABW Database is a crucial tool and reveals information about the diverse social backgrounds and education of Australian Baptist women, their wide range of occupations, the extensive relationships between Baptist women through marriage and family, and their connections to other Baptists and other denominations.[80] The ABW Database contains information about over 2,500 women and informs all chapters of this book.

The relative lack of information on women in the Baptist denomination is not materially different from the amount of information on women in most religious organizations, or in wider Australian society, but this does not make the loss less significant. The extant records are, nevertheless, a rich source for demonstrating the range of work that Australian Baptist women undertook during the period.

CONVENTIONS

Until 1901, when Australia became a Federation of six states, Australia consisted of separate British colonies. It is, therefore, anachronistic to refer to Australian states before then. However, for the sake of convenience, the colonies of Australia are sometimes referred to as states unless specifically referring to an earlier period. Often the Anglican denomination in Australia was called the Church of England, but this book uses Anglican to refer to the denomination.

When Great Britain colonized Australia, there were existing inhabitants who had been on the land for over sixty thousand years—the world's oldest living culture. The term "First Nations people" will be used to refer to Australian Aboriginal and Torres Strait Islander peoples.[81]

79. Stone, "Prosopography," 46.
80. Hilton, "ABW Database."
81. APSC, "Aboriginal and Torres Strait Islander Peoples."

In almost all cases Baptist women are referred to by their first name and their surname at the time of their death. Appendix 1 contains basic known information about the Australian Baptist women included in the book. Footnotes use women's names at the time their work was published and thus there are some differences between names of women in the text and in the footnotes.

To avoid confusion, the book uses the term "denomination" to describe all Australian Baptist people and structures, and "congregation" to describe local Baptist churches. Strictly speaking there is no Australian Baptist denomination, just thousands of Baptists attending hundreds of congregations, which generally are referred to by members as a "church," and connected through six state unions or associations. Baptist Ministries Australia, originally the Baptist Union of Australia (BUA), is a national Baptist organization with no authority over the procedures and practices of congregations or associations.

Most of the names of the state-based Baptist organizations have changed over time as the names of organizations were not officially registered until the mid-twentieth century. For instance, the Baptist Unions in NSW and SA were referred to as both a union and an association.[82] For consistency in this book the state-based Baptist organizations are referred to as unions, following the convention of the BUA at the time it was established in 1926 and reflecting their primary purpose of bringing together independent Baptist congregations.

The name of the Australian mission organization has also changed since its establishment in 1912 as the Australian Baptist Foreign Mission (ABFM). Rather than use its current name (Baptist Missions Australia), the organization will be referred to as the ABFM, as it was called from 1912 to 1959. Indeed sometimes for convenience the ABFM is used as an overall term that may include women's work prior to 1912, although technically women worked for state Baptist missionary organizations before 1912.

The term "foreign mission" is considered ethnocentric but was used extensively by Australian Baptists and accordingly is sometimes used in this book to define mission work undertaken in countries other than Australia, although generally the term "overseas mission" is used. Some spellings of place names changed, particularly of the towns and villages of missions in East Bengal, and so the most accepted spellings are used. Specifically, the region where Australian Baptists first undertook mission will be referred to as East Bengal rather than Bangladesh.

---

82. "South Australian Baptist Association," *South Australian Advertiser* (Adelaide), 30 September 1884, 5; "South Australian Baptist Union Annual Assembly," *TAB*, 6 October 1936, 9; Prior, *Some Fell on Good Ground*, 66.

Many Baptist women and men discussed or quoted in the book have children or other descendants. The book will seek to "tread softly" on the lives and experiences of Baptists by being sensitive and respectful about information obtained from the sources.[83] The words and actions of individuals will not be judged through a twenty-first century perspective as far as possible, particularly with respect to views about women, non-Christian people, and First Nations people.

CHAPTER OUTLINES

The following six chapters focus on different arenas of activity by Australian Baptist women.

Chapter 2. Women in Congregations assesses the demographics and spiritual practices of Baptist women, and illuminates the diversity of Baptist women, evident in the work women undertook within their congregations, including the roles of women's organizations within congregations.

Chapter 3. Women in Mission Outside Australia examines the ministry of more than 250 Australian Baptist women who undertook mission service. One hundred of these women worked in East Bengal for the Australian Baptist missions, and the others worked in a multitude of places around the globe in over fifty other Protestant mission organisations.[84] The chapter evaluates missionary women in Australian Baptist mission history and historiography. Many women considered mission work their calling and vocation, although their work has largely been overlooked and downplayed.

Chapter 4. Women's State and National Baptist Organizations describes the history of the different women's organizations that operated at state and national levels between 1878 and 1945 in Australia. The chapter reveals both their significance for the denomination and how these organizations and their achievements have been largely omitted from Baptist historiography.

Chapter 5. Women's Ordination, Leadership, and Writing discusses why Australian Baptist women could not and did not seek ordination. The chapter analyzes the work of women who preached, undertook evangelistic endeavors, and wrote religious works. The chapter identifies the many leadership, preaching, and ministry roles undertaken by women within and outside the denomination, particularly through women's organizations.

Chapter 6. Women's Social Work and Activities Outside the Denomination assesses the involvement of Baptist women in a range of organizations and activities that were ecumenical or non-denominational in nature. The

---

83. King, *Tread Softly*, 9.
84. East Bengal was the only location for ABFM activity until 1959.

chapter contends that because women did not have, or could not attain, formal leadership positions within the denomination, they sought opportunities to work in religious organizations outside the denomination, particularly CE and the WCTU.

Chapter 7. The concluding chapter consolidates the various themes from each chapter of the book, specifically acknowledging the importance of evangelical and Baptist identity.

2

Women in Congregations

> Baptist women, numbering two-thirds of our congregations, are ready to stand shoulder to shoulder and to help in every possible way the coming of the Kingdom of our Lord.[1]
>
> —Florence Benskin, 1925.

INTRODUCTION

In 1964 Ruth Smith, an Australian Baptist minister's wife and a former missionary, gave a presentation to Victorian Baptists, reflecting on the role of Baptist women in the mid to late nineteenth century:

> There was no organized women's work, but the help one gave to one's neighbour in sickness, trouble and drought was all in the Name of the Master. From Miss [Vera] Horsfall at Lake Charm a letter was written saying there was 'nothing to report' from the women. *But we know they were writing with their lives the history of the Church.*[2]

For the most part Australian Baptist women from the 1830s to 1945 were "writing with their lives" within their Australian Baptist congregations. This

---

1. Benskin, "Through a Woman's Window: Pull Together," *BR*, 16 March 1925, 10.
2. Mrs A. E. [Ruth] Smith, "Women Through the Ages," BUVA (emphasis added). The pageant was performed at the 1964 BUV Assembly meeting on 7 October 1964. See "Of Interest to Women: Vic. BWA Celebrates 40 Years," *TAB*, 21 October 1964, 7.

chapter discusses women's work in Australian Baptist congregations—in what has been defined as the intermediate sphere.[3]

Women established separate women's groups within their congregations to support various causes, most notably in their own congregations but also in their community, or in support of mission activities outside Australia. The roles of women's groups within Baptist congregations need to be identified and examined. Baptist women provided funding for local church projects and supported community members. Women were also involved in mission activities. Within Australian Baptist congregations, women comprised a greater proportion of the membership and adherents than men.[4] Consequently women's work was necessary and vital, both as individuals and in local women's groups.

CHARACTERISTICS OF AUSTRALIAN BAPTIST WOMEN

Demographics

Australian Baptist women reflected the Australian population in that most were white and English-speaking. In the nineteenth century more Baptists were born in the UK rather than Australia, although this proportion decreased from the turn of the century and by the mid-twentieth century over 90 percent of Baptist women whose birthplace is known were born in Australia.[5]

Historically Baptists have been typified as being from lower socio-economic backgrounds—another hangover from the restrictions placed on non-conformists in the eighteenth and nineteenth centuries in England.[6] However various historians show that Baptists in England came from a wide range of socio-economic backgrounds and their socio-economic status increased throughout the nineteenth and twentieth centuries.[7] Aus-

---

3. Wilson, *Constrained by Zeal*, 1, 210.

4. Benskin, "Through a Woman's Window: Pull Together," BR, 16 March 1925, 10.

5. ABS, "Historical Censuses"; Hilton, "ABW Database." The proportion of the Australian population born outside Australia has remained relatively high due to continuing migration to Australia in the twentieth and twenty-first centuries. In 2019 the OECD reported that Australia had the second highest proportion of foreign-born population of OECD countries. For Baptist information, see Hilton, "ABW Database." More women were born in the UK compared to Australia in the nineteenth century but this reversed by the mid-twentieth century: 62 percent of Australian Baptist women were born in Australia, and nearly 94 percent died in Australia. That is, women who came to Australia generally stayed in Australia.

6. West, *Daughters of Freedom*, 143.

7. Wilson, *Constrained by Zeal*, 7.

tralian census data confirm that on average, Baptist women were largely middle-class, although there is some nuance in this, as Australian Baptist women were more likely to be from families in small business or trade occupations than the Australian social or political elite class.[8] Prominent Baptist women tended to be from wealthy middle-class families and rarely engaged in paid employment. Such a scenario occurred in part because women who did not need paid employment had time to undertake voluntary work.

Clearly some Baptist women were poor.[9] From about 1868 to 1872 Norwood Baptist SA supported Rhoda Coates to undertake "domestic missionary" work in an "evangelical mission" in the area, which was then a relatively poor part of Adelaide. In 1871 she is reported as visiting 70 families weekly "and was generally well received."[10] In June 1886 the Norwood Baptist Deaconess minutes record that one of the single women members was financially stressed and arrangements were made to assist her.[11] There were working-class women involved in Baptist work, such as Ada Davis, the Victorian CE Superintendent in 1925, whose occupation was "factory hand."[12] The Collins Street Baptist Members Roll occasionally included addresses of members, some of whom lived in working class or poor areas.[13] Various ministers' wives came from poor or working-class families. Prior to marriage: Edna Bennell was a milliner; Sarah Chapman and Hannah Walton were dressmakers; Martha Harrison was a waitress; Lily Higlett worked as a shop assistant; and Sarah Whale worked in a china factory.[14] Potentially some Baptists valued the notion of financial struggle, as it complemented the notion of Baptist persecution. For example when speaking at the funeral service of Ada Reeves, from Casino Baptist in regional northern NSW, the Rev. Lawrence Jagger "spoke of the heroic faithfulness, the Spartan endurance, and the saintly sacrifice of the mothers of our land."[15]

---

8. ABS, "Historical Censuses"; Hilton, "ABW Database." The database contains 1,325 women whose occupation, father's occupation, or husband's occupation, is known. Less than 5 percent were independently wealthy or active in Australian political life, and many of these were previously in small business or a trade. See, for example, *This Corner*, 20.

9. ABS, "Historical Censuses."

10. "News of the Churches: Norwood," *TP*, October 1870, 118, "Norwood Baptist Church," *Adelaide Observer* (Adelaide), 23 December 1871, 11.

11. Norwood Baptist Deaconesses MM, SABA.

12. Ada L. Davis, in *Handbook of the Baptist Union of Victoria*, 53–54; *Australian Electoral Roll*, 17.

13. Otzen, "Calling the Roll," 49.

14. Hilton, "ABW Database."

15. "Mrs Ada Jane Reeves," *TAB*, 12 January 1943, 5.

Australian historians tend to agree that class was important but not a dominant factor in Australian life, and Australian society was viewed as relatively egalitarian, certainly in comparison to the UK.[16] Women from poor or working-class backgrounds were not excluded from involvement in Baptist congregations. Yet poor women appear to be less engaged than wealthy women, reflecting the available time and resources that middle-class or wealthy women brought to Baptist congregations and the denomination, and also showing that women's social class was rarely made evident unless they were from relatively wealthy families.

Australian Identity

It cannot assumed that Baptist women who were either born in Australia or spent a significant proportion of their lives there thought of themselves as Australian. Political commentator Stephanie Brookes describes Australian identity as "a work of collective and individual imagination, constantly evolving and influenced by the contexts in which it is developed."[17]

Some Baptist women were Australian only by virtue of their location. In the nineteenth century people living in Australia were more likely to identify themselves as belonging to the colony in which they lived, rather than Australia. Many women retained an identity with the country of their birth, particularly when links remained with family and friends.[18] In 1862 Christina Swan went on a "trip home . . . [to Scotland which] was one of the great events of her life."[19] In 1897 Catherine Proctor wrote of her sadness in leaving Scotland to travel to Australia, "away from home and loved ones, away from companionships precious and sweet."[20] Likewise in 1910 Mary Crofts migrated to Australia despite the fact she was "an English woman to the very marrow!"[21] Some Baptist women migrated to Australia but then returned to the UK, including Scottish woman Janet Dobie who "couldna' bear the thought of her auld banes lying in Australie, far from her folk."[22] Being

---

16. See Richardson, *Family Experiments*.

17. Brookes, *Politics, Media*.

18. Arthur, *Migrant Nation*, 9.

19. "In Memoriam: Gathering Homeward One by One," *Queensland Freeman* (Brisbane), 16 February 1888, 4.

20. Catherine Proctor in "In Memoriam: Catherine Proctor, of Sea Lake," *TSB*, 2 September 1897.

21. Crofts, [Reflections on Alice Crofts].

22. Robert Fraser, "They Heard Dr. Boreham," *TAB*, 15 September 1936, 4. See Hilton, "ABW Database."

temporarily in Australia did not stop women wanting to work to improve Australian society. Ethel Spurr lived in Australia from 1909 to 1914 with her husband the Rev. Frederic Spurr, the minister of Collins Street Baptist, Melbourne. While in Australia, she absorbed herself in Australian society, becoming a life member of the Australian WCTU engaged in establishing health centers for poor women and their infant children, and speaking at meetings on social issues.[23]

Throughout the first half of the twentieth century many Australians continued to see themselves, and Australia, as intrinsically British with a shared heritage and strong family links. In 1930 Australian born Stella Stafford expressed a sense of imperial identity when she wrote that Queen Victoria had been a "great and good woman who ruled over our Empire."[24] There was ongoing and strong connections to the UK and the British Empire. Until 26 January 1949 Australian citizenship did not legally exist and all Australian residents were British subjects.[25] Australian passports issued to 1967 included the word "British" on the cover.[26]

Most Baptists identified as being Australian and it was considered their "homeland."[27] Frank Boreham wrote that he and his wife Stella Boreham initially missed England but over time "found that [they] had become citizens of the distant south."[28] In 1906, upon return from an overseas trip, Rosetta Birks said that she "had represented . . . Australia itself in England and America."[29] Elsie Cumming's diaries during her service in the First World War indicated her connection to Australia, writing she was "proud of our Australian boys."[30] In 1937 Esma Venn was traveling through UK and Europe, and wrote to CE members: "I am still thinking about you all back in Australia, which I have proved is the best place to live in after all."[31]

Despite the predominance of English-speaking Australian Baptist women, there were some exceptions, particularly Chinese- and German-speaking Baptists. Inner-city congregations in Sydney, Melbourne, and

---

23. See "Schools for Mothers," *Herald* (Melbourne), 15 November 1912, 6; "The WCTU," *Spectator and Methodist Chronicle* (Melbourne), 20 February 1914, 299.

24. Stafford, *Path of Life*, 2.

25. Klapdor et al., "Australian Citizenship."

26. Doulman and Lee, *Every Assistance and Protection*, 14.

27. See, for example, Edith K. Wilcox, "Baptist Womanhood in Action," *TAB*, 27 September 1938, 4; Pappin, "Furreedpore [sic]," *OB*, February 1895, 4; Gwenyth Harry, "Mymensingh," *OB*, July 1921, 3.

28. Boreham, *My Pilgrimage*, 137–38.

29. "The YWCA," *Advertiser* (Adelaide), 13 December 1906, 8.

30. Tranter, *In All Those Lines*, 102.

31. Esma Durbin, "An Endeavourer in Paris," *TRC*, 1 September 1937, 47.

Hobart formed valuable connections with Chinese Baptists. For example, in the late 1890s the Baptist Union of NSW provided support to a Chinese mission, and Bathurst Street Baptist, Sydney, held baptismal services for Chinese people.[32] There were many German families in Australian Baptist congregations, particularly in SA and Queensland. In the latter half of the nineteenth century in Brisbane, German-speaking Australians were members of Wharf Street Baptist. They had their own church building and conducted their services in German.[33] Although the German congregation had links to the Baptist Union of Queensland, German Baptists were relatively insular, and women appear to have led lives largely within the German community. Johanna Kruegar, the wife of the Rev. Carl Kruegar, lived in Queensland from the age of nine but could not speak fluent English.[34]

First Nations women joined Baptist congregations, such as Mary—surname not recorded—who was one of the first three people baptized in Newcastle in 1864.[35] Unfortunately such occurrences are rarely mentioned, other than on mission sites to First Nations people, and their roles and influence prior to 1945 were not recorded.[36]

Some Australian historians conclude that since 1788 most of the historical notions of Australian identity were endorsed inappropriately as a largely homogenic, white, settler, egalitarian, society.[37] Thus for Baptist women, their sense of Australian identity was focused on masculine notions of Australian identity, specifically through the characteristic of mateship, which was even more prevalent following the First World War. Mateship highlighted an egalitarian Australian identity but it was associated with men, to the exclusion of women.[38] Baptist Lorna Ollif, in her 1981 history of the Australian Women's Armed Services wrote: "Australia [was] a man's country from its beginning."[39]

32. "The Churches: Baptist Chinese mission," *Daily Telegraph* (Sydney) 1896, 11.
33. Parker, *Pressing on with the Gospel*, 11.
34. "Notes and News," *TQB*, 1 March 1900, 29.
35. "The Baptist Church: Year of Jubilee: Historical Sketch," *Newcastle Morning Herald and Miner's Advocate* (Newcastle, NSW), 14 October 1911, 4.
36. Tyler and Tyler, *Mount Barker Baptist Church*, 2; Kathleen Simmons, "Random Reflections from Queensland," *TAB*, 16 October 1928, 7.
37. Arthur, *Migrant Nation*, 2.
38. Grimshaw et al., *Creating a Nation*, 218; Piggin and Linder, *Fountain of Public Prosperity*, 470.
39. Ollif, *Women in Khaki*, 18.

Baptist Identity and Stereotypes of Baptist Women

Baptist distinctives influenced the perceptions of Baptists held by other Australians, and Australian Baptist women were sometimes stereotyped as naysayers, pious, or wowsers, generally because they were opposed to the consumption of alcohol and, by extension, other enjoyable activities.[40] Many Baptist women may have accepted, or even welcomed, some of these descriptions of themselves.[41] In *Daughters of Freedom*, Janet West asserts: "No reference is made in nineteenth-century Baptist publications to women except in terms of a feminine ideal of 'shrinking, delicate modesty.'"[42] This broad statement cay be refuted because there are many articles in early Baptist papers that described women in affirmative terms, such as in 1870 when North Adelaide Baptist women are described as "working vigorously," in addition to the multitude of articles in the late nineteenth century about the valuable work of Baptist missionary women.[43]

Of course, nineteenth-century Baptist denominational papers did have some articles that used "feminine ideals" and restricted women's roles solely to that of wife and mother. In 1881 *The Queensland Freeman* printed a short story by Rose Terry Cook, a North American writer, "In Two Pews," which described a Christian woman as being trained by her mother "in the delicate, gentle ways of her own home ... to do her duty as well as she knew how."[44] In 1902 the editor of *The Baptist* in NSW wrote that suffrage was not something that an "ordinary woman" wanted, as the act of voting was "invading the privacy and quietude of her home life."[45] These articles indicate a somewhat adverse view of women or that women should be relegated to the home, but reflected a societal view rather than a specific Baptist view. In 1880 James Greenwood, a NSW politician and former Baptist minister, wrote an article reflecting opinions on equality, such as women being

---

40. "Wowsers on the War-Path," *Call and WA Sportsman* (Perth), 24 October 1919, 9; "Wit and Humour in the Assembly," *TSB*, 21 November 1912, 763. The term "wowser" probably originated in Australia, as a derogatory term for those—particularly evangelicals—who advocated for restrictions on alcohol, gambling, and other "worldly" or immoral activities. See Piggin and Linder, *Fountain of Public Prosperity*, 366.

41. See, for example, Helen Harry, "The Juniors," *TRC*, 1 January 1898, 8. Helen Harry mentioned piety as a good attribute.

42. West, *Daughters of Freedom*, 143.

43. "News of the Churches: North Adelaide," *TP*, September 1870, 106. See also Silas Mead, "Deaconesses," *TP*, August 1868, 156–60; Henry Coombs, "The Record of a Brief Life," *Queensland Freeman* (Brisbane), March 1881, 34.

44. Rose Terry Cooke, "In Two Pews," *TQF*, July 1881, 106.

45. "Topics of the Month: The Ordinary Woman," *Baptist* (Sydney), 1 November 1902, 2.

physically weaker, and being "compelled by nature to . . . the nurture of her children," yet he believed "whatever a woman can do as well as a man, there is no reason in nature, and there ought to be no reason in social life, why she should not be as free as a man to do it."[46] Generally Baptist women were described in equal terms with men with respect to their ability to work within the Baptist denomination. In *The Australian Baptist*, for example, which commenced in 1912, there are few articles that describe women in deficient or submissive terms.[47]

Being a wife and mother was an important part of most women's identity. In 1917 Elizabeth Baker's spiritual growth was observed: "As she advanced towards young womanhood she grew in those graces of the Spirit, and in that strength and beauty of character which fitted her for the high and sacred offices God designed her to fill—those of wife and mother."[48] In 1944 a similar description was made regarding Emily Lanyon, whose "real sphere was in the home, for she was 'a worker at home,' and there by her influence, she enriched the whole household."[49] Attributes of motherhood were also given to—and taken on by—single women, such as missionary women who were "Mother's in the Lord," or Marion Downes, who wrote a poem about "Every Child's Mother."[50]

In 1912 the Baptist Union of Victoria (BUV) held an evening session celebrating the jubilee of the Union, with two speeches titled "The New Woman and the Old" and "The New Man and the Old" delivered by the Rev. Frederick Harry and the Rev. Arthur Waldock respectively. Frederick Harry affirmed that improvements could, and should, be made by women through courageous and hopeful action, but advised women not to be aggressive about their rights, or to be "militant suffragettes."[51] Ironically Arthur Waldock's speech on men was not significantly dissimilar to Frederick Harry's speech on women.[52] Splitting the discussion of women and men indicates that officials envisaged women and men undertaking different tasks

---

46. James Greenwood, "The Equality of the Sexes, *Sydney Mail and NSW Advertiser* (Sydney), 10 January 1880, 54.

47. Many articles in Australian Baptist papers have been examined and none sought to repress women explicitly. However in the 1960s there are some articles that discuss the inappropriateness of women's ordination, including several written by women.

48. "Death of Mrs. Elizabeth J. Baker," *TAB*, 4 September 1917, 10.

49. "Called Home: Mrs S. E. Lanyon," *TAB*, 29 August 1944, 5.

50. Gooden, "Mothers in the Lord," 5; Marion Downes, "Every Child's Mother," *Kyneton Observer* (Kyneton, Victoria) 1899.

51. Frederick Miles, "Facts and Faith for the Future," *TSB*, 21 November 1912, 760.

52. Miles, "Facts and Faith for the Future," *TSB*, 21 November 1912, 760.

in different ways. Seemingly the greatest difference was that while women were required to undertake work for the denomination, they should not act outside prevailing societal restrictions on women's actions: Women should be "encouragers" rather than acting like men.[53] In 1931 another Victorian Baptist minister, the Rev. Henry Clark, specifically addressed the role of women at the meeting celebrating one hundred years of Baptist worship in Australia, observing that women were part of Jesus' ministry and were the first candidates for believers' baptisms conducted in Australia. He reflected: "It brought to mind also the sacrificial service that had been rendered by godly women to the Church throughout the century."[54]

The ways in which women are written and spoken about reveal stereotypes of hard-working women who did not seek a public role for themselves. Yet women's writings frequently contained themes relating to identity, indicating a difference between harmful stereotypes and Baptist women's perception of themselves as active Australian Baptists.[55] Generalisations about Baptist women demeaned their roles, downplayed their ministries, and reinforced the perception they were not active in the development of the Australian Baptist denomination or wider Australian society, leading to them being overlooked in later historical accounts.

Spiritual Practices

Australian Baptist women's identity was linked to their Baptist faith—a living faith. Baptist women's faith impacted their lives in a variety of ways, particularly through evidence of spiritual practices such as their personal devotions and prayer.[56] Essentially such practices were an additional component of their lives, being more than their recorded actions and activities.

In 1907 Sarah Booth implored readers of her book: "We want to give you an incentive for a noble life. We want you to have spiritual ambition."[57] Philip Sheldrake views spirituality as the intersection of theology, a relationship with God, and Christianity in practice. Spirituality is an approach to life.[58] For most women, their evangelical spirituality was expressed through the desire for an active faith, studying the Bible, an ongoing personal

53. Miles, "Facts and Faith for the Future," *TSB*, 21 November 1912, 760.
54. "Thanksgiving Meeting," *TAB*, 28 April 1931, 10.
55. Hilton, "Australian Baptist Women as Public Intellectuals."
56. Randall, *What a Friend We Have in Jesus*, 42, 86, 91, 183; Sheldrake, *Spirituality*, 163.
57. Booth, *Dinna Forget*, 309.
58. Randall, *What a Friend We Have in Jesus*, 22; Sheldrake, *Spirituality*, 3.

relationship with God through prayer, and reflection on the sacrifice of God through Christ's death on the cross, particularly during communion services.

Women's spirituality, that is the actions in living out their faith, was evident through active participation in their congregation. Worshiping with others was essential and worship services were broadly the same in all Australian Baptist congregations, irrespective of any doctrinal differences.[59] Singing exemplifies this. Australian Baptists encouraged singing—and the use of the Baptist Hymnal from the UK—in Sunday worship services. Singing occurred with the full congregation, by the choir, or by soloists.[60] Interestingly many of the hymns sung by Baptists were written by women from the UK and the USA.[61]

Australian Baptists often worshipped with non-Baptist congregations because of the lack of Baptist congregations in outer suburban and regional locations. The experiences of May Ingram, Edith Penno, and Eliza Walters may be cited as typical in this regard. May Ingram was a Baptist minister's daughter and had been a member of various Baptist congregations in Queensland. In 1905 she married Richard Ingram and in 1909 they moved to Bundaberg, which did not have a Baptist congregation. May and Richard Ingram worshipped with the Bundaberg Presbyterians for over twenty years, but when they moved to Toowoomba they resumed attendance at a Baptist congregation.[62] In 1888 Edith Penno was baptized in Coromandel Valley Baptist SA, and attended the congregation until her marriage in 1893 when she moved to Magill. As there was no Baptist congregation in Magill she worshipped with the Salvation Army until 1907, and when her family moved to Keswick she attended the Baptist congregation located there.[63] Eliza Walters was a member of Bathurst Street Baptist, Sydney, but in 1861 she married and moved to Nundle in northern NSW. The town initially had no church and Eliza Walters and other women established a Sunday School that later became part of the Primitive Methodist Church. By 1889 Eliza

---

59. See, for example, Norwood Baptist Deaconesses MM, SABA; Dorcas Society Bathurst Street Baptist Church Minutes of Meetings (DSBSBM), State Library of NSW, Sydney (SLNSW); Hurlstone Park Baptist Ladies Aid Society Minutes of Meetings (HPBLASM), NSWBA; Ladies Sewing Guild Glen Osmond MM, SABA; Grange Baptist Church Flower Committee MM, SABA.

60. Manley, *From Woolloomooloo*, 1:94, 217.

61. See, for example, *Baptist Hymnal*. At least 16 percent of the hymns were written by women.

62. "Death of Mr. R. H. Ingram," *TAB*, 8 August 1939, 7.

63. "Mrs. H. J. Penno," *TAB*, 15 August 1939, 7.

Walters had moved to Tamworth, where she became a foundation member of Tamworth Baptist.[64]

Even in larger cities women may have not been able to attend a Baptist congregation due to distance and the lack of personal transport.[65] Myra Fuller addressed the lack of a local Baptist congregation by establishing a congregation in Pennant Hills in the early 1920s.[66] Some Baptist women lamented their inability to worship with other Baptists, including Emily Price who worshipped with Congregationalists for many years but said she "could never be other than a Baptist."[67] These examples demonstrate the importance of women's faith: being a Baptist was significant, but regular worship with an evangelical congregation was more important than insistence on Baptist denominational loyalty.[68]

In 1911 Victorian Baptist Cecilia Downing wrote about some of the important ways in which women could express their ministry through their spiritual practices. She considered that women's "ministry for the Church will be futile unless it begins with prayer, praise, and meditation . . . [Prayer] is among the most powerful services that women can exercise for the Church's progress."[69] Women prayed with other women from their congregation, in the home, as part of their private devotions, or in family worship.[70] In 1889 at Mount Gambier Elizabeth Mildwaters died at the age of forty-four. Her obituarist wrote:

> One thing that caused her sorrow was that she had never publicly, or in the family, used her gift of prayer. A few days before her death she said to her husband, "Perhaps you think I cannot pray aloud, but I can." . . . Then she poured her soul out in prayer, committing her soul to Christ, and her husband, child, and loved ones to Him who slumbereth not nor sleepeth.[71]

---

64. J. H. F., "The Late Mrs. Eliza Walters," *TAB*, 31 March 1914, 2.

65. J. A. Packer, "A Happy Transition: Death of Miss E. M. Price," *TAB*, 29 November 1932, 4; Edgerton Long, Eulogy for Olive Grace Collins, 1998, NSWBA.

66. "More or Less Personal," *TAB*, 10 September 1929, 4.

67. Packer, "A Happy Transition," *TAB*, 29 November 1932, 4.

68. Randall, *What a Friend We Have in Jesus*, 17.

69. Mrs J. [Cecilia] Downing, "The Ministry of Woman in the Church," *TAB*, 20 April 1911, 266.

70. "Baptist Union of New South Wales," *TP*, February 1870, 22; John. E. Walton, "In Memoriam: Tasmania," *TSB*, 10 February 1903, 47; Downing, "The Ministry of Woman in the Church," *TAB*, 20 April 1911, 266; Wood, "Leaves from My Life Story," *TAB*, 5 October 1926, 2.

71. "Mount Gambier," *TP*, 1 March 1889, 48.

The anguish of Elizabeth Mildwaters at feeling stifled in praying is heartbreaking and poignant.

Baptist women also engaged in daily devotions and home-based "family worship." Indeed family worship was a feature in many Australian Protestant families in the late nineteenth and early twentieth centuries.[72] Family worship usually took the form of a Bible reading, a short message—or devotional—usually related to the reading, hymn singing, and prayer. Many Australian Baptist households used a book by Charles Spurgeon specifically for this purpose titled *The Interpreter*.[73]

The expectation was that men would lead—the Rev. Alan Webb wrote that family worship was "a church in the house with the father as priest to his family."[74] Yet evidence suggests that perhaps women were more likely to lead than Baptists acknowledged. For instance, the Rev. Frederick Spurr preached about "father as a true priest" of the home and yet recalled that family worship in his childhood was undertaken by his widowed mother.[75] For Mary Gibson the "power and beauty of her prayers at family worship were very great" and she frequently led family worship, although she did not pray out loud when entertaining her obituarist—a Baptist minister.[76] Annie Morling's husband and sons were ministers, and yet her son the Rev. George Morling remembered his mother's words during their regular family worship time.[77] Hugh Dixson acknowledged his father's expectation that all family members attend family worship and yet reflected that his mother Helen Dixson influenced his spiritual life more than his father.[78]

From the early twentieth century onwards family worship appears to have lost its appeal.[79] Efforts by advocates to increase the use of family worship were not successful—a situation lamented by the Rev. Edward Harris as caused by "twentieth-century strenuous life."[80] From the 1920s few Baptist

---

72. Frederick Miles, "Victorian Snapshot," *TAB*, 13 January 1914, 10; Hugh Dixson, "Letter to the Editor," *TAB*, 20 July 1915, 2.

73. Spurgeon, *Interpreter, or, Scripture for Family Worship*.

74. Webb, "Old Ideals," *TSB*, 3 July 1901, 151, quoted in Manley, *From Woolloomooloo*, 1:285.

75. Frederick C. Spurr, "Australian Family Life: Fourth of a Series of Sunday Evening Discourses," *Watchman* (Sydney), 11 August 1910, 3.

76. John E. Walton, "In Memoriam: Tasmania," *TSB*, 10 February 1903, 47.

77. Rogers, *George Henry Morling*, 11.

78. Hugh Dixson, "Early Baptist History," *TAB*, 18 July 1916, 5.

79. S. M. [Sydney] Potter, "Baptist Union of Victoria: The Closing Day," *TAB*, 19 May 1914, 12.

80. Edward Harris, "The Family Alter," *TAB*, 23 June 1914, 3.

families appear to have retained family worship, although many Baptist women continued their own personal devotions.[81]

Baptist women's spiritual lives also impacted their relationships with others. This is beautifully expressed by Clara Crump's obituarist who stated that she was "remembered more for what she was rather than what she did."[82] While very few women left a written record of their theology, their actions confirmed an emphasis on these Christian spiritual traditions.

Tithing and philanthropy

The Baptist denomination was sustained through funding provided by adherents. Baptist women, like many Christians, believed in the principle of tithing, which was initially expressed by an individual giving one-tenth of their income to God.[83] The money was usually given during a specific time in worship services. Baptist leaders—and other denominational leaders—encouraged tithing, although many Baptists did not strictly give one-tenth of their income. Margaret Press, a WCTU activist in Victoria, believed: "One-tenth of the income of God's people consecrated to the service of Christ would effectively solve the financial problems in all our churches, and in the work of His Kingdom throughout the world."[84]

There were several wealthy Baptist women who gave considerable funds to the denomination.[85] Mary Ann Gibson was a key figure in the development of the Baptist denomination in Tasmania. During the nineteenth century Mary Ann Gibson and her husband William Gibson donated land and buildings for Baptist congregations. They paid for Baptist ministers to move from England to Tasmania and guaranteed ministers' wages until congregations were able to financially support the minister.[86] She was crucial to the development of the Baptist denomination in Tasmania. Sophia Barker, from 1890 to 1909, was the sole owner of a drapery shop in Mount Barker

---

81. Mrs A. J. [Christina] Whitbourn, "The Disadvantages of a Minister's Wife," *TAB*, 26 June 1917, 2, 14.

82. "Clara May Crump," *TAB*, 25 March 1970, 4.

83. Rubio, *Family Ethics*. Tithing was law in Jewish culture.

84. Mrs [Margaret] Press, "Should We Give Systematically?," *TAB*, 14 April 1914, 7. Margaret Press was an Australian Wesleyan Methodist but she spoke at Baptist events, and articles she wrote were published in *Australian Baptist*.

85. The Victorian Baptist Archives have records of over twenty-five Victorian Baptist women to 1945 who donated relatively large funds to various Baptist activities during their lives or as part of their estate.

86. Walton, "In Memoriam: Tasmania," *TSB*, 10 February 1903, 47; Rowston, "Spurgeon's Men," 31.

SA, which had been established in 1865 by her husband William Barker. Sophia Barker's choice to be the wife of a draper may have been largely out of her control, as too the continuation of the business after her husband's death in 1890. Yet because of her successful business Sophia Barker made significant financial donations to the Baptist denomination in SA, as did her daughter Florence Barker. Although Sophia Barker operated the business for nineteen years, Baptist articles focused on the initial ownership of the business by William Barker—although she probably assisted in building the business.[87] Ellen Trestrail and Rebecca Bullock donated significant funds to Baptist theological colleges in Victoria and NSW respectively.[88] Other philanthropists donated funds to the denomination, including Lady Emma Dixson and Bessie Greening in NSW, Lady Helen Goode in SA, Laura Grimes and Rachael Phelps in Queensland, and Annie Oliver in WA.[89] Women's philanthropy was usually acknowledged at the time but has rarely been included or acclaimed in Baptist history.

THE FIRST AUSTRALIAN BAPTIST WOMEN

There are few official records regarding women's work in congregations prior to the 1880s. Despite this, there are clear indications that women were involved in the establishment and development of Baptist congregations around Australia, particularly through the records of foundation members of Baptist congregations.[90] The first baptisms that occurred in Australia were two unnamed women baptized by the Rev. John McKaeg in Sydney on 12 August 1831.[91] Meetings of Baptists in the 1830s in Sydney regarding the establishment of a Baptist congregation and building included women, with one report stating that among the 300 people present "the welcome faces of the ladies contributed in no small degree to grace and enliven the coup d'eil" (a quaint way to express the opinion that women brighten a room).[92] In 1823 Mary Ware arrived in Tasmania with her husband Jeremiah Ware: and

---

87. "Obituary: Miss F. J. Barker," *Mount Barker Courier and Onkaparinga and Gumeracha Advertiser* (Mount Barker, SA), 1 February 1951, 5.

88. Prior, *Some Fell on Good Ground*, 235; Otzen, *Whitley*, 49.

89. "The Late Mrs Oliver," *TAB*, 6 December 1921, 8; Lillias Slinn, "New South Wales Union: A Deaconess' Association," *TAB*, 2 October 1917, 6; "Baptist," *Telegraph* (Brisbane), 7 June 1930, 10; "Waverley," *TAB*, 20 May 1930, 11; Trigg and Robertson, "History of Mount Barker"; *These Fifty Years*, n.p.

90. See Hilton, "ABW Database."

91. Manley, *From Woolloomooloo*, 1:3.

92. "Baptist Meeting," *Currency Lad* (Sydney), 29 September 1932, 3.

the first meeting of Tasmanian Baptists occurred in their home in 1835.[93] She was one of the first Baptist woman to provide hospitality in Australia!

Mary Ware, c. 1854. Portrait by Robert Dowling, oil on canvas on board, 34.0 x 29.0, National Portrait Gallery of Australia. Purchased with funds provided by Mary Isabel Murphy and Rosalind Blair Murphy 2014; used with permission.

In 1837 Helen Finlayson and her husband William Finlayson were described as "the first Baptist people" in SA: of her it was written that "much of her time was devoted to deeds of kindness and charity."[94] In Victoria in

93. Rowston, *Baptists in Van Dieman's Land*, 1, 8.

94. "Obituaries," *South Australian Register* (Adelaide), 25 October 1884, 3; Hughes, *Our First Hundred Years*, 17.

1845, when the foundation stone was laid for Collins Street Baptist Melbourne, no women's names were mentioned, but a report on the meeting to discuss next steps noted that of the 200 people attending, "a great proportion" were women.[95] Christina Swan and her husband James Swan arrived in Sydney in 1837, and they were involved in the early work of Bathurst Street Baptist Sydney. In 1846 they moved to Brisbane, initially worshiping with the United Evangelical Church until 1855 when the first Baptist congregation was established in Queensland. Both Christina and James Swan were foundation members, and Christina Swan's work for the congregation was significant.[96] In some cases, women's involvement is later recorded in tributes, such as Hariett Gibbs, who was a "devoted member and worker of the church" from 1869 to 1881 at Lambton Baptist NSW.[97] Further examples are revealed throughout this book, but unfortunately the existence and roles of early Australian Baptist women are under-reported.

WOMEN'S WORK IN CONGREGATIONS

Australian Baptist women undertook a wide range of activities in their congregations such as hospitality and catering, fundraising, preparing the church building for worship services, and Sunday School teaching. These roles facilitated the growth of local Baptist congregations and the denomination. Often individual women undertook many different tasks. Matilda Glassop, for example, was: "Sunday School teacher, organist, Endeavourer [that is, a member of Christian Endeavor], visitor to parents of Sunday School scholars, [and member of the] Ladies' Sewing Guild [and] church choir."[98] Women undertook roles expected of them, but they were able to shape other roles for themselves, such as providing spiritual support to other Baptist women.[99] Women's participation was vital within their Baptist congregations. In 1892 Harriet Gillings wrote of the importance of

---

95. "Port Phillip," *Sentinel* (Sydney), 4 July 1845, 3.

96. "In Memoriam: Gathering Homeward One by One," *Queensland Freeman*, 15 February 1888, 4.

97. "Lambton," *Newcastle Morning Herald and Miners' Advocate* (Newcastle, NSW), 11 February 1919, 5.

98. "Our Baptist Veterans: Mrs Stephen Glassop," *TAB*, 20 January 1949, 4.

99. See, for example, Norwood Baptist Deaconesses MM, SABA; South Australia Baptist Women's Missionary Union, BWMU Minutes 1922–1944, Baptist Mission Australia Archives, Moore Potter House, Melbourne (BMAA); Jireh Branch QBW Union Minutes of Meetings (JQBWUM), Baptist Union of Queensland Archives, Queensland Baptists' Centre, Gaythorne, Brisbane (BUQA); Grange Baptist Church Flower Committee MM, SABA.

Christian work to women: "As to the question whether such sisters as are called to labour in the Lord should be recognised by the Church, it appears evident that they should; if the Lord calls and qualifies, any such to labour in any department of His service, be it in pastoral work, or as deaconesses, helps, or in any other way."[100]

Women undertook much of the work in preparing the church building for worship services, which was particularly evident in floral displays. For women who did not have their own income, being able to "give" flowers to the congregation was an important and meaningful role. Towards the end of Jane Fraser's life she said: "The only thing I can do now is to grow flowers for the church."[101] Flowers provided a ministry to the sick, as many congregations had processes in place to distribute the flowers used to decorate the church building to members of the congregation who were unwell, or to people in hospital.[102] In the late nineteenth century, for example, the Social and Flower Committee at Ipswich Baptist Queensland decorated the church building for Sunday worship and then rearranged the flowers to create around five bunches of flowers each week to be distributed as needed. Convenor Eliza Webb affirmed: "My prayer is that they have been a help and comfort to some, if not to all."[103] In 1931 Enid Mackay wrote an article about "The Ministry of Flowers" declaring:

> There is no need for gorgeous hot-house blooms, for even the humblest blossom has its message for our hearts. Who could think an evil or unkind thought whilst gazing on a flower. They seem to stir within us that which is good. We give flowers to express joy, and we give flowers to comfort in sorrow, and how many hearts have been strengthened by the gift of a flower![104]

The provision of flowers as part of the service, which then became gifts, was an important ministry, and—as Eliza Webb and Enid Mackay's words indicate—those involved viewed it as a crucial part of their ministry.

Australian Baptist women provided input to worship services and other denominational events through music, including playing instruments and singing.[105] From 1892 to 1945 Auburn Baptist, NSW had eight organists, of

100. Mrs W. G. [Harriet] Gillings, "Women's Ministry: Its Legitimacy and Power: Part 2," *TVB*, February 1892, 26.

101. "The Late Mrs Jane Ann Fraser," *TAB*, 6 March 1917, 3.

102. Ipswich Social and Flower Committee, Report Book, 1897–1901, BUQA; Grange Baptist Church Flower Committee MM, BUQA.

103. Ipswich Social and Flower Committee, Report Book, BUQA.

104. Enid Elphinston, "The Ministry of Flowers," *TRC*, 1 January 1931, 105.

105. "New South Wales: Islington," *TAB*, 12 August 1930, 10; Maxwell, *Triumphant Through Trials*, 14.

whom six were women. Some women served as organist for long periods such as Margaret Cousin, who from 1919 to 1946 was organist at Hurlstone Park Baptist, NSW.[106] Choir directors were usually men, but choirs had more women than men.[107] For example a 1940s photo of the Bathurst Street Baptist Choir has twelve women and six men, including the organist.[108]

Women aided other women who were about to be baptized. Such a role was necessary because of the "house-keeping" involved in full immersion baptisms. Baptisms usually occurred in the baptistry at the front of the church building, although some baptismal candidates were baptized in nearby rivers or the ocean. Baptismal candidates required a support person to prepare them for the baptism, such as praying prior to the baptism, and assistance after the baptism, mainly to change into dry clothes.[109] This was an important ministry activity that could not appropriately be undertaken by male ministers or deacons, and indeed it was a stated "duty" of some deaconesses' committees.[110]

Baptist congregations have always valued Sunday School held for children and young people, describing them as "the biggest and most important thing in our church life."[111] Sunday Schools were first established in the late eighteenth century in the UK to provide education to poor and working-class children. Some scholars question whether Sunday School was a way for the middle-class to control the working-class, yet for many children in the UK it was the only formal education they received.[112] In Australia Sunday Schools were a way to spread the message of Christianity through Bible stories and moral teaching. Protestant congregations organized Sunday Schools for children of members along with children in the local area. Some of these families were poor and working class. In 1888 in Bathurst Street Baptist Sydney, women of the congregation assisted in providing new dresses and hats for a family who "could not continue attending Sunday School for the want of

---

106. Stanhope, *Seek Those Things*, 126; *Through These Years*, 19.

107. See, for example, *Footscray Baptist Church*; Photo in the HPBLASM, NSWBA.

108. Starr, "My Words on 180 Years of CBC."

109. Petersham Baptist MM, NSWBA; Gomm, *Blazing the Western Trails*, 75.

110. Glen Osmond Baptist Deaconess MM, SABA; Norwood Baptist Deaconess MM, SABA; North Adelaide Baptist Deaconesses Minutes of Meetings (NABDM), SABA.

111. "The Great Sunday School Demonstration," *TAB*, 21 September 1920, 3. For additional examples, see "Domestic Intelligence," *Colonial Times* (Hobart), 8 January 1839, 7; "Mount Barker Baptist Church," *Mount Barker Courier and Onkaparinga and Gumeracha Advertiser*, 24 October 1924, 5.

112. Souter, "Place and Pedagogy," 14–15.

frocks."[113] Sunday Schools were usually held prior to Sunday worship services and the families of children who attended Sunday School were encouraged to attend worship services. One of the aims of the Griffith Baptist Ladies Guild in regional NSW was that "Mothers of children attending Sunday School be sought after by Ladies' Guild and encouraged to attend their [Guild] meetings with a view to church attendance."[114] Sunday School was seen as a crucial part of the outreach of a Baptist congregation. In 1925 in Greenslopes Baptist Queensland Emily Smith was delighted to report that "more than twenty Sunday School scholars have confessed Christ."[115]

Many women taught and led the Sunday Schools. Nearly one-third of obituaries of Baptist women acknowledge their role as Sunday School teachers as a noteworthy activity.[116] In 1911 Cecilia Downing stated that "the Sunday School and Bible Class work stands second to none in results for good achieved by our consecrated womanhood."[117]

The North Adelaide Baptist Young Women's Bible Class, c. 1914. With their minister, the Rev. Dr Frederick Norwood. Jessie Mellor (back row, second from right) became a deaconess in 1936. Provided by North Adelaide Baptist; used with permission.

113. DSBSBM, SLNSW.
114. Griffith Baptist Ladies Guild MM, NSWBA.
115. Emily (Sister Grace) Smith, "Deeds at Dunellan," *TQB*, 15 November 1925.
116. Hilton, "ABW Database." See Wilson, *Constrained by Zeal*, 189.
117. Cecilia Downing, "Fellowship of Women: Australian Baptist Women's Board," *TAB*, 24 September 1935, 2.

When Flinders Street Baptist Sunday School commenced in 1861 half of the twelve teachers were women.[118] Later lists and photographs of Sunday School teachers from numerous Baptist congregations show that usually more women than men were Sunday School teachers. In 1911 Port Pirie Baptist SA, a regional Sunday School, had an average attendance of 145 children and all the teachers were women, except for the teacher of the Young Men's Bible Class.[119]

Stanmore Baptist in Sydney provides a useful example of one of the larger Sunday School operations with significant women's involvement. In 1927 those involved in Stanmore Baptist Sunday School were a male general superintendent and six "department" superintendents, of whom two were men and four were women. There were also five secretaries, two assistant superintendents, five pianists, and eighty-one Sunday School teachers or helpers. In total, sixty of the ninety "staff" of Stanmore Baptist Sunday School were women.[120] In 1941 Winifred Ingram wrote a poem for the Stanmore Baptist CE paper about the progression through each of the Sunday School "departments" according to age, until "She's now a member, hand in hand / With those who seek to save."[121] That is, Sunday Schools aimed to take an individual from infancy to church membership. Sunday School leaders, called either superintendents or secretaries, were usually men, yet there many instances where women led the Sunday School.[122] In 1905–6 the NSW Baptist Year Book reported that women led 27 percent of the Sunday Schools in NSW congregations. One prominent example was Mary Wells, who led the Sunday School at Bathurst Street Baptist for over forty years.[123] In 1943 in Queensland twelve of the sixty-seven Sunday School Superintendents were women.[124] Australian Baptist women were proud of their involvement in Sunday School.

---

118. "Baptist Sunday School: Fifty Years' Record: Tributes at Flinders Street," *Evening Journal* (Adelaide), 12 September 1911, 4.

119. Eric Mitchell, "Port Pirie Baptist Sunday School: Anniversary Services," *Port Piri Recorder and North Western Mail* (Port Piri), 4 November 1911, 5.

120. *Stanmore Baptist Sunday School: Officers, Teacher and Helpers Installation Service, 1927*. The statistics for 1928 and 1929 are very similar to 1927.

121. Winnie [Winifred] Ingram, "The New Girl at Stanmore," *Rising Tide*, October 1941, 4.

122. *Footscray Baptist Church*; *Stanmore Baptist Sunday School: Officers, Teacher and Helpers Installation Service, 1927*; *Centenary: 1848–1948*.

123. "New South Wales: Called Home: Miss Minnie [Mary] Wells, of Northbridge, NSW," *TAB*, 6 August 1952, 15; BUNSW, *New South Wales Baptist Year Book*, 10.

124. BUQ, *Year Book 1943*, 18–21.

During 1915 George Doery, the President of the BUV, wrote articles for *The Australian Baptist* about visits made to twenty-three Victorian Baptist congregations. These articles provide a means through which different Victorian congregations can be compared at a point in time: from the larger Melbourne congregations to the small congregations in the Mallee district of north-west Victoria. This comparison is useful because it is otherwise difficult to readily document and compare the specific circumstances of Baptist congregations. Baptist congregations operated independently of each other, have inconsistent and incomplete records, and written histories took different approaches, although they are usually descriptions focused on the work of successive ministers. Around three-quarters of George Doery's articles included reference to women's work, albeit "in their own sphere."[125] At Albert Park Baptist, Melbourne, sixteen young women met weekly to sew items for Baptist mission workers in East Bengal.[126] Newmarket Baptist, Melbourne, had a Women's Missionary Prayer Union and a separate sewing group that raised money for the mission and the congregation respectively.[127] The women in Fitzroy Baptist supported a city mission for poor women.[128] George Doery described the activities and management of each congregation and, perhaps unintentionally, also showed the variety and significance of the work being undertaken by women in the congregations he visited.

The roles that Australian Baptist women were able to fulfil depended on the time, structures, and principles of the congregation. From the 1830s until the 1880s, women's ability to participate in the management of congregations and worship services was sometimes restricted. For example in Flinders Street Baptist until 1891 the constitution formally stated that women attending meetings could not speak and so, when appointed to a position in the congregation such as deaconess, women were required to write a letter accepting the position, in contrast to men who were able to verbally agree.[129] In situations like this, as members, women voted in meetings by raising their hands. There are no known Australian congregations in which women could not vote in members' meetings, although at least one man believed this should be the case. In 1867 William Cleaver, at York Street Baptist Launceston Tasmania, wrote that "allowing females to vote

---

125. George Doery, " With the Victorian President: Baptists in the Fighting Line (WVP): The Auburn Church," *TAB*, 16 November 1915, 7.

126. Doery, "WVP: Albert Park Church," *TAB*, 31 August 1915, 5.

127. Doery, "WVP [Newmarket Baptist]," *TAB*, 27 July 1915, 5.

128. Doery, "WVP: Work among the Women at George Street, Fitzroy," *TAB*, 20 April 1915, 3, 14.

129. Flinders Street Baptist Church MM, SABA.

[is] a practice which cannot be defended by the Word of God, and gives the woman a pre-eminence over man as they are more numerous generally in church than man."[130]

By the 1880s generally women could participate in church meetings and some congregations allowed women to undertake executive positions, such as Mount Barker Baptist SA, although in reality few women were appointed until the twentieth century.[131] Women were appointed to executive positions in circumstances where men were unavailable or unwilling to undertake such roles.[132] Traralgon Baptist, Victoria, was a small, regional congregation and the minutes of meetings included situations where men declined the positions of secretary, resulting in women being appointed "temporarily."[133] Archival materials from smaller congregations in rural areas typically include information about women, generally because they were essential to the establishment and maintenance of the congregation due to the small numbers of people involved, and there are many examples of women who worked in leadership positions in new, small, or regional Baptist congregations.[134] For example, in 1849 Kenton Baptist was established in rural SA and four of the eight trustees were women.[135] In 1886 at Blackheath Baptist, NSW "Miss Smith"—first name unknown—was instrumental in the establishment of the congregation, and was the first Secretary.[136] From 1911 to 1926 Edith Dorse was the Secretary of Stroud Baptist, NSW.[137] From 1939 to 1944 Halley Nicholls was the treasurer at Redland Bay Baptist, Queensland.[138] In 1917, when Evelyn Armstrong presented the financial report as Treasurer of Hornsby Baptist, the President of the NSW BU "remarked on the unique position of the Hornsby Church in having a lady treasurer, and who, judging by the reports, was a great success."[139] Yet there were other women during the period who had executive positions including: Mary Batey in Abermain, Sarah Sharp in Goulburn, and

---

130. See Rowston, *Baptists in Van Diemen's Land*, 75.

131. Mount Barker Baptist Church MM, SABA; Mount Barker Baptist Church, Officers' MM, SABA.

132. Moore, *All Western Australia*, 117.

133. Moore, *Ordinary Church in the Country*, 63–65.

134. "Women's Work," *TSB*, 15 January 1907, 13. Adelaide Bamford, "Letter to the Editor: Women in the Ministry," *TAB*, 16 November 1960, 11.

135. *One Hundred Years*, 2.

136. "Blackheath," *Katoomba Times* (Katoomba), 24 May 1890, 2.

137. Harris, *Stroud District Baptist Church*, 116–19.

138. BUQ, *Year Book 1940*, 87.

139. "Church News: Hornsby, NSW," *TAB*, 25 December 1917, 9.

Mary Shoults in Mortdale.[140] Women in executive positions understood the "uniqueness" of their positions. In 1924 Myra Fuller became the first Secretary of Pennant Hills Baptist, but in 1929 she did not accept nomination as secretary again, "feeling that as there are now a number of men members, one of them should fill the office."[141] During the Second World War various women were appointed to executive positions, including Hazel Brainwood, Treasurer of Dee Why Baptist, NSW, and Grace Fildes, Treasurer of Katanning Baptist, WA.[142]

Obviously, under certain conditions, congregations elected women to executive positions usually expected to be undertaken by men. This occurred in all Australian states including Queensland and Tasmania, which tended to provide fewer opportunities for women than men. These ad hoc appointments did not change the status quo whereby—in most congregations—women were excluded from executive positions.

In the main women undertook their assigned tasks in their Baptist congregations willingly and without complaint, although there are some examples of women expressing frustration about their assigned roles. In 1920 the anniversary service and supper for the Knightsbridge Baptist SA, was fully catered by the men of the congregation. *The Australian Baptist* reported that the men had "been challenged" by the women, and, hence, the choir was thirty men, the men arranged decorations including paper and real flowers, and the men provided supper, served beverages, and cleaned up afterwards.[143] Such a challenge seems reasonable, but their successful one-off event made the men feel as if they had proven to the women that they were easily able to undertake the work of women. There is no evidence that the men of the congregation challenged women to run a congregation's meeting or to preach. This was surely a challenge some women would have welcomed.

In 1871 a report of Norwood Baptist noted that the "young women of the Church had been zealously working, the male members had been comparatively inactive."[144] In 1914 a report from Coburg Baptist, Victoria, referred to the women in the congregation who had raised money for the congregation and denominational mission, while the men held a debate.[145]

---

140. "Abermain," *Newcastle Morning Herald and Miners' Advocate* (Newcastle, NSW), 18 August 1917, 6; "In Memoriam: Mrs Stephen Sharp," *TAB*, 31 August 1926, 4; *These Fifty Years*.

141. "More or Less Personal," *TAB*, 10 September 1929, 4.

142. *Baptist Yearbook*. See Hilton, "ABW Database."

143. "South Australia: Knightsbridge," *TAB*, 22 June 1920; Helm, *Baptists of Burnside*, 124–25.

144. "News of the Churches: Norwood," *TP*, January 1871, 9.

145. "Victoria: Coburg," *TAB*, 4 August 1914, 13.

In 1936 Dr Frank Hone, then President of the Baptist Union of SA, was reported as saying "it is men who do the talking, while the women do the work!"[146] In 1937 Gladys Lewis addressed the "Woman's Rally in connection with the opening of Sydney's new Central Baptist Church" and she was forthright in her view that women were ideal Christian workers. She wrote: "Let me suggest to you that when God has wanted some big thing done in the world He has spoken to a woman . . . Great achievements have been accomplished, and new eras have been inaugurated when our Lord has spoken to a woman."[147] Women provided much of the unpaid labor required to sustain Australian Baptist congregations.

WOMEN'S GROUPS IN CONGREGATIONS: FORMATION, AIMS, MANAGEMENT, ACTIVITIES

Many Baptist women chose to be a member of at least one women's group within their congregation. The groups were formed at the behest of women, sometimes encouraged by the diaconate or minister of the congregation.[148] Generally the members appear to have not been in paid employment and the groups represented all age groups. Most women's groups formed when women within a congregation decided to meet regularly for fellowship and friendship and to aid those in need. For instance in 1887 a sewing group was established in Bathurst Street Baptist "to relieve the poor of the congregation and any deserving cases."[149] In 1894 Emily Hone wrote that the women's group at Southwark Baptist SA initially formed because several women wanted to pray together, "so much did the sisters hunger for common communion and prayer."[150] Clearly women wanted to worship and work together in their congregations.

Some congregations, particularly those that were larger, had multiple women's groups. Thus Flinders Street Baptist formed numerous groups for women throughout the congregation's history, including: the Ladies Working Association, which was established when the congregation first formed; Mothers' Meeting; Dorcas Society; Mothers' Union; Women's Guild; Temperance League; Cheer League for Christmas Boxes; Baptist Women's Mission Union; and Mothers' Club, in addition to a Deaconesses' Committee.[151]

146. "South Australian Baptist Union Annual Assembly," *TAB*, 6 October 1936, 9.
147. Lewis, *He Talked with a Woman*.
148. See, for example, *Mitcham Baptist Church*, 4; HPBLASM, NSWBA.
149. DSBSBM, SLNSW.
150. Emily Hone, "A Word for Senior Endeavour," *TGL*, 1 September 1894, 17.
151. Mead, *God Building*, 24.

Often even smaller congregations had two women's groups, such as Ivanhoe Baptist, Melbourne, which in 1912 had one group that raised funds for work within the congregation and another group that raised funds for mission work.[152] Usually Baptist congregations formed a women's group within two years of the establishment of the congregation, although each group differed with respect to its aims and activities.

Few of the women's groups with extant minutes specifically articulated their aims.[153] For example, in 1917 when the women of Hurlstone Park Baptist, Sydney, decided to form the Ladies' Aid Society, their minutes recorded that they "held a meeting for the purpose of forming a society for the ladies of the church and adherents."[154] No further details were provided. An analysis of extant minutes of women's groups indicates the three main aims were to: provide social support for women; increase the biblical or spiritual knowledge of members; and strengthen the Baptist congregation or the denomination through raising money. Many of the groups undertook all these roles.

First, women's groups were social in nature, enabling women to meet with together, as well as with other Baptists, through inviting guest speakers—particularly important for women who had recently migrated to Australia. In 1913 Ethel Palmer wrote about Annie White and the loving friendship that developed between them in a women's Bible class at Petersham Baptist NSW.[155] In 1919 Marion Tranter hinted at the connection between members of a congregation in a poem:

> Still we miss those true and loved ones,
> who were of our Church a part,
> And their portraits hang for ever,
> on the walls of each true heart.[156]

The minutes of women's groups reveal many visiting speakers, such as in 1937 when Jeannie Mursell, from Brisbane Tabernacle visited and spoke at the suburban Clayfield Baptist Women's Union.[157] Naturally, women's groups were particularly interested in hearing from missionaries and in 1944 the Ladies' Guild at Albury Baptist NSW welcomed Freda Tomkinson,

---

152. "New Church at Ivanhoe," *TSB*, 17 October 1912, 670.
153. In most cases this is because the first minute book is not extant.
154. HPBLASM, NSWBA.
155. Miss [Ethel] Palmer, "The Late Miss Annie White," *TAB*, 14 January 1913, 11.
156. A. Marian Tranter, "Eaglehawk Baptist Church," *Bendigo Independent* (Bendigo), 21 May 1918, 6.
157. Clayfield Baptist Women's Union, BUQA.

a missionary from China Inland Mission, to address their meeting.[158] The 1882 report of Wharf Street Baptist Ladies' Sewing Meeting in Brisbane concluded: "Of course a ladies' meeting would not be complete without that refreshing beverage [of tea]."[159]

Second, women's groups provided a time to develop the spiritual life of members through joint worship.[160] All groups spent time in prayer and often included spiritual or biblical studies. This was the case even when the groups were not designed for that purpose. In 1941 the Annual Report of the Victorian Ashburton Baptist Ladies Bright Hour prepared by Doris Woodall stated that "although primarily it was not the intention to stress the spiritual side, this has not been neglected."[161] Of course, hymn singing was a regular occurrence, as on 3 June 1937 when the Ladies' Bright Hour at Ballarat Victoria spent the afternoon "singing favorite hymns."[162]

Third, usually women's groups encompassed the aim of fundraising, and the funds supported evangelistic events and mission activities. Unsurprisingly significant fundraising work was undertaken by women within women's groups in congregations. In 1913 Dorcas Beattie led an evening of 'entertainment' to raise funds for Broken Hill Baptist.[163] During 1934 Lismore Baptist NSW cleared their debt on the building and stressed that "the church was indebted to the ladies for their assistance."[164]

Fetes, often called bazaars particularly prior to 1930, are useful to examine. They were commonly held to raise money through the sale of food and goods and provision of various entertainments. Usually fetes were organized and managed by women, either within the women's group of the congregation, or through a separate committee established for the sole purpose of organising the fete. This arrangement was not limited to Baptist congregations, and several historians have commented on the importance of fetes in fundraising and the involvement of women.[165]

158. Albury Ladies' Guild Minutes, BUVA.

159. "Work for the Ladies," *TQF*, 15 August 1882, 6.

160. Downing, "The Ministry of Woman in the Church," *TAB*, 20 April 1911, 266; HPBLASM, NSWBA; Ipswich Social and Flower Committee, Report Book, BUQA; Grace Taylor, "Ladies' Zenana Baptist Missionary Society of New South Wales," *Banner of Truth* (Sydney), September–October 1885, 142.

161. Doris Woodall, Ashburton Baptist Ladies Bright Hour: Third Annual Report, BUVA.

162. Ballarat Ladies' Bright Hour MM, BUVA.

163. "Beryl Street, Broken Hill," *TAB*, 10 June 1913, 1; Wilcox, *Baptist Women's League*, 12.

164. "Debit Turned to Credit: Baptist," *Northern Star* (Lismore, NSW), 15 September 1934, 7.

165. See Kingston, "Faith and Fetes"; Pitman, "Green and Gold Cookery Book."

One of the earliest recorded Baptist fetes was held in Tasmania in November 1847, where the organization committee for the "Bazaar . . . in aid of the debt on the Baptist Place of Worship, Hobart Town," consisted of nine named women who were "assisted by" several men, only some of which were named. In the months prior to the fete, several women took responsibility for collection of goods made for sale—"fancy goods"—and during the fete women were assigned specific stalls. Goods for sale included stools, ottomans, and cushions, and on the first day a colonial army band played for entertainment. This fete raised £173 at a time when the congregation's debt was £300.[166] This success was replicated in Baptist congregations around Australia, examples from the nineteenth century being: in 1862 Castlemaine Baptist Victoria held a "well attended" fete; in 1868 Morphett Vale Baptist SA women's "working meeting and bazaar" raised £200, nearly 15 percent of the cost of the new church building; in 1872 Eden Valley Baptist SA held a fete "provided chiefly by the ladies . . . which paid off the debt on the chapel," and in 1897 in Auburn Baptist NSW a report on the congregation indicated "the ladies [were] busy in their preparations" for a fete.[167] Fetes remained an important source of fundraising until the late twentieth century.

Many Baptist women formed sewing groups in their congregations, intended to assist the poor rather than to raise money. In the mid to late nineteenth century they were often called a Dorcas Society.[168] Dorcas Societies replicated Societies formed in the UK, named after Dorcas in Acts 9:36, a clothes maker for the poor. The earliest Societies formed in Australia in the 1830s were non-denominational. There was no affiliation between the different Dorcas Societies, the largest of which were the Societies in Sydney and Hobart. Societies provided social welfare to poor women at the birth of a child, usually through the provision of clothing and other supplies, which were then returned to the Society and made available to other women. Society members met regularly to sew together and put together the supplies.[169] Few details have been retained from the early Dorcas Societ-

---

166. "Bazaar," *Courier* (Hobart), 13 November 1847; "Bazaar," *Colonial Times* (Hobart), 6 July 1847.

167. "The Baptist Church Bazaar," *Mount Alexander Mail* (Castlemaine, Victoria), 10 March 1862. "Opening of the Baptist Chapel, Morphett Vale," *TP*, May 1868, 111, "Denominational News: Eden Valley," *TP*, 1872, 148, "Local and District Items: Bazaar at Auburn," *Cumberland Argus and Fruitgrowers Advocate* (Parramatta, NSW), 25 September 1897.

168. DSBSBM, SLNSW.

169. "Debit Turned to Credit: Baptist," *Northern Star*, 15 September 1934, 7; DSBSBM, SLNSW.

ies in Baptist congregations aside from mentions in annual reports.[170] One exception is the Flinders Street Baptist Dorcas Society, whose first minute book has been retained. The Society formed in 1867: twenty-six women from the existing Ladies Association agreed to be "subscribers" providing financial support as they could, meeting on the first Wednesday afternoon each month for "friendship," and "for making and supplying clothes for the poor."[171] The minutes of the first two years of the Society, written by Mary Shaw, the first Secretary, reveal that the Society took some time to institute a suitable model, as the focus was beyond mothers with babies. In Victoria in Collins Street Baptist there is evidence that a Dorcas Society was established around 1870 by Hannah Martin, the wife of the Rev. James Martin, soon after their migration to Australia. Once again, this society did not exactly follow an established model, undertaking a range of activities, such as making slippers for people in hospital and putting together clothing bags for poor families.[172]

From the early twentieth century many of the sewing groups in individual congregations were titled a "Sewing Guild'" or "Sewing Circle."[173] The emphasis was to make good clothing available for poor women at no- or low-cost and at any time of their lives, not just in their "confinement"—the time prior and after childbirth.[174]

Australian Baptist women's groups were managed in a variety of ways, although all women's groups examined were managed by women with women appointed to all executive positions.[175] Women's meetings were chaired by women, except for a small number of meetings that were chaired by the minister of the congregation. Women's committees were usually open to all women of the congregation, except for deaconesses' committees.[176]

---

170. See, for example, "On Sunday," *Express and Telegraph* (Adelaide), 19 December 1871, 2.

171. Flinders Street Baptist Dorcas Society MM, SABA.

172. "Melbourne and Suburban City Mission," *Age* (Melbourne), 24 November 1874, 3.

173. "Work for the Ladies," *TQF*, 15 August 1882, 6; Doery, "WVP [Newmarket Baptist]," *TAB*, 27 July 1915, 5; Ladies Sewing Guild Glen Osmond MM, SABA.

174. Norwood Baptist Deaconess MM, SABA; "North Adelaide Baptist Church," *Adelaide Observer* (Adelaide), 11 November 1876, 12; Wilcox, "Baptist Womanhood in Action," *TAB*, 27 September 1938, 4.

175. Norwood Baptist Deaconess MM, SABA; NABDM, SABA.

176. NABDM, SABA.

UNPAID DEACONESSES IN BAPTIST CONGREGATIONS

From the 1860s to 1945 at least fifty Baptist congregations throughout Australia were supported by unpaid deaconesses, formally elected to their positions by the membership of the congregation.[177] Over twenty were in SA, which was strongly influenced by the Rev. Silas Mead, who encouraged congregations to formally recognize the work of women through appointing unpaid deaconesses.[178] In part he was reflecting the evangelical holiness movement—or Keswick tradition—which emphasized a life of piety and devotion.[179] Appointing deaconesses was an acceptance that women should be formally involved in their congregations, in the intermediate sphere. Deaconesses' committees had limited membership because only elected women attended meetings. The role of deaconesses complemented the role of deacons, who were elected to serve the congregation. Extant records from Baptist deaconesses' committees reveal they were remarkably like deacons.

Baptist deaconesses, like deacons, met once a month. Usually the chair was the minister of the congregation, but in some cases it was the minister's wife, as at Goodwood Baptist SA, or an internally elected president, such as in Glen Osmond Baptist SA.[180] On rare occasions the deaconesses met with the deacons to discuss specific issues, such as evangelistic endeavors to increase membership. Thus in 1913 West Melbourne Baptist deaconesses and deacons met for "mutual consideration of what more could be done to conserve the results of the work and extend the Redeemer's Kingdom."[181]

---

177. Hilton, "ABW Database."

178. "Opening of the Baptist Chapel, Morphett Vale," *TP*, May 1868, 111; Silas Mead, "Deaconesses," *TP*, August 1868, 156–60.

179. Gooden et al., *Silas Mead*, 74.

180. "South Australia: Goodwood," *TAB*, 8 November 1927, 14; Glen Osmond Baptist Deaconess MM, SABA.

181. "West Melbourne," *TAB*, 5 August 1913, 12.

Stanmore Baptist minister's wife and deacons' wives, 1906. Stanmore Baptist, NSW, did not have a deaconess committee, but the wives of deacons were considered significant. Back row: Rosa Tyas; Anna White; Emily Brasnett; Harriett Lumb; Front row: Hannah Buckingham; Mildred Tinsley; Mary Yarrow; Elizabeth Rose. © The Baptist Historical Society of NSW Inc.; used with permission.

Deaconesses were never considered as important as the deacons. All Australian Baptist congregations had a deacons' committee, whereas deaconesses' committees were optional and have been identified in around 10 percent of Baptist congregations. Many histories of congregations may mention the existence of deaconesses, but their roles were not emphasized, and their ministries considered minimal or a supplementary work of the congregation.[182] In 1917 Norwood Baptist released a "jubilee" history, which stated that while most of the minutes of deacons' meetings were extant, "there [was] not so complete an account of the deaconesses."[183] Interestingly, despite this claim, the minutes for Norwood Baptist deaconesses are extant from 1872. Unfortunately, though, around Australia very few minutes from deaconesses' committee meetings are extant, let alone incorporated in the history of these Baptist congregations. The 1985 history of Parramatta Baptist Sydney included one paragraph about women's work in the congregation, including deaconesses, in the chapter titled "Ancillary Organizations," which observed that although the women's work was operating from 1876

182. *Peterborough Baptist Centenary*; Helyar, *Voice in the City*, 17.
183. *Peterborough Baptist Centenary*.

there were "no records extant."[184] The term "no records extant" has become synonymous with a tradition that diminishes the importance of work done by women as elected deaconesses, along with other women's groups in Australian Baptist congregations.

Yet being a deaconess was considered a privilege. In 1926 an obituary for Mary Watson affirmed: "The highest office to which a member of the church can he called is that of deacon or deaconess. To this office Mrs Watson was called many years ago and has consistently carried out its duties."[185] *The Australian Baptist* contained other instances of congregations honoring deaconesses, either through appointment as a "Life Deaconess" or emphasizing women's work in the congregation and their position of deaconess in their obituaries, including those of Alice Garrett, Annie Kennett, and Annie Whittle.[186] The duties of the Glen Osmond Baptist deaconesses allude to their respected position in the congregation, stating that deaconesses "may make recommendations to the Officers, or to the Church concerning matters which they consider to be in the best interests of the Church."[187] Deaconesses undertook varied activities including pastoral care to women and young people who attended worship services.[188] The deaconesses at Grange Baptist SA undertook mission activities outside the congregation, although this was not common.[189] Overall, the deaconesses were considered knowledgeable about the needs of the congregation and evidence demonstrates they fulfilled important tasks within the congregation.

Arguably the work of a deaconess was just as, or even more, important than that of a deacon. Policy within congregations rarely altered an individual's life, whereas funds to provide people with food, clothing, or emotional support could make a significant impact. Deaconesses need to be acknowledged alongside deacons for their ministry to Baptist congregations.

---

184. Watkin-Smith, *Baptists in the Cradle City*, 143–44.

185. "Aberdeen Street Baptist: Memorial Service to Mrs. J. Watson," *Geelong Advertiser* (Geelong, Victoria), 10 August 1926, 2.

186. "Called Home: Mrs. Alice Garrett," *TAB*, 4 July 1944, 2; "South Australia: The Late Mrs. Samuel Kennett," *TAB*, 16 February 1926, 4; "The Late Mrs. E. Whittle," *TAB*, 11 January 1956, 4.

187. Glen Osmond Baptist Deaconess MM, SABA. The duties are written on the first page of the minute book.

188. See, for example, NABDM, SABA.

189. Grange Baptist Church Ladies' Guild MM, SABA.

CASE STUDY: THREE CONGREGATIONS AND THREE WOMEN'S COMMITTEES

The following case study examines the different origins, structures, and features of three city congregations and three women's groups: North Adelaide Baptist; Jireh Baptist Brisbane; and Hurlstone Park Baptist Sydney. North Adelaide Deaconesses' Committee has extant minutes from its formation in 1882 to 1941; minutes of the Jireh Branch of the Queensland Baptist Women's Union (QBWU) are for the period from 1929 to 1948; and the Hurlstone Park Ladies' Aid Society minutes date from the Society's establishment in 1917 until 1929.[190] These congregations represent three of around fifty Australian Baptist congregations for which there are extant minutes of women's groups prior to 1945.

The formation of the three congregations illustrates three different ways in which the Baptist denomination expanded in the late nineteenth and early twentieth centuries. Established in 1848, North Adelaide Baptist was one of the oldest congregations in Adelaide and was formed to provide a local congregation for Baptists in North Adelaide.[191] Jireh Strict and Particular Baptist, known as Jireh Baptist, was established in 1862 and was the third Baptist congregation in Queensland. Jireh Baptist was located close to the center of Brisbane and formed following disagreements between members of the existing Brisbane congregation located at Wharf Street. Those who formed Jireh Baptist believed that Wharf Street Baptist had lost its reformed or Calvinistic position.[192] Hurlstone Park Baptist, located ten kilometres west of Sydney city, was established in 1913 as a branch of the nearby Dulwich Hill Baptist congregation in response to the growing population in the area.[193] These congregations represent growth because of local action, division, and collaboration respectively.

North Adelaide's membership agreed to establish a Deaconesses' Committee in late 1882, with four women initially appointed as deaconesses. The minutes did not include formal requirements for deaconesses, but tasks they undertook included: assisting other women who were being baptized; interviewing prospective members; visiting sick members of the congregation; and undertaking housekeeping tasks on the church property.[194] The Deaconesses' Committee did not organize fundraising events. Over the

---

190. NABDM, SABA; JQBWUM, BUQA; HPBLASM, NSWBA.
191. Hughes, *Our First Hundred Years*, 33.
192. White, *Fellowship of Service*, 36; Parker, *Pressing on with the Gospel*, 7.
193. *Through These Years*, 5.
194. NABDM, SABA.

course of this period there were other women's groups that operated within the congregation, including a Dorcas Society and a Mother's Group, both established in the mid-1870s.[195] In 1896 a Young Women's Class formed, followed in 1902 by a Women's Guild, and in 1925 by a Senior Girls' Missionary Union. These new women's groups undertook additional activities such as social welfare, local mission, fundraising for mission, and teaching other women in the congregation.[196] The work of the deaconesses remained consistent throughout the period, indicating that the other groups did not intrude upon the work of the deaconesses. As the congregation's membership increased, so did the number of deaconesses, so that in 1905 there were ten deaconesses—Jane Mellor, Helen Goode, Jeanie Gilbert, Bertha Cooper, Adelaide Kekwick, Elizabeth Mason; Catherine Neill, Julia Whittle, Mary Moody, and Joanna McLaren—and 1945 there were fourteen deaconesses.[197]

The Ten North Adelaide Baptist Deaconesses, 1905. From the Church Manual. Photo provided by North Adelaide Baptist; used with permission.

195. "North Adelaide Baptist Church," *Adelaide Observer*, 11 November 1876, 12.

196. *North Adelaide Baptist Church: Tynte Street*, 8. The minutes from the other women's groups are not extant.

197. *North Adelaide Baptist Church: Manual*, 16–17.

From 1882 to 1945 North Adelaide Baptist appointed sixty-five deaconesses who served an average of over twelve years each. The women were aged between thirty and sixty at the time of their initial appointment as deaconess. Four were single women, and about one-quarter of those who were married did not have husbands who were members of the congregation. Over time there were different generations of families with women serving as deaconesses, such as: Augusta Smith, one of the first deaconesses, and her daughter Helen Goode; Julia Whittle and her daughter Ethel Ellis, niece Isabella Sorrell, and daughter-in-law Annie Whittle; and Ellen Hale and her daughter-in-law Nancy Hale.[198] The importance of the deaconesses to North Adelaide Baptist is evidenced by the fact that in the church building two deaconesses—Matilda Evans and Augusta Smith—had stained glass windows dedicated to their memory.[199]

Women's groups had operated within the Jireh Baptist congregation prior to 1909; however in that year, following the establishment of the Queensland Baptist Women's Union (QBWU), the Jireh Baptist women's group aligned itself with the QBWU and changed its name to signify that it was a branch of the QBWU. Hepzibah Mirfin, a member of Jireh Baptist, had represented the Jireh Baptist women at the first meeting of the QBWU and was the first Vice-President of the QBWU.[200] The Jireh Branch of the QBWU met monthly with around twelve attendees at each meeting. The president of the group was the minister's wife, although there were periods when other women took on the president's position, presumably when the minister's wife was unavailable.[201] All members were encouraged to participate, and during 1929 and 1930 the group engaged in a unique Bible game whereby the group chose a word at one meeting—such examples being "well," "stone," or "light"—and members were required to come to the next meeting and present a Bible verse using the word.[202] The Jireh QBWU Branch worked within the Baptist denomination, with frequent interactions with the Jireh diaconate, women's groups in other Baptist congregations, and the home mission committee.

In September 1917 nine women met at Hurlstone Park Baptist and formed the Ladies' Aid Society for women in the congregation. The Society aimed to raise funds for the congregation, provide catering for functions,

198. NABDM, SABA; *Centenary: 1848–1948*.

199. Monk, "Stained Glass Windows at NABC." Prior to 1918 the window dedicated to Matilda Evans was removed.

200. JQBWUM, BUQA; QBWU MM, 1909–1911, BUQA. None of the earlier—or later—minutes of women's meetings at Jireh Baptist are extant.

201. JQBWUM, BUQA.

202. JQBWUM, BUQA.

and visit those in the congregation who were unwell. These broad activities were "to assist the church in any and every way possible."[203] Initially this group had an inward focus, which was to reduce the debt on the church building. After several years of operation the Society expanded its area of support to include wider Baptist interests in NSW and the ABFM. The minister chaired the first meeting but rarely attended other meetings. A formal committee was elected and the first president, as was common practice, was the minister's wife.[204] The members reserved the first meeting of the month to discuss any business, and all other meetings were dedicated to sewing clothing to raise money.[205] The group did not provide financial assistance to individual people within or outside of the congregation, although members of the Society visited members of the congregation in cases of illness or bereavement and they distributed flowers used in Sunday services. Most meetings included addresses by Society members or invited speakers, which included women who were well-known in the NSW Baptist denomination, such as Susan Davey, Lily Higlett, Emily Price, and Isabella White. The only men who addressed the Society were successive ministers of Hurlstone Park Baptist.[206] The Society developed connections to other Baptist women's organizations, and met with other women's groups in nearby Baptist congregations at Carlton, Dulwich Hill, and Haberfield. In 1923 the Society affiliated with the state-based Baptist women's mission group.[207] This affiliation did not lead to a change in either the name or aims of the Ladies' Aid Society. By this time the Society had effectively expanded its aims, whereby money raised was donated to overseas mission. Perhaps a formal move to change aims was unnecessary as the women had an implicit understanding of the widening aims of their group.

There were differences and similarities among these three women's groups, which demonstrate the various ways in which women's groups were established within Baptist congregations. North Adelaide Baptist *membership* agreed to establish the deaconesses committee; Jireh Baptist responded to the *state denominational women's organization* in renaming and reshaping the women's committee; and Hurlstone Park Baptist Ladies' Aid Society was established by *women in the congregation*. The women's groups had different aims. North Adelaide Deaconesses' Committee worked solely within

203. HPBLASM, NSWBA.

204. See, for example, "Churchill Baptist Church: History of the Church: 1913–1963," BUQA; Maxwell, *Triumphant Through Trials*, 23.

205. HPBLASM, NSWBA.

206. HPBLASM, NSWBA.

207. HPBLASM, NSWBA.

the congregation and there was no formal interaction with groups outside the congregation. Jireh QBWU Branch and Hurlstone Park Ladies' Society assisted their congregation and the wider denomination through practical and financial support, and the groups welcomed interactions with other groups and people. All groups commenced each meeting with prayer and a Bible reading or study.

The women's groups were an intrinsic part of each of their congregations. They assumed the roles that they were expected to undertake—as women—but they used their roles to style their own ministry, largely in the form and place that suited these women. For example, the Jireh QBWU Branch meeting minutes recorded two instances where they agreed *not* to participate in events as requested by the Jireh Baptist diaconate. In 1929 they agreed they would not be part of the 1930 Jireh Baptist Fete Committee, although they later appointed two women to represent them; and in 1932 they agreed that they would not take up a "suggestion" in a letter from the Jireh Baptist Secretary about providing women to be "responsible for the provisioning" of the tea meeting.[208] Women had a greater control of the activities they undertook because they were part of a formal group in the congregation.

While outside the period considered in this book, the three congregations later demonstrate the somewhat transient nature of many Baptist congregations. North Adelaide Baptist withdrew from the Baptist Union of SA in the early twenty-first century, choosing to operate as an independent Baptist congregation.[209] Jireh Baptist ceased to operate in 1978 due to an unsustainable low number of members. In the 1980s Hurlstone Park Baptist faced closure due to low membership, and the local Vietnamese Baptist community assumed responsibility for the church building. The congregation is now called Hurlstone Park Vietnamese Baptist and remains affiliated with the Baptist Union of NSW. Thus these congregations illustrate the impact of ongoing doctrinal differences, diminishing attendance, and shifting demographics of the Baptist denomination in the late twentieth and early twenty-first centuries.

The women's groups are just three examples of the many women's groups based within Baptist congregations. The North Adelaide Deaconesses' Committee adopted the mode employed by other deaconesses' committees. Likewise most women's groups shared various features of the Jireh QBWU Branch and the Hurlstone Park Ladies' Aid Society. In all cases women mobilized themselves to support Baptist work within their congregation and the broader Baptist denomination.

208. JQBWUM, BUQA.
209. "North Adelaide Baptist Church."

THE MINISTER'S WIFE

One cannot discuss roles within Baptist congregations without discussing the ministers' wives, and their—usually—prominent role, with many women being expected to be unpaid workers in their congregation.[210] Denominational papers included articles about the importance of ministers' wives, such as *The Southern Baptist*, which in 1901 included a long article on ministers' wives and stated that wives "brighten" ministers' lives through various mechanisms such as providing a good home life, understanding and support to him, and actively taking part in his work.[211] Most other protestant denominations would have held an expectation that ministers' wives contributed to their husband's ministry, and such a view continued throughout the twentieth century.[212] The expectations that ministers' wives would actively support their husbands were not unfounded in the Baptist context. Given how many Baptist ministers' wives worked within their local congregation and in the denomination more widely, clearly many ministers' wives considered their position within the congregation as a vocation, which matched the expectations Australian Baptists held regarding the role.

Australian Baptists treated ministers' wives differently to other women members. This is shown in women's organizations such as the women's "Help Society" at Warwick Baptist Queensland, which expected the minister's wife "to take her place as president of the society."[213] Most women's organizations in congregations were not as explicit. Thelma Howard observed that even as a young minister's wife she was expected to be president of the women's organizations at the congregations where her husband was the minister.[214] From 1924 the SA BWL's standing orders included that the "President should one year be a lay woman and the next a minister's wife."[215] Such arrangements were common and confirmed that Baptists viewed ministers' wives as being special and having status in the congregation and denomination.

Most ministers' wives supported their husband's role and their ministries ranged from practical support to assistance in preaching duties. Indeed about 30 percent of women who are known to have preached were ministers' wives. Elizabeth Middleton—an Australian Baptist minister's wife from 1884 to 1907—was "in every sense of the word . . . her husband's unpaid

---

210. See, for example, Wilcox, "Concerning Deaconesses."
211. "The Bright Side of a Minister's Life," *TSB* 1901, 35.
212. Dempsey, *Fate of Ministers' Wives*, 1; Watt, *History of the Parson's Wife*, 99.
213. "News of the Churches: Warwick," *TQB*, 15 September 1931, 14.
214. Maxwell, *Triumphant Through Trials*, 23, 27.
215. Wilcox, *Baptist Women's League*, 11; Benskin, "Through a Woman's Window," *BR*, 15 November 1924, 12.

curate."[216] Elizabeth Wood's role as a minister's wife from 1882 to 1927 was acknowledged by her husband the Rev. Harry Wood who wrote: "My wife was a great help to me . . . in visiting, tract distribution, standing by me at the open-air meetings, sometimes holding an umbrella over my head, and in the inquiry-room."[217] From 1898 to 1924 in rural WA Ada Kennedy was described as a "fit helpmeet" and "her preaching ability was welcomed everywhere."[218] Isabella Miles worked in the five congregations at which her husband, the Rev. Frederick Miles, was minister from 1900 to 1918, including singing in services and undertaking Sunday School teaching. Following their departure from Australia, she remained in contact with various state women's groups through letter writing.[219] In 1914 newly married Stella Churchward Kelly moved to Lithgow, NSW, where her husband the Rev. Thomas Churchward Kelly was the minister. She is reported as saying that she felt "called" to work at the Lithgow church as a "second minister."[220] After their mission service, she assisted her husband in his interim ministries and services, including regular preaching, until his death in 1953.[221]

From the late nineteenth century Baptist minister wives established state unions, which met during the yearly and half-yearly union meetings, generally during the business session.[222] The Queensland Baptist Ministers' Wives Association provides an example of these organizations. The Association was considered part of the Baptist Union's activities.[223] Invited guests included Baptist missionary women—married and single—and visiting ministers' wives such as Ethel Townsend from the UK who spoke at the 1938 meeting.[224] In 1928 Ella Davies declared that Psalm 101 was "the min-

---

216. J. A. Packer, "The Passing of Mrs. R. J. Middleton," *TAB*, 8 September 1931, 3. The term "curate" means someone who assists the minister but was rarely used by Baptists.

217. Wood, "Leaves from My Life Story," *TAB,* 5 October 1926, 2.

218. Gomm, *Blazing the Western Trails*, 62–63.

219. Mrs F. J. [Isabella] Miles, "Among Scottish Baptist Women," *TAB*, 2 April 1918.

220. "Lithgow," *TAB,* 28 April 1914, 13.

221. Stella Mary Churchward MacDonald, Rev. Thomas, and Mrs. Stella Churchward Kelly, 1990, Tasmanian Baptist Archives, University of Tasmania, Hobart; "Mother's Day Observance: Devonport," *Advocate* (Burnie, Tasmania), 15 May 1944, 2.

222. F. M. [Frederic] Cutlack, "By Credo," *Saturday Mail* (Adelaide), 17 June 1916, 4; "Baptist Ministers' Wives," *Telegraph* (Brisbane), 27 September 1932, 14.

223. "The Fifty-First Assembly of the Queensland Baptist Union," *TQB,* 15 October 1928, 6.

224. "Baptist Ministers' Wives Union," *Brisbane Courier* (Brisbane), 26 March 1930, 22. Single missionary woman Gladys Collins spoke at the 1930 meeting. "Mrs. H. Townsend Addresses Baptist Ministers' Wives," *Telegraph* (Brisbane), 22 September 1938, 6.

isters' wives' psalm."[225] Psalm 101 includes the phrases: "I will behave myself wisely . . . I will walk within my house with a perfect heart" (vv. 2, 3). The ministers' wives' organizations were a support group for ministers' wives and their meetings allowed for discussion on issues specifically relating to their position. Information on their discussions is limited to reports in denominational papers as there are no extant records of agendas or other data. Organizations for ministers' wives continued until the late-1940s, when they disbanded, possibly because of the prominence of state and national Baptist women's organizations.

While most women were prepared or eager to support their husband, some ministers' wives found the expectations of their role to be overwhelming and felt unappreciated. In 1917 at the SA ministers' wives meeting Christina Whitbourn presented a paper on "The Disadvantages of a Minister's Wife" including that she: felt judged by members of the congregation; was "expected to lead" the work of women; and did not have time for personal devotions due to the work she undertook in her home and in the congregation. While outlining such negatives, Christina Whitbourn stated that overall it was a "privilege" to be the minister's wife.[226] Edith Wilcox wrote that she had "the greatest respect and admiration for . . . ministers' wives. But our ministers marry the woman they love, and not a curate, as we have grown to expect."[227] Evidently many Baptists were aware of the expectations placed on ministers' wives. Where ministers' wives did not participate in their husbands' ministry, their rationale was either their family responsibilities or poor health. For example, despite being a "faithful helpmeet," Sarah Chapman was not active in the Rev. Samuel Chapman's ministry at Collins Street Baptist, Melbourne: "Her delicate health would not allow it."[228] Likewise in SA Eva McCullough "never cared for publicity, but often regretted that because of ill-health she could not take the part in church work that was expected of the minister's wife."[229] Although somewhat ironically, Eva McCullough strongly advocated on behalf of her husband at a time when his ministry methods were questioned.[230] Prior to 1945 there are no known instances of a Baptist minister's wife making an explicit choice not to support her husband's ministry.

---

225. "Queensland Baptist Ministers' Wives Union," *TQB*, 15 May 1928, 7.
226. Whitbourn, "The Disadvantages of a Minister's Wife," TAB, 26 June 1917, 2, 14.
227. Wilcox, "Concerning Deaconesses."
228. "The Late Mrs. Samuel Chapman," *TSB*, 26 March 1902, 78.
229. "The Late Mrs R. McCullough," *TAB*, 28 July 1925, 4.
230. Mount Barker Baptist Church, Officers' MM, SABA.

An area of anxiety for ministers' wives was the fact that congregations in the Baptist denomination sometimes did not have enough funds to adequately remunerate their minister. At the turn of the twentieth century Ada and William Kennedy endured financial stress in their rural WA ministry, although "with all the hardship and poverty they had never lacked a meal."[231] In 1933 when Thelma Howard married the Rev. Alan Howard his wage was considered low but members of the congregation at Murwillumbah, NSW supported them by providing farm produce and home-made food.[232] Low wages were an issue particularly during the economic depressions in the 1890s and the 1930s. During these times some ministers took on additional work outside the denomination, although there is no evidence that ministers' wives sought paid employment. The Rev. William Tayler stated in 1913: "It certainly was not the money that attracted us [to Baptist ministry]." Phoebe Tayler interjected, saying "we managed . . . but now I often wonder how we did it."[233]

Until the late twentieth century a paid career would not have been viewed as a legitimate activity for a minister's wife. The only time the occupations of ministers' wives were discussed was in respect to women who had an occupation prior to their marriage, or widowed ministers' wives.[234] The involvement of ministers' wives in activities outside the religious sphere was rarely mentioned in denominational papers or records.[235]

Melody Maxwell and Beth Allison Barr postulate that in the USA some women with an interest in ministry chose to marry a minister in the belief that she could undertake ministerial roles in supporting her husband, including pastoral care for members of the congregation.[236] This appears to be the case for several Australian Baptist ministers' wives. Arguably two women who support this case were Emily Hone in SA and Cecilia Downing in Victoria. Both women married Baptist ministers who later left the ministry, yet they continued to be involved in Baptist denominational activities and other religious organizations.[237] Several paid deaconesses were widows

---

231. Gomm, *Blazing the Western Trails*, 48.

232. Maxwell, *Triumphant Through Trials*, 23. His exact wage compared to other ministers is unknown.

233. "Veteran Baptist Minister," *TAB*, 18 February 1913, 10.

234. See, for example, "In Memoriam: Mrs Stephen Sharp," *TAB*, 31 August 1926, 4.

235. Hilton, "ABW Database." Volunteer work outside the religious sphere while being married to a minister was only identified in four cases: two of these were the women active in the Red Cross, and two were board members of hospitals for women or children.

236. See Maxwell, "Winding and Widening Path"; Barr, *Becoming the Pastor's Wife*.

237. Hone, "A Word for Senior Endeavour," *TGL*, 1 September 1894.

of Baptist ministers prior to their service, including Frances Aldridge, Ethel Cronou, and Catherine Phillips.[238] Some widows of ministers remarried a minister, including Catherine Phillips, Sarah Harrison, and Hermine Leeder.[239] Other widows of ministers continued to be involved in Baptist causes, including Matilda Evans, Helen Goode, and May Nelson.[240] It is plausible that these women, who had effectively been working as unpaid ministerial workers, wanted to continue the work they considered their "calling" within the Baptist denomination.

CONCLUSION

Baptist and evangelical distinctives shaped the theological commitments and spiritual practices of most Australian Baptist women and across Australia women undertook many roles in their congregations to fulfill their beliefs: fundraising and Sunday School being two important ministries. Women established groups within Baptist congregations that enabled women to have some control over the work they did and to target their activities. Most of the groups were informal, but about fifty congregations established deaconesses' committees. The women's groups fulfilled several aims such as supporting women, including practical assistance, building biblical and spiritual knowledge of members, and fundraising for the congregation and denomination, significantly for local and overseas missions.

---

238. "City Tabernacle Deaconess," *Telegraph* (Brisbane), 4 March 1939, 7; Slinn, "A Deaconess' Association," *TAB*, 2 October 1917, 7; Parker, *Women Who Made a Difference*, 35.

239. Hilton, "ABW Database."

240. NABDM, SABA; "The Late Mrs. May Nelson," *TWA*, 14 March 1931, 10.

3

Women in Mission Outside Australia

> The cause for rejoicing would be the fact of the army of
> workers being augmented for the extension of Christ's
> Kingdom—for the spread of knowledge of Him![1]
>
> —Bertha Tuck, 1902

INTRODUCTION

MISSION WAS THE ONE activity that united all Australian Baptists. Manley describes overseas mission as the "most important unifying force among Australian Baptists."[2] Australian Baptist women and mission outside Australia—at that time called foreign mission—are inextricably linked: the first ten Australian Baptist missionaries were women.[3] Overseas mission work was a distinct component of women's ministry.

Between 1882 and 1945 over 250 Australian Baptist women have been documented as having worked in overseas mission and on average they worked as missionaries for nearly twenty years. One-hundred women worked specifically in Australian Baptist missions in East Bengal, which was the only location for Australian Baptist overseas mission activity until 1959—in comparison there were thirty-six men.[4] Outside of the Austra-

---

1. Bertha Tuck, "Present Day Needs of Present Day Missions," *TSB*, 17 December 1902, 286.

2. Manley, "Shaping the Australian Baptist Movement"; "Our Own Church," 292.

3. Manley, *From Woolloomooloo*, 1:192.

4. Cupit et al., *From Five Barley Loaves*, 611–54. The women have been identified

lian Baptist missions, over 150 Australian Baptist women worked overseas for various Protestant mission societies, particularly the China Inland Mission (CIM) and Poona and Indian Village Mission (PIVM).

The missionary women saw their work as guided by God and—as Kath Rumbold stressed—was required to bring "Christian freedom" to the local people.[5] In 1894 Emily Chambers wrote, "I am sure you will all not only join us in thanking the Lord for blessing thus far bestowed, but in asking His continued blessing that all may be done for His glory alone."[6] In 1941 Daisy Howard affirmed that the light from a candle "represented the Witness for God in India, for however small, 'God has not left Himself without witness.'"[7] In 1906 Dr Ethel Ambrose quoted a verse of poetry containing the lines: "Do you point to the light that has gladdened your path, cry to the wanderer, Come! . . . Go! Seek ye the souls that are sinking in death, and tell them of Home and Light."[8]

This chapter provides the context for women's involvement within the modern missionary movement and focuses on Australian Baptist missionary women's roles. Missionary women's writings can be used to identify and describe their motivations for becoming missionaries, their roles, and their theological views.[9] Inevitably this chapter focuses on the women who worked for the Australian Baptist missions, although examples from women in other mission organizations are also used. By necessity this chapter briefly discusses some of the key themes in mission studies with relation to Baptist women, particularly colonialism, but cannot assess these issues in detail.

---

through the Staff List. The list includes married women who were not specifically employed by the ABFM. At least five women on the staff list were self-supporting, that is, the ABFM did not give them a regular allowance, but in all other respects they were ABFM staff. Women who went to East Bengal as short-term volunteers are not included on the Staff List unless they were financially supported by the ABFM.

5. Kath Rumbold, quoted in Cupit et al., *From Five Barley Loaves*, 118. Rumbold was a missionary from 1947 to 1954.

6. Emily Chambers, "Mymensingh," *OB*, January 1894, 2.

7. D[aisy] Howard, "Confusion or Communion," *OIF*, 6 August 1941, 8.

8. Ambrose, *White Already to Harvest* (Poona, India), November 1906, as quoted in Hinton, *Ethel Ambrose*, 102. UK poet Anna Shipton wrote the poem alluded to, called "Home! Light! Home!"

9. Robert, *Christian Mission*, 59.

MISSIONARY WOMEN IN AUSTRALIAN BAPTIST MISSION HISTORY

The work that Australian Baptist missionary women undertook in East Bengal between 1882 and 1945 was essential to the operation of the mission. One should expect, therefore, that women would feature predominantly in Australian Baptist mission reporting and historiography. Yet despite prolific extant documentation, women's work as overseas missionaries has been largely ignored, particularly within the historiography of Australian Baptist missions and denominational history.[10] Wilfred Crofts recognized this issue in 1960 when he contacted the ABFM General Secretary asking that his wife, Gwenyth Crofts, be included in reference to the work they did in East Bengal and Assam, writing: "I hope this will always be watched . . . I fear the same mistake is often made . . . the woman is forgotten."[11] The ABFM was not an anomaly in this respect. Prior to 1945 most mission organizations consistently under-reported missionary women's work and, until the late twentieth century, researchers did not seriously acknowledge or consider women's worldwide work in mission.[12]

Women's work was largely ignored in Australian Baptist mission reporting because men undertook most of the formal reporting of mission work. From 1913 missionary women reported information to the ABFM Board through the Field Council, and while women were on the Field Council, as examined below, the reports were written by the secretary, who was always a man.[13] Thus typically a man had oversight of formal reports from the mission field to the mission board. The Field Council's reports focused on issues managed by missionary men, including land acquisitions, building works, technical training for East Bengali men, and East Bengali Baptist organizations.[14] This focus was partly because men's work appears more likely to require approval from the ABFM Board than women's work, but the result was that men's work was discussed more by the Board than women's work.[15] In addition, when missionary women returned to Australia, their activities were less likely to be reported than those undertaken by men.

---

10. Gooden, "We Trust Them"; "Mothers in the Lord."

11. Wilfred Crofts, Letter to John Williams, ABMS General Secretary, 27 April 1960, BMAA.

12. Robert, *Christian Mission*, 114.

13. "Inter-State Board of Baptist Foreign Missions," *TAB*, 11 February 1913, 7; ABFM, Board MM, 1925–1934, BMAA.

14. See, for example, Field Council MM, 18–21 June 1919, ABFM, NSWBA.

15. ABFM MM, BMAA.

The way in which women's work was under-represented in reports is apparent in annual reports of Australian Baptist mission work. Presumably all mission workers were required to submit an annual report, excluding married women. Yet the published annual reports did not include an equitable representation of mission work by women compared to men. As an example, the 1925 ABFM *Annual Report* contained sixty pages of reports: fifteen missionary women contributed twenty-seven pages, compared to eight men contributing thirty-three pages—less than two pages per woman compared to more than four pages per man.[16] When an article about the contents of the 1925 ABFM *Annual Report* was published in *The Australian Baptist*, the only issue mentioned related to training of East Bengali men.[17] In these subtle ways mission officials placed men's work above women's work.

Missionary women were less likely than missionary men to have their writings published in the Baptist mission papers and, more importantly, in the denominational journal. Missionaries disseminated information through the Australian Baptist mission publications and letters to supporters. Women's writings were published in Baptist papers, but less regularly than men's writings. Women's letters were read and distributed through women's mission organizations but appear to have rarely been read at state or national Baptist meetings, where men's letters or reports were highlighted.[18] In addition, due to the gendered nature of mission work, missionary men generally wrote reports on their work with men, and women wrote predominantly about their work with other women. Because men's articles were more likely to be published, men's work was highlighted more than women's work.

Few missionary women presented a session at the Australasian Baptist Missionary Conventions, where Australian and New Zealand (NZ) missionaries met annually to discuss missionary methods, address common issues, and undertake Bible studies.[19] Thus women were somewhat restricted in their ability to convey issues of concern and activities of their work.

The impact of women's work being under-reported flows through to the historiography of Australian Baptist mission. In many cases historians

---

16. ABFM, *Extending the Kingdom in Bengal*. The report contained a sixteen-page summary report from the General Secretary that discussed the work of men and women in equal length, which essentially meant that women's work was discussed less given there were more missionary women. Other Annual Reports have been examined and, while some are more balanced, none has an equitable representation.

17. "The Australian Baptist Foreign Mission," *TAB*, 24 August 1926, 4.

18. See, for example, *TAB* 1913, which included numerous articles summarising meetings of state foreign mission committees.

19. *Our Bond* (Calcutta), 1893–1941.

did not incorporate the work of women missionaries, even though many women had written about their mission work and their missiology.[20] Three prominent examples are: Bertha Tuck, who worked in East Bengal for forty years and wrote extensively on a wide range of topics, many of which concerned missionary practices; Constance Williams, who in 1912 published a book about her experiences of mission; and Bertha Harris, who in 1938 published a book about the history of the ABFM school in Mymensingh, East Bengal.[21] In addition, Baptist missionary women have written biographies about other missionary women, specifically Gladys Collins for Bertha Tuck and Louisa Hinton for Ethel Ambrose.[22] Missionary women published articles in denominational papers and some others published books, but these have rarely been cited extensively in mission histories.

The period from 1882 to 1945 marked the establishment of the missions in East Bengal and was dominated by missionary women, yet the history of Australian Baptist mission published in 2012 provides scant information about the early period and contains very little analysis of women's work, focusing almost exclusively on the work and records of male missionaries.[23] The early history of the mission is written by Gerald Ball, who in 1987 wrote a paper on the Australian Baptist mission's initial policies, which was dismissive of missionary women.[24] In *Five Barley Loaves* he wrote that "motivation [to undertake missionary work] characterized the service of women as diverse as Helen Cousin, Ada Doery, Edith King, Minnie Lamb, Lorna McGregor, Kath Perrin and Flo Harris, previously unmentioned, yet between them they served 180 years."[25] By combining the significant work of these women into a single sentence Ball understated the work of these seven women, not to mention many other women who were not included at all. Gooden and this author have commenced the process of correcting the omission of missionary women through recent scholarship on Australian Baptist missionary women between 1882 and 1950.[26] Certainly this chapter seeks—at least in part—to address the gap in research on Australian Baptist

---

20. Hilton, "Australian Baptist Women as Public Intellectuals."

21. Bertha Tuck, "The Care of Souls," 1928, Speech, BMAA; Williams, *Land of Promise*; Harris, *Mymensingh Mission School*.

22. Collins, *Christ's Ambassador*; Hinton, *Ethel Ambrose*.

23. Gooden, "Mothers in the Lord," 17. The period from 1864 to 1945 represents over half of the timeframe but only 20 percent of the book (119 of 598 pages).

24. Ball, "Patterns of Presentation," 3.

25. Ball in Cupit et al., *From Five Barley Loaves*, 118.

26. Gooden, "Mothers in the Lord"; "We Trust Them"; Hilton, "For the Extension of Christ's Kingdom."

missionary women, while acknowledging that unfortunately not all missionary women's experiences could be included in this chapter.

Baptist women who worked as missionaries for other Protestant mission organizations have rarely been included in Australian Baptist historiography. To some extent this was also the case for men, yet because about one-third of these missionary men were ordained, most men worked in the Baptist denomination on their return to Australia from mission work. Some women were known, particularly those with well-known relatives or those who were active in the denomination, but overall their lives and their work are rarely included in Baptist historiography.[27]

A further issue relates to the way Australian Baptist missionary women have been depicted in scholarship. This is particularly the case with Ellen Arnold, who was one of the first two Australian Baptist missionary women in East Bengal, served for fifty years, and was significant in the growth of the ABFM in East Bengal.[28] While much of the scholarship affirmed her sustained work, within later historiography she has been portrayed as "difficult" and even that mission workers "doubted her sanity."[29] Some of these characterisations stem from personal correspondence by another Baptist missionary, the Rev. William Goldsack. The use of these letters perpetuates an unnecessary stereotype of a missionary woman whose work can be minimized because William Goldsack once privately wrote to a friend that she was "not quite right in her mind."[30] Several Australian Baptist missionary women and men had issues with Ellen Arnold's style and approach to mission work, but these did not result in poor mission work. In 1982 Jess Redman acknowledged that Ellen Arnold had a "reputation of a 'femme terrible'" but Redman believed that Ellen Arnold "felt resentment against anything that kept her from her true course."[31] The continued emphasis on archival material that denigrates Ellen Arnold is unnecessary and

---

27. See, for example, Wilkin, *Baptists in Victoria*. Wilkin lists at least seven missionaries (women and men) who served with other organizations but are identified by surname only. Men are easier to trace given that, usually, there are further references to them in denominational or mainstream papers.

28. Mitchell, *Ellen Arnold*; Crofts, *Our Bond Jubilee Edition*; Breward, *History of the Churches in Australasia*, 211.

29. Frank Marsh, "Ellen Arnold Day," *Vision* (Sydney), July 1956, 5; Piggin and Linder, *Fountain of Public Prosperity*, 562–63; Cupit et al., *From Five Barley Loaves*, 55–56.

30. William Goldsack wrote a letter to his friend James Fowler, dated 16 August 1898, "between our two selves." He had been on the mission for less than one year and she had been working as a missionary for over fifteen years. See Gooden, "Mothers in the Lord," 282–83.

31. Redman, *Light Shines On*, 18–19.

inappropriate, especially when men's poor performance is not highlighted—at least four missionary men between 1882 and 1945 have been identified as lacking judgment, being unable to adequately speak the local language, or behaving inappropriately.[32] Ellen Arnold's work in Australian Baptist mission should be admired, including the fact that she was held in high esteem by the local East Bengali people.[33]

There is strong evidence, then, that Baptists have largely ignored and misrepresented the roles of women in Australian Baptist mission, in an activity that was so important to women and the denomination. Ultimately women's numerical predominance and formal inclusion in mission management did not translate to gender equity. Baptist officials and historians chose not to acknowledge the significant work of women to the Australian Baptist missions. The inclusion of women was inconsistent with the view prevailing within the Baptist denomination that women's work was at the periphery of Baptist mission. In essence, the history of Australian Baptist mission has been a narrative of men's work, albeit with an obligatory—if sometimes disparaging—reference to Ellen Arnold.[34]

MODERN MISSION AND MISSIONARY ORGANIZATIONS

Modern Mission

Australian Baptist women's mission focus was shared with other Christians in Australia, NZ, UK, Europe, and North America.[35] Historians concur that the modern Protestant mission endeavor commenced in 1793 when the first missionaries from the English Baptist Missionary Society (BMS) went to India.[36] One of these BMS missionaries, William Carey, was widely acclaimed as founder of the modern foreign missionary enterprise and a heroic Baptist

---

32. Hilton, "ABW Database."

33. Marsh, "Ellen Arnold Day," *Vision*, July 1956, 5. Material by some East Bengali workers praising Ellen Arnold is in the archives of BMA, but much of the work has not been examined as it is written in Bengali and has not been fully translated.

34. Ball, "Patterns of Presentation," 3–5; Cupit et al., *From Five Barley Loaves*; Piggin and Linder, *Fountain of Public Prosperity*, 426–27. Piggin and Linder's account contained a more gender balanced perspective than other histories but included an account about Ellen Arnold's detractors.

35. Piggin and Linder, *Fountain of Public Prosperity*, 29.

36. Bebbington, *Baptists Through the Centuries*, 81; Robert, *Christian Mission*, 48, 75; Stanley, *History of the Baptist Missionary Society*, 1. The scholarship on modern mission is extensive. Robert provides a helpful overview of recent scholarship. See Robert, *Christian Mission*, 48, 75.

figure—explicitly acknowledged as such by Australian Baptists.[37] While this characterisation appears overstated, the work undertaken by William Carey and his associates in India through the BMS galvanized Baptist and other Protestant mission and subsequently led to an exponential growth in overseas mission for over a century.[38]

Australian Baptists, inspired by the missionary zeal espoused through the British BMS, were proud of their Baptist mission heritage.[39] In 1898 CIM worker, Jessie Warner, affirmed that she "had longed for the time to be able to assist in carrying the gospel to the heathen."[40] Likewise in 1926, at the end of her career, ABFM worker Helen Cousin reflected: "Enthusiasm generally runs high . . . The call of the great non-Christian world is heard, and the prayer is breathed out fervently, 'Here am I, send me.'"[41]

By the 1880s most of the large Protestant denominations in the UK and North America had established missions in Asia, Africa, and the Pacific, yet it was only in 1882 that SA Baptists "sent out" the first two Australian Baptist missionaries—both women—Ellen Arnold and Marie Gilbert.[42] The period from 1882 to 1945 covers the establishment and maintenance of the Australian Baptist missions in East Bengal, and arguably the zenith of Australian Protestant missionary optimism and energy.[43]

Evangelicals and Faith Mission

Evangelicals were an intrinsic part of the growth of modern Protestant missions.[44] Evangelical beliefs of Australian Baptist missionary women can be demonstrated with reference to Bebbington's four marks of evangelicals:

37. Elsie Sutton, "Carey Sunday at Mymensingh," *OB*, January 1925, 3–4; Dutta, *British Women Missionaries in Bengal*, 66; Piggin and Linder, *Fountain of Public Prosperity*, 355.

38. Stanley, *History of the BMS*, 39. In the twenty-first century many Baptists continue to revere William Carey. In 2019 the author was thrilled to sit on "Carey's Couch" in the Angus Library, Regents' College, Oxford.

39. Cupit et al., *From Five Barley Loaves*, xxvi.

40. Jessie Warner, "China Inland Mission," *Goulburn Evening Penny Post* (Goulburn, NSW), 6 September 1898, 2. Non-Christians, particularly those in India, China, and Africa, were often referred to by the—now dated—term "heathens."

41. Helen Cousin, "The Hopes of a Missionary," *TAB*, 28 April 1936. The quote is from Isaiah 6:8.

42. Cupit et al., *From Five Barley Loaves*, xv, 11.

43. O'Brien, "Historical Overview," 374.

44. Cupit et al., *From Five Barley Loaves*, xv; Treloar, *Disruption of Evangelicalism*, 4, 2.

conversionism, activism, biblicism, and crucicentrism.[45] Women often stressed conversions, which became a performance indicator for the work of missions, particularly in the late nineteenth and early twentieth centuries.[46] Ellen Arnold pleaded: "God grant [a member of the community] may be converted and become as a little child in the Kingdom."[47] Bertha Tuck insisted "individuals needed to be 'born again'" to enter the Kingdom of God.[48] The ABFM asked prospective missionaries to provide evidence of conversions they had secured.[49] Missionary women outlined the work they undertook, with activism being a key component. Baptist missionary Minnie Lamb's approach to mission work was described as "intensively evangelical."[50] Annie Lucas commented: "We go on quietly working and praying, we trust for the seed of the Kingdom to spring up . . . we are only limited by time and strength."[51] Missionary women relied on the supreme authority of the Bible. They read and studied the Bible and they held Bible studies with local people. For instance in 1929 the women organized a week-long Summer School camp in Orakandi for East Bengali women to study the Biblical writings of Paul, which included sessions on "Paul's methods of extending the Kingdom of God."[52] Missionary women regularly referred to themes of the cross and the atonement for sin through Christ's sacrifice.[53] In 1909 Ethel Newcombe composed a poem which included the line: "Can you and I still hear the drip—the rain of blood out-pour'd."[54]

Evangelicalism espoused that Christians were responsible for undertaking mission to all people and ensuring they were informed about, and challenged to follow, Christ, especially those living in non-Christian

---

45. A more complete analysis can be found at Hilton, "For the Extension of Christ's Kingdom." See also Bebbington, *Evangelicalism in Modern Britain*, 4; Piggin and Linder, *Fountain of Public Prosperity*, 25; Gladwin, "Mission and Colonialism," 285–86.

46. "Figures," *OB*, February 1901, 2.

47. Ellen Arnold, "Pubna [sic]," *OB*, August 1911, 3–4.

48. Bertha Tuck, "Report of the Sixteenth Annual Convention of Australasian Missionaries Tangail, 1903," *OB*, December 1903, 3.

49. Cupit et al., *From Five Barley Loaves*, 183.

50. H[edley] J. S[utton], "A Tribute to the Late Miss M. F. Lamb," *OIF*, 6 February 1940, 15.

51. Miss [Annie] Farmillo, "Notes from Serajgunge," *OB*, March 1912.

52. Gladys E. Collins, "Lifting the Standard of Womanhood," *OIF*, 6 October 1929, 2.

53. See, for example, Edna Hale, "Taking Up the Cross on Behalf of India," *OIF*, 6 April 1943, 11.

54. Ethel Newcombe, "A Garden of the Lord," *OB*, May 1909, 8.

nations.⁵⁵ Women's missionary work was the practice of a living faith and a Christian, evangelical commitment.⁵⁶ Women's commitment to spread the Gospel through mission work was an expression of their *activism*; their reliance on the Bible exhibited their *biblicism*; they wanted to expand Christianity through *conversionism*; and they believed in *crucicentrism*; and sought to work towards "a civilization dominated by the Cross."⁵⁷

Many Baptists and other Evangelicals were committed to "faith missions" whereby mission workers did not receive a salary but rather relied on their faith in God to provide necessary resources.⁵⁸ Faith missions, including CIM and PIVM, were attractive to Evangelical women and most emphasized evangelism rather than establishing and maintaining institutions such as schools and hospitals.⁵⁹ The ABFM was not a faith mission but wrestled with the principle of faith missions, as discussed below.⁶⁰

Women's Involvement in Mission

Until the mid-nineteenth century, most Protestant missionaries were men, who were usually "accompanied" by their wives.⁶¹ Many married missionary women were as committed to mission as their husbands, and undertook many different tasks, albeit with little formal recognition and accordingly the mission work undertaken by most of the early BMS missionary wives is largely unknown.⁶² Hannah Marshman, who was married to Joshua Marshman, one of the pioneer BMS missionaries, was originally acclaimed for her role in household management. Since the late twentieth century some mission historians have acknowledged her evangelistic work from 1799 to

---

55. Piggin and Linder, *Fountain of Public Prosperity*, 26; Hutchinson and Wolffe, *Short History of Global Evangelicalism*, 11, 20; Porterfield, *Modern Christianity*, 6.

56. Piggin and Linder, *Fountain of Public Prosperity*, 25.

57. See, for example, Miss J. R. [Janet] Hogben, "The NE India CE Convention," *OB*, February 1918, 4.

58. Taylor and Taylor, *Hudson Taylor*, 55; Maughan, *Mighty England Do Good*, 104.

59. Robert, *Gospel Bearers, Gender Barriers*, 13; Robert, *Christian Mission*, 61; Maughan, *Mighty England Do Good*, 138–39.

60. There is significant literature on modern European mission activity and faith missions. See, for example, Maughan, *Mighty England Do Good*; BMS World Mission, "Women in Mission"; Gooden, "Mothers in the Lord"; Seton, *Western Daughters in Eastern Lands*; Lienemann-Perrin et al., *Putting Names with Faces*.

61. Dutta, *British Women Missionaries in Bengal*, 60.

62. Stanley, *History of the BMS*, 228; Dutta, *British Women Missionaries in Bengal*, 66. Most wives were committed to mission, and many worked in the mission.

1847, although her legacy remains undeveloped.[63] In the mid-nineteenth century married missionary women, such as Elizabeth Sale and Marianne Lewis from the BMS, realized the value of evangelistic work among local women.[64] This work was labeled "women's work for women," or "zenana" mission, as it involved missionary women meeting with local women in the zenana—women's area—of their home. Initially it was conducted by married missionary women, who were convinced that women's work for women complemented other mission activities predominantly aimed at men, and that engaging single missionary women would ensure the success of women's work for women.[65] One such woman was Ellen Pigott, who worked alongside her husband in the BMS from 1863 to 1890 in Ceylon, now Sri Lanka. After mission service, she and her husband the Rev. Henry Pigott migrated to Australia, and she spoke in various forums in support mission.[66] She is one of the few Australian Baptist women who worked as a foreign missionary before 1882.

From the mid-nineteenth century numerous zenana mission organizations were formed in the UK and USA to send single missionary women to India and then China. Large numbers of single women were attracted to zenana mission work, which enabled missionary women to evangelize and educate local women, some of whom had no previous contact with people outside their homes.[67]

In the UK the "Ladies Association for the Support of Zenana Work and Bible women in India, in Connection with the Baptist Missionary Society," generally known as the Baptist Zenana Mission (BZM), was one of the larger organizations dedicated to women's work for women. In 1867 it was established as a mission organization separate from the UK BMS and was managed by Baptist women, with all workers being women.[68] Marianne Lewis, one of the founders of the BZM, believed criteria for the missionary women were: "Undoubted piety and a talent for acquiring languages."[69] BZM workers were required to obtain some theological training along with

---

63. Dutta, *British Women Missionaries in Bengal*, 64; Stanley, *History of the BMS*. Dutta outlines the importance of Hannah Marshman, whereas Stanley does not analyse her work.

64. Manley, *From Woolloomooloo*, 2:594.

65. Mrs C. B. [Marianne] Lewis, "A Plea for Zenana," *Leader* (Melbourne), 14 June 1873, 4.

66. "The Cingalese [sic] Mission," *SMH*, 4 Feb 1890, 8.

67. Robert, *Christian Mission*, 127; Seton, *Western Daughters in Eastern Lands*, 18.

68. Kemp, *There Followed Him Women*, 15.

69. Kemp, *There Followed Him Women*, 15.

other skills such as basic medical aid and teaching.[70] Initially the BZM struggled to provide appropriate preparation for missionaries until it established a joint training facility in 1912 with the English Presbyterians and the London Missionary Society called Carey Hall in Birmingham.[71] From 1867 until 1926 over 320 women worked in the BZM. Over 220 women worked in India, 54 in China, 26 in Democratic Republic of the Congo, then called the Belgian Congo, and 18 in Ceylon, now Sri Lanka.[72] At least 4 single Australian Baptist women served in the BZM: sisters Elsie and Ethel Evans, Grace Hickson, and Elizabeth Williams, a sister of an ABFM missionary woman.[73]

Ultimately the designated women's work merged with the general work. In 1914 the BZM handed management of their work to the BMS. The Women's Missionary Association was created to manage finances for missionary women. In 1926 it merged fully with the BMS.[74] Georgiana Kemp, a participant at the time and author of a history of missionary women's work, accepted the need to merge zenana mission into the BMS but expressed the hope that the workers would not be "*sub*-merged."[75] Such a concern was warranted. Certainly she was prescient to the extent that almost a century later the BZM work has not been analyzed separately from the work of the BMS.[76]

In North America from 1861 to 1910 44 different Protestant women's foreign mission organizations were established.[77] In 1910 Helen Barrett Montgomery, a leading North American Baptist mission advocate and preacher, outlined the work of North American missionary women in her book *Western Women in Eastern Lands*.[78] She documented that during 1909 there were at least 2,368 missionary women working in 36 North American foreign mission organizations, with 307 of these women working in 6 Baptist women's mission organizations.[79] Some Australian Baptist women

70. Kemp, *There Followed Him Women*, 20–21; Stanley, *History of the BMS*, 374.
71. Kemp, *There Followed Him Women*, 21.
72. Kemp, *There Followed Him Women*, 117–26.
73. Kemp, *There Followed Him Women*, 117–26; Hilton, "ABW Database."
74. Stanley, *History of the BMS*, 374.
75. Kemp, *There Followed Him Women*, 116.
76. See Stanley, *History of the BMS*. Stanley includes little information about BZM workers notwithstanding that they represented about one-third of the BMS workforce during the period from 1868 to 1927.
77. Montgomery, *Western Women in Eastern Lands*, 243–44.
78. Leonard, *Baptists in America*, 211–12.
79. Montgomery, *Western Women in Eastern Lands*, n.p. Helen Barrett Montgomery attended the 1910 Missionary Conference in Edinburgh and was the first woman elected as President of the Northern Baptist Convention in 1921, in part because of her

worked for these North American Baptist mission organizations.[80] As in Australia, North American women's work remains understated, although recent scholarship has addressed some of the gaps.[81]

Australian Christian women—like women from the UK and North America—were attracted to overseas mission service, and many volunteered in part because there were limited opportunities to work within Australian religious organizations, particularly in the areas of leadership and evangelism. From 1880 to 1945 up to 1,500 Australian women worked for Protestant mission organizations operating around the globe. Baptist women represented about 15 percent of this number—a high proportion given that Baptists represented no more than 5 percent of the Australian population.[82]

Australian Baptist Foreign Mission (ABFM)

In the late 1860s SA Baptists funded a new mission in Faridpur, East Bengal, as recommended by the BMS, and the Victorian Baptists funded a mission in Mymensingh that had been established by the BMS.[83] These missions were operated by local Christian workers with regular visits from BMS missionaries. In 1882 Ellen Arnold and Marie Gilbert went to Faridpur, supported by SA Baptists, being the first Australian Baptist missionaries.[84] Ellen Arnold returned to Australia in 1884 and visited every Australian colony and New Zealand to garner support for the mission work. In 1885 five missionary women, including Ellen Arnold, went to East Bengal, supported by Baptists in SA, Queensland, and Victoria.[85] Australian Baptist poet Hannah Fry wrote: "They have left this southern land / On this October day, / For India coral

---

significant fundraising for foreign missions.

80. See Hilton, "ABW Database." For example, Mary Grimes worked for an "American Baptist mission" organization as a single woman, but the exact organization is unknown.

81. Montgomery, *Western Women in Eastern Lands*, 36–37; Leonard, *Baptists in America*, 213. For recent scholarship, see Maxwell, *Reclaiming Voices*.

82. O'Brien, *God's Willing Workers*, 122. The precise number is very difficult to determine due to the range of foreign mission organizations and incomplete records. Many other women applied for service but were not accepted. See Loane, *Story of the China Inland Mission*, 20.

83. Cupit et al., *From Five Barley Loaves*, 9–10. Further details on the establishment of Baptist missions is outlined in Cupit et al., *From Five Barley Loaves*.

84. Percy Lanyon, "Our Federation," in Crofts, *Our Bond Jubilee Edition*, 7; Cupit et al., *From Five Barley Loaves*, 14. The South Australian Baptist Missionary Society changed its name to Furreedpore Mission in 1886, as there were several people involved in the mission organization who were not Baptists.

85. "Farewell Meeting to Zenana Missionaries," *TP*, 1 November 1885, 135.

strand / The Gospel to convey."[86] In the period from 1882 to 1945 74 percent of Australian Baptist missionaries were women.[87]

Between 1882 and 1899 the Australian colonies and NZ established seven separate Baptist missions in East Bengal. The organizations worked closely with each other, but the arrangement meant that until 1913 Australian Baptist missionaries worked for colonial and then state mission organizations. While in the early years of the work there were more women from SA, over the period the percentage of women from each of the states working in the ABFM broadly mirrored the state Baptist populations.

The ABFM formed in 1913 when Australian state mission organizations federated. The New Zealand Baptist Missionary Society (NZBMS) remained a separate organization, although missionaries retained close connections and all ABFM and NZBMS missionaries attended an annual convention in East Bengal.[88] In Australia the ABFM structure consisted of an Executive Board, a Board, and state mission committees. In East Bengal, as discussed above, a Field Council facilitated contact with the ABFM Board. The Field Council consisted of between eight and ten missionaries with at least three women members, which ensured women's activities were not completely ignored.[89] Through this period the ABFM's work was limited to East Bengal.[90]

The ABFM was not a faith mission as it paid an "allowance"—not a salary—to missionaries, which was set at a level that was deemed justifiable, and it paid for travel, housing, and "uniform" costs.[91] When deciding the governance of the new mission organization some Australian Baptists, including some missionaries, proposed that the ABFM be established as a faith mission. Instead in 1913 the ABFM decided to pay allowances, taking the approach that all Australian Baptists shared faith that the mission was adequately supported.[92] When the ABFM did not specifically adopt

---

86. Fry, *Poems*, 53.

87. Cupit et al., *From Five Barley Loaves*, 15; Hilton, "ABW Database."

88. Lanyon, "Our Federation," in Crofts, *Our Bond Jubilee Edition*, 7.

89. See, for example, Field Council MM, 1, BMAA.

90. Cupit et al., *From Five Barley Loaves*, 16.

91. Cupit et al., *From Five Barley Loaves*, 183; Gooden, "Mothers in the Lord," 10, 141.

92. C. E. [Charles] Wilson, "Faith and Finance: How the Baptist Missionary Society spends its money," *OIF*, 6 October 1931, 1. The Rev. Charles Wilson, a Scottish missionary wrote: "We do not expect [missionaries] alone to exercise faith and accept all the hardship of uncertain and irregular supplies. We seek to share with them their consecration and to exercise faith for them. That is the work of a true Faith Mission." The Editor of *OIF* confirmed his agreement as it "exactly puts the case for our Australian work."

the principle of a faith mission three missionary women and two men left the ABFM and worked with other faith mission organizations.[93] Most Baptists would have shared Lillian Vandeau's spirit of the notion of a shared responsibility, writing in 1896 that the denomination had a "sacred duty to help [the missionaries] go."[94] Nevertheless some ABFM missionary women were committed to faith missions. Marie Gilbert, for instance, became an independent missionary, working alongside the ABFM mission, because she "wanted to serve as the Lord might direct."[95] Marion Fuller remained a Baptist missionary but gave away most of her allowance to demonstrate that "God has promised."[96]

Although the Australian Baptist missionary allowance was significantly lower than a Baptist minister's wage in Australia, it was enough to live on in East Bengal. Initially the allowance was the same for single men and women. Married men received twice the allowance of a single missionary, given that married women were not technically missionaries and did not receive their own allowance. In the early twentieth century mission officials changed the rates. A single man received a higher allowance than that received by a single woman, and married men received more than a single man in recognition that the allowance was supporting two people.[97] Additional allowances were made for missionaries with children. ABFM allowances were less than those paid by other mission organizations, and allowances were sometimes reduced when the ABFM encountered financial stress.[98]

Australian Baptist missions did not engage missionaries from other denominations. All missionaries needed to identify their Baptist congregation before commencing service. Possibly a mission candidate joined a congregation specifically to be considered for Baptist mission work, but even so Baptist beliefs would be expected—from both the mission organization and the congregation. In 1887 Agnes Kiddell's Baptist credentials were described in the following way: "Until lately associated with another denomination she found it not a light matter to take up the cross of Baptism and so throw in her lot with our Baptist Church life."[99] Eleanor Walker is another example: she worked in Papua as a Methodist missionary sister from

93. Cupit et al., *From Five Barley Loaves*, 14.
94. "Baptist Union," *Mercury* (Hobart), 8 May 1896, 3.
95. "South Australian Notes," *TAB*, 24 August 1926, 6.
96. Marion Fuller, "Our Bond," 26 July 1889, (Unpublished editions).
97. Gooden, "Mothers in the Lord," 139–40.
98. Field Council MM, BMAA, 4, 6; Cupit et al., *From Five Barley Loaves*, 183.
99. "The Five Missionaries Who Sailed for India, October 22, 1887," *TP*, 1 November 1887, 167.

1892 to 1902, in East Bengal for the Tasmanian Baptist Missionary Society from 1904 to 1906, and then for the Seventh Day Adventist Missionary Organization in India. In 1904 she "embraced Baptist principles, was baptised . . . [and] was given the right hand of fellowship."[100] At least three Baptist missionary wives—Stella Churchward Kelly, Verna Churchward, and Lilian White—were adherents of other denominations prior to marriage, and all became members of a Baptist congregation around the time of their marriage.[101] All women directly engaged in mission service were technically Australian Baptists, which was appropriate given the focus to evangelize East Bengali people and form Baptist congregations.

Australian Baptist Women in Other Mission Organizations

Between 1882 and 1945 more Australian Baptist women served outside the Australian Baptist denomination than within—in around fifty different mission organizations.[102] Most of these women worked for non-denominational faith mission organizations, such as CIM and PIVM. CIM was founded in 1865 in England by Hudson Taylor, a faith mission pioneer who opened China to mission. In 1890 an Australian Council was formed following a visit to Australia by Hudson Taylor. From 1890 to 1945 forty-eight Australian Baptist women undertook mission work by the CIM—out of the two-hundred-and-five Australian and New Zealander missionary women in the CIM.[103] At least twelve Australian Baptist women worked for the PIVM, which was promoted in Australia in the early 1890s by the Rev. Charles Reeve, a Tasmanian Baptist minister.[104] At least fourteen Australian Baptist women worked for the NZBMS, BMS, or American Baptist mission organizations—five of whom also worked for the ABFM. The remainder of Australian Baptist missionary women worked for other mission organizations operating in India, China, Africa, and in the Pacific.[105] Often

100. "Tasmanian: Hobart," *TSB*, 13 December 1904, 288.

101. MacDonald, Rev. Thomas, and Mrs. Stella Churchward Kelly.

102. Hilton, "ABW Database." The women were identified through examining Baptist records, newspaper articles, and other historical records.

103. Loane, *Story of the CIM*, 6, 21, 35, 49, 66, 80, 104. The CIM had 360 mission workers who were Australian, and 205 were women. Baptist women represented 24 percent of the Australian missionary women. Baptist men represented 18 percent of missionary men.

104. See https://www.sim.co.uk/about-us/history. PIVM is now part of the mission organization "Serving in Mission" (SIM).

105. Hilton, "ABW Database." It is difficult to identify and confirm a full list of missionary women who may have worked for other denominational mission organizations.

women worked for more than one mission organization, including nineteen ABFM missionary women.[106] These Baptist women, who felt called to mission, were unconcerned about working outside the Australian Baptist denomination.[107]

Baptist women chose to work for mission organizations other than the ABFM for a variety of reasons, including their skills and education, their health status, the desire to work for a faith mission, and their "call" to particular fields or activities. Dr. Beryl Bowering, for example, wanted to work as a medical missionary for the ABFM but as the ABFM did not engage medical missionaries she chose to work for the London Missionary Society.[108] Some women volunteered to join the ABFM but were rejected either because they did not fulfill the minimum educational requirements or received adverse health reports.[109] Some of these women volunteered for other mission organizations that had less stringent rules regarding education and health.[110] Some Baptist women chose to work for mission organizations that adopted the principle of faith missions.

Generally missionary women serving in organizations other than the Australian Baptist denomination were not widely known within the Australian Baptist denomination. One indicator of this is in obituaries in *The Australian Baptist*. Most ABFM missionary women had published obituaries. Conversely, reports of the deaths of women who worked in other mission organizations were rarely published, sometimes even when these women were actively involved in the Australian Baptist denomination following their service.[111] Some women working for other missions remained connected to the Baptist denomination, although the extent to which this occurred depended on their profile within the denomination and dissemination of information about their missionary work.

Of course several missionary women who served in non-denominational missions were well-known within the Baptist denomination. Sisters Ethel and Lily Ambrose in the PIVM were the grand-daughters of Helen and William Finlayson, well-known in SA. Kate Allanby commenced mission service with the Queensland Baptist Missionary Society but left and established the Mayurbhanj mission in India. She maintained contact with

106. For details of the women, see Hilton, "ABW Database."

107. Randall, *What a Friend We Have in Jesus*, 17, 112.

108. Redman, *Light Shines On*, 69.

109. Board Meetings held in Sydney (Baptist Church, Petersham) 23–25 August 1933, BMAA. See also O'Brien, *God's Willing Workers*, 124; Hilton, "ABW Database."

110. ABFM, Board MM, BMAA.

111. Hilton, "ABW Database." The death of BMS worker Elizabeth Williams was not reported in *TAB*, despite her sister being an ABFM missionary.

Queensland Baptists, in part because of the advocacy for her mission work undertaken by herself, her mother Mary Allanby, and her sister Grace Selby.[112] CIM workers Ethel Embery and her daughter Winifred Embery were known partly because Ethel Embery's brothers were well-known Baptist ministers in Victoria.[113] Janet Ellem retained contact with the congregation of Stanmore Baptist during her missionary work for the non-denominational South Sea Evangelical Mission in the Solomon Islands.[114] Two women active in the denomination after completing non-denominational overseas mission service were Ella Davies and Louisa Hinton: both were Baptist minister's wives. Ella Davies served in CIM and after mission service preached occasionally to Australian Baptist congregations, was a member of state Baptist mission organizations in NSW and Queensland, and spoke regularly about mission work at women's meetings. Louisa Hinton served in PIVM and after service wrote several books promoting mission.[115] Clearly Australian Baptist women were committed to overseas mission work in whatever form that service took.

MOTIVATIONS FOR MISSION

Australian Baptist women were motivated to volunteer for mission by their Evangelical activism and calling to mission.[116] As an example, Alice Mead "heeded the call of God for India."[117] Lorna McGregor stated that "from childhood [she] felt the call of the mission field."[118] Extant ABFM application forms from the 1940s asked the question "What reason have you to believe that you have been called to work in the Foreign Field?" In 1945 Agnes Alcorn's answer to this question included the statement: "When definitely faced with the call of the Foreign Field, I told the Lord that I was willing to go, if He would send and equip me. I believe He is doing this."[119] Many

112. "Windsor Road," *TQB*, 1 December 1904, 175; G., *Kate Allanby of Mayurbhanj*, 26, 29.

113. "Personal," *Herald* (Melbourne) 1932, 9.

114. "Pages of the Past," *Rising Tide* (Stanmore, NSW), May 1941, 10, 12.

115. "New South Wales Senior Girls' Camp," *TAB*, 2 May 1939, 7; Hinton, *Ethel Ambrose*.

116. See Porterfield, *Modern Christianity*, 3, 6.

117. "The Late Mrs. C. S. Mead," *TAB*, 17 September 1935, 4.

118. "Noted Missioner: Miss Lorna McGregor," *Maryborough Chronicle, Wide Bay and Burnett Advertiser* (Maryborough, Queensland), 22 June 1933, 3.

119. Agnes Trudinger, The Australian Board of Baptist Foreign Mission: Form of Application for Service, [April] 1945, BMAA. The completed application forms for most ABFM missionary women are not extant.

women expanded on their calling to mission work in published articles. In 1933 Jean Harry remarked that when "the missionary is met by the question, 'Why?' [They] can answer that quite readily for [they] know the reason of [the] calling."[120] For many women this call was to engage in work in East Bengal. Agnes Alcorn's application stated: "The Lord was leading me to offer my services to the Baptist Foreign Mission in Eastern Bengal."[121] Her preference to apply for mission work in the ABFM was a departure from her family members connected to the CIM, and she described her decision as being "against old prejudices."[122] Ada Doery felt called to mission work in East Bengal from a young age. Due to concerns about her health, initially she volunteered to work at a mission in Southern India, before ultimately being accepted by the Victorian Baptist Missionary Society.[123] For many Australian Baptist women East Bengal was an obvious choice, given it was the location of Australian Baptist mission activity.[124]

Some Baptist women felt they were called to undertake mission in locations other than East Bengal. Such decisions were often based on familial ties, as many Baptists supported mission organizations outside of the Australian Baptist missions. The families of Elizabeth Chapman, Lorna Fleming, and Gertrude Trudinger were involved with the CIM. Indeed Gertrude Trudinger had strong connections to the CIM, as she and five of her siblings were CIM workers and two other siblings worked with another faith mission, the Sudan United Mission.[125] Most of the Trudinger family were Presbyterians, but Gertrude Trudinger and two of her nieces—Ina Meares and Agnes Alcorn—were members of Baptist congregations and became overseas missionaries. Ina Meares worked as a faith missionary in a school in China, and Agnes Alcorn's experience is mentioned above. Irrespective of where women worked, all attested to experiencing a calling to their missionary vocation.[126]

Women's interest in mission was encouraged by their congregations in various ways. Congregations disseminated information about mission

120. Jean Harry, "Toddlers on the Path Way [sic]," *OIF*, 6 May 1933, 11. Jean Harry did not provide details about her own "why" in this article as she was focusing on the process.

121. Trudinger, Application.

122. Trudinger, Application.

123. A[da] Doery, "Mymensing [sic]," *OB*, March 1921, 5.

124. Effie Baldwin, Letter to Roy Henson, 8 September 1980.

125. Loane, *Story of the CIM*, 17, 91.

126. See, for example, George Menzies, "Foreign Mission Day in New South Wales," *TAB*, 5 October 1915, 3; "The Late Mrs. C. S. Mead," *TAB*, 17 September 1935, 4; Trudinger, Application.

activity, arranged visits by missionaries, and supported overseas mission; often used Sunday School lessons which presented missionary information; established mission groups for women; and encouraged CE societies with a mission focus. Denominational and CE papers promoted mission. In 1905 an article by Mary Foucar implored readers to listen to God's word, as "is it any wonder the Holy Ghost, without any hesitation, prompts one to say: 'Here am I: Send me.'"[127] Missionary women visited Baptist congregations and left deep impreessions. Gwenyth Crofts's autograph book contained words of encouragement from missionary women she had met as a teenager, such as Hilda McLean who in 1915 wrote: "If we live by the spirit, let our steps be guided by the Spirit. Gal 5:25."[128] In 1903, as an eighteen-year-old, Stella Churchward Kelly had attended a missionary conference by John Mott, an evangelist and mission enthusiast from the USA.[129] ABFM worker Elsie Watson wrote that: "from our childhood we have been taught the greatness and glory of mission enterprise."[130]

Another significant reason for the relatively large number of women who volunteered for mission was that most Australian Protestant denominations had few paid roles for women in Australia, and so Baptist women who wanted to engage in work that exemplified their Christian convictions and a calling to leadership had limited options, other than missions.[131] As outlined above, Australian Baptist missionary women were not highly remunerated and thus were not motivated to be missionaries because of financial benefits.

It is likely that some women volunteered for service to advance their own ambitions for leadership and autonomy.[132] William Carey expressed ambition in his statement: "Expect great things from God, Attempt great things for God."[133] Women did not explicitly state such personal ambitions. Yet some women's writing reveal hints of ambition, perhaps also relating to their belief in their calling to the work. Jess Redman's history of the ABFM refers to: Ellen Arnold's resolute strength of character; Marie Gilbert's desire

127. Miss M. O. [Mary] Pigott, "The Home Circle," *TRC*, 2 October 1905, 89.

128. Gwenyth Harry Autograph Book.

129. "Home and Foreign Missions Australasian Students' Conference," *Argus* (Melbourne), 14 April 1903, 6.

130. Elsie Watson, "India for the New-Comers," *OIF*, 6 August 1928.

131. West, *Daughters of Freedom*, 296.

132. Bhattacharya, "Zenana Missions and Christian Missionaries," 6.

133. Walker, *William Carey*, 9. This quotation is attributed to William Carey, although historians have debated the exact form of the quotation. There are examples of Australian Baptist women using this expression, or variations. See Mrs. C. A. [Marion] White, "Character Building and Education," *TAB*, 10 September 1929, 17.

to "strike out on her own"; Jean Harry's preaching ability; and Hilda McLean working "closely with experts in Islamics."[134] Missionary women in the ABFM held leadership positions such as: Grace Thomson, who managed the Orakandi dispensary; Iris Seymour and Janet Hogben, who managed the Mymensingh school and orphanage consecutively for over fifty years; and Florence Harris, the principal of Birisiri school.[135] They had opportunities that were not available to most Australian women, such as being able to have a career in the Australian Baptist denomination, to preach, and to travel.[136] Women's desire for these opportunities cannot be completely ruled out as a motivation for undertaking mission, despite the lack of explicit evidence of such ambition.

SOCIAL BACKGROUND AND TRAINING

Australian Baptist missionary women came from a variety of backgrounds with diverse skills and life experiences. While the family situations of over half of the ABFM missionary women are unknown, about one-third had fathers who were professionals, were in business, or were teachers, including eleven women whose fathers were Baptist ministers.[137] ABFM missionary women were more highly educated than average Australians, as one-third had institutional training, with 8 percent of these possessing university degrees at a time when less than 1 percent of the total Australian population attended university.[138] A further 13 percent of women had worked as nurses or teachers prior to volunteering for mission service. Less information is known about Baptist women who worked outside the denomination, yet several of these women are known to have been financially supported by other family members.[139] Thus the available evidence, albeit incomplete, appears to indicate that Baptist missionary women were more likely to be from financially stable families and educated or trained in a specific profession than were most Australian women.[140]

---

134. Redman, *Light Shines On*, 14, 18, 77, 124.

135. Cupit et al., *From Five Barley Loaves*, 26, 34; Frank Marsh, Letter to whom it may concern: Re. Miss Florence S. Harris, 7 January 1950, BMAA.

136. O'Brien, *God's Willing Workers*, 162.

137. Hilton, "ABW Database."

138. ABS, "Historical Censuses"; DETYA, *Higher Education Students*, 5.

139. See, for example, G., *Kate Allanby of Mayurbhanj*, 28; Varley, *Henry Varley's Life-Story*, 111, 193.

140. ABS, "Historical Censuses."

Mission organizations tried to engage women who had the necessary skills, temperament, and health to undertake mission work, yet until the mid-century the ABFM did not have a consistent approach to the minimum training required for missionary women. This issue was in direct contrast to missionary men, for whom the ABFM—and many other mission organizations—required ordained ministers.[141] In 1927 in the UK Georgiana Kemp stated that "of all the shining qualities of [Baptist zenana missionary women], none is more conspicuous than a superb courage leading to audacious daring."[142] Such a statement reiterates the position within the ABFM. Until the 1920s many Baptist missionary women did not undertake formal mission training. Women received on-the-job training once they were engaged in the mission work. Missionary women were expected to have specific skills to support their work, including a basic education: essentially this was proficient reading and writing skills, and an ability to learn another language.[143] Some women relied on their track record of volunteer work or personal qualities such as "courage" and "daring" when applying for mission work.[144]

Obtaining adequate training for Australian missionary women was not an issue limited to the ABFM, and from the late nineteenth century various women's training facilities were established in Australia. Australian mission organizations, including the Australian Baptist missions, encouraged prospective missionary women to obtain training at these facilities.[145] In 1892 a Baptist woman Charlotte Warren and her husband Dr William Warren established one of the first Australian women's training facilities in Melbourne.[146] Members of Charlotte Warren's family were connected to the CIM, and many of the students prior to 1900 volunteered for the CIM. At least eight Australian Baptist women attended Warren's Missionary Training Home, five of whom undertook overseas mission for the CIM or the Australian Baptist missions.[147] The Training Home was operated under the

141. Minutes of the Annual Meeting of the Australian Baptist Foreign Mission Board, Sydney, 24 August 1926, BMAA. Will Johnson, who was a carpenter, was advised that he would not be considered for service unless he took the "full course of College Training as in the case of all other candidates."

142. Kemp, *There Followed Him Women*, 17.

143. Baptist missionary women needed to be able to read and write. In 1891 the ABS estimates that one-third of Australian women were not able to read and write. Census data from 1911 indicates that this had improved and only about one in five Australian women were not able to read and write. See ABS, "Historical Censuses."

144. Kemp, *There Followed Him Women*, 17.

145. "Reports for 1896," 37; Loane, *Story of the CIM*, 14.

146. Loane, *Story of the CIM*, 14.

147. See, for example, "Two Lady Missionaries," *Western Mail* (Perth), 24 February 1900, 28. Missionary women who received training included Ethel Embery and

principle of a faith mission, although some of the Baptist attendees were supported by relevant Baptist Unions.[148] Rolland House, a Presbyterian deaconess and missionary training facility in Melbourne, opened in 1916. By 1926 "most" Australian Baptist missionary women completed its training program.[149] Through the period Australian Baptist missionary women attended other facilities including Hope Lodge in Adelaide, the Sydney Missionary and Bible College, and the Melbourne Bible Institute.[150] From 1899 New Zealand Baptist missionary women could attend the Dunedin Missionary Training Home, which was established by Annie Driver. She had been an Australian Baptist missionary until forced to resign because of her poor health, and she lived in New Zealand following marriage to the Rev. Harry Driver.[151] Students undertook classes in "Bible study, Christian ethics, evidences [sic] of Christianity, Christian doctrine, physiology, medicine, English, and Music."[152] By the mid-twentieth century the ABFM expected that prospective missionary women had attended a mission training facility.

The ABFM wanted missionary women's training to be in a facility that was in line with Baptist principles, and that women acquired the necessary skills to provide "leadership among the women of the Orient."[153] In the 1920s the ABFM did not have the money to establish a Baptist training facility for women and so relied on those established by other Protestant denominations. Women's mission training was usually for two years and they studied a variety of subjects incorporating pastoral work, church history, ethics, and biblical studies. Women undertook practical and pastoral work in schools or hospitals as part of the course.[154] Australian Baptists did not establish a missionary training institution for Baptist women until 1949.[155]

Australian Baptist women's missionary training requirements differed among the states, particularly before federation of the ABFM in

---

Jessie Warner (CIM), and Eliza Reid, Lily Soundy, and Annie Lucas (Australian Baptist missions).

148. John C. Martin, "The Training of Women for Indian Service: What Australia Is Doing," *OIF*, 6 April 1926, 5.

149. Foreign Mission Board Annual MM, 22–24 August 1934, BMAA. See Cupit et al., *From Five Barley Loaves*, 190.

150. Hilton, "ABW Database."

151. "Obituary," *Timaru Herald* (Timaru, New Zealand), 18 January 1943, 3.

152. "Dunedin Missionary Training Home," *Otago Witness* (Dunedin, NZ), 26 June 1901, 12.

153. Martin, "The Training of Women for Indian Service," *OIF*, 6 April 1926, 5.

154. Martin, "The Training of Women for Indian Service," *OIF*, 6 April 1926, 5; Clack, *We Will Go*, 121.

155. Cupit et al., *From Five Barley Loaves*, 190.

1913. Presumably differences occurred because of demand and supply. Some states did not have many volunteers and accordingly they engaged women whose credentials may not have been acceptable in states with more volunteers. Examples of this are evident in both WA and Tasmania, which had smaller numbers of Baptists and volunteers were well-known within Baptist circles. For instance, Edith King had not completed any training and exhibited poor health, yet she was accepted by the WA mission committee.[156] Likewise in 1896 the Tasmanian Baptist mission annual report by Lillian Vandeau stated: "Our committee have long felt more interest would be aroused and sustained in our churches if someone went from our midst to represent us."[157] That year they had been pleased to accept a local woman, Lily Soundy, as a Tasmanian Baptist missionary. Prior to this Tasmanian Baptists had financially supported Lucie Thompson, from SA. These situations illustrate the importance placed on state representation and the belief that local representation ensured ongoing donations to the mission, even in cases when there were reservations regarding skills and experience.[158] SA and Victorian Baptists did not appear to have a problem attracting women to volunteer for missionary work. In the nineteenth century NSW had some difficulties in obtaining missionary workers, but by the twentieth century there were many suitable volunteers.[159]

Overall the level and quality of training undertaken by missionary women prior to service increased over time and targeted the skills required for missionary work. From 1882 to 1900, eleven of the thirty-three Australian Baptist missionary women in East Bengal are known to have had formal training: three from Charlotte Warren's facility; four as nurses; and five as teachers. From 1901 to 1920 the proportion of the thirty-five missionary women who commenced service with formal training increased, including four women with university degrees, two of whom were doctors. The training itself varied significantly in this period: university or college education; attendance at various missionary training facilities; or the absence of formal training aside from working alongside a Baptist minister and obtaining basic medical skills.[160] From 1921 to 1945, most of the thirty-two women

---

156. "Goalundo Mission," *TSB*, 10 May 1904, 10. The details of the health issue were not discussed.

157. "Baptist Union," *Mercury*, 8 May 1896, 3.

158. At some points the relationships among the state mission committees were tense, involving some rivalry and distrust. See Cupit et al., *From Five Barley Loaves*, 14; Prior, *Some Fell on Good Ground*, 194; Moore, *All Western Australia*, 35.

159. ABFM, Board Minutes, BMAA.

160. "Goalundo Mission," *TSB*, 10 May 1904, 10.

had received formal mission training, usually at Rolland College.¹⁶¹ In 1926 the ABFM Board agreed that all prospective missionary women needed to undertake formal missionary training.¹⁶² Thus while often missionary women who commenced mission work before 1920 were engaged on the basis of their personal qualities, by the mid-1920s the ABFM had a process in place to assess prospective missionary women's applications, which comprised interviews between the applicant and Board members, inspection of references from ministers or teaching staff, and written responses to a set of questions regarding attitudes, education, and Christian activities.¹⁶³ As the ABFM matured as an organization the skills and training required for missionary women became more explicit and rigorous and consequently the skillset for missionaries was applied consistently across Australia.

MISSIONARY WOMEN'S WORK

Roles Undertaken

Australian Baptist missionary women undertook all the roles required for establishing and maintaining a mission, including those of evangelist, preacher, teacher, administrator, interpreter, nurse, doctor, and contract manager.¹⁶⁴ Although Australian Baptist missionary women undertook many different roles there were a number of key activities, and these did not change significantly over the period from 1882 to 1945, particularly within Australian Baptist missions.¹⁶⁵

Missionary women's writing was not a specified activity per se but was vitally important in fulfilling women's mission commitments. Missionary women were avid and competent writers. Missionary communication was necessary to ensure continued interest, prayer, and financial support for the mission work.¹⁶⁶ Missionary women wrote letters for reading in Baptist congregations, in meetings of their support base, and to specific individuals.

161. Martin, "The Training of Women for Indian Service," *OIF*, 6 April 1926, 5; Hilton, "ABW Database."

162. ABFM, Executive Minutes, 28 June 1926, BMAA.

163. Cupit et al., *From Five Barley Loaves*, 183. Some applications from the mid-1920s are in the BMA Archives. For example, Jean Harry's file contains a hand-written application addressing set questions, references from Baptist ministers, and a supporting medical certificate.

164. Gooden, "We Trust Them," 132, 41.

165. See, for example, Redman, *Light Shines On*, 61.

166. Lily Higlett, Notes for Meetings of the NSW Women's Missionary Society, 1939–1943 (Notes), NSWBA.

In 1945 ABFM worker Nola Hodgson sent seventeen-year-old Gladys Bergersen a letter about her life working at various East Bengal missions, and she valued the letter so much that she kept it for eighty years.[167] Missionary women also wrote update reports to the mission boards and for annual reports, as well as articles for the Australian Baptist mission papers, and other denominational papers.[168] Women engaged by other mission organizations wrote for their relevant papers, particularly *China's Millions* for CIM and *White Already to Harvest* for PIVM.[169] Missionary women wrote books about their own or other missionary experiences, including: ABFM workers such as Gladys Collins, Stella Churchward Kelly, Annie Driver, Bertha Harris, and Jess Redman; and PIVM worker Louisa Hinton.[170] Missionary women wrote stories about local people who had accepted or rejected the Christian message. Thus Constance Williams and Gwenyth Crofts published books about East Bengali people and Winifred Embery published a story about Chinese people.[171] Some women wrote for the local people to address specific needs. In 1912 Mary Grimes wrote a book of gospel songs for the BMS in southern India; in 1930 Gwenyth Crofts and Elfrida Hill contributed Bengali hymns to a BMS hymnbook; and in the early 1940s Beryl Bowering wrote an adaptation of Lydia's conversion in Act 16:14–16 in simple language.[172] Australian Baptist missionary women's lives, roles, and experiences can be interpreted and understood because many of their writings have been retained.

Mission establishment was an essential activity that required vision, negotiation skills, and good management. Australian Baptist women established at least four Australian Baptist missions in East Bengal.[173] In southern India in 1895 Kate Allanby established the Mayurbhanj Mission with assistance from Agnes Kiddell.[174]

Evangelism was a key reason why most women volunteered for mission service and was their most important role. In *Our Bond Jubilee Edition* both

167. Nola Henderson, Letter to Gladys Heather, 25 November 1945.

168. *OIF*, 1915–1949. *OB*, 1893–1941. *TAB*, 1912–1972.

169. *China's Millions* (London), 1875–1952. *China's Millions* (Melbourne), Australasian Edition, 1935–1987. *White Already to Harvest* (Puna, India), 1898–1968.

170. Stella M. Churchward Kelly, Recollections of a Missionary Life, 1949, Tasmanian Baptist Archives, University of Tasmania, Hobart; Collins, *Christ's Ambassador*; Driver, *Missionary Memories*; Harris, *Mymensingh Mission School*; Redman, *Light Shines On*; Hinton, *Ethel Ambrose*.

171. Crofts, *Bengali Brownies*; Williams, *Land of Promise*; Embery, *Those That Endure*.

172. Bowering, "Lydia"; Redman, *Light Shines On*, 77.

173. Gooden, "We Trust Them," 132, 41.

174. G., *Kate Allanby of Mayurbhanj*.

Hilda McLean and Gwenyth Crofts stressed the importance of evangelistic work undertaken by women over the first fifty years of Australian Baptist mission service.[175] Evangelism was intended to result in the conversion of local people, and to equip them to evangelize other people. Women worked to evangelize the local women in their homes (the zenanas), schools, markets, and events held on the missions. They traveled to small villages surrounding their main mission centers, and they undertook extensive itineration, which involved from two-weeks to two-months of traveling throughout a region to speak with women in their local language about Christianity.[176] CIM worker Ella Davies summarized a two-month itineration through Western China: "We went about to all places within our reach, visiting thirteen villages in all, staying a day or two, or even more, at each. Our whole time was occupied in teaching and preaching."[177] Lorna McGregor described her itineration work in the following way: "It is a wonderful privilege to be able to go on these tours, visiting lonely, distant places, giving the people the opportunity of a special gathering together for fellowship . . . Touring in the villages brings to one a happiness too deep for words."[178] Many missionary women preached regularly in mission congregations, such as: Ellen Arnold, from 1882 until her death in 1932; Edith King, from 1904 to 1918; and Jean Harry in the 1930s and 1940s.[179] Opportunities for missionary women in the ABFM to preach declined from the 1920s, particularly as the number of missionary men increased and more East Bengali men were engaged as preachers. If men were available to preach, demarcated gender roles meant that a man preached in preference to a woman. However missionary women often referred to their evangelistic work with women in schools or their homes as "preaching."[180]

Teaching was an important part of Australian Baptist mission work and many women undertook teaching activities as part of their mission work. Teaching was usually undertaken in the local vernacular, although older children in mission established schools were also taught English. The missionary women believed that without education people were not capable of understanding Christian beliefs. Hilda McLean wrote: "Education helps

---

175. Crofts, *Our Bond Jubilee Edition*, 19–20.

176. Log book of NSW Zenana Work, Comilla, 1914–1940, NSWBA.

177. Ella Godbold, "Kuei-Cheo," *China's Millions* (Melbourne), January 1907, 3.

178. Lorna McGregor, "Birisiri Women's Evangelistic Report," in ABFM, *Annals of Victory*, 31.

179. Ellen Arnold, "Correspondence," *OIF*, 6 January 1923, 124; Edith King, "Faridpur," *OB*, March 1906, 6; Redman, *Light Shines On*.

180. Hilda McLean, "Our Fifty Years of 'Preaching,'" in Crofts, *Our Bond Jubilee Edition*, 19–20. Her inverted commas.

evangelism... Evangelism brings in the recruits, 'teaching' trains them."[181] Education was initially conducted as a part of the zenana mission, but by the turn of the century missionary women established Sunday schools and had arrangements with local schools to teach Scripture.[182] Australian Baptist women in other mission organizations rarely worked as teachers; instead they undertook medical work as a component of their evangelistic work.[183]

All missionary women provided some type of medical assistance to local people, either through dispensaries located on the missions or as part of itineration and zenana visits.[184] Within the Australian Baptist missions from 1882 to 1945 medical services were considered "subsidiary" to evangelistic work.[185] In the 1945 ABFM annual report Janet Hogben inserted an explanation for her provision of "social service":

> Should this report in some parts seem to be one of social service rather than of definite missionary activity I would point out that we and the members of our staff are called upon during these abnormal days to witness for Christ in many previously unthought-of ways and we have reason to believe that our witness is telling for Him through these avenues.[186]

Despite the reluctance of the ABFM Board to support medical missions or other social services, most missionary women provided such services to East Bengali people and about 15 percent of ABFM women were qualified nurses or doctors.[187] The reality of mission work was that medical and social services were required to undertake evangelistic work, and missionaries needed to have the ability to treat common illnesses, if only for the needs of other missionaries when required. Certainly Alice Barber's medical

---

181. Hilda McLean, "Our Fifty Years of 'Preaching,'" in Crofts, *Our Bond Jubilee Edition*, 20.

182. Ellen Arnold, "From a Zenana Missionary's Point of View," *TSB*, 13 January 1898, 13; Stella M. Churchward Kelly, "Serajgunje: A New Walla's Welcome," *OIF*, 2 June 1917, 1–3.

183. Hilton, "ABW Database." Only one Australian Baptist woman working in other mission organizations has been found to have teaching qualifications.

184. Grace Thomson, "The Ministry of Healing," in Crofts, *Our Bond Jubilee Edition*, 22.

185. Victorian Baptist Foreign Mission, quoted in Cupit et al., *From Five Barley Loaves*, 44.

186. J. R. Hogben, "Mymensingh Girls' School Report," in ABFM, *Forward Area*, 28.

187. Redman, *Light Shines On*, 69; ABFM, Board Minutes, BMAA. Missionary women asked that the ABFM consider establishing a facility to provide local women with medical services.

skills were used by Australian Baptist missionaries.[188] Missionary women received training in basic medical treatments before leaving Australia.[189] The Australian Baptist women's commitment to medical assistance demonstrates a broad definition of "evangelism" in their missionary work.[190] In the mid-twentieth century the ABFM formally acknowledged that mission was more than evangelism, and mission policy changed to incorporate medical assistance and other social services.[191] Clearly mission practice had preceded the policy.

Over 20 percent of Australian Baptist mission women working in other mission organizations were engaged to undertake medical work alongside evangelism, including Dr Ethel Ambrose and Lily Ambrose, a nurse, in PIVM; Dr Eleanor Varley and Ethel Varley, a pharmacist, in Sudan Inland Mission; Louisa Pike, a midwife in CIM; and Dr Beryl Bowering in the London Missionary Society.[192] In addition Dr Laura Hope, together with her husband Dr Charles Hope, worked as independent medical missionaries alongside Australian Baptists in East Bengal from 1903 to 1933.[193]

Women undertook other work depending on the needs of the specific mission. For instance, the ABFM did not undertake regular translation work—the Bible had been translated into Bengali and Garo before 1882—but some missionary women did translations at various times, particularly Hilda McLean, and women in other mission organizations, such as Kate Allanby, also undertook translation work.[194] Sisters Annie and Susie Garland in the CIM worked on a new Chinese Braille method.[195] In several missions the women enabled "child sponsorship," where congregations, mission groups, or individuals supported a local child attending a mission school or orphanage, and missionary women sent updates on the child's progress.[196] This type of support was a precursor to formal arrangements later introduced

---

188. Grace Thomson, "The Ministry of Healing," in Crofts, *Our Bond Jubilee Edition*, 22.

189. Stella M. Churchward Kelly, "Beside All Waters," 8–10, BMAA; Daisy Grace, "Under Canvas with the Children," *OIF*, 6 April 1925, 6.

190. Robert, *Gospel Bearers, Gender Barriers*, 20.

191. Cupit et al., *From Five Barley Loaves*, 119. Later changes in mission practices discussed below may have been another reason for this shift.

192. Hilton, "ABW Database."

193. Secomb, "Borne in Empire."

194. "Miss McLean's Last Book," *OIF*, 6 September 1938, 8; Redman, *Light Shines On*, 77; G., *Kate Allanby of Mayurbhanj*, 59.

195. Loane, *Story of the CIM*, 86.

196. "New South Wales: Petersham," *TAB*, 26 March 1925, 10.

by various mission agencies. Women planted vegetables to provide fresh food for those living on the mission, and thereby saved money.[197]

Women had to deal with changes caused by political unrest, war, famine, and ongoing sickness. Missionary work in China was interrupted by the 1900 Boxer Rebellion, which resulted in the death of an estimated 30,000 Chinese Christian converts and around 200 foreign missionaries.[198] CIM worker Marion McKie was reported as having been murdered, but she had gone into hiding during an ambush. A letter to her parents outlined the terrible situation for local Christians: "They appeal to us to help them, but what can we do? Truly we are cast upon God."[199] Missionaries in India dealt with ongoing unrest due to the independence movement, which fought for Indian independence from the British Raj. In 1931 an English magistrate was shot in Comilla, and the ABFM missionary women arranged for his wife to return to England.[200] The women outlined their actions in the mission Logbook, yet in *Our Indian Field* the ABFM General Secretary laconically described Comilla as "rather a political storm centre lately."[201]

Missionary women's work was hampered by two world wars. During times of war missionaries had a shortage of general supplies including food, and reduced shipping led to restricted movements, a loss of correspondence, and fewer goods being sent from Australia. Funds from Australian Baptists were given to the war effort rather than the missions.[202] During the First World War Grace Brown appealed for funds through Australian Baptists' belief in the importance of evangelism:

> In the homelands the question is being raised in various forms: "Ought we to send so much to India and work keenly for her at this time of strain and need for the war?" We reply with another query: "Has India meted out her help to the Empire in men and money for the war, according to this standard of grudging

---

197. Alice Hawkyard, "Birisiri," *OB*, March 1923, 7; Janet Hogben, "Mymensingh," *OB*, November 1928, 8.

198. Loane, *Story of the CIM*, 28–29; Treloar, *Disruption of Evangelicalism*, 4, 36. Two Australians and one New Zealander were among the CIM workers killed in the 1900 Boxer Rebellion.

199. Marion Elizabeth Chapman, "Missionary Perils: Miss Chapman's Adventures," *Mount Barker Courier and Onkaparinga and Gumeracha Advertiser*, 1 February 1901, 3.

200. Log book of NSW Zenana Work, Comilla, 27–28, NSWBA.

201. John C. Martin, "Indian Unrest and Its Reaction on Our Work in Bengal," *OIF*, 6 April 1932, 3.

202. See, for example, F. W. [Frederick] Norwood, "Mission Advance in Time of Crisis," *OIF*, 21 November 1915, 2. Throughout 1915 there were several articles discussing the impact of reduced funds.

calculation? . . . Shall we not repay in our best coin, giving her the knowledge of the love of Christ, and help her to become the great nation we have been through the Gospel."[203]

During the Second World War Florence Harris wrote: "We think war, we dream war, but it is useless mentioning it in our letters."[204] During 1943 in East Bengal there was a severe famine, which resulted in the death of an estimated one and a half million people on the Indian sub-continent, and further impacts on food availability and quality. Gwenyth Crofts wrote that when they received bags of flour they "had to sift it again and again to remove weevils, and bake it to remove the smell of mould."[205] Jess Redman described the combined impact of war and famine as "appalling."[206]

Sickness of missionaries was an ongoing and common issue in overseas mission. Of the one-hundred ABFM women workers, twenty-four resigned due to ill health and two died while serving. Other Australian Baptist women died in service, including Ethel Ambrose in India, Janet Ellem in the Solomon Islands, and Sarah Liddy in China.[207] Mission work was disrupted because of ill-health, and missionaries were required to move between missions to cover "gaps."[208] Where possible, mission organizations encouraged missionaries to have an annual holiday for their health. Most missionaries in East Bengal went to the cooler mountain areas of India or Nepal during the hottest months of the year.[209] In 1923 Gwenyth Crofts wrote a poem called "On Holiday," which commenced:

> "You've been so very good this year,"
> Said our Home Board one day.
> "We'll give you leave to go and rest,
>
> "Where mountain breezes play."
> "There perspiration is no more,

---

203. Miss Grace Brown, "'Your Jesus Not for Us': The Women's Own Argument and Appeal," *OIF*, 21 November 1915, 15–16.

204. Florence Harris, Letter to Frank Marsh, ABFM General Secretary, 18 June 1940, BMAA.

205. Crofts, *Glimpses into the Life of a Missionary Wife*.

206. Redman, *Light Shines On*, 104.

207. Hinton, *Ethel Ambrose*, 238; Loane, *Story of the CIM*, 156; "Miss J. G. Ellem," *SMH*, 21 June 1933, 17.

208. Martin, "Indian Unrest and Its Reaction on Our Work in Bengal," *OIF*, 6 April 1932. 3.

209. See, for example, Minutes of the Foreign Mission Board Executive meeting, 1901, BMAA; Hogben, "Mymensingh," *OB*, November 1928. The ABFM purchased cottages in Darjeeling for the use of families with children at Mount Herman School.

"Nor 'pokes' nor smells intrude,
"Go, maidens fair, rest, meditate,
"Return with health renewed."[210]

Mission organizations relied heavily on the service of women, but often controlled aspects of their lives. In the ABFM the Board guided the movements of missionaries' locations, the number of missionaries, and funding allocations.[211] The Board expressed displeasure at those missionary women who did not comply with ABFM directives, although in most cases the women who disputed directives already intended to leave the ABFM. For example, Martha Plested in 1918, Ellen Arnold in 1931, and Hilda McLean in 1936 were instructed to retire and return to Australia because of their age and health. Each decided they wanted to remain in East Bengal, effectively as faith missionaries.[212] Yet overall missionary women—and men—did not publicly question the authority of the ABFM Board. For instance in 1926 the ABFM delayed sending the fiancées of two missionary men to East Bengal because of scarce finances. Likewise missionaries accepted that the ABFM determined their mission locations, as articulated by Edna Hale in November 1937, cheerfully stating: "I'm just wondering where I'll be located [next year]."[213] Most missionaries appear to have been compliant, even when decisions had a direct disruptive impact on their lives.

Experience of Furlough

Furlough, or leave from mission work, was granted to all missionaries following a period of service. Mission organizations had different criteria about furlough and sometimes missionary women worked for many years before returning to Australia, often at their own expense. A case in point was Louisa Pike in the CIM. She and her husband Douglas Pike could not afford to come back to Australia regularly, and on one of their furloughs they only had enough money for the travel costs of two of their five children. Sadly one child died in boarding school in China while they were on furlough.[214] From 1913 the ABFM Guidelines were that following five years of service,

210. Gwenyth Harry, Mussourie Mountain Musings, 1923, BMAA.

211. ABFM, Board Minutes, BMAA. Lack of funds in the ABFM was a constant issue.

212. ABFM, Board Minutes, August 1934, BMAA; H. [Hilda] McLean, "Tangail Transplanted," *OIF*, 6 May 1936, 4.

213. Edna Hale, Letter to Frank Marsh, ABFM General Secretary, 22 November 1937, BMAA; ABFM, Board Minutes, 18 August 1926, BMAA.

214. See, for example, Calvert, "Douglas Pike," 45.

paid furlough of twelve months was granted.[215] The ABFM organized a deputation program for missionaries which generally involved about three months of their furlough. The missionaries visited different congregations and attended meetings promoting mission work.[216]

Some of the deputation work undertaken by ABFM women is referred to in *The Australian Baptist* and it indicates how this work enabled a much more personal exchange of information than articles written in mission or denominational publications. When Florence Harris addressed Hornsby Baptist in 1926 the Secretary wrote that: "All were touched by her stories of the children and women of India."[217] Yet Florence Harris, along with most missionary women, had previously addressed issues about the children and women of India in published articles.[218] In 1938 *The Australian Baptist* acknowledged the burden of furlough work on ABFM missionaries, but then wrote: "can we do without this personal touch?"[219] The spoken word and the presence of missionaries was seen as more influential than an article.[220] While furlough work appears to have been relentless, most women seem to have appreciated the opportunities to maintain personal connections and to talk about their work.[221]

Not all women were required to undertake furlough work. Elizabeth Williams, a missionary with the UK BMS, wrote to a fellow worker about promotion of mission work, remarking "I am glad that I have very little of that sort of work to do!"[222] The BMS did not expect Elizabeth Williams to undertake any furlough work in the UK or Australia. In contrast, the ABFM relied on mission workers to promote mission work in Australia, as did faith mission organizations.

Baptist missionary women working in mission organizations other than the ABFM maintained contact with their local Baptist congregations, and this connection allowed missionary women to visit their Baptist congregation during their furlough.[223] For instance in 1914 Mary Abbott, a

---

215. Minutes of District Committee Meeting, 29 April–1 May 1925, BMAA.
216. ABFM, Board Minutes, BMAA.
217. "New South Wales: Hornsby," *TAB*, 25 May 1926, 10.
218. Florence Harris, "The Children's Message: 'Prize Day,'" *OIF*, 6 April 1924.
219. "The Personal Touch," *TAB*, 19 May 1936, 6.
220. West, *Daughters of Freedom*, 210.
221. Iris Seymour, "Mymensingh," OB, January 1895, 3.
222. Elizabeth Williams, Letter to Ella Lockhart, Foreign Secretary, Women's Missionary Association, 30 June 1925, IN / 88, Angus Library and Baptist Archives, Regent's Park College, Oxford (ALA).
223. Susan Davey, "New South Wales: Ladies' Zenana Society," *TAB*, 8 February 1938, 12.

PIVM worker, returned to Brisbane for furlough. She spoke at a missionary event at Taringa Baptist, Queensland, and received money donated at the event.[224] In 1926, when the ABFM was experiencing a period of financial stress, the ABFM Board strongly advised Australian Baptist congregations not to invite or accept offers from missionaries in organizations other than the ABFM to speak to Baptist congregations, stating: "Our home constituency is being constantly exploited by undenominational [sic] missions over whose message, field methods, and home management the Baptist Churches of Australia can exercise no control . . . Sift most carefully applications for entrance to our Churches which may be made by other missions than our own."[225] The Board did not want mission donations to be directed to organizations other than the ABFM. However individual congregations were unlikely to reject a visit from a missionary who had connections to the congregation. This pattern of Baptist people working in faith missionaries and relying on support of Baptist congregations or individuals continued throughout the twentieth century and into the twenty-first century.

Australian Baptist missionary women were less visible on furlough than missionary men for several reasons, two of which specifically related to married missionary women. First, the ABFM expected married men to undertake extensive furlough work, yet missionary wives were not expected to undertake such deputation work. To illustrate, Lilian White appears to have not accompanied her husband, the Rev. Victor White, when he undertook deputation work in regional NSW. In contrast active missionary wives such as Alice Mead, Stella Churchward Kelly, and Gwenyth Crofts, while not expected to undertake deputation work during furlough, deliberately chose to do so.[226] Of course married women may have attended events and promoted mission during their furlough but these activities failed to be mentioned in published reports. Second, missionary women's care of children quite likely reduced their capacity to undertake deputation work in Australia. When in East Bengal school-aged children attended boarding school, yet during furlough children returned to Australia with their parents. While the missionaries and their children may have welcomed additional time together, the responsibility of childcare could have curtailed some women's activities and reflected expectations within the broader Australian culture—that a mother should be at home with her children.

224. "Taringa Union Baptist Church," *Daily Standard* (Brisbane), 28 October 1914, 2.
225. Board meeting 18–20 August 1926, ABFM, Board Minutes, BMAA.
226. See for example, "Alberton," *TAB*, 9 March 1920, 8; "A Visiting Missionary," *North Western Advocate and the Emu Bay Times* (Burnie, Tasmania), 29 September 1916, 2; Cutlack, "By Credo," *Saturday Mail*, 17 June 1916, 4; Susan Davey, "Ladies Zenana Society," *TAB*, 14 December 1937, 12.

Other factors that impacted the extent of furlough work undertaken by women relate to promoting and reporting women's furlough work. An example of the promotion of furlough work is contained in the minutes of the ABFM Executive Board meeting on 12 March 1926. The minutes detailed furlough arrangements for Victor White and Allan Grace, then recorded an agreement "that if possible an itinerary be arranged by the Executive officers for Miss [Grace] Brown."[227] Grace Brown does not appear to have undertaken any work outside SA and WA, in contrast to the extensive furlough work by Allan Grace and Victor White.[228]

Missionary women's furlough work was promoted less than men's furlough work in *The Australian Baptist*. Florence Harris serves as an example. Both she and Victor White were in NSW on furlough in 1926. Victor White had printed forms with his itinerary, but Florence Harris did not. Likewise in 1938 Florence Harris undertook furlough work in NSW for much of her year in Australia but at no stage was her itinerary published. Wilfred Crofts visited the state for two weeks and his itinerary was published in *The Australian Baptist*.

Many Baptist missionary women's furlough activities are only known about through their correspondence with the ABFM General Secretary. Men's words were also reported in more detail than women's words. This was partly because they were more likely to preach at Sunday worship services than women. Yet missionary men's speeches appear to have been reported more than missionary women even when both spoke at women's meetings. To illustrate, in 1938 Susan Davey wrote summaries of the monthly meetings of the NSW Ladies Zenana Society for publication in *The Australian Baptist*. In twelve articles published during 1938, on average her summaries of speeches by missionary women were two thirds the length of speeches by missionary men.[229]

Australian Baptist missionary women are known to have preached during their furloughs, at a time that women preached rarely in Australia. Significantly, during 1884 Ellen Arnold preached to many Australasian Baptist congregations when she was stimulating interest in Baptist mission.[230] About half of the women documented as having preached in Australian Baptist congregations worked as overseas missionary women, including Gwenyth Crofts, Florence Harris, Stella Churchward Kelly, and Edith King,

227. ABFM, Executive Minutes, BMAA.

228. See *TAB*, 1926. Allan Grace and Victor White have well over twenty references each to work undertaken on furlough while Grace Brown has only seven references.

229. See, for example, Susan Davey, "New South Wales: Ladies' Zenana Society," *TAB*, 8 February 1938, 12; *TAB*, 1 November 1938, 4.

230. Ellen Arnold, "Letter from Miss Arnold," *TP*, 1 June 1885, 71.

plus women outside the ABFM such as Kate Allanby, Charlotte Bailey, and Thora Parker.[231]

Resignation From Mission Work

Australian Baptist women resigned from mission organizations for reasons such as breakdown of health, conflict with other missionaries, lack of funds, disagreement with mission policy, desire to join another mission organization, personal issues, inability to learn the language, or marriage. Only one-third of missionary women resigned due to age.[232] Baptist missionaries agreed to repay the cost of training, outfits, and transportation if they did not serve for a minimum of five years, for any reason other than ill-health.[233] This arrangement was not dissimilar to other occupations in Australia such as that of teaching. Yet the application of this rule annoyed some families, including the family of Agnes Kiddell who resigned to marry in 1889, but continued to undertake volunteer missionary work.[234] Often mission organizations and missionaries found it difficult to manage resignations, particularly where there was conflict between missionaries and the ABFM Board, or if missionaries were reluctant to resign.[235] The unplanned loss of staff put remaining missionaries under stress, an instance being in 1938 when Florence Harris was concerned about her role in the forced retirement of Helen Cousin.[236] Missionary women who had worked with the ABFM long enough to obtain a meagre pension were appreciative of the support, but their financial situation was often precarious. As Florence Harris in 1964 wrote: "You may wonder why I am still working . . . I live with an elderly sister and her elderly sister-in-law and want to help keep the home going for them (one is 88, the other is 83)." Florence Harris was seventy.[237]

Many missionary women continued involvement in mission support in Australia after resignation. In 1916 Minnie Morphett was forced to retire from mission service after she started to lose her hearing. Her obituary in

231. Hilton, "ABW Database." In part this is because missionary women's activities are more likely to be reported than those of non-mission workers.

232. Hilton, "ABW Database"; Loane, *Story of the CIM*, 72.

233. "Furreedpore [sic] Mission," *TP*, 1 November 1889, 192.

234. Gooden, "Mothers in the Lord," 163.

235. See, for example, Minutes of the Foreign Mission Board Meetings, Sydney, 28–30 August 1935, BMAA.

236. Florence Harris, Letter to Frank Marsh, ABFM General Secretary, 11 July 1938, BMAA.

237. Cupit et al., *From Five Barley Loaves*, 183. See also Florence Harris, Letter to John Williams, ABMS General Secretary, 15 April 1964, BMAA.

1937 explained that while this was "a deep disappointment to her . . . she worked for India at home. Her love for the mission field never grew cold."[238] Other women become state or national board members, or members of women's mission organizations. In NSW both Helen Cousin and Florence Harris joined the NSW mission committee on returning to Australia after ABFM service. They both continued to visit Baptist congregations: Helen Cousin was described as "an evangelistic missionary [who] gave a fine address."[239] Likewise Florence Harris was well-liked. Her minister at Petersham Baptist Sydney, the Rev. Roy Henson, later wrote:

> Flo would have been the first to acknowledge her shortcomings, whatever they were, and equally the first to reject the favourable image presented . . . the remarkable fact is that the unanimous verdict of all who know her . . . is that she was a woman who walked in love and left behind her a track record difficult for most of us to equal.[240]

Some women became involved in other Baptist denominational activities, such as Elsie Sutton, who supported Carey Grammar School, Melbourne.[241] To 1945 over 25 percent of Australian Baptist missionary women were also ministers' wives, and a few single women who returned from the mission field then married a Baptist minister: Vera Cross and Mary Pope married widowers who had been their ministers prior to service in East Bengal.[242] Doris Rogers had gone to the mission field anticipating that her fiancé would join her on completing his studies. He did not pass the medical test, so after she finished one term in East Bengal she resigned from mission work to marry him.[243] In most instances Australian Baptist missionary women's identity, irrespective of their marital status, was linked to mission, even after they retired: being a missionary was esteemed above other attributes.[244]

Not all missionary women continued to be involved in activities of the Baptist denomination on their return from mission work. Kath Perrin commenced mission service in 1928 and during the Second World War requested leave to enable her to work with the Young Men's Christian Association.

---

238. "South Australian Notes: Miss Minnie Morphett," *TAB*, 14 September 1937, 7.

239. "Box Hill Missionary Effort," *Box Hill Reporter* (Box Hill, Victoria), 30 August 1929, 5.

240. Henson, "Florence Susannah Harris."

241. "The Triumph of Mrs. Sutton," *Vision* (Sydney), June 1951, 12.

242. "Miss M. Lord," *OIF*, 6 January 1926, 2; Starling, *They Went Before Us*, 12–13.

243. Doris Rogers, Letter to Roy Henson, 25 May 1980. Private Collection held by Rebecca Hilton.

244. Gooden, "Mothers in the Lord," 175.

After the war she returned to Australia and worked as Matron of the Women's Prison Pentridge, showing compassion to the women incarcerated and helping them to gain life skills.[245] A small number of former missionary women appear to have lost their missionary zeal.[246] It is to be expected that some women's faith and missionary zeal changed following mission service, although this seems not to have been a common experience.[247]

Most missionary women did not find resignation or retirement from their "life work" easy, and for several reasons.[248] They were loathe to leave their work and the people with whom they had formed relationships, and some were concerned about their financial security on return to Australia. Several women were instructed to resign by the ABFM General Secretary due to age or ill-health. Most of these women reluctantly returned to Australia, such as Helen Cousin, who felt like "everything [had] been cut from under her."[249] As earlier mentioned Ellen Arnold, Hilda McLean, and Martha Plested chose to live in East Bengal after their retirement.[250] Women who did return to Australia may have felt that they lost status and mission identity within the denomination. Possibly most women felt like Bertha Tuck, who on retirement lamented: "One truly needs comfort for one's soul when passing through the ordeal of retirement from a life work."[251]

CASE STUDY: EDITH KING AND STELLA CHURCHWARD KELLY

Edith King, a single woman, lived in regional towns in Victoria and WA, with an unknown level of education, and Stella Churchward Kelly, originally from a Methodist family in Adelaide, who completed a Bachelor of Science degree from Adelaide University before marriage to a Baptist minister, are two Australian Baptist missionary women whose lives are interesting to examine and

---

245. Geraldine Turner, "Gaol Bid to Make Women Better," *Herald* (Melbourne), 17 July 1952, 5.

246. "South Australian Notes," *TAB*, 26 August 1924, 2; *TAB*, 16 September 1924, 6. Ada Archer's obituary implied that her faith was jaded, stating "her religious views changed, and she gradually withdrew from her earlier associations." Two weeks later, a clarification appeared in *Australian Baptist* that Ada Archer had "a happy close to a life which had for a period felt the buffeting of the storms."

247. See Hilton, "ABW Database."

248. Bertha Tuck, Letter to John Martin, ABFM General Secretary, 21 April 1928, Letter, BMAA.

249. Harris, Letter to Frank Marsh, ABFM General Secretary.

250. Cupit et al., *From Five Barley Loaves*, 612, 637.

251. Tuck, Letter to John Martin, ABFM General Secretary.

compare. Both women spent many years on the Australian Baptist mission field: Edith King from 1904 to 1921, with three years on furlough, and Stella Churchward Kelly from 1916 to 1943 with ten years on furlough. Both had relatives involved in overseas mission and expressed a strong calling to mission work. Edith King described her call as being "the call of the young in India; and the call from the outcasts."[252] Stella Churchward Kelly eloquently described her calling: "as distinctly as it ever came to Abraham, 'Get thee out of this country, and from thy kindred,' and we said, 'Yes, we will go.' I feel overwhelmed. Alone we can do nothing. He, through us, can do many things."[253] Although—as a married woman—her acceptance was based on her husband's suitability, rather than her qualifications and experience.

Stella and Thomas Churchward Kelly, 1916.
Photograph provided by Beth Barber; used with permission.

Both women wrote numerous articles for mission publications. Edith King's rudimentary education is evident through some of the simple expressions used in her articles, for example, that she felt "privileged in . . . being brought into touch with the people,"[254] and "we have been received into sev-

---

252. "Baptist Union of Western Australia," *TAB*, 18 November 1913, 12.
253. Menzies, "Foreign Mission Day in New South Wales," *TAB*, 5 October 1915, 3.
254. Edith King, "Faridpur, the Camp, Baliakandi," *OB*, February 1907, 7.

eral of the big homes here and have found the ladies very friendly."[255] Stella Churchward Kelly was more expressive in her writing, an example being her first itineration. She wrote:

> We had a splendid time. We camped in three different centres, each of which offered a good field for work. Mr. Kelly and our preacher Nobin Babu had splendid times in four large hats, besides bazaars, schools, etc., while books sold "like hot cakes." The women were not neglected either, in fact we two raw recruits marvelled more than once at our boldness, yet how could we hold back.[256]

Both women suffered personal hardship because of their mission work. Edith King was forced to resign due to ill-health and died at the age of 41. Stella Churchward Kelly was asked by the ABFM Board to stay in Australia for two years with her son while her husband undertook language training, and later she was asked to leave her children in Australia and return to her teaching work in East Bengal—despite the fact that she was not technically a paid employee of the ABFM, rather the wife of a missionary.[257] These missionary sacrifices were considered part of the missionary calling. Edith King and Stella Churchward Kelly were not unique, nor were they stereotypical: they demonstrate the diversity of missionary women and their experiences.

KEY THEMES IN MISSION STUDIES AND THE ABFM

Ecclesiology

The ABFM established Baptist congregations on mission sites and usually these congregations reflected the style and organization of Australian Baptist congregations. Thus the first Australian Baptist missionary women organized Sunday worship services that reflected the style in Australian Baptist congregations, with Bible readings, an address for children, a sermon, and hymn singing.[258] Likewise most of the missions held Sunday Schools and CE meetings following the worship services, and provided a weekday Bible study. In the late nineteenth and early twentieth centuries many East Bengali congregations did not have a minister who was appointed by the congregation.

---

255. See, for example, Edith King, "Pabna II," *OB*, May 1907, 8; "Faridpur," *OB*, June 1909, 4.

256. S. M. Churchward Kelly, "Serajgunj," *OB*, May 1918, 5.

257. ABFM, Executive Minutes, 26 June 1936, 1, BMAA.

258. See, for example, Daisy Grace, "Field Notes: Pubna [sic]," *OB*, February 1921, 4.

In most cases missionary men acted as the ministers, although by 1945 most congregations appointed local ministers. As in Australia and the UK, the Baptist congregations in East Bengal formed unions with each other.[259]

East Bengali women had limited opportunities to undertake a formal role in their congregations, due to their cultural setting and to the use of an Australian Baptist congregational model.[260] East Bengali women undertook fundraising and pastoral support, such as visiting women who were unable to attend worship services. In 1933 at Comilla the missionary women reported: "Our Bengali workers are co-workers in the true sense, taking their part in the life of the community as Deaconesses of the congregation, secretary, and treasurer of the women's auxiliary."[261] A patriarchal culture was considered the norm, and so inherent gender inequalities in a western congregational structure were not considered a constraint on East Bengali women. Indeed East Bengali women experienced more restrictions on their congregational activities than Australian Baptist women. For instance in 1929 at the meeting of the Women's Auxiliary of the Baptist Union of East Bengal, Bertha Harris reported that East Bengali women enjoyed attending the women's organization within the East Bengali Baptist Union as: "Those who previously were afraid to pray in public have advanced in this respect."[262] That is, twentieth-century East Bengali women felt constrained in their ability to pray aloud with men—something that had been an issue in the late nineteenth century in Australia. While local women spoke at women's meetings, there was no suggestion that any of the Bengali women undertook preaching or sought ordination.

Australian Baptist missionaries incorporated some local cultural practices in the worship services arranged for East Bengali congregations. For instance, worship services were conducted in the local language and the gendered East Bengali society meant that East Bengali women and men sat in different parts of the church building.[263] In addition missionaries accepted that the local people "swayed their bodies backwards and forwards as

---

259. Cupit et al., *From Five Barley Loaves*, xii, 45.

260. Within East Bengal culture, women did not have a high status. Garo society was slightly different as it was both matrilineal and patriarchal: that is, Garo property was inherited through the female line, yet the society was governed and controlled by men. This does not appear to have influenced the formation of Garo congregations. See A. [Ada] Doery, "Missionary News," *TSB* 1904, 152.

261. Log book of NSW Zenana Work, Comilla, 33, NSWBA.

262. Bertha Harris, "The Ninth Annual Meeting of the East Bengal Baptist Union: The Women's Auxiliary," *OB*, April 1929, 5.

263. Redman, *Light Shines On*, 83.

they sang."²⁶⁴ At that time such movements were not a feature of Australian Baptist worship, perhaps because it was considered too close to dancing. In these ways some cultural distinctives were incorporated, when appropriate, into local Baptist congregations.

Colonialism

From the mid-twentieth to the early twenty-first-century some academics have been critical of mission work. Predominantly the criticism relates to missions being part of a larger colonial and imperial project, where western culture was seen as an ideal and missionaries worked to convert local people to a western form of Christianity and culture, or capitalist economic arrangements.²⁶⁵ Revisionist scholarship by mission historians examines the complex interplay between mission and colonialism, concluding that overseas missionaries were less racist that other westerners and often advocated for the rights of local people.²⁶⁶

British colonial themes emerge in Australian Baptist women's missionary writings and are evident through interactions between missionary women and local women. Australian Baptist missionary women seem to have assumed, even if subconsciously, that western Christian culture was superior to other cultures.²⁶⁷ Indeed non-Indigenous Australian culture, which included the Australian Baptist denomination, only existed because of British colonialism in Australia: First Nations people were dispossessed of their land and mistreated by the British colonizers.²⁶⁸ Thus Australian Baptist missionary women were linked to British colonialism through being Australian and of British descent. Missionary women were able to preach or lead mission work partly because of their presumption that they were from a superior western culture with a superior message for local people.

Missionary women's belief in their superior culture was reflected in the way they referred to East Bengalis. There are examples of patronising references. In 1894 Ellen Arnold described the people living in Pabna as

---

264. Edith King, "News from Rajbari," *OB*, February 1913, 7.

265. For an overview, see Gladwin, "Mission and Colonialism," 282.

266. See, for example, Robert, *Christian Mission*, 48; Gladwin, "Mission and Colonialism," 283; Bhattacharya, "Zenana Missions and Christian Missionaries."

267. Secomb, "Borne in Empire."

268. Piggin and Linder, *Fountain of Public Prosperity*, 38. There is significant scholarship on Australian colonialism and treatment of First Nations people. See John Harris, *One Blood*.

"intensely dark and stupid."[269] In 1899 Iris Seymour asserted that the people in a nearby village were "poor, ignorant and quarrelsome."[270] In 1912 Constance Williams described Muslim women in Mymensingh as "uneducated" and "ignorant."[271] In 1913 Annie Barry compared Indian women to caged birds: "You happy women of our own land cannot realize the radically different position and conditions of the dear Indian women . . . We can weep with them in their sorrows, but how little there is of true joy with which to rejoice! . . . we pity [Indian women]."[272] The imagery of caged birds was used by missionary women in the ABFM and other mission organizations to highlight Indian women's lack of freedom in their repressive patriarchal culture.[273]

These descriptions need to be viewed as reflecting a certain style adopted in mission articles along with a desire for Australian Baptists to continue to donate funds to missionary organizations. The motivation for missionary women's writings about the lives of East Bengali women was to elicit sympathy about difficulties inherent in local women's lives. Descriptions such as "ignorant" were possibly made to underscore the potential for improvements to local people's lives through literacy and engagement with missionaries. That is, the sharp contrast of the "darkness" of their lives versus the "light" of Christianity.[274]

Most missionary women demonstrated a desire to understand the perspectives of local women and develop good relationships with them. In 1938 Effie Baldwin observed: "One must understand their viewpoint, learn what they revere."[275] Alongside conversions, missionary women wanted to improve the lives of local women with respect to education, hygiene, and status within a society that did not value women.[276] Missionary women within the ABFM employed local East Bengali women to work with them in the mission as teachers or Biblewomen. Biblewomen accompanied missionary women undertaking itineration or zenana mission, where their knowledge of the local vernacular enabled better connections with local women. ABFM women believed that East Bengali women could work in their local Baptist congregations, and they were committed to helping local women

---

269. E. A. [Arnold], "Pubna [sic]," *OB*, January 1894, 3.

270. Iris Seymour, "The Mymensingh Orphanage and School for Girls," *OB*, January 1899, 1.

271. Williams, *Land of Promise*, 67–68.

272. Annie Barry, "NSW Foreign Missionary Society," *TAB*, 6 May 1913, 7.

273. See, for example, Driver, *Missionary Memories*, 49.

274. Collins, *Christ's Ambassador*, 13, 29.

275. E. H. [Effie] Baldwin, "The Retreat," *OIF*, 6 April 1938, 12.

276. See, for example, Cousin, "The Hopes of a Missionary," *TAB*, 28 April 1936, 2.

experience social, moral, and physical uplift.²⁷⁷ Missionary women—and Australian Baptists more generally—believed that mission work allowed East Bengali women to receive an education, convert to Christianity, and be freed from constrictive cultural practices.²⁷⁸

Indigenization

The process of indigenization and the transfer of the mission work to the local Christians was regularly discussed by missionaries and the ABFM Board.²⁷⁹ Indigenization was independently conceived by mission theorists Henry Venn (UK) and Rufus Anderson (USA) in the mid-nineteenth century and advocated that local Christians determine policy and undertake leadership of their local congregations, including the process of adapting Christianity to suit the local culture. Iorganization only occurred when missionaries accepted that a western ideal of theology, ecclesiology and missiology was not appropriate in other cultures, and local people were empowered to create their own culturally appropriate expressions of Christianity.²⁸⁰

Australian Baptist missionary women were aware of the importance of aligning their western style of Christianity with East Bengal culture. In the nineteenth and early twentieth centuries one could interpret some of the missionary women's activities as demonstrating subconscious prejudices and a western view of Christianity, as seen in earlier examples. However from the 1920s missionary women supported indigenization efforts—at least theoretically. Florence Harris asserted that India needed "not to be westernised, but Christianised."²⁸¹ Gwenyth Crofts composed a poem on "Indianisation," a play on words for indigenization in India, in which one stanza reads: "If you can see through Indian eyes, / Be brotherly and kindly wise / And let the Indian church arise. / You're doing your bit to Indianise."²⁸²

Mission historians observe that from the 1950s iorganization policies within Christian overseas mission organizations changed, or were forced to change, due to the independence of former colonized countries and

277. Janet Hogben, Letter to Home Folk, 2 March 1935, BMAA.

278. See, for example, Crofts, *Bengali Brownies*; Miss L. [Lorna] McGregor, "Cold Season Touring in Garo-Land," *OIF*, 7 April 1941, 9.

279. Cupit et al., *From Five Barley Loaves*, 22, 115.

280. Hutchinson and Wolffe, *Short History of Global Evangelicalism*, 187. This is referred to as the Three-Self Principle: Self-Governing, Self-Supporting, and Self-Propagating. There is significant scholarship on this principle.

281. Florence Harris, "Babu Jogendra Nath Pundit," *TAB*, 26 April 1938, 26.

282. Gwenyth Crofts, "Let's Indianise," *OIF*, 6 July 1944.

anti-western sentiments.[283] In 1954 the ABFM transferred responsibility and ownership of Garo Baptist assets in East Bengal to the Garo Baptist Union.[284] In contrast, when the CIM withdrew from China in the early 1950s, all assets were compulsorily forfeited to the Communist Government.[285] Mission organizations had various approaches to iorganization, although the issue of how Christianity can be expressed within different cultures in a largely postcolonial and globalizing world continues to be debated into the twenty-first century.[286]

Stereotypes

Robert describes a stereotypical missionary woman from the late nineteenth or early twentieth centuries as "the spinster in her unstylish dress and wire-rimmed glasses, alone somewhere for thirty years teaching non-Christian children."[287] A second stereotype was the gaunt missionary's wife who deferred to her husband's demands, as portrayed in the character of Orleanna Price in Barbara Kingsolver's 1998 novel *The Poisonwood Bible* (observing that this book was set in the 1950s and 1960s).[288] Australian Baptist woman Lilian Brown, in her missionary novel, *A Brother's Need*, wrote of one character's experience with missionary women:

> And every single one of those [missionary women] was in a blue serge uniform, without a frill or ruffle about it . . . I felt as if my dress were horribly unsuitable, somehow. And that started me wondering if I would have to give up wearing pretty things in India . . . I found that the whole of [a missionary's] salary wouldn't buy many such dresses in a year.[289]

These stereotypes portray missionary women as eccentric or as unthinking subordinates. As with most stereotypes, some missionary women exhibited stereotypical attributes, such as working with children in remote areas, having poor health, wearing old clothing, and being unmarried. Yet few women worked alone as "it was felt undesirable that any lady should be committed to

283. Robert, *Christian Mission*, 91.
284. Cupit et al., *From Five Barley Loaves*, 110.
285. Loane, *Story of the CIM*, 105.
286. Robert, *Christian Mission*, 77–78; Lienemann-Perrin et al., *Putting Names with Faces*, 65.
287. Robert, *American Women in Mission*, xvii.
288. Kingslover, *Poisonwood Bible*.
289. Mead, *Brother's Need*, 12.

labour in loneliness amidst the heathen population of India."[290] Further, the stereotype of a spinster who became a missionary because she did not find a husband is not applicable. Missionary women were, on average, twenty-five-years old at the time they began mission service, having commenced missionary training in their early twenties.[291]

As already established, missionary women represented a wide range of backgrounds, skills, training, and beliefs. Mission historians challenge the adverse stereotypes because the evidence clearly indicates missionary women transcended misrepresentative stereotypes.[292]

Gender

Australian Baptist missionary women were not treated as equal to missionary men, as evidenced earlier with respect to mission reports and historiography.[293] A striking example may be cited from 1887 in an article published in denominational papers, *Truth and Progress* and *The Baptist*, on five Baptist missionaries commencing service, which stated that the only man, Arthur Summers, was the "the first Australian Baptist missionary to India."[294] In 1966 Alan Prior reasoned that "it was evidently meant that he was the first male missionary. The women missionaries were usually referred to as 'zenana workers.'"[295] Both the original report and Alan Prior's defense of the statement reflect the inequality between women and men on the Australian Baptist mission field and in Australia—and other examples abound. A 1903 article in *The Queensland Baptist*, probably written by the Rev. William Whale, stated: "It is simply marvellous what a lady worker can do . . . but the mission is incomplete for proper working except where others are doing work on a large scale and the Zenana work is supplementary."[296] In 1930 an article in *The Australian Baptist* lamented the resignation of several missionaries—women and men—and stated that "the mission is likely to be seriously weakened in personnel until the younger men make good."[297]

290. "Victorian Baptist Zenana Mission," *Argus*, 1 September 1885, 10.
291. Hilton, "ABW Database."
292. Robert, *American Women in Mission*; Lienemann-Perrin et al., *Putting Names with Faces*.
293. ABFM, Board Minutes, BMAA; ABFM, Executive Minutes, BMAA.
294. "The Five Missionaries Who Sailed for India, October 22, 1887," *TP*, 1 November 1887. The report was also published in the December 1887 edition of *Baptist*.
295. Prior, *Some Fell on Good Ground*, 2.
296. W. W., "Married Missionaries," *TQB*, 1 August 1903, 104.
297. "More or Less Personal," *TAB*, 17 April 1928, 4.

There is no evidence that missionary women believed their work was less important than men's work, but with reports such as these it is difficult to imagine that women were not aware of how others perceived their position in the mission compared to men.

Missionary women adapted to changes in mission work arising from changes in mission policies over time. In the period from 1882 to the early 1920s, women in the Australian Baptist missions had relative autonomy in the work they undertook. This was partly because most of the women's evangelistic work occurred away from the mission buildings, in the zenanas of East Bengali women's homes or in local schools.[298] From the 1920s ABFM women's work shifted from being largely evangelistic work based outside of the mission to a focus on institutional work based inside the mission. The shift transpired due to the interaction of several factors, including the 1930s economic depression, political instability in East Bengal, and the ABFM management and funds being increasingly centralized from 1913 until 1926, at which point the ABFM Board managed financial and operational decisions.[299] Overtime the ABFM missions contained institutions such as schools and orphanages. Usually these institutions were built in the larger missions led by men, and so although missionary women managed the institutions, ultimately the missionary men were in charge.[300] Inevitably these changes led to a loss of missionary women's autonomy in the ABFM and it was a typical experience within many mission organizations, not just the ABFM.[301] In 1946 Mildred Cable, an English missionary, addressed mission students in Melbourne about women being "shut into a compound" and stated: "It has to be thought out, and I suggest you talk to your Boards about these things. We must get out of the rut we are in if we are going to keep abreast of the times."[302] There was inherent tension between women's missionary vocation, including their leadership qualities, and the restrictions placed on them.

---

298. Crofts, *Our Bond Jubilee Edition*.

299. ABFM, Board Minutes, BMAA; Cupit et al., *From Five Barley Loaves*, 86; Edith King, "The Rajbari Record," *OIF*, March 1917, 9.

300. See, for example, "Locations," *OIF*, 6 February 1931, 8; "Missionary Locations," *OIF*, 6 April 1944, 16.

301. Seton, *Western Daughters in Eastern Lands*, 100–101.

302. Cable, "Missionary in Relation to God."

Married Missionary Women

Within the ABFM married missionary women were treated differently from single women. The ABFM expected married women to work as missionaries. Most married women wanted to work, although obviously women with young children on the mission field had periods of time where they were limited in their ability to undertake mission work. Yet, in many instances married women were excluded from mission records. From 1926 reports by married women were not included in the Annual Reports.[303] Tributes and obituaries for married missionary men usually minimized the work their wives had undertaken.[304]

In 1956 mission historian Stephen Neill identified a subtle distinction between a *missionary's* wife and a *missionary* wife.[305] A missionary's wife described a woman who viewed missionary work predominantly as her husband's vocation, while a missionary wife was a married woman who was a missionary: that is the woman and the mission organization understood that her vocation was that of a missionary. Most married Australian Baptist missionary women considered themselves a "missionary wife"—nearly half worked as missionaries prior to their marriage to a missionary man.[306] While mission organizations relied on missionary wives to work on the mission, they were not officially considered missionaries. Numerous ABFM annual reports illustrate this. Sometimes names of missionary wives are stated, but rarely are written reports from them included, especially after 1920.[307] Gwenyth Crofts—a missionary prior to her marriage—wrote: "For the past twenty years I have been, officially, not a missionary but a missionary's wife. In practical politics there's little difference except that, as a wife and mother, care of my family was my first duty."[308]

---

303. Prior to 1926 a very small number of reports by married women were included, but none appears after 1926.

304. See, for example, ABFM, Executive Minutes, 27 November 1931, BMAA.

305. Neill, *History of Christian Missions*, 256.

306. Hilton, "ABW Database." This number includes twenty women in the ABFM plus another thirty women about whom is it known they had gone to the mission field as single women.

307. See, for example, *Labourers Together with God*; *Furreedpore [sic] Mission*; ABFMVC, *Story of a Year's Work*; ABFM, *Extending the Kingdom in Bengal*; *Facts from the Front Line!*, 5; *Annals of Victory*, 5.

308. Crofts, *Glimpses into the Life of a Missionary Wife*.

Alice Mead with Her Daughter Dorothy, 1902.
Provided by Ros Gooden and the Wilson family; used with permission.

Gwenyth Crofts with Her Daughter Ruth, 1928.
Provided by the Joyce Family; used with permission.

Many married missionary women wrote about their calling to mission work, some did not have children, and most of those who had children worked for lengthy periods of time on the mission field while their children attended boarding school.[309] Of course the use of boarding schools was occasionally an issue, and some children of missionary women were critical of their mothers for the perceived choice of being a missionary rather than a "mother."[310] Mission papers attest to the work undertaken by married missionary women: Alice Barber and Annie Barry engaged in medical work; Gwenyth Crofts taught language and sewing; Stella Churchward Kelly taught science; Alice Mead was a teacher and assisted in the dispensary; Lillian White taught music; and Effie Baldwin, Lucie Thompson, and Elsie Sutton—none of whom had children—undertook zenana mission.[311] Of Alice Barber, Grace Thomson wrote: "She has been as a ministering angel to many of us."[312] Women who arrived in East Bengal to be married to ABFM missionary men received training in Bengali and zenana work.[313] Likewise married women in other organizations also appear to have consciously worked as missionary women, as demonstrated through the work undertaken in the CIM by Ella Davies as a zenana worker and Louisa Pike as a midwife.[314]

Married women were able to pursue a wide range of work activities precisely because they were not directly controlled by the relevant mission organization. While single women had defined roles and activities to undertake, married women had the freedom to engage in tasks that they believed were important. For instance, even though the ABFM did not have a focus on healthcare or translations, Alice Barber was active in medical work and Gwenyth Crofts did various translation work.[315] In addition, in the East Bengali culture, married women were more readily accepted than single women.

---

309. See, for example, Crofts, *Glimpses into the Life of a Missionary Wife*; Menzies, "Foreign Mission Day in New South Wales," *Australian Baptist*, 5 October 1915, 3; Calvert, "Douglas Pike," 14.

310. Calvert, "Douglas Pike," 14; Macdonald, *My First Ten Years*. This issue is discussed further in Moxey and Devereux, *Exploring Boarding School Challenges*.

311. Mrs C. D. [Effie] Baldwin, "The Blocked Way," *OIF*, 6 May 1933; Florence Harris, Letter to Frank Marsh, ABFM General Secretary, 2 August 1946, BMAA.

312. Grace Thomson, "The Ministry of Healing," in Crofts, *Our Bond Jubilee Edition*, 1932, 22.

313. Bertha Harris, Letter to "Friends" in Australia, 30 November 1928, BMAA.

314. "Baptist," *Brisbane Courier* (Brisbane), 22 July 1933, 5; Calvert, "Douglas Pike," 45.

315. Crofts, *Our Bond Jubilee Edition*, 22.

CONCLUSION

Australian Baptist missionary women had a strong sense of their roles within their respective missions, and being a missionary was essential to their identity, although their roles were influenced and shaped by gender, marital status, and the context of the place in which they were missionaries. Australian Baptist women responded to the foreign missionary "call" in relatively greater numbers than Baptist men or other Evangelical women.

Missionary enterprise gave women opportunities to undertake unique roles within the denomination and women were involved in all aspects of establishing, building, and maintaining missions. Most of the work by Australian Baptist missionary women could not have been pursued had they remained in Australia. Their roles were prominent within the Australian Baptist denomination; they had autonomy—albeit limited—in their work; and they had status within the local community in which they worked. Clearly being a missionary was an important part of their lives and identity—probably more so than being Baptist.

Missionary women appear to have been content to fit within the cultural norms and expectations for an Australian Baptist woman, and perhaps partly because of this, their missionary work has, until now, been under-reported and under-appreciated within the historiography. Any analysis of Australian Baptist mission work must include an appropriate representation of women's work to ensure a balanced view of Australian Baptist mission.

For Australian Baptist women, and their interaction with the missionary movement, there are many paradoxes to observe. Women held positions of leadership in the missions because of imperialistic beliefs held by western society that western culture was superior to non-Christian cultures. Women had significant responsibilities, autonomy, and variety, in their positions, particularly when compared to other Australian women at that time, yet they possessed limited authority within the mission or the ABFM. Women's work was significant but was not valued as highly as that of missionary men. Missionary women who married lost their formal identity as "missionaries" but married women experienced more freedom in their choice of work. Women wanted to "free" the local women from cultural patriarchal practices, yet western patriarchal foundations were not acknowledged or challenged.[316] Of course another paradox of missionary women is that they were the only women in the denomination who were accorded significant public recognition and status, particularly when compared to the "home" women who provided crucial support for the mission. It is the roles and work of these women that are the focus of the next chapter.

316. O'Brien, *God's Willing Workers*, 120.

4

Women's State and National Baptist Organizations

The women thus banded together for service had proved to be the backbone of the whole body, and a body was a poor thing without a backbone.[1]

—Ruth Lawton, 1935

INTRODUCTION

Australian Baptist women actively developed and participated in state-based and national Baptist women's organizations supporting foreign and home mission, and this chapter outlines the formation and activities of these organizations. The state organizations developed at different times, and for different reasons, yet they all provided a formal mechanism for women to work cooperatively across their congregations. The organizations offered individual women opportunities to develop and demonstrate their administrative and leadership skills. While women's organizations formed within congregations were important, state-based and national women's organizations had a greater impact. They developed and managed various large projects, such as childcare or aged care facilities, along with raising significant funds for foreign and home missions. Despite the extensive activities and achievements of these organizations, their work is rarely included or recognized within Australian Baptist historiography.

1. "Baptist Women's Union: President Entertains," *Evening News* (Rockhampton, Queensland), 21 May 1935, 10.

THE CONTEXT

Australian Women's Church Organizations

State-based and national women's organizations existed in all mainstream Christian denominations and influenced their respective denominations through their ingenuity, unpaid labor, and fundraising.[2] Depending on the denomination, the scope of the organizations was different. The largest women's organization in the Australian Catholic Church is the Catholic Women's Association, formed in Sydney in the early twentieth century to allow women to socialize with each other and provide various classes, concerts, and social events for members.[3] As the century progressed the Association expanded its scope and became more involved in social welfare activities, including hostels for homeless women and assistance to families in "distressing circumstances."[4] From 1892 Anglican women's organizations, called Mothers' Union, were established in Australian colonies, based on the British Mothers' Union.[5] These state-based groups focused on assisting women within the family unit and stressed personal morality. Single or divorced women were unable to become members. The Mother's Union became more active from the 1920s, particularly with respect to opposing laws that made it easier to obtain a divorce. Meetings included prayers, speeches on Christian themes, and time for fellowship.[6] Women in the Methodist, Congregational, and Baptist denominations established similar state women's organizations, which focused on mission work and service, and were open to all women.[7] Australian Christian women thus created separate structures—a "parallel church" or "female sub-culture"—for women.[8]

Why did so many Baptist women volunteer to work in state women's organizations? Two conclusions from twenty-first-century studies of volunteerism, group dynamics, and gender apply to Baptist women. First, altruistic behaviour leading to volunteerism occurs when people are committed

---

2. O'Brien, *God's Willing Workers*, 65.

3. "Catholic Women's Association," *Freeman's Journal* (Sydney), 13 November 1919, 31; O'Brien, *God's Willing Workers*, 83–84.

4. "Catholic Women's Association," *Catholic Freeman's Journal* (Sydney) 9 November 1939, 26.

5. See https://www.muaustralia.org.au.

6. O'Brien, *God's Willing Workers*, 69–71.

7. Pitman, *Our Principle of Sex Equality*, 63; O'Brien and Carey, *Methodism in Australia*, 73.

8. Hilliard, "Methodism in South Australia," 73, Wilson, *Constrained by Zeal*, 210.

to a cause and are satisfied that the organization aligns with their beliefs.⁹ Second, women appear more likely than men to seek opportunities to work within groups.¹⁰ There are several different explanations for this, including that women are more likely than men to prefer social interactions and to work with others to achieve shared outcomes.¹¹ In addition to 1945 many women did not undertake paid employment and therefore had time for volunteer work, and being part of a women's organization gave women the opportunity to lead. In 1885 in NSW, Grace Taylor, Secretary of the women's mission society, stated: "We have found it good to meet together, and while seeking to benefit others, we have received a blessing ourselves."¹² This expression may have become a mantra to the women as it was also expressed by Lily Higlett in 1942.¹³ Undoubtedly the sentiment was shared by other women in the other states—and other denominations.

The Significance of Women's Overseas Mission Organizations

Within Australia most of the earliest state Baptist women's groups were established with a focus on overseas mission, and there are three reasons for this. Firstly, women supported home mission from within their congregations and so, at least initially, there was less need for a state-based organization targeting women's support of home mission—until home mission needs expanded into large projects in the mid-twentieth century. A second reason was linked to Ellen Arnold's actions. Her expansive missionary career was stated in chapter 3, but her work to ensure ongoing financial support for Baptist mission was vital. In 1884, having returned to Australia due to poor health, Ellen Arnold visited all Australian colonies and New Zealand and promoted support for Baptist mission, especially encouraging the formation of women's state-based organizations.¹⁴ However the third and most significant reason for the emergence of women's mission organizations

---

9. Merrilees et al., "Volunteer Retention Motives," 43.

10. Croson et al., "Groups Work for Women," 411.

11. Croson et al., "Groups Work for Women," 411.

12. Taylor, "Ladies' Zenana Baptist Missionary Society of New South Wales," *Banner of Truth*, September–October 1885, 142.

13. Higlett, Notes, NSWBA. Lily Higlett wrote the identical phrase in her notebook in January 1942.

14. Arnold, "Letter from Miss Arnold," *TP*, 1 June 1885, 71; S. [Stephen] Howard, "Victorian Association, 1885," *TP*, 1 February 1886, 24; Wilkin, *Baptists in Victoria*, 117; Prior, *Some Fell on Good Ground*, 191.

was the importance of the Protestant overseas mission endeavor in the late-nineteenth century.

The emphasis on overseas mission was not a phenomenon limited to Australian Baptist women. Given the importance of mission, it is useful to briefly examine the context for women's foreign mission organizations in the UK, the USA, and Australia, and their growth and change over time.[15] The increasing number of missionary women who undertook "women's work for women" from the late nineteenth century required support from women in the sending countries. In the UK and the USA new women's mission organizations supporting only missionary women were established at a time when the existing mission boards were reluctant to fund missionary women: they failed to recognize that women's work was strategic to the mission.[16] By the end of the nineteenth century over forty different women's mission societies operated in the UK and the USA. These organizations had more combined members than suffrage organizations, which indicates the extent of women's commitment to mission.[17]

The larger women's missionary organizations had significant mission support structures in place, and some published their own journals.[18] One such organization was the Baptist Zenana Mission (BZM) in the UK, which from 1904 to 1911 published the *Baptist Zenana Magazine*.[19] The BZM had linkages with Baptist individuals and women's mission groups in Australia.[20] By 1930 most of the women's missionary organizations in the UK and USA had merged with general missionary organizations. The BZM is a case in point, becoming a department of the Baptist Missionary Society (BMS) in 1914 before being fully merged in 1926.[21] Such mergers were justified on the basis that resources were used more effectively and efficiently in one large organization than two—or more—smaller organizations. Although this reasoning had some merit, the reality was that women who had previously been managing missionary women's work competently were inevitably sidelined from the management of the larger organization.[22]

---

15. Robert, *Christian Mission*.
16. Gooden, "We Trust Them," 128; Beaver, "Pioneer Single Women," 12.
17. Montgomery, *Western Women in Eastern Lands*, n.p.; Robert, *American Women in Mission*, 129.
18. See, for example, ZMS, *India's Women*; WFMSPC, *Woman's Work for Woman*.
19. Stanley, *History of the BMS*, 231; "Victorian Baptist Zenana Mission," *Argus*, 1 September 1885, 10.
20. See Elizabeth A. Lush, "Zenana Mission," *TQF*, June 1881, 85–86.
21. BMS World Mission, "Women in Mission."
22. Seton, *Western Daughters in Eastern Lands*, 95.

Most Australian Protestant denominations, including Baptists, created women's mission organizations that supported mission work undertaken by missionary women *and* men.[23] For instance, women in the Congregational denomination established a Federated Women's Guild with state auxiliary committees, and Methodist women instituted a Women's Missionary Auxiliary. In the Australian Anglican denomination overseas mission activity was linked to England until the late nineteenth century, and it was not until 1910 that the Women's Auxiliary Board was established following a request from the Anglican Australian Board of Missions, with the intention of ensuring the support of women in Anglican mission. A male member of the Board publicly stated that mission societies understood that women raised the necessary money for mission activities for both missionary women and men, although the women in the Auxiliary did not consider their primary role to be fundraising.[24] Australian Presbyterian women established distinct Presbyterian Women's Missionary Associations in most Australian states during the 1890s, specifically to support missionary women. This model was an exception in Australian mission although by 1912 these associations had been subsumed within the Australian Presbyterian Foreign Mission Committee and women engaged in fundraising rather than management of missionary women.[25] The Presbyterian women previously involved in managing missionary women did not question the change in their focus and the loss of their power and autonomy.[26] As in the UK and USA, mission organizations relied on women's fundraising, but most organizations had limited roles for women in the management of mission activity.[27]

Women were an intrinsic part of the support of Australian Baptist mission work in East Bengal. Australian Baptist women were a formal part of mission administration in both East Bengal and Australia. From the establishment of the Victorian and NSW Baptist Foreign Mission groups in the mid-1880s, the committees had a formal requirement that women be members, and this was not a requirement of any other state union committee.[28] When the state missions merged in 1913, the structure of the new Australian Baptist Foreign Mission (ABFM) required that the Executive Board include at least two women. Australian Baptist officials needed to

23. West, *Daughters of Freedom*, 214.
24. Mitchell, *Working Together*, 11–12.
25. Godden, "Containment and Control," 88.
26. Godden, "Containment and Control," 89–90.
27. Mitchell, *Working Together*, 15.
28. BUV, *Victorian Baptist Union Yearbook*; BUNSW, Minutes of Proceedings, NSWBA.

include women in the mission structure to ensure women's continuing involvement, particularly through fundraising. In the period from 1913 to 1945, at the annual meetings of the ABFM Board, which managed mission policy and finances, over 33 percent of attendees were women.[29] The state mission committees managed recruitment of missionaries and raised funds, and formally had women members.

Women did not have representation in executive positions. In the nineteenth and twentieth centuries no women held the positions of General Secretary, Chair, Secretary or Treasurer of the ABFM, a pattern mirrored by the state mission committees with only two known exceptions: Lillian Vandeau was Secretary in Tasmania; and Edna Marsh was Treasurer in WA.[30] Possibly this occurred because these states had a smaller number of Baptists than other states.

Australian Baptist women did not create a separate mission organization in the way that Baptist women in the UK and the USA did.[31] The small Australian state Baptist mission organizations, and even the ABFM, was only viable if all Baptists worked for and supported one organization. Certainly one of the reasons the missions federated in 1913 was to streamline resources used for mission management. So Australian Baptist women created mission *support* organizations, which were managed and run by women and operated alongside the general state mission organizations: the formation of these is expanded below.

Women's representation on mission boards was important, and arguably the women on the ABFM Board made a constructive influence on mission administration. Specifically in the 1920s Ellen Shepard was an executive member of the ABFM and she conducted interviews of prospective missionary women.[32] Presumably this created a better interview experience for those women. The photograph of the first ABFM Board meeting in 1913 portrays five women and eleven men. Only two women were present as members, another woman was the wife of a member but had previously been a missionary, and the two other women were ABFM workers. None of the eleven men had been or were missionaries. This demonstrates that Baptists accorded a higher status to missionary women than other women in the denomination. Former missionary women were often state representatives and attended annual ABFM meetings.[33]

29. ABFM, Executive Minutes, BMAA.
30. Cupit et al., *From Five Barley Loaves*, 655.
31. Kemp, *There Followed Him Women*, 108–11.
32. ABFM, Executive Minutes, December 1924, BMAA.
33. ABFM, Board Minutes, BMAA.

While women were an accepted, albeit small, part of the ABFM management, this was not the case for other Australian mission organizations. From its establishment in 1890 to 1945 the Australian Council of the China Inland Mission (CIM) did not have any women in executive positions.[34] The Methodist Overseas Mission Board consisted only of men until 1918 when membership to one representative of the Women's Auxiliary of Methodist Overseas Mission was granted.[35] The Anglican Board of Missions reluctantly allowed for women to be co-opted from the Women's Auxiliary from 1917.[36] Thus Australian Baptist women were more involved in the leadership and management of Baptist overseas mission activities than women in the aforementioned overseas mission organizations.

Notwithstanding this, Baptist women created separate women's mission organizations, which provided the mechanism for them to undertake a wide range of activities to support missionaries.[37] In 1925 Mabel Stephen, a SA mission supporter, affirmed there was: "the certainty of God's promises being fulfilled, if only we [women] do our part."[38] A 1968 paper on the role of the women's mission organization in Victoria claimed that for many of the members, the involvement in supporting mission became "the absorbing passion of their lives."[39] In effect, supporting overseas mission enabled women to share the financial costs of, and spiritual commitment to, mission with the missionaries.[40]

FORMATION OF BAPTIST WOMEN'S STATE-BASED ORGANIZATIONS

Six Different States and Twenty Different Organizations

The history of Australian Baptist women's organizations from 1872 to 1945 presents a distinctive, if uneven, development. This chapter—as far as possible—describes events chronologically, and moves between states. Baptist

---

34. Loane, *Story of the CIM*, 145. State committees may have had women members, but the book did not include such information.

35. O'Brien and Carey, *Methodism in Australia*, 183.

36. Mitchell, *Working Together*, 15.

37. See, for example, "NSW Baptist Assembly: Foreign Mission Reports," *TAB*, 30 September 1930, 10.

38. Mabel Sarah Stephen, "Central Prayer Meeting: 5 May 1925," South Australia Baptist Women's Missionary Union, Volume 6, 43, SABA.

39. Victorian Baptist Women's Fellowship Missionary Committee, BUVA.

40. See, for example, "Baptist Union," *Mercury*, 8 May 1896, 3.

women in the six Australian states formed twenty different Baptist women's organizations to facilitate state-based work for the Baptist denomination and to form connections with each other. Table 1 lists women's organizations established to 1945. This list only includes women's organizations and accordingly is not a complete list of Baptist organizations. Where there were minor name changes, organizations are grouped by state rather than in chronological order.

Table 1. Baptist women's state and national organizations until 1945				
Year estab.	State/ Territory	Organization titles	Year of change	Type *
1872	Vic	Victorian Auxiliary of the Zenana Mission		O
		Victorian Zenana Mission Society (new focus)	1885	
		Baptist Women's Missionary Union (BWMU)	1895	
1878	NSW	Baptist Evangelist Society Ladies' Auxiliary		H
		NSW Ladies Auxiliary of the Baptist Home Mission (new focus)	1886	
		Baptist Women's Home Mission Deaconess Association (new name and focus)	1918	
		Women's Home Mission Auxiliary (new name and focus)	1925	
1884	NSW	Ladies' Zenana Missionary Society (LZMS)		O
1885	SA	Ladies' Zenana Committee		O
		BWMU (new name)	1910	
1885	Qld	Young Women's Mission Class (until about 1917)		
1892	NSW	Girls' Zenana Aid Society (until about 1916)		O
1906	WA	Baptist Women's Goalundo Auxiliary (until 1913)		O
		Home Mission Ladies' Auxiliary (until 1913)	1910	H
		Baptist Women's Missionary Auxiliary (new name and focus)	1913	H/O

Table 1. Baptist women's state and national organizations until 1945

Year estab.	State/ Territory	Organization titles	Year of change	Type *
1909	Qld	Queensland Baptist Women's Union (QBWU)		H/O
1922	Vic	Senior Girls' Missionary Union (SGMU)		O
1923	Qld	SGMU		O
1924	Vic	Victorian Baptist Women's Association		H
1924	SA	Baptist Women's League		H
1925	SA	SGMU		O
1926	NSW	SGMU		O
1926	Tas	Tasmanian Baptist Women's Auxiliary		H
1929	National	Federal SGMU		O
1935	National	Australian Baptist Women's Board (ABWB)		H
1935	NSW	NSW Baptist Women's Federation		H/O
1938	Tas	SGMU		O

* O signifies that the group mainly focused on overseas mission activities, and H signifies a home mission focus.

Women's state-based organizations focused on at least one of three aims: to support overseas mission; to support home mission; or to provide a mechanism to unite Baptist women. Most fulfilled all three aims: they had an interest in, and directly supported, both overseas and home missions, and by their nature brought Baptist women together.

Baptist Women's State-Based Organizations: 1872 to 1915

Victoria had the earliest known state-based women's organization, established in 1872 when Hannah Martin formed the Victorian Auxiliary of the Zenana Mission to support the English Baptist Zenana Missionary Society.[41] On her death in 1902 her obituary stated: "No one was so intimately associated with the Foreign Mission of our Victorian churches as Mrs. Martin."[42] Money raised by the Victorian Auxiliary was forwarded to Eng-

---

41. Wilkin, *Baptists in Victoria*, 116; Victorian Baptist Women's Fellowship Missionary Committee, History of 72 years of BWMU of Victoria, BUVA.

42. "Editorial Notes on Passing Events: Victorian: Mrs Martin," TSB, 2 May 1905,

land. In 1873 an article was published in the Melbourne *Leader* promoting zenana mission and requesting funding for the work. Written by Marianne Lewis, one of the leading English Baptist missionary women, she stressed that: "As a merely philanthropic effort, such a work must commend itself to Englishwomen; but when, in addition, the higher aim of carrying life, eternal life, to those who are now so evidently sitting in the shadow of death is considered, we believe we shall not appeal for help in vain."[43] As Hannah Martin's contact details were listed at the end of the article, she almost certainly submitted the article to the *Leader* to garner ongoing support from Victorian women. The reference to "Englishwomen" reflected how Australian women at this time viewed themselves as being inextricably linked to the UK, and the notion of Australians supporting an English-based organization was not deemed unusual. The records of this initial committee are not extant and details about funds raised were not reported in Victorian Baptist papers, presumably because the funding went directly to the English Baptist Zenana Missionary Society.

In 1878 the first women's home mission organization was established for Baptist women in NSW and named the Baptist Evangelist Society Ladies' Auxiliary.[44] There are no extant records of either the Evangelist Society, which was established in 1876, or the Ladies' Auxiliary. For many years the NSW women's home mission organizations referred to the establishment year of the Ladies' Auxiliary as the year that women commenced support of home mission work. The Ladies' Auxiliary's establishment and ongoing meetings are mentioned in the NSW Baptist paper, then called *The Banner of Truth*. However no precise date was ever celebrated by NSW women in various iterations of the organization.[45] While *The Banner of Truth* contains several articles regarding the Evangelist Society, little reference is made to the Ladies' Auxiliary, except to indicate that in 1885 the Auxiliary raised £25 for an Evangelist to work in NSW.[46] Emma Dixson held an executive

---

97. This was the leading article of the 2 May paper.

43. Lewis, "A Plea for Zenana," *Leader*, 14 June 1873, 4.

44. The organization's name reflects the intention that *an* Evangelist received funding rather than evangelism as an activity.

45. "Our Denomination Chronicle," *Banner of Truth* (Sydney), September–October 1885, 142; "NSW Women's Home Mission Auxiliary," *TAB*, 18 September 1945, 3. There were few references to the establishment of the women's organization, and later articles in *Australian Baptist* do not mention anniversary years.

46. "The Treasurer in account with the Ladies' Baptist Zenana Mission Society, for the year ending 3rd September, 1884; and The Baptist Missionary Society of New South Wales in account with the Treasurer," *Banner of Truth* (Sydney), September–October 1885, 145. All extant copies of the *Banner of Truth* were examined in the NSW Baptist Archives.

position in the Auxiliary and she remained associated with successive NSW women's home mission organizations until her death in 1922.[47] In 1886 the Auxiliary changed both its focus and name following the meetings of the Baptist Union of NSW, which agreed that the Evangelist Society should merge with the Home Mission Society, and that: "A ladies' auxiliary society for raising funds for home mission work was thought desirable, and its formation urged."[48] Such a statement confirms that Baptists understood women's organizations were well-placed to raise funds for Baptist projects.

NSW was the only Australian state to form a home mission organization prior to an overseas mission organization. One possible reason for this may relate to the motivation of the individual women who established the Auxiliary. Three of the five members of the first executive were born in NSW, and they may have felt closer ties to the local community than other women who had migrated from the UK.[49]

In 1885 SA Baptist women established the Ladies' Zenana Committee to coordinate overseas mission activity being undertaken by women within their congregations.[50] It is not known why a women's committee was not established prior to this time, given that the first two missionary women had commenced work in 1882. Perhaps the Baptist Union of SA believed that as the number of missionary women increased in the mid-1880s it was necessary and appropriate to have a state level women's organization. This organization undertook tasks such as interviewing prospective zenana missionaries. The tasks were beyond that of fundraising previously undertaken within individual congregations. The Ladies' Zenana Committee supported the SA Baptist Missionary Society, whose annual report for 1885 acknowledged "the valuable services rendered by the Ladies' Zenana Committee . . . [who] have taken up departments of service that could be efficiently performed only by them especially in connection with the reception and departure of lady missionaries."[51] It was not until 1926 that SA women become members of the SA Baptist Missionary Society.[52]

In NSW Ellen Arnold's visit in August 1884 resulted in women forming the Ladies' Zenana Missionary Society (LZMS), with the aim to channel

47. "Our Denomination Chronicle," *Banner of Truth*, September–October 1885, 142; "Death of Lady Dixson," *TAB*, 18 April 1922, 4.

48. "The Baptist Jubilee: Meeting of the Baptist Union," *Daily Telegraph* (Sydney), 17 September 1886, 6.

49. "Our Denomination Chronicle," *Banner of Truth*, September–October 1885, 142.

50. "Annual Meeting of the South Australian Baptist Missionary Society," *TP* 1886, 89.

51. "Annual Meeting of the South Australian Baptist Missionary Society," *TP* 1886, 89.

52. "South Australian Notes: Miss Barker," *TAB*, 27 April 1926, 10.

efforts in NSW to support and promote foreign zenana mission work.[53] The minutes for the first meeting on 3 September give the reasons for establishing the LZMS as "the great necessity for increased interest, and more direct effort on behalf of the women of India, in a social as well as a religious point of view, which work could only be effected by woman herself. The deep need for the establishment of such a Society was felt by all present."[54] This statement illustrates how these women strongly believed that the mission work needed to be undertaken by women—"women's work for women"—with the aim to convert local women in zenanas to Christianity and improve their lives.[55]

Representatives from most of the congregations in Sydney and surrounds attended the meeting. An executive committee was formed, with the key executive positions being filled by: Isabel Hibberd, President; Margaret Taylor, Vice-President; Elizabeth Reid, Treasurer; and Grace Taylor, Secretary. Grace Taylor wrote letters addressed to the women in every NSW Baptist congregation requesting that they provide a representative to attend meetings, or to be a contact for information. Each associated congregation nominated a woman to "collect" funds.[56] This structure enabled information to be shared to all Baptist congregations and facilitated maximum fund collection. The LZMS believed that one of their key roles was "the raising of money needed to maintain a missionary field [and that this work] will devolve to a large extent upon our sisters."[57]

The LZMS was a "branch" of the NSW Baptist Missionary Society, which had only been established in 1883, one year earlier.[58] The minutes of both organizations show that both committees agreed the women's work was important and that the women's organization would retain its own identity. One week after the first meeting of the LZMS, the Baptist Union of NSW met and agreed to send a letter to the LZMS expressing their "hearty congratulations to the ladies for the missionary spirit they have manifested" along with a recommendation that the two mission organizations discuss "amalgamation."[59] However the meeting subsequently decided "that the word cooperation be substituted for amalgamation."[60] This latter decision

53. "Zenana Missionary Society," *TAB*, 21 September 1920, 3.

54. Ladies' Zenana Missionary Society MM, 1884–95, NSWBA. Grace Taylor underlined the word woman in the original minutes.

55. Lewis, "A Plea for Zenana," *Leader*, 14 June 1873, 4.

56. Ladies' Zenana Missionary Society MM, NSWBA.

57. Grace Taylor, "1886 Annual Report," in Ladies' Zenana Missionary Society MM, NSWBA.

58. "Baptist Union of New South Wales," *SMH*, 16 September 1884, 7.

59. BUNSW MM, 116, NSWBA.

60. BUNSW MM, 116, NSWBA.

was significant because it allowed for the LZMS to operate as a distinct organization. Initially women from the LZMS met monthly, with "cooperative" meetings with men in the NSW Baptist Missionary Society four times a year. By the 1890s these meetings were no longer required because women were members of both mission organizations, as the by-laws of the Baptist Union of NSW stated that the "Foreign Mission Committee [was] to consist of thirty persons... fifteen of whom shall be ladies previously nominated by the Ladies' Zenana Missionary Society."[61]

In 1885 Victorian women changed the focus of their support and fundraising from English missionaries to the two Victorian zenana missionaries, Ruth Neville and Marion Fuller, who commenced work in Mymensingh, East Bengal. The two women were supported by the Victorian Baptist Foreign Mission Society, which was formed through merging of Hannah Martin's women's Auxiliary with the overseas mission organization that had been established in 1865 to support a mission worker in Mymensingh.[62] Initially the women members were reluctant to become a "subsidiary" of the Victorian Foreign Mission Society, for reasons that were not recorded. In 1886 they agreed to be "merged" into the Mission Society whose standing orders allowed for two women members.[63] The renamed Victorian Zenana Mission Society was a committee of the main society.

In 1895 Victorian Baptist women created a new organization named the Baptist Women's Missionary Union (BWMU), which was outside the management of the general mission society.[64] This action appears to suggest that the Victorian approach to merge the women's and men's committees was less effective than the NSW cooperative approach. The aim of the BWMU was to broaden women's involvement in mission by establishing branches of the BWMU within congregations to "interest the women, young and old, by giving them fresh missionary news, and urging them to work and sell and subscribe towards the Mission."[65] Clearly Victorian Baptists believed that women were more effective operating through a separate women's organization, although the first meeting was chaired by the Rev. Allan Webb, in his role as Secretary of the Victorian Foreign Mission Society.[66] Hannah

61. "The Baptist Union New South Wales Constitution," *Baptist* (Sydney), 3 November 1894, 179; "NS Wales Assembly: The Business Session," *TAB*, 3 October 1916, 9.

62. Cupit et al., *From Five Barley Loaves*, 10.

63. Howard, "Victorian Association, 1885," *TP*, 1 February 1886, 24; BUV, *Victorian Baptist Union Yearbook*.

64. "Notes and Comments: the BWMU," *TSB*, 18 April 1895. The Victorian Zenana Mission Society was effectively disbanded.

65. "Notes and Comments: the BWMU," *TSB*, 18 April 1895, 85.

66. Allan Webb had sent a letter to the women on behalf of the Victorian Foreign

Martin was the chair of the Victorian BWMU until her death in 1905.⁶⁷ The BWMU expanded its scope over the first ten years of operations, and thus by 1901 the BWMU had a subcommittee for home mission, although the focus of the organization continued to be overseas mission.

Ellen Arnold's missionary trip to promote Australian Baptist mission included a visit to Tasmania in 1884. Although Baptists in Tasmania formed congregations from 1834, the Baptist Union of Tasmania was only formed in 1884 and at the time of Ellen Arnold's visit the Union had no committees or firm structure. As a result of the "enthusiasm" of Ellen Arnold, Tasmanian Baptists established a Tasmanian Baptist Missionary Committee, which was formally part of the SA Baptist Missionary Society.⁶⁸ Two Tasmanian men were nominated for membership of the SA Baptist Missionary Society, and likewise two women, Lillian Vandeau and Mary Ann Gibson, were "Honorary Members" of the SA Ladies' Zenana Committee, where they represented Tasmanian women until 1890 when the Tasmanian Baptist Missionary Committee became part of the Victorian Missionary Society.⁶⁹ Arrangements for Tasmanian women to be honorary members of the Victorian Zenana Mission Committee do not appear to have continued in the twentieth century.

From 1886 until 1901 Lillian Vandeau was Secretary of the Tasmanian Baptist Missionary Committee. Her appointment arose because of the small size of the denomination in Tasmania rather than because Tasmanian Baptists were more willing than other Australian states to appoint women to executive positions in key committees. Lillian Vandeau wrote the annual report of the Committee and, until the late 1890s, her reports were read aloud at the Union meetings by various men.⁷⁰ In 1901 Lillian Vandeau ceased her connection with the Committee when she married.⁷¹ The Baptist Union of Tasmania affirmed that "the young ladies . . . are the chief workers in the association."⁷² From 1885 to the early 1900s the Committee operated with men holding the positions of President and Treasurer—chairing the meetings and controlling the finances—but otherwise activities were undertaken by women.

Mission Society requesting they establish the BWMU, which adds credence to the notion that the previous arrangement was not working as well as expected. See "The Baptist Women's Mission Union," *TSB*, 16 May 1895, 115. Allan Webb did not have an official role in the BWMU after the first meeting.

67. BWMU of Victoria MM, BUVA.
68. "Farewell Meeting to Zenana Missionaries," *TP*, 1 November 1885, 136.
69. "The Annual Meeting of the Furreedpore [*sic*] Mission," *TP*, 1 June 1887, 88.
70. Lillian Vandeau in "Baptist Union of Tasmania," *TP*, 1 May 1886, 71.
71. "Wedding," *Examiner* (Launceston, Tasmania), 13 July 1901, 11.
72. "Baptist Union of Tasmania," *TP*, 1 May 1886, 71.

Accordingly Tasmanian Baptist women had less autonomy than women in women's mission organizations in other Australian states. Lillian Vandeau's reports of the Committee's work communicated this operational arrangement.[73]

In 1906 WA women established the Baptist Women's Goalundo Auxiliary. Its motto was "Ye also helping together by prayer," although its activities were always broader than prayer.[74] Nineteen women attended the first meeting, which was chaired by the Rev. Silas Mead, then a member of the WA Foreign Mission Committee.[75] The Auxiliary's aim was to promote the work of the Baptist mission in Goalundo, East Bengal, and to undertake fundraising "for schemes approved by the [WA mission] committee."[76] This clarification indicates that the women wanted to show their support for the general committee, which, incidentally, included women in its membership.[77] From a twenty-first-century perspective the inclusion of the aim that schemes would be "approved" may seem irrelevant, but it indicates that the women considered their activities to be part of the Foreign Mission Committee and needed to fit within this framework. WA was in a unique position in that most Baptist missionaries visited the mission supporters in Perth as they transited through the port at Fremantle on their way to and from East Bengal. Women in the Auxiliary provided meals for the missionaries and hosted events, which allowed missionaries to speak about their work.[78]

The Goalundo Auxiliary provides a vivid example of the involvement of family members. In 1906 when the Auxiliary was formed there were five women involved in the committee who had a family link to three Australian Baptist missionary workers: the two WA workers, Grace Brown and Edith King, and Dr Cecil Mead from SA. Grace Brown's mother, Marie Brown, was the organization's first president. Grace Brown's sister, Caroline Hall, was active in the committee and was a determined mission supporter, having worked in East Bengal as a missionary in 1900 but returning to Australia in 1901 due to ill-health.[79] She provided support for Baptist missions including

73. "Baptist Union of Tasmania," *TP*, 1 May 1886, 71–72.

74. Baptist Women's Goalundo Auxiliary Minutes of Meeting (BWGAM), 1906–1909, Baptist Union of Western Australia Archives, Perth, Western Australia (BUWAA). Goalundo was the location of the East Bengal mission supported by Western Australia. "Ye also helping together by prayer" is taken from 2 Corinthians (1:11).

75. Cupit et al., *From Five Barley Loaves*, ix; BWGAM, BUWAA. Silas Mead attended Auxiliary meetings intermittently, but he did not chair further meetings.

76. BWGAM, BUWAA.

77. "Baptist Union," *Western Mail* (Perth), 1 June 1901, 73.

78. "Baptist Foreign Mission," *TWA*, 31 October 1933, 12; Moore, *All Western Australia*, 109–10.

79. BWGAM, BUWAA. Caroline Hall chaired meetings when her mother was not available.

representing WA on the ABFM Board, writing mission papers, and visiting congregations to discuss mission activities.[80] Edith King's mother, Ada King, was involved in distributing correspondence from the missionary women. Blanche Wilson and Sarah Hann, the sister and aunt respectively of Cecil Mead, were also on the Committee.[81] Caroline Hall's obituary observed that through her sister's work she "felt she was able to express something of her own missionary zeal."[82] It is likely that other women supporting mission work had similar convictions.

In 1913 the members of the Goalundo Auxiliary changed the organization's name to the broader Baptist Women's Missionary Auxiliary. Around 1910 the Home Mission Ladies' Auxiliary was formed as a separate organization, although in 1913 it became a subcommittee of the Baptist Women's Missionary Auxiliary.[83] Thus from 1913 the Baptist Women's Missionary Auxiliary supported both home mission and overseas mission.

The Queensland women's state-based Baptist organization supported both home and overseas mission from its conception. On 12 October 1909 women from nine different Baptist congregations around Brisbane met to form a Queensland Baptist Women's Union (QBWU). Jeannie Mursell—whose husband, the Rev. James Mursell, was the minister of the Brisbane Tabernacle—organized this initial meeting as she believed that a women's group provided benefits to members "if they became banded together for prayer and other service."[84] "Prayer and other service" became the motto of the QBWU and their objective was: "to inspire and encourage women's work in the churches of the Denomination, and to bind together Baptist women in a fellowship of prayer, and service for the Kingdom of God in Queensland, and throughout the world."[85] Within the first year of operation the QBWU undertook fundraising and other activities which supported foreign and home mission, as well as catering at the annual Baptist Union of Queensland meetings.[86] Annual meetings of the QBWU were popular and generally over one hundred women attended.[87]

80. Jess Redman, "Mymensingth Convention," *OIF*, 6 February 1936, 4.
81. BWGAM, BUWAA.
82. "The Late Mrs Caroline Hall," *TAB*, 18 July 1956, 5.
83. WA BWMU highlights of history, 4 October 1966, Script, BUWAA.
84. QBWU MM, BUQA.
85. QBWU MM, BUQA; QBWU MM, 1920–1934, BUQA. The first minute book does not outline the motto or object. However the second minute book contains a typed copy of the constitution on the front page.
86. QBWU MM, BUQA; QBWU Executive MM, 1909–1920, BUQA.
87. QBWU MM, BUQA.

Baptist Women's State Organizations: 1918 to 1945

From 1918 to 1925 in NSW the women's home mission organization was especially active due to a new focus on supporting paid deaconesses. The organization was renamed the Baptist Women's Home Mission Deaconess Association and the members actively recruited and supported deaconesses to work within various locations or congregations where a need for women workers had been identified.[88] While the Association's main role at this time was to financially support the deaconesses, it continued to undertake and fund other denominational work such as catering for state union meetings. In 1925 the organization became the Women's Home Mission Auxiliary as the women took on a broader focus for home mission.[89]

In SA and Victoria women's organizations for home mission were not established until 1924. This simultaneous timing appears to be a coincidence as there is no evidence to indicate that either state followed the example of the other. In SA this organization, titled Baptist Women's League (BWL), was formed along the lines of the English Baptist Women's League. On 8 April 1924 Florence Benskin—whose husband the Rev. Frederick Benskin was the minister at Flinders Street Baptist—organized a meeting of women representing Baptist congregations in SA to form a women's organization.[90] This BWL became the state level organization representing women's organizations within congregations, and most Baptist congregations in SA were formally or nominally associated with the BWL.[91]

The BWL used the same structure as the English League, as Florence Benskin had been involved with this organization before coming to Australia. A formal affiliation between the SA BWL and the English League was established in 1927, at the time Florence Benskin returned to England.[92] In 1928 Maria Harrison represented the SA BWL at the annual meetings of the English League in London. A widow since 1916, she was the first Secretary of the BWL and continued in this role until 1929. Annual picnics were held on her property.[93] She was "very active" as a motivational speaker to women in SA Baptist congregations, the BWL, and the WCTU. She believed that

---

88. "N. S. Wales Annual Assembly: Home Mission Day," *TAB*, 8 October 1918, 6.
89. E. J. P., "Baptist Women's Home Mission Association," *TAB*, 6 January 1925, 10.
90. Wilcox, *Baptist Women's League*, 11.
91. See, for example, "Churches and Church Affairs," *Register* (Adelaide), 13 September 1924, 4.
92. Wilcox, *Baptist Women's League*, 12.
93. "Veteran Worker Passes," *TAB*, 10 January 1950, 4.

women's groups "by God's blessing … were helping to make the world better and happier."[94]

The motto of the BWL was "Happiness is great love and much serving," which set the tone for work undertaken by the women.[95] One of the first tasks agreed by the BWL was to organize catering for the annual meetings of the Baptist Union. Edith Wilcox observed that the catering had "been the means of splendid fellowship, as the women from the various Churches work harmoniously together during these three days of meals."[96] One perceives that the women strengthened their networks through this activity. Throughout the period from 1924 to 1945 the BWL provided practical support and funding to the SA Baptist denomination. Specifically from 1940 to 1945 the BWL provided financial assistance to Margaret Speck to support her work at Hilton Baptist, and to Florence Hogan and Myrtle Stribling to support their work at Port Kenny Baptist.[97]

In 1924 the Victorian Baptist Women's Association (VBWA) was established with the aim of bringing Victorian Baptist women together. The VBWA made a deliberate decision not to be affiliated with the Baptist Union of Victoria and so maintained a degree of independence from denominational influences. Perhaps the experience of the earlier mission "merger" led to the women creating an independent structure. The VBWA focused on home mission, overseas mission, Carey Grammar School, and Carlton Free Kindergarten, but the creation of the Association did not lead to consolidation of existing committees supporting these different causes. Instead separate committees worked with the various existing organizations supporting mission, the school, and the kindergarten. Thus from the commencement of the VBWA, there was close collaboration with all the women's ministries.[98] By 1928 the VBWA had created new committees managing the relationship with the Australian Council of Churches, Pennstone—a holiday house that it managed for missionaries and ministers,—and the work with immigrants, which involved providing assistance to help new immigrants settle into Australian life, specifically those from the UK.[99] Fundraising events were held targeting these different interests, such as in 1928 when the VBWA held a fete to raise funds for Carey Grammar and "Church House," a building for Baptist

94. "Temperance Worker Delegate to Lausanne: Mrs Harrison Returns," *News* (Adelaide) 3 January 1929, 9.

95. Wilcox, *Baptist Women's League*, 11.

96. Wilcox, *Baptist Women's League*, 11.

97. Wilcox, *Baptist Women's League*, 19; "Baptist Manse at Port Kenny," *West Coast Sentinel* (Streaky Bay, SA), 22 October 1937, 7.

98. Victorian Baptist Women's Association (VBWA) MM, 2, BUVA.

99. VBWA MM, 77, BUVA.

activities in Victoria.[100] The VBWA sought to maintain effective cooperation between the various women's committees to reduce duplication.[101]

Victoria Steel was an influential member of the VBWA. From 1924 to 1932 she was the first Secretary, apart from 1928 when she was President. From 1933 to 1935 she was a Vice-President. She addressed the women's meeting at the 1927 Baptist Union Assembly on "The Influence of Christian Womanhood" where she outlined the value of social welfare undertaken by women. She challenged women to "attempt and achieve yet greater deeds."[102] She supported both foreign and home mission and was involved in activities inside and outside the Baptist denomination. She was married to Percy Steel, a Baptist layman who was the President of the Victorian Baptist Union in 1926, and they had five children.[103]

The VBWA was committed to raising funds for Victorian Baptist work, but in 1929 unnamed sources criticized it for being too focused on fundraising, and consequently the Association agreed to have a specific study element during each of its quarterly meetings, and to create a study guide for women's groups to use in Baptist congregations. In 1930 the subject of "Home Life" was chosen, and various women—and men—addressed the meetings on the subject, although there are no extant records on the content of the speeches.[104] While the speakers were warmly received, there is no record or other evidence that a study guide was prepared.

In 1935 NSW women created a similar over-arching organization called the NSW Baptist Women's Federation, which met quarterly. The Federation provided the means to bring together the seven women's organizations operating at that time: the Women's Home Mission Auxiliary, LZMS, SGMU, the Theological College Housekeeping Committee, Ministers' Wives Union, the Luncheon Committee (which provided catering at meetings of the Baptist Union of NSW), and the Voluntary Aid Detachment.[105] NSW Baptist women regarded all these organizations as part of women's denominational work.[106]

100. VBWA MM, 74, BUVA.

101. "Victoria: Baptist Women's Association," *TAB*, 3 December 1929, 3.

102. F. J. [Frederick] Wilkin, "Victorian Baptist Union," *TAB*, 14 June 1927, 12. Victoria Steel paraphrased a statement attributed to William Carey, as previously referred to.

103. "Woman's Realm," *Argus*, 23 March 1926, 14; "Baptist camp at Ocean Grove," *Geelong Advertiser* (Geelong, Vic), 23 April 1927, 6.

104. VBWA MM, 99, BUVA.

105. Voluntary Aid Detachments commenced during the First World War and initially were not a Baptist organization, nor a woman's committee, although women undertook delivery of the service. See "The Australian Women's Register."

106. Women's Auxiliaries [NSW], *Annual Reports and Balance Sheets 1947–48*, 2. The Federation also elected NSW representatives on the Australian Baptist Women's

By the mid-1920s Tasmanian Baptists had still not formed women's organizations despite various efforts to do so. In 1916 Stella Churchward Kelly visited Baptist congregations in Tasmania prior to joining her husband in East Bengal. Stella and Thomas Churchward Kelly were from SA but their mission work was paid for by Tasmanian Baptists. Stella Churchward Kelly wanted Tasmanian women to form a state Women's Missionary Auxiliary.[107] Some congregations had women's mission groups, but these were quite small, such as the Devonport Baptist's Women's Missionary Working Guild, which operated in the early 1920s.[108] While Tasmania is geographically small by Australian standards, the various Baptist congregations were spread throughout the state with minimal transport infrastructure. Consequently there was no convenient central location for women from different Baptist congregations to meet. Of course, the lack of transport was an issue in other states, but usually there was one large center, the capital, where women met. This was not the case in Tasmania, where Hobart had a small population.[109] In 1926 the Tasmanian Baptist Women's Auxiliary was established, aiming to support both home and overseas mission.[110] The Auxiliary had a relatively narrow focus, meeting twice a year during the Baptist Union meetings. All fundraising and other activities were organized by women's groups within congregations. An important function of the Auxiliary was to elect two women to represent the Auxiliary—and Tasmanian Baptist women more generally—at the executive meetings of the Baptist Union of Tasmania.[111]

A significant event in the history of Baptist women's organizations was the introduction of the Senior Girls' Missionary Union (SGMU) established between 1922 to 1926 in Victoria, Queensland, SA, and NSW. Clearly young women were volunteering for mission, and organizations for young women provided both a place to recruit women for overseas mission and a mechanism for women to actively support other missionary women. At the end of the nineteenth century missionary some organizations were formed for young Australian Baptist women in NSW and Queensland. In 1892 in NSW around ten congregations in Sydney established mission groups for women called the Girls' Zenana Aid Society. A state Executive Committee met

Board, discussed below.

107. "Baptist Union: Second Day," *North Western Advocate and the Emu Bay Times* (Burnie, Tasmania), 28 October 1916, 3.

108. "Devonport," *Advocate* (Burnie, Tasmania), 29 May 1924, 4.

109. ABS, "Historical Censuses." The population of Tasmania was about 50,000 in 1830 and about 250,000 in 1945, representing 3 percent of the Australian population.

110. David Mitchell, "Tasmanian Baptist Union," *TAB*, 16 November 1926, 2.

111. "Tasmanian Baptist Assembly," *Advocate* (Burnie, Tasmania), 1 November 1935, 2.

annually from 1896 until 1916, although the first two annual meetings were chaired by men.[112] From 1916 the Society continued operating but only in around five congregations. Likewise in Queensland from 1885 at least two congregations had groups for young women called the Young Women's Mission Class.[113] These NSW and Queensland groups aimed to educate young women about mission activity, and during meetings the women worked on sewing or embroidering items they sold to raise funds to support Baptist mission. Neither of the young women's organizations gained significant traction at the state level and they remained restricted to a small number of congregations. From 1914 John Martin, then the General Secretary of the ABFM, encouraged young women to become involved in mission support as he was convinced that it was advantageous to have separate organizations for young women.[114]

In 1922 Dr Alice Barber, with the assistance of Margaret Findlay, established the Victorian SGMU, which was supported by branches in Baptist congregations. The aim was "To bring India to Christ, and Christ to India."[115] They mirrored a structure used by Victorian Presbyterian women.[116] The SGMU was to become an important organization in the Australian Baptist denomination through its ability to appeal to young women who then worked together to raise funds for the ABFM. It was state-based but with consistent structures and aims across all states.

SGMU branches were quickly established in congregations throughout Victoria through the efforts of Alice Barber and Margaret Findlay.[117] Both women were on furlough from their ABFM work in East Bengal and were expected to visit congregations in Victoria. This ability to speak to congregations, along with Baptist women's overall enthusiasm for mission and mission support, created an ideal environment for promoting the new organization. By the end of 1922 SGMU branches had been established in twenty-two Victorian congregations, and the Victorian SGMU had agreed to cover all costs of supporting Ruby Brindley, a Victorian-born Baptist who was about to commence ABFM work in East Bengal. As Alice Barber advised, Ruby

---

112. "Girls' Zenana Aid Society," *Cumberland Argus and Fruitgrowers Advocate* (Parramatta, NSW), 12 March 1898, 2.

113. Hughes, *History of the Queensland Baptist SGMU*.

114. John C. Martin, "Australian Board of Baptist Foreign Mission," *TAB*, 6 October 1914, 2.

115. "Earnest Work: Girls' Missionary Union," *Brisbane Courier* (Brisbane), 25 September 1929, 22.

116. "Victorian Notes," *OIF*, 6 October 1922, 5.

117. "A Year of Testing and Achievement: Missionaries on Furlough," *OIF*, 6 September 1922, 2–3.

Brindley was the SGMU's "own missionary," demonstrating the organization fulfilled its intended role to engage women in overseas mission activity.[118]

SGMU branches were established in congregations in three other states—Queensland (1923), SA (1923), and NSW (1926). It was recognized that "the girls in the other States were . . . following the Victorian girls' example."[119] While ABFM workers on furlough visited SGMU branches in these states to offer encouragement and support, overall the establishment and management of the SGMU through Australia was due to the constant efforts of Baptist women within congregations.

During 1923 several Baptist congregations in Queensland formed SGMU branches. Louise Grimes from the Brisbane City Tabernacle, and Charlotte Wilkins from Fairfield Baptist, had both independently visited Victoria to observe how the Victorian SGMU operated. They replicated SGMU branches in their own congregations.[120] The appeal of mission then led other congregations to set up their own branches. In 1923, in an editorial about how to keep young women in the church, the Rev. William Bell, editor of *The Queensland Baptist*, wrote: "When linked up with the missionary enterprise, our girls are in direct touch with the command of Christ. The missionary interest is broad, and if properly cultivated, will take them into new worlds. Above all, the missionary motive is purely unselfish."[121] William Bell's remarks reinforced John Martin's view that young women were—effectively—a resource to support mission. To an extent it illustrated how young women could believe that the support of mission enabled them to be "unselfish" and taken "into new worlds."[122] In September 1923 Queensland Baptist women representing seven SGMU branches met during the Baptist Union of Queensland's annual meetings and created a state level SGMU, which subsequently met monthly.[123] The only minor change between the Queensland and Victorian SGMU rules and by-laws was that the Queensland SGMU Central Executive had a representative from the QBWU, and consequently the SGMU and the QBWU were formally linked.[124]

The Queensland Baptist Women's Union continued to operate alongside the new organisations. Women such as Ruth Lawton exemplify Union

118. "Victorian Notes," *OIF*, 6 October 1922, 5.
119. "Senior Girls Missionary Union," *TAB*, 16 September 1924, 9.
120. "Fairfield," *TQB*, 1 March 1923, 14.
121. William Bell, "Timely Topics: Our Girls," *TQB*, 1 May 1923, 4. William Bell's previous two editorials addressed training for those wanting to become ministers—men—and he felt it was appropriate to acknowledge opportunities for women.
122. Dzubinski and Stasson, *Women in the Mission of the Church*, 211.
123. Ralph Sayce, "Foreign Mission Session and Demonstration," *TQB* 1923, 13.
124. Hughes, *History of the Queensland Baptist SGMU*, 14.

leadership. She was President of the Union in 1930 and 1935 and was committed to women's groups—both the Union and the SGMU—believing that women were stronger when they worked together. She visited many different congregations to encourage women to support the work of Queensland women's organizations and was described as an "inspiring" and "vigorous" speaker.[125] She was married to James Lawton, manager of various sawmills in south-east Queensland, and they had six children. When her husband retired they moved to Sandgate in Brisbane, and she was one of the foundation members of the women's group in Sandgate Baptist. Anna Abbott, president of the Sandgate women's group and wife of the minister the Rev. A. Hedley Abbott, acknowledged that Ruth Lawton's appointment as president of the Queensland Baptist Women's Union was "conferring an honor upon the local branch."[126] Ruth Lawton also donated funds to the Baptist Union of Queensland to establish new Baptist congregations in south-east Queensland.

In SA women such as Bessie Brice and Dorothy Mead had been agitating for congregations to form SGMUs.[127] The state SGMU formed in 1925 with ten congregations and members taking a solemn pledge: "Desiring to show my appreciation of the love of Jesus Christ for me, I gratefully pledge myself to give time, money, and prayer for the forwarding of His Kingdom, especially concentrating upon the work in Eastern Bengal and Australia."[128]

In 1926 the NSW SGMU formed and quickly became a vibrant organization and a large contributor to mission funds, and by 1930 had raised sufficient funds to support five missionary women.[129] Ruth Mungomery was the NSW SGMU Secretary from 1928 until her death in 1934 at the age of 35. She was involved in several different Baptist women's groups within her congregation at Parramatta Baptist and in the NSW LZMS, but she embraced the work of the SGMU, visiting NSW Baptist congregations to promote overseas mission. When she died the SGMU organized a memorial service at which two men participated, but, unusually, the key addresses were given by representatives of various women's organizations including Lily Higlett from the LZMS, Marion White from the Home Mission Auxiliary, and Isabel Church and Marjorie Hercus from the SGMU. A report of the service noted:

125. "Baptist," *Brisbane Courier* (Brisbane), 11 May 1929; "Baptist Women's Union: President Entertains," *Evening News*, 21 May 1935.

126. "Sandgate," *TQB*, 15 November 1929, 12.

127. "The Baptist Union," *Advertiser*, 19 April 1924, 11.

128. Mrs A. J. [Edith] Wilcox, "Baptist Womanhood in Action," *TAB*, 27 September 1938, 4.

129. ABFM, Board Minutes, BMAA.

Without exception each one [of the women] spoke of the wonderful Christian personality and influence of Miss [Ruth] Mungomery, and how her whole life just simply spoke "service" for others. Whatsoever her hand found to do, she did it will all her might. We will truly not need to remember her, for she will never be forgotten.[130]

While the SGMU was significant in the four most populated states, Baptist women in Tasmania and WA did not eagerly embrace the SGMU. During the late 1920s in Tasmania SGMU branches were formed only in the Devonport and Burnie congregations. In 1937 the Baptist Union of Tasmania encouraged more congregations to form branches and the state SGMU was established the following year, although in 1945 it was still relatively small with branches in only nine congregations, which represented about 30 percent of Tasmanian congregations.[131] Similarly in the mid–1920s several WA congregations established branches of the SGMU following Alice Barber's visit promoting the organization. Proponents of the SGMU made numerous attempts to establish a state organization in WA, most particularly in 1930 when missionaries Grace Brown and Grace Thomson visited.[132] It was not until 1947 that an executive committee formed following a visit by missionary Florence Horwood, who reinvigorated SGMU interest.[133] Arguably young women in WA had opportunities to be involved in the state mission committees.[134] The SGMU was only required once young women were not able to undertake meaningful roles in these other mission committees. Of course as WA is the largest Australian state geographically, with a relatively small population, making for expensive and long travel times, and this may have been another reason for the delay.[135]

The activities undertaken by the SGMU across the state unions were similar. State level SGMUs held well-attended monthly and annual meetings.[136] Many SGMUs supported their "own" missionary women. For in-

130. "Miss Ruth Mungomery," *TAB*, 30 October 1934, 4.

131. "Baptist Union Concludes," *Examiner* (Launceston, Tasmania), 29 October 1937, 6.

132. South Australian Senior Girls' Missionary Union MM, SABA.

133. Miss L. Moorehead, "Senior Girls in the West," *TAB*, April 1952, 19.

134. BWGAM, BUWAA.

135. ABS, "Historical Censuses." In 1949 the population of WA was about 500,000, being about 6 percent of the Australian population. Geographically, WA comprises one third of the Australian continent.

136. For example, during the 1930s monthly SGMU meetings in Sydney had around one hundred women in attendance. See Florence Harris, Letter to Frank Marsh, ABFM General Secretary, 4 October 1930, Letter, BMAA.

Women's State and National Baptist Organizations

stance, Florence English was supported by the NSW SGMU at Hurlstone Park Baptist, and Margaret Findlay was supported by the Victorian SGMU.[137] The SGMU executive committees provided advice and study resources to the SGMU branches, and coordinated larger fundraising events, including slide shows, fetes, concerts, and pageants. In contrast to the earlier organizations for young women, the SGMU did not undertake sewing. All activities were designed to raise money for, and knowledge about, mission.

The SGMU provided opportunities for younger Baptist women to deepen friendships with other women through the state SGMU annual camps—the highlight of the SGMU calendar—usually held at Easter. Camp numbers fluctuated between the 1920s and 1945. In 1924 a photograph of the SGMU camp in Victoria depicted 35 attendees, and in 1938 the first SGMU camp in Tasmania had 20 attendees. In the 1930s SGMU camps in Victoria, SA and NSW regularly had around 100 attendees, with the largest known attendance of 170 reported in 1939 in NSW.[138]

The South Australia Senior Girls' Missionary Union Easter Camp, 1927. Two women have been identified: Beryl Bowering in the back row, far right, and Elizabeth Gooden to her left. The photo was published on page 10 in *The Record* (Adelaide), 14 May, 1927; used with permission of the Baptist Churches of South Australia and Northern Territory Association.

---

137. "Night of Rejoicing: Women's Missionary Triumph," *TAB*, 19 August 1930, 4; "Church News: Hurlstone Park," *TAB*, 4 April 1944, 7.

138. "New South Wales Senior Girls' Camp," *TAB*, 2 May 1939, 7. Most SGMU camp reports did not indicate the number of attendees.

Some Women at the New South Wales Senior Girls' Missionary Union Easter Camp, c. 1941. Lily Higlett was one of the "Camp Mothers" and is in the front row, second from right. Photo provided by John Church; used with permission.

Camp attendees enjoyed Bible studies, addresses about the work of mission, and sunrise prayer services, as well as time for sport and recreation such as tennis tournaments, scavenger hunts, and indoor games.[139] The camps were held in various facilities depending on the numbers attending and the available options. Sometimes the Victorian SGMU was held in two different locations because one larger adequate facility to accommodate all participants was not available.[140] For many years the Queensland SGMUs were held at the large home of Laura Grimes.[141] Each camp appointed a "Camp Mother" who was often a missionary woman on furlough or a respected woman in the denomination. In 1927 in SA Margaret Gowans was Camp Mother: she was a former mission worker. In 1936 in Queensland Ruth Goodman was Camp Mother: she was active in the Queensland denomination. In 1941 in NSW two women were Camp Mothers for the 125 attendees: Lily Higlett, mission enthusiast, and Annie Nall, a former ABFM missionary.[142] Camp attendees used mission study resources. The seventy-five attendees at the 1930

139. Adeline Sturgess, "New South Wales: SGMU Camp," *TAB*, 16 April 1940, 7.
140. "Victoria: SGMU Camp," *TAB*, 20 May 1930, 10.
141. "Baptist," *Telegraph*, 7 June 1930, 10.
142. "Religious Notes," *Register*, 9 April 1927, 7; "Baptist Camp," *Courier Mail* (Brisbane), 20 April 1936, 20; Adeline Sturgess, "SGMU Easter Camp," *TAB*, 22 April 1941, 4.

Victorian SGMU Camp used a book titled "The call of God."[143] In SA the SGMU camps had a theme: in 1936, "Come, let us build"; in 1940, "Behold I make all things new"; and in 1945, "The great adventure: follow the Christ, the King."[144] The camps provided an opportunity for young women to meet for social interaction, study, and fellowship, and provided motivation to women to continue to support mission through fundraising efforts. Inevitably some women felt called to volunteer for mission work because of their involvement in the SGMU. Mabel Burgess was one such SGMU member who became a missionary in the Solomon Islands with the South Sea Evangelical Mission. She was described as "one of our own Senior Girls" by Adeline Sturgess, who was on the NSW SGMU Executive.[145]

In 1929 the first Baptist congregation commenced in Canberra, then the Federal Capital Territory, and a Women's Fellowship was quickly established.[146] Geographically and administratively the Canberra Baptist congregation was part of the Baptist Union of NSW. However the Canberra Women's Fellowship did not formally affiliate with the NSW Women's Home Mission Auxiliary. The reason for this is unknown although, given the number of women in the congregation who were originally from Victoria, they may have wanted to be independent from NSW and there was no necessity for them to join the Auxiliary. Some women from the Fellowship regularly attended the NSW Auxiliary's annual meetings, notably Charlotte Waldock, the Canberra Baptist minister's wife.[147] These women's desire to remain independent was another small example of how women maintained a particular type of autonomy within the denomination.

In the early 1940s the Victorian and SA women's organizations were well-established and each sought to commemorate twenty-one years of operations in 1945 through a significant project. Both organizations chose to raise funds to purchase separate aged care facilities—"Strathalan" in Melbourne and "Illoura" in Adelaide. They were the first two aged care homes managed by the denomination and, at least for a time, raised the profile of both women's organizations.[148] Women's interest in aged care facilities is understandable because from the mid-twentieth century advances in medicine

---

143. "Victoria: SGMU Camp," *TAB*, 20 May 1930, 10.
144. Senior Girls' Missionary Union South Australia, 1931–1963, BMAA.
145. Sturgess, "New South Wales: SGMU Camp," *TAB*, 16 April 1940, 7.
146. Arthur Waldock, "Canberra Church," *TAB*, 25 June 1929, 12.
147. Waldock, "Canberra Church," *TAB*, 25 June 1929, 12. Charlotte Waldock established the Fellowship and was president for many years. She was from NSW.
148. Edith K. Wilcox, SA BWL, SABA; VBWA MM, BUVA.

led to people living longer, on average women lived longer than men, and generally society expected that women would care for their elderly relatives.

The Baptist Union of Victoria (BUV) had discussed the possibility of a social welfare project but up to 1944 no action had been taken.[149] In early 1944 Mary Pope, as President of the Victorian Baptist Women's Association (VBWA), spoke to the General Secretary of the BUV "to expedite matters" regarding the purchase of a suitable property for aged care facilities.[150] At a subsequent special meeting on 10 May 1944, the members of the VBWA agreed to present the proposal at the upcoming BUV Assembly meeting, and to encourage as many members of the VBWA as possible to attend the meeting to ensure the project was accepted.[151] At the BUV Assembly meeting in mid-May 1944, Mary Pope put forward the proposal that: "this assembly approves the establishment of a home for aged people in celebration of the 21st birthday of the VBWA." Dr Eleanor Varley spoke about why the facility was so important—presumably from a medical point of view.[152] Following agreement by the BUV Mary and her husband, the Rev. William Pope, identified an appropriate site for the future aged care facility and in July 1944 the BUV purchased this site in the then rural township of Macleod, fourteen kilometres north-east of Melbourne. *The Australian Baptist* stated that "Our confidence in our ladies to make good in the matter of establishing a home for the Aged, is being fully vindicated. They have lost no time in locating a suitable property."[153] Thus Baptists at the time understood that this project originated from women's agitation. The facility, called Strathalan, opened in February 1945, with the VBWA funding the purchase price. Several women were appointed to the first management board, and ongoing funding was provided through a bequest from Ruth Wilkins.[154] While both Victorian Baptist men and women have been part of ongoing management, clearly women's involvement was critical to the establishment of the facility, particularly by Mary Pope whose leadership in the project was essential. This activity stimulated interest in the Women's Association and during the late 1940s and early 1950s a monthly newsletter was produced containing updates on women's work.[155]

---

149. Manley, *From Woolloomooloo*, 2:551; Clarke, *Making a Difference*, 10.

150. VBWA MM, BUVA.

151. VBWA MM, BUVA.

152. Sydney. M. Potter, "Baptist Union of Victoria," *TAB*, 23 May 1944, 4.

153. "Victorian News and Views, *TAB*, 18 July 1944, 4.

154. Clarke, *Making a Difference*, 11, 22.

155. See, for example, Mrs W. G. [Mary] Pope, "The President's Message," *Baptist Woman* (Melbourne), 1 April 1946, 1–2.

The beginnings of the Baptist aged care facility in SA involved—as with Victoria—a project undertaken with significant input from women. In 1944 SA women, through the SA BWL, committed to raise £4,000 for the aged care facility. According to Ken Webb's history of Illoura prepared in 1999, the Baptist Union of SA agreed to this fundraising, so long as the funds were lodged directly with the Union, whereby the Union, Webb wrote, could "keep a steadying hand on this wild female enthusiasm."[156] In hindsight Webb's statement trivializes the work of the committed SA Baptist women; certainly the process used by the Union is evidence of the control that men sometimes exerted over Baptist women. The fundraising appeal was officially launched at the twenty-first anniversary meeting of the BWL in April 1944—Mary Pope attended this meeting. The BWL raised the funds and, after some delays, Illoura was opened in 1949.[157] It is clearly evident that women were essential in the project, which was driven by a strong woman—Edith Wilcox. She was Secretary of the BWL from 1929 to 1953, and President in 1940–41, and was described as "the originator of the proposal to provide the home."[158]

Common Features of Australian Baptist Women's Organizations

While the women's state organizations developed at different times, all organizations operated similarly. Meetings were held regularly, either once a month or once a quarter, and most congregations within each state union were formally represented. Country congregations unable to attend nominated a correspondent, who was sent information on decisions and activities.[159] The organizations held annual meetings at which members were elected to executive roles of president, vice-president, and secretary. Further positions were elected such as pianist, "press correspondent," and "country correspondent."[160] Each position was valued. For instance in 1933 the NSW Women's Home Mission Auxiliary celebrated the work of Emma Steed. She had been deaf since early adulthood and had written over 150 letters during the year to Baptist women in remote locations in Australia. She

---

156. Webb, *Illoura*.
157. Webb, *Illoura*.
158. "South Australia: The Assembly," *TAB*, 20 October 1954, 5.
159. BWL MM, SABA; Bamford, "New South Wales: Home Mission Women's Auxiliary," *TAB*, 22 August 1933, 11; QBWU Executive MM, QUBA; VBWA MM, BUVA.
160. "Queensland Baptist women," *TAB*, 1 November 1938, 9.

was lauded as having "done splendid work as the country and immigration correspondent."[161]

Women's organizations provided a means for dissemination of information about a variety of mission activities and other denominational events and highlighted Baptist work to encourage other women to direct their time, effort, and funds to assist. Interactions occurred between the women's organizations in different states. The state women's mission groups shared letters and articles, and hosted visits from all Baptist missionary women regardless of their "home" state, especially after the federation of the ABFM in 1913. Women held events to promote mission work, often in conjunction with state Baptist union meetings. Some of these events were large, such as the 1932 "View Day" in Melbourne, which attracted over six-hundred people.[162] Women provided goods for "Christmas boxes" sent to Australian Baptist missionaries, which contained items for the use of both missionaries and local people, including food and clothing.[163] Women's organizations were expected to organize and provide catering for the state and national Baptist union meetings.[164] In reality, hospitality, catering, and event management were tasks that women were obliged to undertake, although this does not diminish their obvious commitment to, and the importance of, their role in this area.

The Australian Baptist denomination relied on women's organizations because of the funds they raised.[165] Unfortunately while it is not possible to accurately calculate the full extent of funds raised by women's organizations, an examination of financial details from the state Baptist unions highlights the significant contributions by women. For instance, in 1885 women in NSW raised £77 of the £182 allocated to overseas mission, representing 42 percent.[166] In 1938 the NSW SGMU raised over £750 of the £3800 allocated to overseas mission, being 20 percent, which was significantly more than the £79 raised by the Young Men's Missionary League. In 1943 the NSW

---

161. Bamford, "New South Wales: Home Mission Auxiliary," *TAB*, 22 August 1933, 11. The immigration correspondent communicated with new arrivals from the UK to help them settle into Australia.

162. See, for example, "Victorian Notes," *OIF*, 6 October 1922, 5; *Baptist Yearbook*; "BMWU of Victoria," *OIF*, 6 October 1932, 4; "Lockyer District: Blenheim," *Queensland Times* (Ipswich, Queensland), 18 September 1940, 3.

163. "Christmas Boxes: Mrs. Pieper," *OIF*, 6 May 1935, 5.

164. Miles, "Among Scottish Baptist Women," *TAB*, 2 April 1918, 4; "Queensland Baptist Union: The Opening Day," *TAB*, 1 October 1929, 5.

165. Cupit et al., *From Five Barley Loaves*, 192.

166. "The Treasurer in Account with the Ladies' Baptist Zenana Mission Society, for the Year Ending 3rd September, 1884; and The Baptist Missionary Society of New South Wales in Account with the Treasurer," *Banner of Truth*, September–October 1885, 145.

SGMU contributed £1,106; the Zenana Society £1,132; and the Young Men's Missionary League £97.[167] In 1934 the two women's mission organizations in Queensland directly contributed £330 of the £1440 allocated to overseas mission, representing 23 percent of funds.[168] Women also organized some of the general appeals, so these examples do not reflect the total funds that should be attributed to work by women.

The women's organizations cost little to operate as women donated their time, meetings were held at Baptist facilities that were made available at no cost, and catering was usually undertaken on a roster. Members paid an annual fee to be part of the organization, either personally or through their Baptist congregation, and the fees were part of the funds raised. Significantly meetings opened and closed with prayer, and contained activities such as singing of hymns, Bible studies, discussions, speeches, and time to socialize through morning or afternoon tea at the conclusion of the meetings. In this way women's groups fostered the spiritual and social lives of Australian Baptist women.

The myriad Baptist women's organizations that existed between 1872 and 1945 reflect the independence of Baptist congregations and the state unions. The changing of names of the home and overseas mission organizations further reflects the way overseas mission was a nationally cohesive activity, whereas home mission was specific to each state. The names of the women's mission organizations initially varied between the states but by the mid-twentieth century the women's mission organizations around Australia were all named Baptist Women's Missionary Unions (BWMU) or Senior Girls' Missionary Unions (SGMU). Conversely, home mission organizations largely retained their historical names. As late as 1973 the Australian Baptist Women's Board, discussed below, "instigated" action to have consistent naming of all women's organizations throughout Australia, yet some state organizations resisted because they did not want to change their name.[169] In effect the state home mission organizations operated separately, while Australian Baptist women continued to be united nationally through overseas mission.[170]

---

167. "Baptist Union of NSW," *TAB* 1938, 2; "Baptist Union of New South Wales: Annual Assembly," *TAB*, 28 September 1943, 8.

168. BUQ, *Year Book 1934*, 47.

169. "State Bodies Are Considering Change of Name," *TAB*, 22 August 1973, 10.

170. This reflected the broader denomination, where states operated independently in almost all areas except in overseas mission work, which occurred through the ABFM.

CASE STUDY: LILY HIGLETT AND THE NSW LADIES' ZENANA MISSIONARY SOCIETY

This case study examines the activities of the NSW LZMS between 1938 and 1943, and the life and beliefs of Lily Higlett, the President of the Society, and her commitment to mission support, and includes a discussion on the retention of material written by women.[171] Lily kept notebooks with information to guide her during the meetings and one of the notebooks for the period from 1938 to 1943 surfaced in 2019. The notebook is a rare extant archival document from a Baptist woman expressing her faith and illustrating her leadership and organizational skills in her role as President of the LZMS.

The notebook's journey to the Baptist Association of NSW Archives illustrates the randomness of the retention of material pertaining to Baptist women. Following Lily's death her notebooks were kept by her husband, the Rev. William Higlett, and then her daughter, Isabel Church, who kept some of the notebooks but offered others to friends. The notebook used for this case study had been given to Edna Hale, an ABFM missionary, who subsequently gave the notebook to Bernice Cardwell, who was the NSW BWMU President between 1973 and 1981.[172] In 2019 Bernice Cardwell's family deposited her writings and other documents, including Lily's notebook, into the Baptist Association of NSW Archives. The location of other notebooks is not known. A loose-leafed typed letter at the front of the extant notebook expressed a common misconception about women's records. It indicated that this specific notebook did not contain any information of significance, and perhaps was "not worth keeping."[173] This raises the probably that Lily's other notebooks—which *were* valued for their content—contain additional material of theological significance, including sermons, and consequently their likely loss is unfortunate. By contrast, most of the diaries and papers written by William Higlett, were retained in Baptist archives.[174] The fact that Lily's work was dispersed reflects a lack of foresight in 1943 regarding the value of women's written works—and the value of archives and archivists who *do* value such work.

Lily's notebook outlines the LZMS's operations and consideration of mission at a time when Australian Baptist mission was at its zenith during the 1930s and 1940s. Monthly meetings of the LZMS had around

---

171. In this Case Study Lily Higlett will be referred to as Lily.
172. "News of Our Women's Work," *TAB*, 22 August 1973, 10.
173. Higlett, Notes, NSWBA.
174. Parker, *True Pastor*, 177–78.

fifty attendees. Women from congregations from Sydney city and suburban groups sent representatives and women outside the greater Sydney area were kept informed of the Society's operations through summaries of the meetings written by Susan Davey and published in *The Australian Baptist*.[175] In 1942 Lily's notes for a meeting stated: "Mrs [Susan] Davey as reporter has given her best, helping not only women in the suburbs to know something of our monthly meetings but giving information to the women in our country districts and in other states."[176] Unsurprisingly Susan Davey did not include that statement in her report of the meeting! The Society meetings were formal, with agendas consisting of prayer, singing, Bible studies, and speeches from members of the Society, other mission enthusiasts, and missionaries on furlough.[177]

Lily was the daughter of Fredrike Low, née Hafner, who was born in Germany, and John Low, a Baptist lay-preacher who was born in Scotland. Lily grew up in Brisbane, and in 1909, married William Higlett, a Baptist minister and widower with three adult sons. They moved to Grafton, NSW, where their only child, Isabel Church, was born in 1911. In 1914 they relocated to Sydney, where William Higlett was pastor of Haberfield Baptist until his semi-retirement in 1929.

Lily was active in several different Baptist organizations including her Haberfield Baptist's women group, the NSW CE Union, the Women's Home Mission Auxiliary, and the LZMS. William shared Lily's commitment to overseas mission and in retirement he was the Secretary of the NSW Foreign Mission Committee.[178] Lily was an effective public speaker and visited many Baptist congregations in NSW to address their women's committees.[179] Although there is no evidence that she ever preached to a Baptist congregation during a Sunday worship service, she may have preached when William Higlett was traveling or unavailable. Nevertheless many of her speeches to women's groups should be considered preaching.

---

175. See Davey, "New South Wales: Ladies' Zenana Society meeting," *TAB*, 1 November 1938.
176. Higlett, Notes, NSWBA.
177. Higlett, Notes, NSWBA.
178. Parker, *True Pastor*, 103, 56.
179. Helen Cousin, "Late Mrs W. Higlett," *TAB*, 22 June 1943, 5.

Lily Higlett, Isabel Church, Dorothea Burnett (Lily's Niece), and William Higlett. Photo provided by John Church; used with permission.

Lily's surviving notebook contains some of her speeches and prayers for meetings of the LZMS and demonstrate her Evangelical beliefs and her commitment to overseas mission.[180] In her speech at the July 1942 meeting, she stated:

> While fully conscious of pending crisis [of war], [overseas missionaries] have the complete and adequate answer for every problem that could arise. They have Christ, and He is sufficient for every crisis. It is our privilege at home to provide the means

180. Higlett, Notes, NSWBA.

for the carrying on their difficult task, and to pray more earnestly than ever before that whatever else falters the Christian Missionary Work will go on . . .
We are called to a life that is God mastered.
A life dominated by the purpose of God
A life dedicated to the witnessing for God.
Doing Christ's work in the world.[181]

This speech contained rhetorical features common in public speeches or sermons, especially through the repeated emphasis on the phrase "called to a life" as well as its rhythmic cadences.[182]

Lily believed in the power of prayer.[183] In July 1941 her introductory comment to a prayer was: "I have often said whenever you meet a strong Christian woman you know behind that life, there is much prayer."[184] Meetings of the Society during her time as president contained at least three prayers. While some were led by other women, Lily appears to have led at least one prayer each meeting. Lily crafted her language to target women. For example, in March 1939 she stated: "We are daughters of the King of Kings through a loving faith in our exalted Lord."[185] Notwithstanding the name of the Society, it focused equally on missionary women and men, and any missionary guest was "warmly greeted."[186] Perhaps Lily's active faith is the most enduring feature highlighted in her notebook, with every prayer, speech, and comment revealing the extent to which she was prepared to work for the promotion and funding of overseas mission. Her speech notes for the meeting of the Society in June 1942 centered around Acts 20:35. She wrote:

> How grateful we are to Paul that he has preserved this great saying of His Master for us . . . There is a blessing in giving which can be gained in no other way. Let us put the emphasis where it belongs. It is more blessed to give than to receive. [From the second half of Acts 20:35.] . . . There is a thrill in the things we receive. But life will never reach to its highest level if we have not reached to the blessedness of giving.[187]

---

181. Higlett, Notes, NSWBA. Lily Higlett had underlined "will go on" in her notes.
182. See, for example, E. [Ernest] A. Kirwood, "Christmas Musings," TQB, 15 December 1927, 1–2. The Rev. Ernest Kirwood wrote: "Man reconciled to God and called to a life of devotion and obedience."
183. Randall, *What a Friend We Have in Jesus*, 79, 83.
184. Higlett, Notes, NSWBA.
185. Higlett, Notes, NSWBA.
186. Higlett, Notes, NSWBA.
187. Higlett, Notes, NSWBA.

One cannot deny that in her life, Lily practiced "the blessedness of giving." On 9 June 1943 Lily died unexpectedly at the age of sixty-three. William Higlett died a year later. *The Australian Baptist* published three different obituaries for Lily. One was written by the Rev. John Deane, which was spoken at her memorial service; and two others were written by Helen Cousin and Elizabeth Dovey, women who undertook Baptist mission support alongside Lily.[188] The contents of Lily Higlett's notebook provides evidence of a woman in a leadership position, who was confident in expressing her Christian beliefs.

NATIONAL ORGANIZATIONS

Australian Baptist women created two national women's organizations through the establishment of the SGMU Federal Committee in 1929 and the Australian Baptist Women's Board in 1935. The fact that the SGMU Federal Committee was the first national Australian Baptist women's group reinforces again the importance of mission to Australian Baptist women.

In 1910 some state women's mission organizations tried to meld together as a single organization within the Australian denomination, to "make all our Baptist women missionary enthusiasts."[189] Yet women did not form a national organization: as they judged there was no need. State Baptist Unions—and links to each state—remained strong. Australian Baptists came together at triennial assemblies from 1908, and these meetings usually had a session for women. The ABFM formed in 1913 and women had a formal voice in the organization, but federation of the state mission organizations had little impact on the support work that women's state mission organizations undertook. A further impediment was the expense and time to regularly travel the long distances between state capitals.

In 1929 young Baptist women established the first national women's group, the Federal SGMU which was approved by the Baptist Union of Australia (BUA).[190] The Federal SGMU gave young women a national platform. It did not sponsor projects or seek to influence state SGMUs. Essentially the Federal SGMU was a mechanism to enable each of the state SGMUs to report annually, and a consolidated report then to be submitted to the BUA.

188. John Deane, "The Home-Call of Mrs. W. Higlett," *TAAB*, 15 June 1943, 4; Helen Cousin, "The Late Mrs W. Higlett," *TAB*, 22 June 1943, 5; Elizabeth Dovey, "The Late Mrs. W. Higlett," *TAB*, 22 June 1943, 5.

189. "The Women's Meeting," *TSB*, 29 September 1910, 633.

190. "Earnest Work: Girls' Missionary Union," *Brisbane Courier*, 25 September 1929, 22.

In 1935 the Australian Baptist Women's Board was formed and, again, the relatively late development of this group illustrates how Baptist women did not see a need to be united with each other at a national level. Until 1935 the SA and Victorian home mission women's organizations had formal connections with the English Baptist Women's League—in the "homeland"—but only informal, albeit regular, contact with each other.[191] Discussions among Australian Baptist women regarding the formation of a national organization occurred during the early 1930s at a time of polarising political and religious ideologies and threats of war.[192] The issue of world peace appears to have been discussed by all state-based Baptist women's organizations, but the impetus for a national body was led by Cecilia Downing.[193] In 1932 a letter published in the women's column of *The Australian Baptist* by "C. D."—almost certainly Cecilia Downing—requested that Australian Baptist women consider collaborating at a national level to be part of the League of Nations' call for world peace.[194] Perhaps promoting peace was a way that some women believed the country could recover from the 1930s economic depression. Certainly women such as Cecilia Downing and Elizabeth Rees expressed this view.[195] Cecilia Downing obtained agreement from the state women's groups to form an Australian Baptist women's group that represented all Baptist women in both meetings of Baptists in the Asia-Pacific region and the women's committee of the Baptist World Alliance. Cecilia Downing was in turn responding to a resolution by the Baptist World Alliance in 1932 that more women be involved in that organization, and she was adament that Australian Baptist women were best represented by a national group.[196]

The 1935 Australian Baptist Assembly agreed to amend the constitution of the Baptist Union of Australia to include the Australian Baptist

---

191. *Coming-of-Age*, 7; Wilcox, *Baptist Women's League*, 12.

192. "World Peace and Social Questions: Baptist Assembly Attitude," *Advertiser* (Adelaide), 27 September 1935, 14; Pargeter, *For God, Home and Humanity*, 83.

193. Carrie Chapman Catt, "Steps to Abolish War," *AWRS* (Melbourne), 1 January 1932, 14; "Devonport Baptist Church," *Advocate* (Burnie, Tasmania), 28 October 1933, 9; "Men Have Failed: Women Must Save the Country," *Courier Mail* (Brisbane), 3 October 1935, 22.

194. C. D., "Letter to the Editor of 'For Our Women,'" *TAB*, 2 August 1932, 6. While Celia Downing is not identified as the author of this letter, she was currently writing to each of the state Baptist women's organizations on this issue, so it is probable that she also wrote to *Australian Baptist*.

195. Elizabeth Rees, "'Peace on Earth': And in Our Own Hearts," *AWRS*, 1 December 1937, 223.

196. Cecilia Downing, "Fellowship of Women," *TAB*, 24 September 1935, 2.

Women's Board (ABWB).[197] The ABWB had formal representation of six Australian states and the Australian Capital Territory. The Northern Territory did not become affiliated until 1965. Cecilia Downing, appropriately appointed as the first President of the ABWB, called the amendment of the constitution an "epoch-making event."[198] The ABWB had two aims, the first of which was wide-ranging, beginning with the statement: "To inspire and encourage women's work in the churches of the denomination, and, by coordinating existing work, to bind together Baptist women in a fellowship of prayer and service for the Kingdom of God in Australia and throughout the world."[199] There were eight subsections detailing actions to achieve this aim, centring on themes of friendship, Bible study, links to Baptist women outside Australia, and women's interest in the "spiritual life and progress of the Baptist Church in Australia."[200] The second aim of the ABWB was: "To perform such other functions as may be remitted to it by the Assembly or Executive Council of the Union and/or by any state Union."[201] There is no evidence regarding the origins of this aim—that is, whether it was proposed by the women, or whether it was imposed by the Assembly. In any case the aims of the ABWB were very broad and, as a result, somewhat ambiguous.

The ABWB and the SGMU intended to work together, and Gladys Cooper, the President of the Federal SGMU, stated that "the heartiest cooperation is desired between the two bodies."[202] Nevertheless, opportunities for the organizations to work together proved to be somewhat limited because they had different purposes. As stated above, the Federal SGMU was a formal reporting mechanism. In contrast the ABWB enabled Australian Baptist women to be represented within national and international women's organizations outside the Baptist denomination. As Cecilia Downing stressed: "The view taken by Baptist women in Australia . . . is that the Baptist denomination must take its place in social and national activities beside other denominations . . . We feel that we can make a name for ourselves and extend the Kingdom of God by doing our Christian work by the aid of the most efficient organization that it is possible to set up."[203] Essentially the

---

197. Ham, *History*.
198. Downing, "Fellowship of Women," *TAB*, 24 September 1935, 2.
199. Downing, "Fellowship of Women," *TAB*, 24 September 1935, 2.
200. Downing, "Fellowship of Women," *TAB*, 24 September 1935, 2.
201. Downing, "Fellowship of Women," *TAB*, 24 September 1935, 2.
202. "Baptist Women's Board," *TAB*, 15 September 1936, 5.
203. Cecilia Downing, "Aspirations of Australian Baptist women," *TAB*, 31 October 1939, 1.

only shared features of the Federal SGMU and the ABWB were that they were national organizations, and their members were Baptist women.

Ultimately the ABWB was not influential within the Australian Baptist denomination and is not even mentioned in Manley's 2006 history of the denomination. In part the lack of influence stemmed from the fact that the Baptist Union of Australia, of which the ABWB was a part, was itself not influential.[204] Baptist women were more likely to support state women's organizations, and at that time most of these had significant power and resources. Nevertheless, the ABWB continued to operate until the end of the twentieth century.

Despite this seemingly harsh but realistic assessment of the outcomes of the ABWB, the organization was important for the women involved. It fostered useful linkages among Baptist women around Australia, as the executive positions rotated through the states. Most importantly it enabled women to connect with Baptist women outside Australia, particularly in the Asia Pacific, the UK, and the USA.[205] The "ABWB Honour Roll" provided information about some of the women who were involved in the ABWB and their indisputable commitment to its aims. Life members included Elsa Warner and Ruth Smith from Victoria, and Agnes Beetson from Queensland. These three women were active in other Australian Baptist organizations, and represented Australian Baptist women within the Women's Department of the Baptist World Alliance, particularly in the South West Pacific Continental Union.[206]

LEADERSHIP

Many women devoted years of service to the support of various parts of the Baptist denomination through their leadership positions within state or national Baptist women's organizations. In most cases women's involvement commenced when they became involved in organizations in their congregations. Women acquired the skills to undertake executive positions through watching others, or through taking up executive positions in organizations for young people, particularly the Junior CE.[207] It was not until the 1950s

---

204. Manley, *From Woolloomooloo*, 1:645.
205. Ham, *History*.
206. Australian Baptist Women's Fellowship Honour Roll, BUVA. Most of the women on the Honour Roll held positions within the South West Pacific Continental Union.
207. See, for example, Maxwell, *Triumphant Through Trials*, 23.

that the Australian Baptist Women's Board established formal training for women to obtain skills in managing meetings.²⁰⁸

Baptist meetings and financial and annual reports assessed the work by women and congratulated women on their fundraising achievements.²⁰⁹ Many reports contrasted the contribution of men and women. When the 1930 Queensland Baptist Union Foreign Mission Report was presented, for instance, delegates highlighted the fundraising undertaken by women and concluded that "the young men of the denomination were not doing their share."²¹⁰

The total number of women involved in leadership within women's organizations is difficult to calculate, although nearly 200 women held the position of president within state and national organizations.²¹¹ This chapter has highlighted details of the roles of women across Australia whose work and leadership through various Australian Baptist women's organizations was significant.²¹²

ARCHIVAL RECORDS AND USE IN BAPTIST HISTORIOGRAPHY

Baptist women's state-based organizations share a regrettable feature in that their histories and details of the women involved have been largely ignored in Australian Baptist historiography. In 1927 Ralph Sayce, the Secretary of the Baptist Union of Queensland, did not include the establishment of Queensland women's organizations in "a bunch of Baptist dates... marking some [of] the stages in the development of Baptist work in Queensland."²¹³

208. "Training course helpful to women," *TAB*, 30 November 1977, 14.

209. See, for example, "New College," *TSB*, 21 March 1912, 1; "New South Wales: Islington," *TAB*, 12 August 1930, 10.

210. A. H. B., "Queensland Baptist Union: Assembly Meetings," *TAB*, 30 September 1930, 6.

211. The number is based on the known women who held the position of president and the average number of years they held that position. As examples, the SA Baptist Women's League changed president every two years. Whereas NSW women's organizations were more likely to appoint a president for a longer period. Not all the minutes from all state organizations are extant. In addition, the role of secretary was important and possibly an additional 150 women held this position in Baptist women's organizations throughout Australia.

212. Hilton, "ABW Database."

213. Ralph Sayce, "The Jubilee Assembly," *TQB*, 15 August 1927, 5. Ralph Sayce only included one event that referenced a woman, which was Martha Plested commencing mission work in 1885. Other dates included: the "suggestion" of forming a Queensland Baptist Union; and when *Queensland Freeman* became *Queensland Baptist*."

The SA Baptist Women's League's work and influence was acknowledged by Escourt Hughes in his 1937 history of SA Baptists. He commented: "The BWL has done nobly. In more than one direction the women have put the men to shame. In all sorts of ways they have rendered fine service."[214] Notwithstanding this statement, Escourt Hughes did not include any details about the work the BWL undertook or acknowledge women's financial contribution to several important Baptist projects in SA.[215] Given the large amount of funds provided by women's organizations for home and mission work, the omission of their work typifies how Baptists took for granted the important work of women's organizations. The roles and impacts of the organizations remain largely unknown and unacknowledged. The failure to incorporate state and national women's organizations in Baptist histories is acute when assessing the ways in which women's involvement in particular activities are either excluded or downplayed.

Australian Baptist women involved in women's organizations did not have a regular mechanism for documentation of their perspectives and activities apart from summaries of meetings, but these were generally concise. Thus general discussions and individual women's speeches may have been alluded to but were neither summarized nor retained.[216]

Did women at the time perceive that their organizations' achievements were being ignored by those reporting on the work of the denomination? It is impossible to discern this, although the existence of written histories in the 1940s of women's groups in SA and Victoria may indicate they wished to highlight work they had undertaken and outcomes achieved and to address this deficiency.[217] In 1918 Isabella Miles alluded to women's work in Australia being seen as "a 'side show' . . . or an 'extra'" and she compared Australia to Scotland, where she believed women's work was "an integral part of the Union's life and work."[218] During the 1940s the women of NSW commenced producing a yearly annual report outlining the work of the various organizations. Possibly this may have been instigated to combat the neglect elsewhere in reporting women's work and ministries. Some of the actions of groups and minutes of meetings hint at annoyance about their unappreciated place in the denomination. This is particularly evident in Victoria and SA. As observed earlier, the VBWA specifically decided not to be affiliated with the BUV, and the minutes of the VBWA meeting in

214. Hughes, *Our First Hundred Years*, 245.
215. Hughes, *Our First Hundred Years*, 197.
216. See, for example, "More or Less Personal," *TAB*, 12 July 1938, 4.
217. Wilcox, *Baptist Women's League*; *Victorian Baptist Women's Association*.
218. Miles, "Among Scottish Baptist Women," *TAB*, 2 April 1918, 4.

February 1925 recorded pointedly that future quarterly meetings would be held on Wednesdays as "we inconvenienced the authorities of the Collins Street Church by holding our meetings on Tuesdays."[219] In 1958 Edith Wilcox's speech about the SA Baptist Women's League hints at the organization's status in the denomination, when she stated: "Some of you may be asking, 'Just what is the Baptist Women's League? . . . Have we any history at all?'"[220] Such statements imply a certain level of frustration at the dismissive attitude towards women's work.

Unfortunately Baptist women's organizations are not alone in being largely omitted from relevant historiography as most women's organizations are ignored in Australian Protestant historiography. Women's work is viewed as an "additional theme."[221] Incorporating records of the state and national women's organizations gives a fuller and balanced understanding of the development, structure, and dynamics of the Baptist—or any other Australian—denomination. Likewise the strong leaders of these groups should be recognized for their ministries. They, and many other women, are a key component of Australian Baptist history.

CONCLUSION

State-based and national women's organizations played a significant role in the Australian Baptist denomination in the first half of the twentieth century, although this chapter has provided only a brief overview. Women's organizations created a parallel church body for women that enabled women's involvement in the support of foreign and home mission and other denominational activities. Women's organizations also provided an opportunity for leadership roles to women who were unable or not encouraged to speak in groups that comprised both women and men.[222] Their activities

---

219. VBWA MM, BUVA.

220. Wilcox, *South Australia Baptist Women's League*, 1.

221. See, for example, Rowland, *Century of the English Church in NSW*. Rowland does not reference any women's organizations and does not have a reference for "women" in the index. In *Methodism in Australia*, Anne O'Brien's chapter on women includes reference to the Women's Auxiliary for Methodist Foreign Missions and Deaconess Order, yet the roles these organizations played in the wider denomination are not detailed. The state chapters largely ignore women's organizations except for David Hilliard's chapter on SA Methodist history. He incorporates women's organizations seamlessly. See O'Brien and Carey, *Methodism in Australia*, 209, 220.

222. See, for example, Hone, "A Word for Senior Endeavour," *TGL*, 1 September 1894, 17; Walton, "In Memoriam: Tasmania," *TSB*, 10 February 1903, 47.

were an important part of the denomination in initiating and managing the burgeoning Baptist social service agencies.[223]

After 1945 the women's organizations continued for around twenty years with little change. From the 1960s, partly due to social change in Australia, Baptist women were not as interested in joining and fostering exclusively women's organizations, and consequently memberships declined. In 1967, as the NSW SGMU was being wound up, 180 women held a "reunion dinner" to celebrate highlights and achievements, particularly with respect to the funds raised for Baptist mission activities and the fellowship provided by annual camps.[224] Perhaps one can consider that these achievements broadly reflect the legacy of all foreign and home mission women's organizations. They provided a mechanism to foster shared aims, and created a place for women to meet, work, and worship together, thus deepening their Christian faith and giving enriched meaning to their lives.

---

223. West, *Daughters of Freedom*, 253; Kelshaw, *BaptistCare*, 9.
224. SGMUNSW, *Reunion Dinner*.

5

Women's Ordination, Leadership, and Writing

> A friend ... wrote this in my autograph book, "Faithfulness in littles is by no means a little thing." Who wants to do little things, thought I! That advice is far too cramping ... [yet] in God's plan for your life and mine, the littles count up into greatness.[1]
>
> —Adelaide Bamford

INTRODUCTION

ADELAIDE BAMFORD WAS NEARLY forty-five years old when she commenced writing a weekly column in *The Australian Baptist*. Prior to this she had been active in the NSW Baptist denomination through singing and speaking at Baptist services and events, and preaching at country congregations that were part of her father's pastorate around Wellington.[2] Yet her writing makes it clear that she felt "called" to do more.[3] Adelaide Bamford and the other women documented in this chapter are examples of Australian women whose Baptist ministries were influential. Some of this work was in leadership or public ministry roles, or writing, tasks they performed with skill and

---

1. Bamford, *Sunlit Road*, 13, 15.
2. Bamford, "Letter to the Editor: Women in the Ministry," *TAB*, 16 November 1960, 11.
3. Bamford, "One Woman to Another (OWTA): 'Commit, Trust, He Worketh,'" *TAB*, 11 July 1939, 7.

vitality. Baptist women confronted the explicit and implicit gender barriers that existed within the denomination to enable their voices to be heard.

Women's roles in leadership and public ministry challenge the narrow stereotypes of Baptist women. Yet there is evidence of women speaking or writing about their faith, or other religious themes, in every Australian state.

ORDINATION

Until the mid-twentieth century most Australian Baptists, along with most other mainstream Christians worldwide, considered that women had ministry roles distinct from men, a major difference being that women should not undertake roles ministering to men or leading a congregation.[4] In 1894 Emily Hone expressed this outlook, writing: "We always depended on men taking the lead, and, I think, none of the women dared to take any part aside from singing, unless the brothers were all absent."[5] Emily Hone wrote this in the past tense, intimating that she—and other women—had reconsidered this position. In Australia exclusion of women from the ordained Baptist ministry was by assumption rather than specific rules. There were no ordained Australian Baptist women ministers until the Rev. Dr Marita Munro was ordained in Victoria in 1978, and it was not until 6 March 2025 that all Australian states had ordained women ministers when the Rev. Karen Haynes was ordained in Queensland.[6] However prior to this some women were able to preach and to serve in leadership positions. Some women were eager to work in the denomination through these means. Their belief in the priesthood of all believers and a desire for activism were, after all, tenets of their evangelical Baptist faith.[7]

One of the impediments to ordination of Baptist women ministers was the structural nature of the denomination. Those "called" to the ministry were usually supported by their congregation, to gain relevant experience, and the Baptist colleges, to undertake theological training. Australian Baptists did not establish a pathway for women to feel supported or secure in seeking ordination, through either of these avenues. Consequently women who may have felt called to the pastoral ministry pursued other paths and

4. Bebbington, *Baptists Through the Centuries*, 158. From the late twentieth century this is referred to as the complementarian view, but this was not a description used before 1945.

5. Hone, "A Word for Senior Endeavour," *TGL*, 1 September 1894, 17.

6. "Air Force Chaplain Makes History." The Queensland Baptist Assembly voted to allow women's ordination in May 2024, the final Australian state to do so.

7. In the twenty-first century there is evidence that some Australian Baptist congregations would not consider calling a woman minister.

remained silent about their calling. In 1941 in England the Rev. Violet Hedger, one of the first Baptist women ministers, affirmed that for women "the urge to use one's powers in this holy service [of Christian ministry] is not enough, unless the Call be reinforced by the Call of a Church . . . There is a tragedy in the lack of encouragement here."[8] Of course, missionary women described their calling to mission and, for many Baptist women, this calling was able to be fulfilled, either overseas or in Australia. Whether any of these missionary women might have pursued ministry in Australia—if this had been a possible path—is unknown. There is no conclusive evidence that women left the Baptist denomination because they were unable to pursue their calling to pastoral ministry.[9] However some Baptist women who preached, including Emilia Baeyetz, Adey Janes, and Margaret Vernon, worked with different evangelical churches. Whether this was a choice or a necessity is unknown.

By comparison, in England in the early 1920s the Rev. Edith Gates, the Rev. Maria Living-Taylor, and the Rev. Violet Hedger were the first three women ordained to the Baptist ministry.[10] Discussion among women in the UK regarding women's ministry had occurred prior to this, particularly when the merits of women preaching during the First World War had been debated by the Church of England. Katherine Rose, a member of the English Baptist Women's League—and an Australian Baptist minister's wife between 1899 and 1904—said that "nothing had so entirely shown the State Church to be obsolete as the recent division concerning the status of women in the National Mission. The State Church had shown herself to be hopelessly mediaeval and out of date."[11] In 1918 Edith Gates commenced her ministry in the pastorate of Little Tew and Cleveley, Oxfordshire, although she was not ordained until she completed the Baptist Union requirements in 1922.[12] Maria Living-Taylor was ordained in 1920, when she was called as the joint minister with her husband the Rev. John Living-Taylor to Linton Road Baptist, Barking, near London.[13] These Baptist congregations called the women to enter into ministry despite the fact they were not ordained at that time. Violet Hedger was the first woman to receive ministry training in an English theological training facility, and was encouraged by Dr

---

8. Hedger, "Some Experiences of a Woman Minister," 5.

9. West, *Daughters of Freedom*, 143, 253.

10. Gouldbourne, "Baptists, Women, and Ministry."

11. "Personal," *TAB*, 21 November 1916, 3.

12. As part of the English Baptist Union's guidelines for ordination, probationer ministers were required to pass Baptist Union Examinations before ordination.

13. Gouldbourne, "Baptists, Women, and Ministry."

George Pearce Gould, then principal of Regent's Park College, London. She undertook the same entrance process as that of her male colleagues. Before her graduation Dr Henry Wheeler Robinson became principal and refused to pay the five pounds for Violet Hedger's final examination fees, as was common practice for all students. He did not think she would pass her examinations or work as a minister.[14] In 1990, on Violet Hedger's ninetieth birthday, Dr. Deborah Rooke, then a first-year student at Regent's Park College, gave Violet Hedger a framed apology from the College and a cheque for £5 affirming the ministry of women and celebrating Violet Hedger's ministry. Violet Hedger appreciated the gesture, although she did not cash the cheque.[15] Despite the fact that the three women were ordained by their respective congregations and fulfilled the requirements of ordination set by the relevant Baptist Unions, they were not included in the "List of ministers" in the annual Baptist handbooks; instead they were identified separately as "Women Pastors."[16]

The reasons why Baptist women in England were ordained earlier than women in Australia are worthy of further investigation. Possibly Baptists in England retained more of a non-conformist flavor in that many congregations deviated from cultural norms, including those regarding the roles of women. In contrast, the imported Baptist denomination in Australia was more aligned with other denominations, including the Anglican Church, and operated within the patriarchal culture that socially limited women's roles.[17] The Baptist denomination followed the pattern of the large mainstream Australian denominations, most of which did not ordain women until late in the twentieth century.

Baptist congregations in the USA were more likely to take the approach of Australian Baptists, where women were recognized for their invaluable ministries but were not ordained. However some Baptists were open to ordaining women and the first known ordination of a woman was the Rev. M. A. Brennan in 1876. There were many other women in active ministry from this time.[18] In the Southern Baptist Convention (SBC), the largest Baptist group in the USA, the Rev. Addie Davis was the first woman to be ordained, and this occurred in 1964. Historian Elizabeth Flowers

14. Hedger, "Some Experiences of a Woman Minister."
15. Deborah Rooke, email to Rebecca Hilton, 10 November 2020.
16. See, for example, BUGBI, *Baptist Handbook for 1927*, 290.
17. Of course, English society was also patriarchal, but because the Baptist denomination remained somewhat apart from other Protestant denominations and cultures, the patriarchal structure was probably less of an issue for Baptists in England than it was in Australia.
18. Durso, "Baptist Women Ministers."

concludes that at the time her ordination was downplayed because SBC officials and the women leaders of the SBC's Baptist Women's League did not want to draw attention to her ordination. The SBC leaders—men—did not want to openly reprimand a congregation for calling a woman to ministry, given the Baptist distinctive of religious liberty, and the women did not want to jeopardize their tenuous position and power in the SBC through the Baptist Women's League.[19] While there has been a small number of women ordained in congregations in the SBC, into the twenty-first century the SBC does not support women's ordination. The issue remains contentious, has divided congregations, and people have left the SBC because of the policy.[20] Other Baptist Unions in North America, such as the American Baptist Churches USA, ordain women.[21]

Australian Baptist women were aware of other women who held leadership positions in churches in the first half of the twentieth century, such as women officers in the Salvation Army or Catherine Spence in the Unitarian Church; indeed Catherine Spence refers to several Baptist women in her diary and letters.[22] However Catherine Spence and Salvation Army Officers were in relatively small denominations. In 1927 the Rev. Winifred Keik was the first woman ordained by SA Congregationalists, one of the larger denominations. Eight women were ordained by the Australian Congregationalists before 1945.[23] Australian Baptist women knew of Winifred Keik, as she addressed various Baptist groups, particularly the SA Baptist Women's League.[24] So why did Baptists, who shared the independent structure of the Congregationalist denomination, not have women seeking ordination? One possibility is that Winifred Keik, as the wife of the Principal of the Congregational Theological College, and supported by the newly established Colonel Light Gardens Congregational Church, was well-positioned to seek ordination: she had access to tertiary theological training, and she was supported by a congregation. Other women followed because they could see ordination was achievable.[25] There was no such precedent in the Baptist denomination.

19. Bebbington, *Baptists Through the Centuries*, 173; Flowers, *Into the Pulpit*, 27.
20. Flowers, *Into the Pulpit*, 192; Barr, *Making of Biblical Womanhood*, 3.
21. Durso, "Baptist Women Ministers."
22. "Baptist Union of New South Wales: Assembly Meetings at Lithgow," *TAB*, 20 April 1915, 4. The report of this event in NSW records the representatives of various denominations and names them, except for "the lady Captain of the Salvation Army." Spence, *Ever Yours*, 316.
23. Pitman, *Our Principle of Sex Equality*, 174–201.
24. Wilcox, *Baptist Women's League*, 18.
25. Pitman, *Our Principle of Sex Equality*, 10.

Given that women were being ordained by some English and North American Baptists and in some Australian denominations, it is likely that Australian Baptist women discussed the ordination of women from the 1920s, although such discussions were not recorded in minutes of women's meetings. An article by an unnamed author in *The Australian Baptist* in 1920 was critical of the Anglican Church in England rejecting the notion that women could be ordained. The author suggested that some women were called to ministry but that: "Women will, therefore, continue to devote themselves to the age-long task of training up Bishops and Deans and Rectors during the nursery stages, knowing that later on their divine instincts will be repudiated by men whom they have nursed and fed."[26]

In 1928 the Baptist Union of Victoria changed its constitution to allow women to be ordained. The Rev. Richard Dobbinson raised the issue because he believed proposed revisions of the Constitution needed to account for the possibility of women ministers. *The Australian Baptist* reported that "a notable addition to the constitution was made under the heading 'Ordination of Ministers,' in so far that any lady qualifying herself for the ministry could be ordained. By this vote it was made possible for women to enter the Baptist ministry in Victoria."[27] *The Argus* wrote about the event in a somewhat different way, reporting there had been much laughter regarding the insertion of the clause to allow ordination of women, indeed: "Despite the protest of one delegate [presumably Richard Dobbinson], members of the Baptist Assembly refused to be serious when it was pointed out yesterday that no provision had been made in the new constitution for the ordination of women to the ministry."[28]

Given that the first ordination of a woman in Victoria occurred fifty years after this event, perhaps it took those fifty years for the laughter to subside, and for women to be seriously considered for the ministry. In 1928 Australian Baptist theological colleges did not accept women to undertake training for the ministry.[29] In addition any women wanting to be a minister of a Baptist congregation needed to be "called" by the congregation, and it is

26. "Convocation and Corinth," *TAB*, 4 May 1920, 6. The article was not attributed to anyone, suggesting it was written by an editor of *Australian Baptist*.

27. "Victorian Annual Assembly: Evangelism and Home Missions: Admission of Women to the Ministry," *TAB*, 6 November 1928, 3.

28. "Baptist Ministry: Women Eligible for Ordination," *Argus*, 26 October 1928, 10; Hilton, "Women in the Australian Baptist Denomination."

29. Otzen, *Whitley*, 47; Eldridge, *For the Highest*, 35, 102; Condie, "Views of Queensland Baptists," 94; Queensland Baptist College Committee, Minute Book, BUQA. The Baptist theological colleges located in Brisbane, Melbourne, and Sydney each accepted only one woman student before 1945. These women were not accepted for ministry training, rather for mission or "other Christian work."

likely that only a small number of congregations would have been willing to consider appointing a woman as their minister.

In 1931 the Rev. William Hurst, a Queensland Baptist minister, was not aware of any woman seeking ordination, although he "did not see why women should be shut out of the ministry just because they were women ... We have never had an offer here [from a woman in Queensland] so I do not know what would be our attitude."[30] This was not entirely true as in 1911—prior to William Hurst's arrival in Australia—Mary Dixon, from Maryborough Baptist, was successful in the entrance examination for the Queensland Baptist Theological College.[31] It is not clear whether she was seeking training for the ministry, but the Queensland College Committee "encouraged" her to study for missionary or other Christian work.[32] Mary Dixon did not complete her theological training and no reasons were given for her withdrawal. Despite this she was "ever willing to help" Maryborough Baptist.[33] To 1945 no Australian Baptist women appear to have sought ordination through official channels.

It is interesting that when the question of women's ordination was raised in the 1960s, several people wrote to the editor of *The Australian Baptist* to express their opinions. Adelaide Bamford's letter against women's ordination was published, in part declaring: "For a period of eight years this writer ministered to a Church by taking a monthly Sunday morning service in a district where there were few lay preachers. This experience taught the lesson: as a *temporary* measure women could be used successfully in the ministry during a 'drought' time."[34] The position taken by Adelaide Bamford is somewhat incongruous. In 1939 her writing indicated that she felt called to work—minister—within the denomination. She wrote: "My own path had been unsettled, and though my prayers were for a wider and greater sphere of services, it seemed impossible from my limited human viewpoint ... [I was] content to trust [God's] guidance. Then in a totally unexpected way [God] worked the miracle."[35] One assumes that her "miracle" is that she was able to serve the denomination through her writing and her regular

---

30. "Women Ministers: Should They Be Ordained," *Daily Mercury* (Mackay, Queensland), 15 October 1931, 11.

31. "Maryborough District," *Brisbane Courier* (Brisbane), 19 December 1912, 8.

32. Queensland Baptist College Committee, Minute Book, BUQA; Condie, "Views of Queensland Baptists," 94.

33. "Maryborough Baptist Church Social," *Maryborough Chronicle, Wide Bay and Burnett Advertiser* (Maryborough, Queensland) 1946, 6.

34. Bamford, "Letter to the Editor: Women in the Ministry," *TAB*, 16 November 1960, 11. Bold is as published.

35. Bamford, "OWTA," *TAB*, 11 July 1939, 7.

preaching. Indeed it is difficult to fathom why Adelaide Bamford held a position against women's ordination, given her work and that she sought a "greater sphere."

Almost certainly there were Baptist women who wanted to apply their calling and skills in ministry work, and for those roles to be recognized through ordination. Yet such explicit reference to callings are absent from the records. One conclusion is that such Australian Baptist women were so driven by an evangelical activist mentality that they were willing to undertake whatever roles were available to them, either within or outside the denomination. For some a calling to ministry became a calling to mission. Although there is a lack of evidence, it seems that some Australian Baptist women, like women in most mainstream Australian denominations and Baptist women in the SBC, did not want to pursue new or controversial roles—particularly ordination—if there was a risk that the opportunities then available to them would be curtailed.[36]

WOMEN WORKING IN BAPTIST ORGANIZATIONS

Until 1945 the Australian Baptist denomination had few paid positions for women. Only 163 women have been identified as working in paid positions, and this includes the one hundred women who worked for the Australian Baptist missions. The ABFM also employed some women in administrative positions in Australia. For instance, from 1934 to 1954 Clara Crump worked for the ABFM in Melbourne, initially as assistant to the General Secretary, and from 1939 was responsible for the ABFM book depot and managed the other female office workers.[37] Presumably there were some other paid positions held by women as clerical assistants either for large congregations or state unions. Certainly there is evidence of women undertaking such roles on a voluntary basis.[38]

The Baptist theological training facilities employed some women—predominantly in catering or cleaning roles—but there is no complete record of the names of these women. Given that few women received ministry training at Baptist theological training facilities until 1945, it is somewhat ironic that from 1907 to 1941 one of the Victorian Baptist College teachers was a woman, albeit a Methodist, rather than a Baptist woman. Florence Sims was the first woman to be awarded a Bachelor of Divinity

---

36. Flowers, *Into the Pulpit*, 28.

37. Cupit et al., *From Five Barley Loaves*, 191. Other women who worked for the ABFM with Clara Crump have not been identified.

38. Manley, *Swayed by Life's Storms*.

from Melbourne College of Divinity and she was employed to teach Greek, on the basis that language was not a theological subject.[39] In addition from 1937 to 1946 there was a group of eight women who tutored prospective male students at the NSW Baptist Theological College: Mary Bowie; Irene Doust; Heather Drummond; Ruth Gladwin; Elsa Lowe; Florence Small; Alice Smith; and "Miss" Hayden—first name not known.[40] The 1945 Annual Report of the Baptist Union of NSW included a report of the College stating: "No word of praise would adequately express the appreciation of the Board when it considers the work being done by the Tutors under the guidance of the Supervisor of Studies, Mrs J. J. [Mary] Bowie, BA."[41] These women have, nevertheless, been ignored and omitted from histories of the College.[42] The women were unpaid for their tutoring, yet they provided their services at a time when the College was struggling to find competent tutors to assist students.

PAID DEACONESSES

While Australian Baptist women were not ordained until 1978, several women undertook pastoral ministry work in Baptist congregations. While only thirty-two women in this category have been identified, their work is important to document within the history of the Australian Baptist denomination.[43] In many cases, women in paid positions undertook the same roles as ordained ministers. Their title and their gender were the only differences between their roles and those of ordained ministers.

Australian Baptist women in paid positions were engaged in a haphazard manner in each of the states, perhaps reflecting their anomalous position. While most of the paid women workers were referred to as "deaconesses," this was also a title given to unpaid elected positions in congregations. Other titles were used: in the early twentieth century Stanmore Baptist NSW, employed a "Bible Woman"; from 1909 to 1919 Launceston Baptist Tasmania, supported a "Church visitor"; and in the 1930s and 1940s women employed by the Baptist Union of SA were referred to as "Sisters"

---

39. Otzen, *Whitley*, 48, 87. Further discussion on theological training for women follows below.

40. Coe, Mary Louisa Bowie née Grey.

41. BUNSW, *Annual Report*, 57.

42. There is no mention of this work or the women in the history of the College or the biography of George Morling, who was the Principal of the College at the time of the women's work. The subjects they tutored are also unknown. See Rogers, *George Henry Morling*; Eldridge, *History of Morling College*.

43. See Hayward, "Baptist Deaconesses," 2.

or "home mission workers."[44] By the 1930s most states applied the term deaconess, and women in this section are referred to as paid deaconesses.

In 1936 Edith Wilcox described the paid deaconess position as: "Women for the most part, who, hearing the call of Christ to serve upon the Home Mission field, are willing to give their time and talents to the smaller churches or other spheres of service in the homeland, much on the lines of overseas mission service."[45] Cecilia Downing articulated the difficulty of defining the work: "The term to be applied seemed to be rather obscure, whether a deaconess was a female deacon, a visitor only, or a member of a sisterhood for mission work and social service. Consideration will clarify the position."[46] Ultimately paid deaconesses performed various roles, such as preaching, visiting, building maintenance, and administration. They worked under diverse conditions, depending on the needs of the congregation and the skills of the worker. Only a small number of Australian Baptist congregations employed paid deaconesses, and they either supplemented the work of the minister or, in some cases, were effectively the minister. Evidence exists of paid deaconesses within Baptist congregations in all Australian states.

Paid deaconesses were less common and introduced at a later date in the Australian Baptist denomination compared to the UK, where the Deaconess Order of the Baptist Union of Great Britain and Ireland commenced in 1891.[47] This Deaconess Order came from an interdenominational appeal by the Rev. Frederick Meyers, a Baptist, and the Rev. Hugh Hughes, a Methodist, for women to enter into "cooperation" with men who already worked in "dark slums" in London.[48] The Baptist Deaconess Order was established for women who felt a "call . . . to serve the Church in any way her Lord shall choose."[49] The women undertook two years of training in the Women's Training College in London, in subjects including Biblical studies, Christian doctrine, church history, and homiletics—the art of the sermon.[50] Like other Protestant Orders, paid British Baptist deaconesses received low salaries, and their roles were not clearly defined, with their work ranging from

---

44. *Stanmore Baptist Church Year Book*, 10; Manley, *From Woolloomooloo*, 1:305.

45. Wilcox, "Concerning Deaconesses."

46. Cecilia Downing, "Baptist Women's Board," *TAB*, 15 September 1936, 5.

47. Baptist Deaconesses' Home and Mission, *Report of the Committee for the Year 1901*, 7, ALA.

48. Mrs. H. Rowntree [Harriett] Clifford, "The Baptist Deaconess," 2.

49. Baptist Women's Training Sisterhood Committee, *Grey Veil*, 11. Baptist Deaconesses wore a grey veil, hence the name of the book.

50. *Order of Baptist Deaconesses and Women's Training College*, 1.

fixing doors to preaching.⁵¹ Some deaconesses sought ordination. This was problematic as while deaconesses were supported financially by the Baptist Deaconesses Order, ordained ministers were not, so newly ordained women needed a congregation to call them to ministry and financially support them. Unfortunately some women left the ministry because of the lack of available ministry positions for women: there was a limited number of congregations willing to ordain women.⁵² The Deaconess Order continued until 1975, when the remaining deaconesses were offered ordination as Baptist ministers.⁵³ These ordinations warrant the conclusion that paid deaconesses were Baptist ministers for all intents and purposes. The Rev. Margaret Jarman, a leading English Baptist who worked as a deaconess before being ordained in 1967, wrote: "When is a minister not a minister? . . . When they are a Deaconess."⁵⁴

In Australia the larger denominations, notably the Catholics, Anglicans, and Methodists, established opportunities for paid work for women through various religious orders or groups.⁵⁵ Catholic orders were established much earlier than other denominations and were significantly larger than Protestant orders. In 1838 five Catholic nuns from the Sisters of Charity arrived from Ireland and established Australia's first women's order called the Sisters of the Good Samaritan. Indeed prior to the mid-twentieth century a large proportion of Australian nuns were migrants from Ireland. Other Catholic orders in the colonies were established in the nineteenth century, the most significant being the Sisters of St Joseph of the Sacred Heart, whose co-founder, Mary MacKillop, was canonized in 2010.⁵⁶ In 1880 over 800 nuns worked around Australia, and by 1945 there were over 10,000 nuns. Although there were some closed orders, where the nuns

---

51. Baptist Women's Training Sisterhood Committee, *Grey Veil*, 12, 18.

52. Aylward, "Order of Baptist Deaconesses."

53. Women in the Ministry: Facts and Figures, 1986, The Baptist Union of Great Britain and Ireland, London, ALA. Not all the deaconesses in 1975 chose to be ordained. Some women resigned from the Deaconesses Order rather than become ordained Baptist ministers.

54. Aylward, "Order of Baptist Deaconesses." Margaret Jarman visited Australia in 1968. She was the second woman and first woman minister to be President of the Baptist Union of Great Britain and Ireland.

55. Champness, *Servant Ministry*, 28; Henderson, *Mary MacKillop's Sisters*, 9; O'Brien, *God's Willing Workers*, 97–99; O'Brien and Carey, *Methodism in Australia*, 219; Piggin and Linder, *Fountain of Public Prosperity*, 502–4. For more information on deaconesses, see Hilton, "Evangelical Deaconess Orders in Australia."

56. Franklin, "Women in the Australian Church."

separated themselves from society, most of the work of Catholic nuns was undertaken in schools and hospitals.[57]

The first Australian Protestant orders were not established until the 1880s when Anglican clergy in NSW discussed women's ministry. They formed a society for deaconesses based at Deaconess House, Sydney, which was a training facility established in 1891. Between 1901 and 1915 only fifteen deaconesses were appointed but the society continued throughout the twentieth century.[58] Anglicans established a small deaconess order in Victoria and later in other states.[59] Methodist Orders were larger than the Anglican activities and by 1915 one-hundred women worked as deaconesses throughout Australia. Initially in 1891 a Methodist Order called "Sisters of the People" commenced in NSW because Laura Francis threatened to leave the denomination if she was not employed, and during the 1890s further orders were established in most colonies, based on Hugh Hughes's West London mission.[60] Australian women in Protestant orders—much like Catholic orders—worked mainly in hospitals, schools, and social welfare provisions.

In all orders, nuns and deaconesses identified seem to have encountered various recurring issues, including poor working conditions, a lack of clarity in roles, and their activities being regarded as significantly less important than equivalent tasks undertaken by men.[61] Women's duties in the orders were invariably at the behest of men, and many women found this situation difficult.[62] Their main roles were teaching, nursing, or assisting poor women and children. Accordingly most deaconesses did not have opportunities for preaching or public speaking. As Anne O'Brien observes, "professionalism formalised their marginalisation."[63] And what of the salary for these important roles that deaconesses were undertaking? In the case of Australian Baptists, "paid deaconesses" received between one third to a half the salary of a Baptist minister.[64]

---

57. Franklin, "Women in the Australian Church."
58. Piggin and Linder, *Fountain of Public Prosperity*, 502.
59. O'Brien, *God's Willing Workers*, 97.
60. O'Brien and Carey, *Methodism in Australia*, 219.
61. George, *That They Which See*, 14; O'Brien and Carey, *Methodism in Australia*, 219-20.
62. Champness, *Servant Ministry*, 28, 31.
63. O'Brien, "Australian Methodist Women," 219. This outcome was similar to what occurred in the British Baptist Deaconess Order.
64. "Deaconess Wanted," *TAB*, 13 March 1917, 10. The salary for a deaconess was up to £91 per annum and an Australian Baptist minister's salary was around £250 per annum.

Only Baptists in NSW adopted a formal deaconess order, and it was operational from 1917 until 1925, with six paid deaconesses being engaged. In September 1917 the Baptist Union of NSW agreed that paid deaconesses be employed to undertake home mission work with management by the NSW home mission organization. Emma Dixson donated funds to pay for the deaconesses' first year of salary and the cost of uniforms, with ongoing salaries to be paid by congregations.[65] The focus on deaconesses led to a name change of the women's organization to Baptist Women's Home Mission Deaconess Association but this was not a long-term change, and in January 1925 the name again changed to the Baptist Women's Home Mission Association and no further deaconess appointments were made by the organization.[66] The Baptist Women's Deaconess Association in NSW was created and controlled by women, whereas other deaconess societies, including the British Baptist Deaconess Order, were largely established and managed by men.[67] Women's management of the NSW Deaconess Association was not a factor in its short existence. The evidence suggests that it struggled for various reasons, including unclear roles, the small number of suitable applicants, uncertain ongoing funding, and few Baptist congregations being prepared to financially support paid deaconesses. Yet, with the support of the NSW Deaconess Association, these six women in NSW ministered to Baptists through their roles as paid deaconesses.

In September 1917 three women—Jean Allen, Catherine Phillips and Bertha Jarrett—had already been appointed to work as paid deaconesses.[68] Jean Allen worked for the Newcastle Baptist Tabernacle, NSW, and later the Rockhampton Baptist Tabernacle, Queensland, but did not attend the Association's meetings. Both Catherine Phillips and Bertha Jarrett spoke at the initial meeting to garner support for the establishment of a Deaconess Association.[69] Catherine Phillips was the aforementioned Biblewoman at Stanmore Baptist.[70] She had been married twice—both husbands had been Baptist ministers—and possibly she worked because her second husband was unable to work. Stanmore Baptist may have chosen to support her,

65. Slinn, "A Deaconess' Association," *TAB*, 2 October 1917, 6.
66. "N. S. Wales Annual Assembly: Home Mission Day," *TAB*, 8 October 1918, 6.
67. Baptist Deaconesses' Home and Mission, *Report of the Committee for the Year 1901*, ALA. The Committee had a mixture of men and women, but all executive positions were held by men. In 1940 the Deaconesses formed a Council consisting of deaconesses.
68. Although to that point the women were not consistently referred to as deaconesses.
69. Slinn, "A Deaconess' Association," *TAB*, 2 October 1917, 6.
70. *Stanmore Baptist Church Year Book*, 10.

being aware of these circumstances. Bertha Jarrett was another paid deaconess—usually called "Sister Bertha"—who worked from 1907 until 1919 for three different Baptist congregations at Wellington and Parramatta in NSW, and the Brisbane Tabernacle in Queensland, before taking up work for the non-denominational Sydney City Mission. There is no evidence to determine whether her preference was to continue working for the Baptist denomination; however she remained an active member of Cronulla Baptist until her death in 1964.[71]

By the end of 1917 three additional women—Emily Pocknall, Eva Stark, and Lillian Wilkins—were engaged as paid deaconesses. Reports about the work of the deaconesses were encouraging, although there was no reference in *The Australian Baptist* regarding the departure of Lillian Wilkins. In 1924 Lillias Slinn, the Secretary of the NSW Deaconess Association, effectively acknowledged that the work was not as successful as first envisaged, when she wrote: "Should any of our people know of a scheme that will mean a larger and greater influence in the women's share of the Home Mission work, we shall be only too happy to learn of it or accept any suggestions for the more effective working of Home Mission interests in our churches."[72]

Despite a subsequent article in *The Australian Baptist* by English deaconess Harriett Clifford promoting deaconess work in NSW, the Society did not engage any additional women.[73]

In Queensland the only Baptist congregation that appears to have engaged paid deaconesses on a long-term basis was the Brisbane Tabernacle. Over the period from 1911 to 1945 five different deaconesses served the congregation. The deaconesses were expected to have "some training"—not specified—and experience, and to undertake a wide variety of tasks, including preaching where required.

The first appointment at the Brisbane Tabernacle was Ethel Butters in 1911. She had undertaken missionary training in Melbourne, and her parents were members of the congregation. She served until 1916 and "her work in connection with the City Tabernacle [was] quite a feature . . . She [was] a fluent and interesting speaker."[74] Bertha Jarrett was the second appointment, working in the congregation from 1916 to 1919 before returning

---

71. "Cronulla," *TAB*, 15 July 1964, 14.

72. "New South Wales: Baptist Deaconesses' Association," *TAB*, 15 January 1924, 4.

73. Mrs. H. Rowntree [Harriett] Clifford, "The Vocation of the Deaconess," *TAB*, 11 November 1924, 5–6.

74. "The Churches: Gympie Baptist Church," *Gympie Times and Mary River Mining Gazette* (Gympie, Queensland), 22 August 1914, 6.

to Sydney.[75] Mary Abbott was the third appointment. She had trained in Melbourne with Ethel Butters before working as a missionary woman for PIVM.[76] She was the Brisbane Tabernacle deaconess for nineteen years. Ethel Cronau, widow of the Rev. Christian Cronau, was the fourth deaconess appointed.[77] She had been a missionary in Solomon Islands, where she met and married her husband. They had returned to Australia and he had been the minister of four regional Queensland Baptist congregations, and two Baptist congregations in Sydney, before his death. Ethel Cronau worked as deaconess from 1939 to 1942.[78] In 1943 Ethel Butters returned to the position.[79] Frances Aldridge, the widow of the Rev. Frank Aldridge, was the fifth woman appointed and served as deaconess from 1944 to 1966.[80] Thus between 1911 and 1945 deaconesses appointed by the Brisbane Tabernacle either had been trained as missionaries or were the widows of Baptist ministers. The Brisbane Tabernacle deaconesses worked predominantly at the Tabernacle but visited other Baptist congregations, generally to address women's meetings. There is evidence that some preached at Sunday worship services when required.[81] The 2005 history of the Brisbane Tabernacle devotes only slightly more attention to the deaconesses than it does to the organ. Indeed a separate history on the organ was written, whereas the work of the paid deaconesses is largely undocumented.[82]

Other Queensland Baptist congregations engaged paid deaconesses, but these appointments were short-term. In 1911 the Rockhampton congregation appointed Jean Allen, called Sister Allen. Her role was described as "deaconess and district visitor."[83] At the annual meeting of the congregation Jean Allen presented an effusive report in which she stated that: "Praise is

75. "Personal Pars," *Wellington Times* (Wellington, NSW), 24 April 1919, 4.

76. "Churchill Baptist Women," *Queensland Times* (Ipswich, Queensland), 17 October 1936, 7.

77. "City Tabernacle Deaconess," *Telegraph*, 4 March 1939, 7. Ironically in 1939 the advertisement for the position of deaconess at the Brisbane Tabernacle was on the same page as Christian Cronau's obituary.

78. "Lockyer District: Blenheim," *Queensland Times*, 18 September 1940, 3.

79. Ball, *Grow the Vision*, 33. It is evident by the wording in the history of the Brisbane City Tabernacle that Leslie Ball did not recognize that Ethel Hiron and "E. Butters" were the same person. Ethel Butters had married and been widowed between her initial service in 1911 and her later service in 1943.

80. Parker, *Women Who Made a Difference*, 37.

81. "The Churches: Gympie Baptist Church," *Gympie Times and Mary River Mining Gazette*, 22 August 1914, 6.

82. Parker, *Pressing on with the Gospel*, 32–34; Ball, *Grow the Vision*; Hughes, *Centenary of the City*.

83. "Rockhampton," *TQB*, 1 April 1911, 62.

given to God for the privilege of ministering to the sick and dying."[84] However despite this she remained in Rockhampton for only a year. In 1920 the newly established Greenslopes Baptist congregation was supported by Emily Smith, called Sister Grace.[85] Emily Smith was a former missionary with Australian Inland Mission and lived in the Greenslopes area with her parents. In the early 1920s she was employed by the Queensland Baptist Home Mission, who sought "men of the very best stamp" while acknowledging that "Sister Grace [was] rendering good service."[86] Emily Smith appears to have only been a paid employee in the early 1920s, as the "first minister [was] officially appointed in 1924."[87] She continued to provide services to the congregation until 1955. For all intents and purposes Emily Smith was the first minister of Greenslopes Baptist, and her 1925 report of the work demonstrated the roles she undertook, including "conducting meetings, visiting the sick, and the 200 homes of our Sunday school scholars, inviting people to church services, and enlisting new members for the CE Societies, Sunday school and Cradle Roll Department, Women's Guild, and WCTU."[88] Emily Smith's extensive work to establish and maintain the congregation is recognized through a stone tablet at the entrance to Greenslopes Baptist.[89] The 2020 centenary history of Greenslopes Baptist mentions "Miss E. Smith (Sister Grace)" as a church visitor and the first foundation member, but does not credit her role in establishing the congregation, especially in comparison to some work by the men involved in its establishment.[90] Emily Smith's history and ministry has been minimized, perhaps because her ministry role did not fit within expectations of women in the Queensland Baptist denomination.

During the 1930s Victorian Baptist women attempted to establish a Deaconess Order but were unsuccessful. Some women were engaged, including Emily Pocknall, who later moved to Sydney, although they were called "sisters" rather than deaconesses.[91] However the Victorian denomination appears to have relied on unpaid workers, such as Margaret Bean (called "Sister Grace") and "Sister" Margaret Vernon.[92] These women under-

84. "Baptist Church Anniversary," *Morning Bulletin* (Rockhampton, Qld), 2 June 1911, 8.

85. Parker, *Women Who Made a Difference*, 30–32.

86. Benjamin Hewison, "Concerning Home Missions," *TQB*, 15 March 1925, 6.

87. "Sister Grace of Greenslopes (Qld)," *TAB*, 9 September 1964, 9.

88. Smith, "Deeds at Dunellan," *TQB*, 15 November 1925, 11.

89. Parker, *Women Who Made a Difference*, 30.

90. Young, *Greenslopes Baptist Church*, 4.

91. Lillias Slinn, "The Late Miss Pocknall: Sister Emily," *TAB*, 30 December 1924, 4.

92. While information is available about the work of Margaret Vernon, very little personal information can be found about her.

took a range of different roles, including some evangelistic and ministerial activities.[93] As their work was concentrated in inner Melbourne, most of the workers appear to have not undertaken regular preaching, with the exceptions of Margaret Vernon and Alice Skeels, whose roles as an evangelist and minister respectively are discussed below.

In Tasmania Mary Lamb and Margaret Vernon were the only women known to have been employed by a Baptist congregation prior to 1945. Mary Lamb was active in Launceston Baptist from the turn of the century, until her death from influenza in 1919. Mary Lamb's work for the congregation included organising church activities, and she preached on numerous occasions in Launceston and in other Tasmanian congregations.[94] The Launceston congregation did not have a minister during 1909, and a report stated: "So far the Church seems to have suffered but little from not having a pastor, probably owing to the esteemed and incessant labours of the Church visitor, Miss Lamb."[95] Mary Lamb served as a pastoral minister, and her obituary described her as a "ministering angel."[96] Margaret Vernon was appointed to the work following the death of Mary Lamb but she remained in Tasmania for less than two years.

In SA the Halifax Street Mission in Adelaide provided paid employment for one or two women from its commencement in 1891. While this was not strictly ministry work, Eleanor Koehncke worked for the mission for twenty-eight years undertaking "ministry among the poor."[97] SA Baptists discussed the establishment of a Deaconess Order in 1936 but, as in Victoria, it never formed. Instead women in SA, mainly through the Baptist Women's League, raised funds to employ "sisters" for pastoral ministry. In 1940 the League engaged Margaret Speck to work as "a leader" in various congregations.[98] She had previously volunteered her time, predominantly through work in CE.[99] Her work in Whyalla, four hundred kilometers northwest of Adelaide, was so successful that the congregation was able to employ a minister and at his ordination Margaret Speck was "thanked . . .

---

93. Doery, "WVP: Work among the Women at George Street, Fitzroy," *TAB*, 20 April 1915, 3.

94. "Bracknell," *Daily Telegraph* (Launceston, Tasmania), 23 March 1900, 4.

95. "The Launceston Church," *TSB*, 1 December 1909, 266.

96. "Ministering Angel Dead: Forty Years' Work in Slums," *World* (Hobart), 19 September 1919, 7.

97. "Flinders Street, Adelaide," *TAB*, 4 January 1916, 12.

98. Wilcox, *South Australia Baptist Women's League*.

99. "Endeavorers' Day at Brighton Baptist Church," *Glenelg Guardian* (Glenelg, SA), 5 April 1933, 4.

for her work for the church up to the time [the new minister] arrived."[100] In 1941 the Baptist Union engaged Florence Hogan and Myrtle Stribling to undertake home mission work six hundred kilometres west of Adelaide, called the Mount Cooper Circuit. Baptist Union officials were reluctant to appoint them, as the preference was for a man to undertake the work, "but they went there and made good with self-sacrifice and devotion."[101] The women lived in the Port Kenny Baptist manse, conducted worship services in four different locations, were accredited by the Baptist Union of SA to undertake marriages, officiated at funeral services, and described themselves as "acting pastors."[102] They successfully continued in this role for twelve years until Myrtle Stribling resigned to marry, and Florence Hogan returned to Adelaide to work at the Baptist West End Mission. Florence Hogan's move was the decision of Baptist Union officials who did not believe she was able to continue working in Port Kenny on her own.[103] Florence Hogan and Myrtle Stribling were not "acting" but were Baptist pastors—unordained ministers. Although highlighted by Gordon Crabb's 2020 history of the circuit, the women's roles as ministers remain largely undocumented. In 1941 Florence Hogan and Myrtle Stribling were engaged because of a lack of men available for the position. Their continued employment suggests they were accepted by the members of the congregations in the Mount Cooper Circuit.

Alice Skeels was another woman who undertook ministry work in various Baptist congregations. From the late 1890s until 1919 "Sister" Alice Skeels established and led Baptist congregations at Ariah Park, Mimosa, Marrar, and Temora in regional NSW, and Traralgon and Warracknabeal in Victoria. She was described as "a wonderful preacher."[104] She was also a "splendid horsewoman," which was a necessary skill as often she rode fifty kilometres on Sundays to preach at different congregations in the area.[105] In 1914 she was attacked by a man while traveling near Marrar, in regional NSW: she managed to escape after he tried to throw a rug over her.[106] An article in *The Southern Baptist* stated that Alice Skeels undertook her

---

100. "Forward Step by Baptists," *Whyalla News* (Whyalla, SA), 29 August 1941, 3.

101. "South Australian Notes: Sister F. Hogan," *TAB*, 5 October 1960, 5. During this period there were fewer men available for pastoral work because of the Second World War.

102. L. Morris et al., "Letter to the Editor: Social Behaviour," *West Coast Sentinel* (Streaky Bay, SA), 16 April 1943, 2.

103. Crabb, *Mount Cooper Baptist Circuit*, 156.

104. "Small Country Church Closes in NSW," *TAB*, 15 March 1985, 1.

105. "Baptist Union," *Age*, 22 November 1907, 7.

106. "Woman Attacked: Struggle in the Dark," *Argus*, 22 June 1914, 11.

Wimmera work "through the liberality of the South Wimmera district."[107] This wording implies that Baptist officials were being generous in allowing her to undertake the work, rather than an affirmation of her ministry and that she was fulfilling a position that may well have been vacant without her. In any case, she received half the salary of a man engaged in home mission.[108]

Alice Skeels ceased her work in 1919 when she was required to nurse her dying mother. Potentially the necessity of having to leave this ministry work was part of her motivation for later establishing aged care facilities. Alice Skeels's view on ordination is unknown, but her funeral notice inserted by her adopted daughter concluded: "She walks with God. He'll understand."[109] These sentences allude to a strong faith, and perhaps the frustration of being unable to serve as she felt called.

The ministry of the women described above—along with others—is not well-known. Yet they ensured the establishment and maintenance of several Australian Baptist congregations.

PREACHERS

Many women preached and led services in Baptist congregations on an ad hoc basis. Most Baptists accepted some women preaching in certain circumstances, although such acceptance was explicitly not extended to ordination.[110] Between 1880 and 1945 over forty-five Australian women—including Adelaide Bamford, Florence Hogan, Alice Skeels, Emily Smith, and Myrtle Stribling—are known to have preached in Australian Baptist congregations, in all Australian states. In addition most Australian Baptist missionary women preached to Australian congregations to promote their mission work.[111] Well-known women from England and North America toured Australia and preached to Baptist congregations, particularly on the subject of temperance such as: Scottish woman Harriett Warne from 1859, who then migrated to Victoria; Englishwoman Margaret Hampson in 1883; and Scottish woman Helen Barton in 1916.[112] Reports of many of the

---

107. "Women's Work," *TSB*, 15 January 1907, 13.

108. "Home Mission Notes: Salaries," *TSB*, 12 February 1907, 41.

109. "Family Notices: Deaths," *Gippsland Times* (Sale, Victoria), 17 October 1961.

110. "South Australian Baptist Association," *South Australian Advertiser*, 30 September 1884, 5. At this meeting in 1884 South Australian Baptist ministers concluded that it was acceptable for women to publicly pray, lead, and preach. See Briggs, "She-Preachers, Widows and Other Women," 337.

111. Hilton, "ABW Database."

112. "Temperance Meeting," Bendigo Advertiser (Bendigo, Vic), 21 May 1859, 1;

sermons delivered by women observed that they were effective speakers.[113] However few of the sermons preached by any of the women are extant.[114]

The second Sunday in May, Mother's Day, was a common time for women, particularly ministers' wives, to preach in various congregations. For example, Stella Churchward Kelly, a minister's wife and former missionary, regularly preached on Mother's Day.[115] On 13 May 1945 five of the fourteen Baptist congregations in Perth had women preaching for Mother's Day: three ministers' wives—Lillian Redshaw, Ella Stark, and Edith Hall—and two missionary women—Thora Parker, a Baptist woman in the South Sea Evangelical Mission, and Florence Freeth, an Anglican woman in the London Missionary Society.[116] This "regularity" suggests that perhaps some women let their husbands know that their best Mother's Day gift was to preach, or perhaps ministers were acknowledging that these women were subject specialists.

In some instances when women spoke in Sunday services their messages were downplayed as "addresses" or "connective remarks," as opposed to preaching or leading the service.[117] A 1928 article in *The Australian Baptist* remarked that Alice Barber "was the speaker" at a Sandringham Baptist service, whereas on the same page of the paper the report on Ringwood Baptist described two men as "preachers" despite them not being ordained.[118] It is likely that some Baptist congregations did not accept women preaching or speaking in any circumstances, but these congregations were largely silent, and the views of Baptist officials on preaching by women were not discussed in denominational meetings.[119] Australian Baptist women's preaching was just downplayed. Retrospectively—even into the twenty-first

---

"Notes for the Month," *TP*, 1 August 1883, 6; "Church Notes," *Barrier Miner* (Broken Hill, NSW), 28 October 1916.

113. "Notes for the Month," *TP*, 1 August 1883, 86; "Two Lady Missionaries," *Western Mail*, 24 February 1900, 28.

114. In SA John Walker also noted there were few unpublished sermons by both men and women, see Walker, "Baptists in South Australia." One exception was Edith Wilcox. See Wilcox, *Rainbow of Hope*; "Concerning Deaconesses."

115. "Mother's Day Observance: Devonport," *Advocate*, 15 May 1944, 2.

116. "Advertising," *TWA*, 12 May 1945, 10.

117. "Baptist," *Western Mail* (Perth), 2 March 1901, 65.

118. "South Australia: Sandringham," *TAB*, 7 August 1928, 14.

119. See, for example, Flinders Street Baptist Church MM, SABA; Ballarat Baptist Church, Church MM, BUVA. None of the minutes from these congregations discussed women preaching.

century—most Baptists ignore preaching undertaken by women in this earlier period.[120]

Women addressed state and national Baptist Union meetings, and most meetings had a presentation from a woman. Most commonly the speakers were Baptist missionary women, although other women spoke, including ministers' wives and women who had tertiary education, particularly as doctors, which by the nature of their work represented a level of leadership.[121] In 1908 the first Australasian Baptist Congress was held in Sydney.[122] The two official delegates from WA were women and the state's welcome speech was somewhat patronisingly called "A Lady Speaks for WA."[123] The only two papers given by women were part of the overseas mission discussion.[124] Given that women made up a significant proportion of missionaries in the ABFM, this was deemed appropriate. In 1911 the second Australasian Baptist Congress was held in Melbourne and a separate meeting for women was held, which coincided with a session for men on denominational management.[125] Separate arrangements such as this appear to have been common at state union meetings.[126] Although men did not attend these sessions for women, those women's meetings resulted in Australian Baptist women hearing the views and theologies of other Baptist women. In 1938 Edmund Jenkin, the President of the Baptist Union of Australia, commented that he thought it was a shame that men did not attend the sessions

---

120. Manley, *From Woolloomooloo*, 1:303–4; Walker, "Baptists in South Australia," 152–54; Petras, "Across the Frontier," 112. Manley does not address women preachers in this period except to note the work of Deaconesses and Biblewomen. Likewise John Walker does not refer to the question of women preaching, instead listing the various reasons why SA Baptists did not ordain women. Michael Petras concludes that "there is no evidence [women] were ever regular lay preachers." Yet reported information contradicts this conclusion.

121. Gertrude Mead, "Medical Missions," *WA Baptist* (Perth), 15 April 1907, 75; Potter, "Baptist Union of Victoria," *TAB*, 23 May 1944, 4.

122. Packer, *First Australasian Baptist Congress*, 9. Seventy-six official delegates attended, of whom four were women (and forty-one were male ministers), although other men and women attended the meeting in an unofficial capacity.

123. Packer, *First Australasian Baptist Congress*, 31.

124. Lucie Thompson, "India's Need"; Bertha Tuck, "The Problem of a Great Opportunity," in Packer, *First Australasian Baptist Congress*, 111–19.

125. *Souvenir of the Second Australasian Baptist Congress*. There were eighty-three official delegates, six of whom were women.

126. "South Australian Baptist Union Annual Assembly," *TAB*, 6 October 1936, 9. In 1936 the first session of the Baptist Union of SA Assembly consisted of two separate meetings: The women held a meeting of the Baptist Women's League and the men held the business meeting.

for women, as the issues discussed were relevant to all Baptists.[127] Likewise although some women may have welcomed the opportunities to attend the business sessions, separate meeting arrangements did not change in most state denominational meetings until later in the twentieth century.[128]

EVANGELISTS

Exactly what is an evangelist? The *Oxford Dictionary of the Christian Church* defines an evangelist as a "proclaimer of the gospel," contending that modern usage applies the term to those who "undertake popular preaching."[129] Most Baptist history scholarship does not explicitly define the term. In 1937 Escourt Hughes used the word to describe people, not always ordained ministers, who spoke "ardently" to a congregation, or engaged in outreach activities that were designed to elicit conversions and adherents to Baptist congregations: To "put some heart" into individuals.[130] Eleven women have been identified who were explicitly described as evangelists within the Australian Baptist denomination to 1945. Yet in analyzing Baptist women's work there emerge many other examples of Australian Baptist women who were evangelists if a broader interpretation is applied.

In 1900 the Baptist Union of WA paid for Ellen Harris to undertake a year's study in Melbourne for evangelistic work. A Perth newspaper reported that Ellen Harris was "trained with a special view to home mission work, either as a church missionary or in a still more public capacity as a lady evangelist."[131] Clearly WA Baptists were prepared to recognize the talents of a woman as an evangelist, and encourage and financially support her training, although their Baptist Union was small, isolated, and had limited funds.[132] From 1901 until at least 1907 Ellen Harris undertook evangelistic work in WA. Her activities from 1907 until her death in 1946 are undocumented and, despite her work being mentioned, she is not in the index of Richard Moore's history of Baptists in WA.[133]

127. Edmund Henry Jenkin, "Melbourne, 1938: Fourth Triennial Assembly, Baptist Union of Australia," *TAB*, 5 July 1938, 1.

128. "Baptist Union of New South Wales: 105th Annual Assembly," *TAB*, 11 April 1973, 15. The 1973 annual Baptist Union of NSW Assembly had a separate women's meeting, but this was not held during the business session.

129. "Evangelist," in Cross and Livingstone, *Oxford Dictionary of the Christian Church*.

130. Hughes, *Our First Hundred Years*, 78, 94.

131. "Two Lady Missionaries," *Western Mail*, 24 February 1900, 28.

132. Moore, *All Western Australia*, 25.

133. Moore, *All Western Australia*, 69. In an unindexed reference Moore writes:

There are other cases of Baptist state unions employing Baptist women to undertake evangelistic work. From August 1881 until January 1884 the Baptist Union of SA engaged Emilia Baeyertz for evangelistic work, and she preached in SA Baptist congregations.[134] Several of her addresses were published, which enables her distinct evangelistic voice to be assessed. She sought to deepen Christian beliefs, and particularly focused on the importance of conversion to Christianity.[135] From 1898 to 1924 Ada Kennedy undertook evangelistic work with her husband in regional WA.[136] In 1906 and 1907 sisters Adey Janes and Minnie Thomas were engaged by the BUV to undertake evangelistic work in regional areas of Victoria. Their "evangelistic meetings" combined "the Gospel in song and story," and they were described as "gracious, gifted women."[137] Minnie Thomas married, and Adey Janes continued her work as an evangelist for organizations outside the Baptist denomination.[138] Like other Baptist women, Adey Janes was committed to converting any non-Christian Australian, writing:

> Shall they see Jesus? Souls in darkness lying
> Have waited long for shining of the light.
> We who are dwelling in the Gospel sunshine,
> May, by its rays, dispel their darksome night.[139]

Other Australian Baptist women were described in various sources as evangelists including Elizabeth Eustace, Annie Green, and Margaret Vernon. The evangelistic work of these women was undertaken both within and outside the denomination. It appears that Baptist women evangelists had more opportunities outside the denomination than within, although this may be related to the reporting of women's evangelistic work. Elizabeth Eustace migrated to Australia in 1897 with her husband the Rev. Arthur Eustace, and after his death in 1903 she embarked on evangelistic work. While it is possible she undertook this work for financial security, it is more likely that her evangelical Baptist beliefs compelled her to engage in the work,

---

"For several weeks Miss Harris of Ewlyamartup (east of Katanning) supplied the pulpit at Woodanilling."

134. Evans, *Emilia Baeyertz Evangelist*, 22–23.

135. Baeyertz, "Six New Addresses," 20.

136. "West Australian Baptist Union: Half-Yearly Meetings," *TSB* 1898, 175. She was probably not paid for this work as her husband was a Baptist minister.

137. "The Gospel in Song and Story," *TSB*, 16 May 1906, 117. Isabella Adey Janes was sometimes incorrectly referred to as Isabella Adey Jones.

138. "Evangelistic Services," *Ballarat Star* (Ballarat, Victoria), 31 July 1906, 6.

139. I. Adey Janes, "Pilgrimage Jottings," *Australian Aborigines* [sic] *Advocate* (Sydney), 31 July 1924, 3.

initially as a missionary with a non-denominational mission to Pacific Islanders, many of whom had been coerced to come and work in Australia, and then in Brisbane.[140] In the late 1890s Annie Green undertook evangelistic activities in SA with Wesleyan Ruth McDowell, including in several Baptist congregations. Southwark Baptist wrote that they "cannot speak too highly of the evangelists' efforts."[141] In the 1920s Margaret Vernon was engaged as an evangelist in Baptist congregations in Tasmania, Queensland, and NSW.[142] The evangelistic ministries of these women were welcomed by Baptist congregations. Yet the success of the Baptist women evangelists did not lead to other women being encouraged to train as evangelists, nor to any women seeking ordination.

The best-known women evangelists in the Baptist denomination were Louisa Ardill and Emilia Baeyertz, although for both women identifying them as Baptists is debatable. From the early 1880s until her death in 1920 Louisa Ardill was known through her work in social welfare, particularly in NSW. Louisa Ardill worked as an evangelist before and during her marriage. A WCTU report observed that: "As an evangelist, also, Mrs Ardill does excellent service."[143] While Louisa Ardill attended worship services at Parramatta Baptist there is no evidence that she was a *member* of a Baptist congregation. Similarly, while Emilia Baeyertz, a Jewish woman, was baptized in 1875 in Geelong Baptist, she is not known to have become a member of a Baptist congregation despite her associations.[144] Even if Louisa Ardill and Emilia Baeyertz were not in Baptist membership, they both influenced many Australian Baptist women and men.[145] They are examples of how Baptist identity was sometimes difficult to ascribe to women whose work was largely outside the denomination. It is likely that for both Louisa Ardill and Emilia Baeyertz—as with many evangelical women—a denominational label was not important.

The Baptist women evangelists identified were for the most part engaged in the Baptist denomination for a short period of time. Baptist

---

140. "Petrie Terrace," *TQB*, 1 April 1905, 60. She worked for the Queensland Kanaka Mission. The term "Kanaka" is an offensive description that has not been used since the mid-twentieth century.

141. "Southwark," *TP*, 20 July 1893, 219.

142. "Dinmore Baptists' Revival," *Queensland Times* (Ipswich, Queensland), 10 July 1926, 8.

143. "Women's [sic] Christian Temperance Union," *Daily Telegraph* (Sydney), 21 September 1895, 9.

144. "Report of the Annual Meetings of the South Australian Baptist Association," *TP*, 1 October 1880, 120.

145. Mrs W. [Emily] Brown, "Our Baptist Veterans," *TAB*, 9 December 1930, 2.

congregations and the state Baptist unions did not have funding to engage evangelists on an ongoing basis, and where there were long-term paid opportunities, these were offered to men.[146] None of these women documented their experiences as evangelists. Methodist evangelist and women's advocate, Serena Lake, wrote that she received hate mail and sometimes doubted her choice to work instead of caring for her parents.[147] Possibly Baptist women encountered similar issues.

There were three additional groups of women who worked as evangelists, comprising: missionary women who spoke to Australian women's groups; women in leadership positions in women's organizations, including Baptist women's organizations; and women who undertook social welfare tasks and spoke to people about the Christian message. Generally reports did not describe women who spoke in these positions as evangelists. The main reasons were that most articles were written by men, and Australian Baptists took a narrow view of what constituted an evangelist.[148] Yet the work that these women undertook must be seen as legitimate evangelistic activity. Therefore a list of Australian Baptist women evangelists must include Adelaide Bamford, Lilian Brown, Elizabeth Dovey, Cecilia Downing, Lily Higlett, Ada Kennedy, Margaret McLean, and Edith Wilcox. These women regularly spoke to large numbers of people—mainly women—about issues they passionately believed in, and their beliefs stemmed from their Baptist faith. For instance, in 1900 Elizabeth Dovey spoke at the Ashfield WCTU meeting on "the Seven Fold Characters of a Christian Worker."[149] She was still speaking at meetings in 1933, and Susan Davey described Elizabeth Dovey's "helpful and heartfelt talk on our 'Christian Assets' . . . pointing out how many opportunities of service are within the reach of all of us."[150] Many Australian Baptist women were evangelists, with their audience largely being women.

From the late 1930s Australian Baptist congregations struggled to maintain membership, with most states adopting a variety of methods to increase membership, including engaging evangelists from within and outside the Baptist denomination.[151] Yet there is no evidence that state unions considered deploying Baptist women evangelists. Many Baptist

---

146. Prior, *Some Fell on Good Ground*, 243–44.

147. O'Brien and Carey, *Methodism in Australia*, 218.

148. Beth Barr argues that definitions of preaching have been narrowed to discount women's ministries. See Barr, *Making of Biblical Womanhood*, 150, 213.

149. Woman's Christian Temperance Union in Ashfield NSW MM, SLNSW.

150. Sarah Davey, "New South Wales: Ladies' Zenana Society," *TAB*, 5 September 1933, 11.

151. Manley, *From Woolloomooloo*, 1:466, 470.

women were described as good speakers at various forums, but often such pronouncements implied surprise that women were skilled speakers. As an example, Lilian Brown was described as having "confidence as a platform speaker which many of her hearers envied and proving that she had at least many of the charms of oratory."[152] In reality training in verbal communication or the art of preaching—rhetoric and homiletics—was not available to most women. Some congregations encouraged women to develop verbal communication skills, but this was not common.[153] Apart from missionary women there are few examples within the Baptist denomination of a woman being supported and trained for evangelistic service.

Through evangelism, speeches, and occasional preaching, women's voices were heard in Australian Baptist congregations. Their work was not generally considered significant, and ordination of women was not legitimately supported, due to reluctance by both men and women to challenge the status quo.

CHRISTIAN ENDEAVOR (CE)

From the mid 1880s many Australian Baptist women were members of CE societies, which were established within many Australian Baptist congregations.[154] CE commenced in Portland USA in 1881 when a group of young people met with their pastor, the Rev. Francis Clark, and adopted the title Young People's Society of Christian Endeavor.[155] Members signed a pledge and agreed to the motto "For Christ and the Church." Other nearby congregations established their own CE societies, which joined together to form CE unions. In the early twentieth century CE was one of the most well-known worldwide evangelical inter-denominational organizations.

From the mid 1880s CE grew in Australia and was enthusiastically adopted by Baptists, Methodists, Congregationalists, and other evangelicals.[156] Baptist CE societies joined with CE societies from other evangelical

---

152. "Christian Endeavour Convention: Stirring Addresses," *SMH*, 18 September 1896, 5.

153. See, for example, "Girls' Literary Association," *Evening Journal* (Adelaide), 9 February 1884, 4; "Baptist Girls' Guild," *Geelong Advertiser* (Geelong, Vic), 11 September 1908, 6.

154. As Christian Endeavor commenced in the United States the worldwide organization used this spelling, but Australian societies used the Anglicized spelling. This book uses USA spelling but does not change the spelling of materials referenced.

155. Bush and Kerrison, *First Fifty Years*.

156. Wilkin, *Baptists in Victoria*, 156; Gomm, *Soul of the Society*, 1. See also "Directory," *TRC*, 1 November 1943, 64. There were small numbers of CE societies in

congregations and formed local, state, and national CE unions. CE was an important component of many congregations, and it was used to educate and engage non-Christian children and young adults through regular meetings that included Christian teaching. CE enabled Australian Baptist women and men to undertake activities that furthered both Baptist and Australian religious life.[157]

CE provided opportunities for women to be in fellowship and take leadership roles within their congregations. In 1888 the third Australian CE society was established at Flinders Street Baptist.[158] In 1890 a photograph was taken of the members, and the membership illustrated women's involvement, with nineteen of the twenty-six members being women. Six women in the group were well-known by other Australian Baptists, particularly for their work in mission: Bertha Tuck and Anne Summers worked in the ABFM; Jane Middleton undertook missionary training, although poor health prevented her from being accepted as a missionary; Eleanor Koehncke and Ada Tapson worked for Flinders Street Baptist as city missionaries in Adelaide; and Blanche Wilson was the daughter of the Rev. Silas Mead, the sister of missionary Dr Cecil Mead, and a minister's wife, and involved in ABFM mission support.[159] In 1894 the editor of the CE paper, *The Golden Link*, supported women's participation wholeheartedly:

> Question: Is it right for women to testify at Endeavour meetings?
> Answer: It is too late in the day to trouble about this question. They do it, and God has wonderfully blessed them in every testimony that they have borne.[160]

Thus from the beginning of CE in Australia, mission was a key component and women's participation was expected and accepted.

Women's leadership roles in their local congregation's CE society are documented in many Baptist congregations. In 1903 the CE society of Barraport Baptist took the service, and two of the four leaders were women

---

Anglican, Church of Christ, and Presbyterian congregations.

157. See, for example, "Christian Endeavour Convention: Stirring Addresses," *SMH*, 18 September 1896, 5; "Christian Endeavour: The Junior Demonstration," *TWA*, 15 October 1928, 15; Maxwell, *Triumphant Through Trials*, 14, 23; Chambers, *Centenary of Christian Endeavour in Australia*, 75.

158. Chambers, *Centenary of Christian Endeavour in Australia*, 48. In 1883 the first CE Society was a group of young women at the Hope Street Church of Christ in Geelong. In 1888 the second group was established at Wharf Street Baptist in Brisbane.

159. In addition to the roles of the women, two of the seven men later undertook mission work.

160. "Answers to Correspondents," *TGL*, 1 September 1894, 17.

("Miss [Louise] Genat, Miss E. [Elsie] Tudball").[161] Likewise in 1932 at Cabramatta Baptist the CE Society organized the Mother's Day service, undertaken by five women and two men. Caroline Steel was the "leader" of their CE Society.[162] Many other women were involved in executive positions in their congregation's CE society. In the late 1890s Blanche Wilson was President of the Perth Baptist CE and Grace Brown was secretary.[163] In 1926 fifteen-year-old Esma Venn was elected Secretary of the Junior CE at Newcastle Baptist Tabernacle.[164] Thelma Howard, who left school at thirteen in order to financially assist her family, believed that CE had given her important training in running meetings, which she felt was essential for her work as a minister's wife.[165] Many Baptist women continued to be involved with CE throughout their lives, including Esma Venn and Thelma Howard, who led her congregation's CE group until the age of seventy-seven.[166] Similarly Anna White's obituary declared that as she aged she considered giving up the work but because she "felt the power of [young people's] appeal, she felt she must keep on as long as she could manage it."[167] Many other Baptist women undertook leadership roles and obtained valuable experience within their local congregation's CE group. CE provided leadership opportunities for women that were otherwise unavailable.

Australian Baptist women were also involved in CE outside the Baptist denomination.[168] CE distributed publications, held annual conventions that addressed major issues, and took up social causes. Baptist women became involved in other organizations and causes, particularly mission, due to their initial involvement with CE. In the late nineteenth century in NSW Margaret Long, the founder of the Aboriginal Inland Mission (AIM), became involved in mission through a local CE union, and in the early years of her AIM activities provided regular updates through the CE paper, *The Roll Call*.[169] In the 1930s in Queensland the Baptist CE Societies in Brisbane congregations agreed to support a Brisbane city missionary, with the work being supervised

---

161. "Christian Endeavour: Barrapoort [sic]," *TSB*, 27 January 1903, 36.

162. "Mother's Day," *Biz* (Fairfield, NSW), 13 May 1932, 4.

163. Perth Baptist Christian Endeavour Society," *Western Mail* (Perth), 8 October 1904, 23; "Church News," *Western Mail* (Perth), 22 July 1898, 45.

164. Esma Durbin, "Letter to the Children's Page," *TAB* 1926, 12.

165. Maxwell, *Triumphant Through Trials*, 23.

166. Maxwell, *Triumphant Through Trials*, 54.

167. "Death of Mrs. William White," *TAB*, 1 July 1919, 3.

168. Manley, *From Woolloomooloo*, 1:167.

169. See, for example, Retta Dixon, "A Missionary Tour amongst the Aborigines [sic] Scattered along the South Coast," *TRC*, 1 March 1899, 211–13; Retta (Mrs L. W.) Long, "Christmas Gifts for the Aborigines [sic]," *TRC*, 1 February 1915, 132–33.

by Esther Malyon and Elsie Martin.[170] Likewise in SA, Margaret Speck was state superintendent of CE prior to becoming a paid worker.[171] Many ABFM workers and other missionary women were members of CE.[172]

CE encouraged and enabled women to undertake leadership roles in the formal structure of the unions. In 1891 Julia Stuckey, a Congregationalist and the first Secretary of the SA CE Union, was quoted as saying that CE members "ignored the question of sex in the Society. It was the best institution she knew of for Church work."[173] Allowing women to hold executive positions was unusual at that time, although no women were appointed to the position of state president of the CE unions. Several Australian Baptist women were elected to executive positions of CE societies within their congregations, and in the regional or state CE unions.[174]

In 1896 in NSW the Maitland paper printed an account of a CE union meeting and the author observed that: "A pleasing feature in the reports [from the local CE groups] was that the majority of the secretaries were ladies, who showed that they more than held their own with the gentlemen holding similar offices." Unusually Helen Harry's speech at this meeting was highlighted in the article, rather than speeches by the men who addressed the meeting.[175] From 1894 to 1897 Helen Harry was on the executive committee of the NSW CE Union and spoke at many CE meetings.[176] She was committed to CE as a vehicle for young people, and she stressed that young people in CE demonstrated "persistent work for Jesus Christ" and she was "sure that we are doing much for the future of our country by fostering among the young a goodness that is not superficial and a piety that is not fickle."[177] She was assisted by Anna White, who affirmed: "No one should take up this

---

170. B. H., "Random Reflections from Queensland: A Lady of Grace," *TAB*, 3 February 1931, 3.

171. "Endeavorers' Day at Brighton Baptist Church," *Glenelg Guardian* (Glenelg, SA), 5 April 1933, 4.

172. Hilton, "ABW Database."

173. "Half-Yearly Meetings of the Baptist Association," *TP* 1891, 52.

174. See, for example, "The Christian Endeavour Union," *Maitland Daily Mercury* (Newcastle, NSW), 24 January 1896, 3; "Death of Mrs. William White," *TAB*, 1 July 1919, 3; "Christian Endeavour: The Junior Demonstration," *TWA*, 15 October 1928, 15; Maxwell, *Triumphant Through Trials*, 14–15.

175. "The Christian Endeavour Union," *Maitland Daily Mercury*, 24 January 1896, 3.

176. "Christian Endeavour Convention," *Australian Star* (Sydney), 8 September 1894, 3; "Christian Endeavour Convention: Stirring Addresses," *SMH*, 18 September 1896, 5.

177. Harry, "The Juniors," *TRC*, 1 January 1898, 8.

work unless prepared to give their very best to it."[178] From 1897 to 1906 the NSW CE paper, *The Roll Call*, had a photograph on its front page—called the "Portrait Page"—and while most individual photographs were of men, several NSW Baptist women were featured because of their work in the state or local CE unions, including Helen Harry and Anna White, along with Lily Ardill, Mary Foucar, A. Hutson, and Mildred Tinsley.[179]

During the 1890s sisters Lilian Brown and Blanche Wilson were on the executive committee of the SA CE Union and actively worked to expand the membership of CE.[180] In 1896 Lilian Brown presented a paper on "Literature" at the Australian CE Convention in Sydney, and said that "She had a hobby, and she had been asked to speak of her hobby, which was Christian Endeavour literature."[181] Given the openness of CE to women's work, it is surprising Lilian Brown described CE literature as a hobby—an activity undertaken in one's free time—rather than her calling or her ministry. In 1897 Lilian Brown spoke at a session of the World CE Convention in San Francisco on "The world's prayer chain."[182] Francis Clark, the founder of CE, claimed that the prayer chain was an "important feature of CE societies."[183] The prayer chain allowed all members of the CE society to participate in prayer, and thus was another mechanism through which women were involved in the meetings.[184]

In the early twentieth century, there are many example of women's continued to be involvement in CE. In 1928 Marjorie Hendry, superintendent of the junior work in the WA CE, organized the Junior Demonstration at the Australasian CE Convention.[185] In Queensland Esther Malyon was coordinator for the Taringa Baptist CE society, and from 1916 to 1930 she was the Intermediate Superintendent for CE in Queensland.[186] CE continued as an

178. "Death of Mrs. William White," *TAB*, 1 July 1919, 3; Mrs. Wm. [Anna] White, "Junior CE Methods," *TRC*, 1 December 1899, 126–27.

179. See *TRC*, 1897–1905.

180. "South Australian Union Young People's Societies of Christian Endeavour," *Christian Colonist* (Adelaide), 27 November 1891, 3; "Rally of Christian Endeavourers," *South Australian Register* (Adelaide), 28 December 1896, 6.

181. "Christian Endeavour Convention: Stirring Addresses," *SMH*, 18 September 1896, 5.

182. "Church Intelligence," *Express and Telegraph* (Adelaide), 17 September 1897, 2.

183. Clark, *Christian Endeavor Manual*, 74.

184. Clark, *Christian Endeavor Manual*, 74.

185. "Christian Endeavour: The Junior Demonstration," *TWA*, 15 October 1928, 15.

186. H., "Random Reflections from Queensland: A Lady of Grace," *TAB*, 3 February 1931, 3.

influential feature of Baptist congregations, although after 1945 its popularity gradually diminished.[187]

Despite many women having formal roles in Australian CE, historical scholarship on CE does not explicitly describe the leadership opportunities for women.[188] Potentially this omission occurred because the most expansive history of CE was written in 1938, while a 1983 history was a pamphlet.[189] Neither publication deemed it necessary to specifically address the issue of women's roles, although Murray Chambers commented in the 1983 Australian CE history that the organization was "years ahead of its time in its emphasis on participation."[190] The role of CE in enabling women to be involved in religious activities was important and women's ministries were a significant reason CE was so successful. Yet the initial openness of CE did not translate to a willingness to extend opportunities to women to fill broader CE leadership positions. Indeed, the opposite occurred. As CE became more established in congregations and Australian religious life, women continued to be involved within the CE of a congregation but appear to have been less involved in the management and leadership of CE unions. This phenomenon can be seen in the above examples, where women were part of the establishment of the societies in the late nineteenth and early twentieth centuries, but became less involved in the 1930s and 1940s, particularly in executive positions.[191]

RELIGIOUS WRITERS

Baptist women's writings are an important source to understand their thoughts and convictions about Christian life, service, and identity, and have been used extensively throughout this book. Prior to 1880 only seven women's writings have been discovered. Five of these were from SA, being Lilian Brown, Matilda Evans, Mary Goode, Annie Mead, and Eliza Randall. The other two women were Victorian Amelia Wheeler and Tasmanian Mahala Clark. Further writings may be extant but privately held. In the

---

187. In the twenty-first century, Christian Endeavour Australia provides support to congregations for youth ministry. See https://www.ce.asn.au.

188. Bush and Kerrison, *First Fifty Years*; Chambers, *Centenary of Christian Endeavour in Australia*.

189. Bush and Kerrison, *First Fifty Years*; Chambers, *Centenary of Christian Endeavour in Australia*. The 1938 history celebrated fifty years of CE in Australia, but after this a Victorian congregation showed evidence that their CE group was established in 1883 and accordingly the centenary of CE was celebrated in 1983.

190. Chambers, *Centenary of Christian Endeavour in Australia*, 75.

191. See Hilton, "ABW Database."

nineteenth century Baptist denominational papers had few articles written by anyone other than ordained ministers or theologians from Britain or North America. So while women's writings were sparse, so were those of unordained Baptist men.[192] A balanced assessment of women's writing within Baptist denominational papers cannot be undertaken prior to 1880 because there were too few papers extant to analyze.[193] Yet in the period from 1880 and into the twentieth century there is a significant body of writing by women. Potentially some women were encouraged, or were more confident, in their ability to write about their religious beliefs rather than to seek approval to speak, although there are some addresses by women that were later published. Public and private extant religious writings from Australian Baptist women include articles, addresses, books, letters, and diaries.[194] Research for this book has analyzed over three hundred pieces of writing from over two hundred different Baptist women who wrote between 1880 and 1945.

It is evident that women made a significant contribution to Australian Baptist thought, particularly through their articles in denominational papers. While most of the extant writing of Australian Baptist women is by missionary women, nearly 120 women who were *not* overseas missionaries either wrote religious articles in Baptist denominational papers or published religious books. Often women's articles included a statement of identity, which situated the writer as a Baptist woman and provided justification for their published work.[195] The following account focuses on this work, although women's writings are also discussed in other sections of this book, including those who wrote in WCTU or CE papers.

In the late nineteenth century at least two women wrote articles for Baptist denominational papers about equality between men and women, using religious arguments. In 1892 two articles by Harriett Gillings—titled "Women's Ministry: Its legitimacy and power"—were published in *The Victorian Baptist* on women's roles in the church.[196] Harriet Gillings argued for

192. See, for example, "Index to 'Queensland Baptist,'" 1892, *TQB*, 1 December 1892, 179. The contributors during the year comprised: sixteen ordained men (most of whom were Australian Baptist ministers), eleven non-ordained men (only five of whom were Australian men), and seven women (two Australian women, both of whom were missionaries).

193. As chapter 1 discusses, Australian colonial Baptist papers were only published for a total of twenty-two years prior to 1880, and not all copies of these publications are extant.

194. Hilton, "ABW Database."

195. Hilton, "Australian Baptist Women as Public Intellectuals." See, for example, Miles, "Among Scottish Baptist Women," *TAB*, 2 April 1918, 4.

196. Mrs W. G. [Harriet] Gillings, "The Ministry of Women: Part 1," *TVB*, January

the equality of women and men in Baptist congregations and stated that both men and women were able to speak about Christian issues in public since "whether male or female, which same distinction is lost in Christ."[197] Yet Harriet Gillings was not advocating for women to be ordained or to have full equality in her articles. She simply wanted to ensure that women were able to speak at Baptist meetings. Subsequent editions of *The Victorian Baptist* did not contain letters to the editor denouncing the conclusions reached by Harriet Gillings as most Australian Baptists accepted women's participation in meetings.[198] In 1894, Fanny Brown's address to the Baptist Union of NSW on "Women's Work in the Church" was reprinted in the NSW denominational paper *The Baptist*. Fanny Brown argued that women should be "speaking for God and praying in public" and that women's work was broader than simply that which occurred within "the walls of the building."[199] Despite the strong language, whether Harriet Gillings and Fanny Brown believed in full equality of men and women—including ordination of women—cannot be determined.

Several Australian women wrote religious articles in the first half of the twentieth century, and many sought a greater role for women in religious life, or at least a wider range of roles women could undertake in the denomination. For example, in 1906 Marion Doyle's address to the Baptist Union of NSW emphasized that women are "to be [man's] equal."[200] Yet Marion Doyle reiterated that women's work in the home was essential: "Home . . . needs most the gentle influence of womanly patience."[201] In 1911 Cecilia Downing spoke to the Baptist Union of Victoria about "The Ministry of Women in the Church."[202] She observed that women in the Bible had ministered to others and that "the word 'minister' has somewhat departed from its original meaning of 'servant,' 'officer,' 'deacon,' or 'deaconess,' and has been exalted so that the serving has been rather lost sight of. It is to the original and scriptural use of the word that I shall refer—the idea of serving more or less actively in the Church."[203] Her focus, accordingly, applied a broad definition of minister to women's work, and she did not discuss—at least in the

---

1892, 16–17; Gillings, "Women's Ministry: Its legitimacy and Power: Part 2," *TVB*, February 1892, 26–27.

197. Gillings, "The Ministry of Women," *TVB*, January 1892, 16.

198. Wilson, *Constrained by Zeal*, 210–11.

199. Mrs Lewis [Fanny] Brown, "Women's Work in the Church," *Baptist* (Sydney), 3 November 1894, 174.

200. Mrs W. [Marion] Doyle, "Woman's Work," *Baptist* (Sydney), 1 October 1906, 4.

201. Doyle, "Woman's Work," *Baptist*, 1 October 1906, 4.

202. Downing, "The Ministry of Woman in the Church," *TAB*, 20 April 1911, 266.

203. Downing, "The Ministry of Woman in the Church," *TAB*, 20 April 1911, 266.

published version of her speech—women as preachers or ordained ministers. In 1929 Marion White wrote an article on "Character Building and Education," wanting more emphasis to be placed on religious education in the home, which was often undertaken by women, stating:

> Now, while I believe with all my soul that God can use the simplest and most ignorant of us, at times, to accomplish great things for Him, yet I do most earnestly assert that the culture of a trained mind is a most precious gift to lay upon the altar in consecration to God, and for that reason the "pursuit of knowledge" is encouraged in our home.[204]

In 1937 Gladys Lewis's published speech followed this theme but with slightly stronger language, extolling the virtues of women: "What Australian citizens of tomorrow will be, depends to an enormous extent upon what the mothers of Australian children are today. If they are good and pure and true, and teach their children the fear of the Lord, then the Australia of tomorrow will grow up strong and noble in the things that make for national well-being, because supremely through the women of Australia God's voice has been heard speaking."[205] Overall these women had broad views of the scope of women's work, yet were careful not to over-extend the boundaries of women's roles in the denomination—clearly a common pattern of advocacy by women event towards the mid-twentieth century.

Two significant women writers in Baptist denominational papers were Florence Benskin and Adelaide Bamford, who wrote regular columns in the SA Baptist paper, *The Baptist Record*, and *The Australian Baptist* respectively. Further examination of their work is outlined in a following case study. Adelaide Bamford also published two books of short messages, which can be read as religious instructions, or sermons. Her book titled *The Sunlit Road* was published by the Australian Baptist Publishing House and it provides further evidence of her "preaching" capacity and her considered Christian beliefs.[206] Adelaide Bamford used well-known themes such as the use of time, the definition of home, and the importance of undertaking regular family worship, and the Christian element she added drew on her life experiences. *The Sunlit Road* contains twenty-one messages and some of the themes have ongoing relevance. Her message titled "Stir up the gift" was about recognizing and using one's skills. She stressed that young people needed to be encouraged to develop their skills, because many people only

---

204. White, "Character Building and Education," *TAB*, 10 September 1929, 17. Marion White paraphrased a statement attributed to William Carey.

205. Lewis, *He Talked with a Woman*, 7–8.

206. Bamford, *Sunlit Road*; *Hills of Home*.

started using "the gift of God" as they aged and became more confident. She perceived: "An inferiority complex, fear of criticism, fear of failing, self-consciousness, pride, are some of the weaknesses which keep us from using 'the gift of God' within us . . . Never mind about what you have not; use what you have to the limit, and Christ will do the rest."[207] Adelaide Bamford may have believed that she had not used "the gift of God" as a young person given that she was forty-five years old when she started her column in *The Australian Baptist*, and fifty years old when she published her first book.

From 1933 to 1945 Victorian Stella Stafford published at least seven books with most being "specially written for the young," and comprising short messages in a similar format to Adelaide Bamford's.[208] Stella Stafford was a member of the well-known Victorian Baptist Harris family. Her father was the Rev. Edward Harris, and two uncles, her brother, and brother-in-law were Baptist ministers. An aunt, Elizabeth Whalley, was a known preacher, and a cousin, Bertha Harris, was an ABFM missionary. As a young woman she was Secretary of the Geelong Baptist Girls' Guild—led by her mother, Ruth Harris—that encouraged young women to develop spiritual and physical skills.[209] At one of their meetings Stella Stafford presented a paper titled "A Business Girl's New Year Endeavour."[210] Like other Baptist women's published material, Stella Stafford's books were evangelical in focus and tone. *The Path of Life* was first published in 1936 by the Keswick Book Depot, an evangelical organization. The book contained twenty-one chapters, each being a separate study backed by various Bible passages, with Stella Stafford affirming that the Bible was "the most wonderful book in all the world."[211] The aim of the book was to convert young people, "to show [her] readers their need of a Saviour, and to point them to the Lord Jesus."[212] Several chapters focused on salvation through the death of Jesus: "That Jesus Christ, God's son, came to this earth, and after living a life of perfect obedience, died for the sins of all."[213] Stella Stafford also implored her readers to be active in their faith, as they were "Saved to Serve."[214]

---

207. Bamford, *Sunlit Road*, 34.
208. See, for example, Stafford, *Path of Life*; *Best for All*.
209. "Geelong, Aberdeen Street," *TSB*, 16 June 1908, 146.
210. "Baptist Girls' Guild," *Geelong Advertiser*, 11 September 1908, 6. No information was given on the content of Stella Stafford's presentation.
211. Stafford, *Path of Life*, 45.
212. Stafford, *Path of Life*, 3.
213. Stafford, *Path of Life*, 21.
214. Stafford, *Path of Life*, 38, 41.

Baptist women also wrote obituaries or letters after the death of family members or friends containing strong Christian themes.[215] In 1887 Sarah Harlen wrote an obituary about her mother, Mary Warren, who "delighted to meet with God's people, and nothing but ill health ever kept her away from Church."[216] In 1902 Janet Webb's letter to friends was published after her husband's death, and stated that, while she was sad, she had faith in the sustaining love of God who "will give us strength for what lies before us."[217] Personal letters to relatives from Lilian Brown in 1909 and from Helen Harry in 1930 indicated their thanks for the Christian witness of their father and husband respectively.[218] In 1913 Ellen Cordiner wrote about the noble attributes of Margaret Ashworth, a former missionary and minister's wife, who died at the age of thirty-one: "In all these things my late friend was outstanding in her earnest perseverance and loyalty to principle and God. Bright as a comrade, yet possessed in a marked degree with the Holy Spirit's power, two very powerful agents."[219] Obituaries by women highlighted the importance that Baptist women placed on evangelical and Baptist beliefs and practices.

Women such as Susan Davey and Elizabeth Sturgess submitted reports of women's meetings for publication in *The Australian Baptist*.[220] Other reports of women's meetings were published in state denominational papers.[221] The women who wrote these reports were enthusiastic about their ability to work in the denomination.

Several Australian Baptist women managed children's columns in Baptist denominational papers. From 1903 to 1908 *The Southern Baptist* published a regular children's column from "Cousin Flora" whose identity, sadly, is unknown.[222] In England from about 1908 to 1927, the regular column for children in the English Baptist paper, the *Baptist Times*, was written by "Cousin Joyce"—identity unknown—who had lived in Australia, and her

---

215. See Hilton, "ABW Database."

216. Mrs John [Sarah] Harlen, "In Memoriam," *TQF*, 15 June 1887, 13.

217. Mrs [Janet] Webb, "A Letter from Mrs Webb," *Baptist* (Sydney), 1 May 1902, 9.

218. Brown, Letter; Harry, Letter.

219. Cordiner, "Personal: The Late Mrs. Ashworth, of Mosman, NSW," *TAB*, 11 March 1913, 4.

220. For example: Davey, "New South Wales: Ladies' Zenana Society meeting," *TAB*, 1 November 1938, 4; L. [Elizabeth] Sturgess, "New South Wales: Ladies' Zenana Society," *TAB*, 9 May 1939, 11.

221. For instance, Emily Griffiths, "To Those Interested in Mission Work," *TSB*, 3 January 1895, 11; Grace Taylor, "Zenana Society," *Baptist* (Sydney), 1 November 1900, 15.

222. Cousin Flora, "Boys and Girls," *TSB*, 30 June 1903, 152.

columns were often reprinted in *The Australian Baptist*.[223] In 1932 and 1933 another unknown woman wrote a regular column for women under the pen name "Felicity."[224] Women who wrote using pseudonyms was a common occurrence in this time period, but it is unfortunate that their identities are unknown. From 1939 to 1947 Lorna Lloyd was "Cousin Jill" for the children's column in *The Australian Baptist*.[225] Lorna Lloyd commenced her column for children when Adelaide Bamford began a column for women. In 2020 the author contacted Melody Markby, the granddaughter of Lorna Lloyd, who was initially unaware of Lorna Lloyd's published work—an unknown heritage.[226] Both Adelaide Bamford and Lorna Lloyd were the daughters of the then editor, the Rev. Frederick Dunkley.

Lorna Lloyd, c. 1940. Photo provided by Melody Markby; used with permission.

---

223. Cousin Joyce, "Uncle John's Corner: A School Captain's Motto," *TAB*, 12 April 1927, 11.

224. See, for example, Felicity, "For Our Women: Conducted by Felicity," *TAB*, 11 October 1932, 6; Felicity, "For Our Women: Conducted by Felicity: Train Them to be Competent Wives," *TAB*, 6 December 1932, 6.

225. Lorna Lloyd, "The Children's Page: Calling all Girls and Boys!" *TAB*, 11 April 1939, 9.

226. Melody Markby, email to Rebecca Hilton, 30 October 2020.

Many Australian Baptist women appear to have written religious poetry, some of which was published in both the denominational papers and books.[227] Marion Downes was a poet and novelist who volunteered to work as secretary for Samuel Chapman, then minister of Collins Street Baptist. He was the inspiration for one of the characters in her novel *Swayed by the Storm*, and she wrote a five-hundred-word poem on his death.[228] Hannah Fry's religious poems were published in the late nineteenth century. The subjects of the poems included deceased friends, memories of childhood, and temperance organizations.[229] Victorian Marion Tranter composed poems and short stories, some of which were published in denominational and local papers or in her book, *The Call of the Bush and Other Poems*.[230] She had well-known Baptist relatives: her grandfather and brother were Australian Baptist ministers, and her sister was an Australian Baptist missionary. Marion Tranter's poem on the anniversary of Bendigo Baptist Sunday School includes the lines:

> Let us faithful be in small things.
> Mighty trees from seedlings grow
> And the truths in child hearts
> planted in good time rich fruit will sow.[231]

Other women published books of religious poetry including Caroline Telfer and Lilian Wooster Greaves.[232] Most of these women's poetry were simple rhymes and some were written as hymns. Women viewed these poems as an effective way to convey religious messages.

Between 1859 and 1885 Matilda Evans published religious fiction using the pseudonym Maud Jeanne Franc. She was the widow of the Rev. Ephraim Evans, a Baptist minister. After the death of her husband SA Baptists provided financial assistance to enable her to establish a small school, and she taught and wrote books to support her own two children and two step-children from her husband's first marriage. She published fourteen

---

227. Some poetry by women is alluded to in various articles or is unpublished. See, for example, "Girls' Literary Association," *Evening Journal*, 9 February 1884, 4. Meetings of this association included women presenting original poems.

228. Downes, *Swayed by the Storm*; Manley, *From Woolloomooloo*, 1:312.

229. Fry, *Poems*, 44, 84, 99.

230. Tranter, *Call of the Bush and Other Poems*.

231. Tranter, "Eaglehawk Baptist Church," *Bendigo Independent* 21 May 1918, 6.

232. See, for example, Telfer, *Occasional Verses*, 31; Lilian Wooster Greaves, "Remembrance," *Western Mail* (Perth), 22 April 1926; *Two Doves and Other Poems*. The case study below notes that Adelaide Bamford quoted the lines from one of Lilian Wooster Greaves' poems.

fiction stories with a Christian message, so-called "religious novels." Her stories were set in Australia and contained Christian themes including God's provision and promises. In *Beatrice Melton's Discipline* the main character addresses belief saying: "Ah, how can I ever be thankful enough to my Heavenly Father for not leaving me in my dark distrust of Him, and of His ways!"[233] The religious novels of Matilda Evans—and Lilian Brown, Marion Downes and others—achieved success at the time, but religious novels lost their popularity from the mid-twentieth century and so their work has been largely forgotten.[234]

Jeannie Gunn was the most well-known Australian Baptist woman writer to 1945. Jeannie Gunn was the daughter of Anna Taylor, née Lush, whose family were well-known Baptists in England and Victoria, and Thomas Taylor, son of a Victorian Baptist minister. In 1901 she married Aeneas Gunn, and they moved to a Northern Territory cattle station. Her husband died after two years of marriage, and she moved back to Melbourne and lived with her widowed father. Her life at the station provided inspiration for two books: *The Little Black Princess: A True Tale of Life in the Never-Never Land* and *We of the Never-Never*.[235] They included timeless descriptions of the Australian landscape and people, such as: "Shut in on all sides by bush and tall timber, with the rushing river as sentinel, we seemed in a world all our own—a tiny human world, with a camp fire for its hub."[236] Jeannie Gunn's books were not religious novels, although there is evidence of implicit Christian elements, including that God is present everywhere. As Jeannie Gunn wrote: "'Be still, and know that I am God,' is still whispered out of the heart of Nature."[237]

Evangelical themes emphasized in women's writing also changed over time. Activism remained the dominant theme of women's writing. This is understandable given that much of the writing was about work that women were undertaking in their congregations and the denomination. Biblicism was the second most common theme, and it became more of a feature after the First World War. Conversionism permeated much of the work through the period, particularly because of the predominance of writings by missionary women whose work was designed to convert non-Christians. Yet the focus on conversions was more prevalent in the late nineteenth and early twentieth centuries and was less of a feature in the period after the

---

233. Franc, *Beatrice Melton's Discipline*, 235; Finnis, "Evans, Matilda Jane."
234. Manley, *Marion Downes*, 4.
235. O'Neill, "Gunn, Jeannie."
236. See chapter 3 in Gunn, *We of the Never Never*.
237. See chapter 18 in Gunn, *We of the Never Never*.

First World War. Crucicentrism was the evangelical theme least engaged with but was more likely to be included in women's writing after the First World War than before.[238] This result broadly correlates with assessments made by Stuart Piggin and Robert Linder that by 1880 evangelical's primary beliefs focused on the importance of the Bible, and by Geoff Treloar that in the period prior to the First World War activism and conversionism were important, and that later in the twentieth century biblicism and crucicentrism were emphasized.[239]

The broad religious themes that women wrote about did not change over the period. Many women stressed the importance of prayer as a significant spiritual practice. In 1894 both Fanny Brown and Emily Hone encouraged women to "pray audibly," in 1915 Lilian Wooster Greaves wrote "pray more faithfully," and in 1946 Mary Pope urged women to "pray earnestly."[240] Unsurprisingly mission support was another dominant theme in the work by women.

Australian historiography has rarely engaged with Baptist women's religious writings.[241] Men's writings have typically been used to elucidate Baptist religious thought.[242] One obvious reason for this was that most Baptist religious work was undertaken by ordained men who had usually been theologically educated. Additionally, in the early twentieth century some Baptist women's writings were published in WCTU or CE papers because those organizations accepted and encouraged women's participation. Such papers were not examined for their religious content, as the organizations were not seen as part of the denomination. Frustratingly, some women's published work has not been retained. For instance, Elizabeth Dovey's 1938 book *Messages to sick and shut-in folk*, based on her letters and her regular radio segment, is not extant.[243] The unpublished work by many women,

238. Hilton, "Australian Baptist Women as Public Intellectuals"; "ABW Database."

239. Treloar, *Disruption of Evangelicalism*, 4, 9; Piggin and Linder, *Fountain of Public Prosperity*.

240. Brown, "Women's Work in the Church," *Baptist*, 3 November 1894, 174; Greaves, *Road to Glory*, 34; Mary Pope, "Words of Inspiration for 1946 from Baptist Leaders," *TAB*, 8 January 1946, 1.

241. There have been some recent papers on Baptist women written by Barbara Coe, Ros Gooden, Ken Manley, and Rebecca Hilton. See, for example, Manley, *Marion Downes*; Hilton, "Australian Baptist Women as Public Intellectuals."

242. See, for example, Manley, *From Woolloomooloo*, 1:360.

243. "More or Less Personal," *TAB*, 12 July 1938, 4; D. [Denis] C. Harper, "She Walked with God: The Late Mrs. E. Dovey," *TAB*, 24 April 1945, 4. The State Library of NSW has several study guides written by Elizabeth Dovey's husband and son, including an unpublished manuscript "Living Treasures or Thoughts for Mothers," but does not have her published work.

which was often presented within women's groups, can be presumed to no longer exist.[244]

CASE STUDY: FLORENCE BENSKIN AND ADELAIDE BAMFORD

Florence Benskin and Adelaide Bamford published regular columns in denominational papers. These were remarkably similar, despite being written at different times within the twentieth century. The women were born twenty years apart and they lived in different cities. It is unlikely they ever met.[245]

Emily Florence Benskin was born in 1874 in London, England and in 1900 she married the Rev. Frederick Benskin in England. They came to Flinders Street Baptist and remained for four years from 1922 until 1926 before returning to England. Florence Benskin died in Bath, England in 1953. From 1923 to 1925 Florence Benskin wrote a regular column titled "Through a Woman's Window" in *The Baptist Record* in SA. Florence Benskin's final regular column was published on 15 December 1925, but she wrote at least one additional column in July 1926. The column continued until March 1927 with no author identified.[246]

Adelaide Bamford was born in 1895 in Sydney, NSW. Her parents, Jessie Dunkley, nee Chidgey and the Rev. Frederick Dunkley, were members of the Salvation Army until 1904 when her father was ordained as minister of Bodangora Baptist, NSW.[247] Adelaide and Reginald Bamford married in 1915 in Tamworth Baptist, NSW. Adelaide Bamford's column was titled "One Woman to Another" and commenced in *The Australian Baptist* in 1939 when her father was the editor. While Frederick Dunkley was the editor for three years, Adelaide Bamford wrote her column for twenty-one

---

244. Women's groups in congregations and the denominations often had speeches or papers presented by women. See, for example, "Girls' Literary Association," *Evening Journal*, 9 February 1884, 4; "Baptist Girls' Guild," *Geelong Advertiser*, 11 September 1908, 6; "Under the Clock: Baptist Young People's Christian Endeavor," *Shepparton Advertiser* (Shepparton, Victoria), 24 October 1929, 4.

245. There is no evidence in Australian newspapers or Baptist denominational papers that Florence Benskin traveled to NSW when living in Australia, and nor that Adelaide Bamford or the Dunkley family traveled to SA between 1922 and 1926. Adelaide Bamford may have read or heard about Florence Benskin's columns.

246. Mrs F. G. [Florence] Benskin, "Through a Woman's Window: My Best," *BR* (Adelaide), 15 July 1926, 12.

247. Albert Leeder, "The Passing of Rev. F. J. Dunkley," *TAB*, 8 January 1946, 4. Bodangora is near Wellington, NSW.

years until 1960.[248] This author believes that she wrote more words than any other contributor to *The Australian Baptist*. She died in 1969 in Sydney.

Both women used Biblical pen names. Probably Florence Benskin's use of the pen name Priscilla, the name of a respected co-worker of Paul in the life of the early church (Acts 18:2, 18), reflects her belief that women were equal to men.[249] Adelaide Bamford used the unusual pen name Keturah, the woman Abraham married following Sarah's death (Gen 25:1–4). Books about people in the Bible rarely discussed or included Keturah and the name has multi-layered meanings.[250] Possibly Adelaide Bamford's use of Keturah acknowledged a freedom to write.[251] While Adelaide Bamford's understanding of the name is unknown, she took on the persona of Keturah, and others referred to her as Keturah.[252]

Both women were actively involved in their local Baptist congregations as well as in other denominational activities. Florence Benskin established the SA Baptist Women's League. Adelaide Bamford was a well-known Baptist speaker, including preaching, and she was a member of several Baptist women's groups including the Women's Home Mission Auxiliary of which she was President in 1943.[253] Both women were mothers: Florence Benskin had one son and Adelaide Bamford had two daughters.

The columns had similar formats and themes, and both columns changed during the first year of publication. Each column was about one thousand words on average. Both women asked other women to contribute to the column. Florence Benskin specifically stated that the aim of her column was to provide a place to "have accounts of meetings . . . [and] new

---

248. This case study only examines columns published by Adelaide Bamford from 1939 to 1945, which is about 350 articles.

249. Priscilla, sometime referred to as Prisca, is usually named before her husband Aquilla.

250. Five books on Bible characters from the late nineteenth and early twentieth century were examined for references to Keturah, and only one included her, as the second wife of Abraham. While there were some Australian women named Keturah, the only references to Keturah in *Australian Baptist* prior to Adelaide Bamford's column were in the light-hearted "Parables of Safed the Sage," by William Barton, a North American writer, which were printed in *Australian Baptist* from 1921 to 1933. The wife was called Keturah, and thus regular readers may have recognised the name.

251. Adelaide Bamford may have believed that Keturah was Hagar renamed, as speculated by some Biblical commentors. Galatians responds to the freeing of Hagar with the words: "For freedom Christ has set us free. Stand firm, therefore, and do not submit again to a yoke of slavery" (5:1). See also Bamford, "OWTA: 'Commit, Trust, He worketh,'" *TAB*, 11 July 1939, 2.

252. Raymond Farrer, "Gossiping the Gospel," *TAB*, 1 July 1941, 3.

253. Wilcox, *Baptist Women's League*, 11.

methods of doing a particular piece of service."²⁵⁴ Adelaide Bamford wanted women to send in questions or advice, writing: "I am afraid [the column] cannot be managed unless you help me."²⁵⁵ Ultimately both women largely wrote their own columns. Florence Benskin and Adelaide Bamford included evangelical themes in their writing. For instance, both women believed in the supreme authority of the Bible. Florence Benskin implored readers to convert others, "to introduce others to the One who changed our lives."²⁵⁶ Adelaide Bamford wrote a prayer that included activist and crucicentrist themes: "I thank Thee that Thou didst not draw back from the Cross, which brings the world blessing, and freedom from sin. Help me not to draw back from any work which Thou dost put into my heart to do for Thee."²⁵⁷

The columns were aimed at Australian Baptist women and contained Christian themes such as friendship, mission, and prayer, and did not challenge normal expectations of women's roles.²⁵⁸ Their straight-forward messages were just as likely to be read by men as by women. This was a conclusion reiterated by the editor of *The Baptist Record*.²⁵⁹ Adelaide Bamford's columns were written as a letter to "Dear Sister Women," signed off with "God bless you all, dear sister women."²⁶⁰ Adelaide Bamford's salutations ensured she would not be accused of preaching to men and overstepping her boundaries, yet the articles were read by Baptist men.²⁶¹

Florence Benskin's writings indicated that she identified herself with Australian Baptist women, despite only being in Australia for a short time.²⁶² One outcome—potentially unintended—was to promote the newly formed SA Baptist Women's League. Florence Benskin's columns included notices about up-coming meetings, summaries of meetings held, and encouraged women's participation in the new organization.²⁶³ Florence Benskin appeared to be pragmatic about her life, and in numerous columns she stressed the importance of looking forward, affirming, "We are on a journey," and, "We do need to realise that there is no standing still in the Christian life."²⁶⁴

254. Benskin, "Priscilla's Portion," *BR*, July 1923, 12.
255. Bamford, "Women's Column: OWTA," *TAB*, 31 January 1939, 11.
256. Benskin, "Through a Woman's Window: In Society," *BR*, 15 February 1924, 14.
257. Bamford, "OWTA: A Prayer," *TAB*, 13 October 1942.
258. Benskin, "Through a Woman's Window: Stunted," *BR*, 15 January 1925 1925, 7.
259. "Through a Woman's Window," *BR*, 15 January 1926, 9.
260. Bamford, "OWTA," *TAB*, 17 October 1939, 5.
261. Farrer, "Gossiping the Gospel," *TAB*, 1 July 1941, 3.
262. Benskin, "Through a Woman's Window: Pull Together," *BR*, 16 March 1925, 10.
263. See, for example, Benskin, "Through a Woman's Window," *BR*, 15 May 1924, 12.
264. Benskin, "Through a Woman's Window," *Baptist Record*, 15 November 1924,

Like many women, she trusted that God provided guidance but she was essentially led by her husband's calling as a Baptist minister.

Adelaide Bamford also wrote about looking forward: "We should review and renew our lives... Life is never monotonous where God is. [God] is constantly providing new pasture, new roads, new and greater desires and service. With [God] it is always better farther on."[265] Her early columns contained "homely hints," such as the 18 July 1939 column that included instructions to dry celery leaves for use as flavoring, and a recipe for a ring cake.[266] From 1940 the format of the column changed and had one theme, usually based on a Bible passage and examining a Christian attribute, like Florence Benskin's columns.

Adelaide Bamford's columns show that over time she grew more confident in her ability to write and to discuss biblical and theological issues. She referenced a range of writers, many of whom were women. The column on 10 April 1945 was based on Deuteronomy 33:25 and quoted writings by hymnwriters Fanny Crosby and Sybil Partridge, and author Grace Stratton.[267] Adelaide Bamford quoted other Australian Baptist women writers such as Elizabeth Dovey, Jessie Hancey, Irene Pocknall, Dulcie Welch, and Lilian Wooster Greaves: some of these women had sent her material, specifically poetry.[268] She wrote about women whom she believed demonstrated exemplary attributes, including author and disability rights advocate Helen Keller, Salvation Army evangelist Evangeline Booth, and Australian Baptist deaconess Bertha Jarrett, whom she would have known. The prevalence of women authors and examples suggests that Adelaide Bamford intentionally used the work and words of women. Sometimes she adjusted Bible passages to make them more relevant to women, either through removing gendered personal pronouns or adding feminine pronouns.[269] She took the term "gossip," an undesirable attribute often ascribed to women, and turned it into an action that was constructive, suggesting that women started "gossiping the Gospel."[270] Adelaide Bamford exercised an important ministry among Australian Baptists.

12; "Through a Woman's Window: What of the New Year?," *BR*, 15 January 1924, 14; "Through a Woman's Window," *BR*, 15 June 1925, 9.

265. Bamford, "OWTA," *TAB*, 2 January 1945, 5.

266. Bamford, "OWTA: Homely Hints," *TAB*, 18 July 1939, 7. The recipe for the ring cake has been tested and was tasty but slightly crumbly.

267. Bamford, "OWTA," *TAB*, 2 February 1943, 5; "OWTA," *TAB*, 10 April 1945, 5.

268. Bamford, "OWTA," *TAB*, 2 February 1943, 5. Adelaide Bamford also quoted Baptist men such as Leslie Gomm and Frank Boreham.

269. Bamford, "OWTA: Schofield Bible," *TAB*, 19 September 1939, 7.

270. Bamford, "OWTA: The Old Story," *TAB*, 7 May 1940, 5.

Given both the national reach of Adelaide Bamford's articles, along with the length of time that she wrote her column, Adelaide Bamford was more influential in the Australian Baptist denomination than Florence Benskin. Despite their significant writings, neither woman's writings have been closely examined in Baptist historiography.[271]

CONCLUSION

Australian Baptist women sought opportunities to communicate their religious beliefs in a variety of ways. Women's willingness to undertake leadership positions shows how the notion of religious work occurring within the intermediate sphere allowed for such activities.[272] In various circumstances women preached; worked in ministry roles, such as paid and unpaid deaconesses or as evangelists; and established and maintained congregations. Women spoke at Baptist union meetings, wrote in the denominational papers, and published books. Where Baptist women's religious writings are extant they provide strong, confident, and intelligent evangelical theological viewpoints, often using biblical arguments and including justification for their positions on women's ministries within the Baptist denomination. Women also took up opportunities for leadership roles in CE groups. None of these activities outwardly challenged the status quo, nor did women seek ordination, yet they creatively exercised leadership and public roles.

The Australian Baptist denomination prided itself on evangelistic work, but this rarely extended to encouraging or allowing women to undertake such work. Thus while a few women worked as evangelists within and outside the denomination, their work does not appear to have been encouraged or supported on an ongoing basis.

The Australian Baptist denomination through its practices and traditions restricted women's roles in leadership and preaching. Australian Baptist women chose to work in the Baptist denomination despite their inequality with men. Nevertheless, many women in the denomination possessed skills that were not fully utilized. Indeed, there are a few women whose actions and written words hint at their frustration. They needed to believe that "God [would] understand" their work and ministries.[273] Inevitably some of these women also undertook significant social welfare and

---

271. Manley, *From Woolloomooloo*, 1; Prior, *Some Fell on Good Ground*; Walker, "Baptists in South Australia."

272. Wilson, *Constrained by Zeal*, 210.

273. "Family Notices: Deaths," *Gippsland Times*, 17 October 1961, 5.

reform activities, most of which occurred outside the denomination, and this is the focus of the next chapter.

6

Women's Social Work and Activities Outside the Denomination

It is not in the power of any one to improve matters, only God. I can do this great thing. I want to be linked in to Him in a very special manner for this work. I will love them but I must also speak very straight. So help me God![1]

—MARGARET BEAN, 1910 (upon commencing her social welfare work in Melbourne).

INTRODUCTION

IT MAY SEEM INANE to include a chapter on Baptist women's activities outside the Baptist denomination. To what extent can these ministries be linked to the denomination? Yet Baptist women to 1945 worked in the areas of evangelism, social welfare, and social reform in Australia in a variety of ways, many—indeed most—of which were outside Baptist structures. They believed their ministries were consistent with their evangelical Baptist faith.[2] In addition, other activities they undertook were also linked to their faith, and it is important to understand how external ministries were incorporated into women's Baptist faith.

---

1. Margaret F. Bean, "A Record of the Work of 'Sister Grace' at Gospel Hall," BUVA.

2. See, for example, McLean, *Womanhood Suffrage*; Booth, *Dinna Forget*, 308; Silas Mead, "The Late Miss L. Paqualin," *TP*, 1 March 1888, 45.

PARTICIPATION IN CHRISTIAN ORGANIZATIONS OUTSIDE THE BAPTIST DENOMINATION

Talented evangelical Baptist women, determined to have an active faith, joined religious organizations outside the denomination to effect change in Australian society. They sought meaningful roles when there were limited opportunities for service within the small Australian Baptist denomination. Many Australian Baptist women were involved in social reform and welfare through membership of, or volunteering in, Christian organizations. Historians and theologians emphasize relationships that developed between evangelicals from different denominations—or pan-Evangelicalism—enabled Baptist women to cooperate with women from different Australian denominations, particularly in the WCTU and YWCA.[3] Baptist women's work in these organizations were generally in unpaid roles and therefore the women volunteers tended to be from the middle-class who did not need to undertake paid employment.[4]

Many Baptist women's actions in social reform and welfare demonstrated elements of a social gospel, or "practical Christian work."[5] Yet evangelical Australian Baptists were considered to have a focus on evangelism—converting non-Christians—and tended to be less interested in social reform and welfare, as evidenced by policies of the ABFM.[6] Baptist women's engagement in an extensive range of social reform and welfare activities is somewhat contrary to this notion. Indeed, Australian Baptist women's considerable involvement in social reform and welfare activities should influence discourse regarding Baptists' Evangelical beliefs, and belies the notion that Australian Baptists were less focused on social reform or welfare.

There is evidence of some Baptists objecting to other Baptists being involved in organizations outside the denomination, and to some extent this attitude was understandable. The denomination was small, and so those who wanted to see the denomination grow believed active Baptists should devote their time and energy inside the Baptist denomination.[7] In

---

3. McGrath, "Anglicanism and Pan-Evangelicalism," 314, 20. There were other religious organizations that originated during the period, but these were not a major feature in Baptist women's lives. For example, Girls Brigade was not popular until after 1945.

4. Carey, "National Woman's Christian Temperance Union"; West, *Daughters of Freedom*, 151.

5. Bebbington, *Evangelicalism in Modern Britain*, 212.

6. Manley, *From Woolloomooloo*, 1:359; Bebbington, *Baptists Through the Centuries*, 124; Treloar, *Disruption of Evangelicalism*, 4, 18–23, 94; Piggin and Linder, *Fountain of Public Prosperity*, 28–29.

7. Richard Woolcock, "The Minister and His Church in their Relation to Outside Organizations," *TP*, 1 November 1894, 333; "Baptist Church, Ballarat," *TSB*, 16 March

1894 Richard Woolcock expressed his belief that Baptists should respond to important issues by creating organizations inside the denomination rather than outside.[8] The ABFM discouraged congregations from allowing missionaries working outside the denomination to address Baptist congregations, essentially because they might redirect interest and funding to mission organizations outside the denomination.[9] Similarly the diaconates of some congregations suggested ministers focus on their own congregational or Baptist denominational work rather than participate in outside organizations.[10] Despite this attitude, many women became involved with religious organizations outside the denomination. However women appear to have been careful to deflect criticism about working in organizations outside the Baptist denomination. In 1901 Margaret McLean wrote that the WCTU "ask[s] no woman to give up her work as a Church member."[11] As Australian Baptists focused on men's activities, women may have engaged in outside activities because their interests and work was not valued as highly as men's activities. In turn women were advancing broader religious work and did not restrict themselves to building up the small Baptist denomination. In any case, women took advantage of the opportunities provided through their involvement in non-Baptist religious organizations.

MISSION TO FIRST NATIONS PEOPLE

In 1922 Emily Price reported on a speech by Margaret Long about the appalling situation of First Nations people and wrote that "many of us felt shamed."[12] First Nations people were treated atrociously by British colonizers from 1788 through to the twentieth century, and elements of this

---

1899; "The Church of the Future," *TAB*, 19 September 1916, 8; Robert Goodman, "Denominational Efficiency," *TAB*, 25 April 1933, 2; "The Use of Baptist Money," *TAB*, 18 July 1934, 3.

8. Woolcock, "The Minister and His Church in Their Relation to Outside Organizations," *TP*, 1 November 1894, 333.

9. ABFM, Board Minutes, BMAA, 18–20 August 1926. This attitude was largely ineffective because Baptists were so committed to mission they supported agencies outside the denomination.

10. "Baptist Church, Ballarat," *TSB*, 16 March 1899, 3; Doery, "WVP," *TAB*, 3 August 1915, 3. In 1899 the deacons of Ballarat Baptist requested that the new minister "refuse all outside work for twelve months." In 1915 the deacons of Clifton Hill Baptist, Victoria, told the minister "that he could devote himself entirely to the spiritual affairs of the church, as they thought that quite enough."

11. Margaret McLean, "Letter to the Editor," *TSB*, 17 July 1901, 168.

12. Emily M. Price, "Zenana Society NSW," *TAB*, 7 February 1922, 3.

disadvantage continue into the twenty-first century.¹³ In the nineteenth and early twentieth centuries Australian Baptists generally did not demonstrate an interest in mission to First Nations people, for which there were several reasons. The denomination was neither well-established in Australia nor well-financed, so the focus was on building the denomination. In addition, Baptists usually prioritized evangelism before social reform or social welfare. Many non-Indigenous Australians, particularly in the nineteenth century, considered that First Nations people were not intellectually capable of understanding Christianity, and the missionary zeal that provided significant support for Evangelical mission outside Australia—which largely followed the mission focus of UK Baptists—was not applied to First Nations people.¹⁴ Mission to First Nations people was not considered as important as overseas mission and missionary women engaged in the work did not have a high status among Baptists, and Protestants more generally.¹⁵ Australian Baptists supported mission overseas and some mission among non-Indigenous Australians, but initially with little acknowledgement that this implicitly ignored the needs of First Nations people.

The first known Australian Baptist women to interact with First Nations people were Eliza Davies and Helen Finlayson in SA. In 1839 Eliza Davies was one of the first non-Indigenous women to sail north on the Murray River SA. In her memoirs published in 1881 she was harsh in her assessment of the First Nations people she saw on this trip but her opinions reflect prevailing views of colonial settlers at that time.¹⁶ In 1839 Helen Finlayson and her husband William Finlayson migrated to SA hoping to undertake mission work to First Nations people. This did not eventuate, but she was reported as sometimes being "in the absence of her husband, . . . alone with hundreds of savages, who, however, never attempted to molest her, but treated her with profound respect and submitted themselves implicitly to her directions."¹⁷ This is a slightly more helpful account than that of Eliza Davies, although still condescending. Notwithstanding such views and widespread apathy, between the 1830s and 1945 Australian Baptists supported various missions to First Nations people.

13. Piggin and Linder, *Fountain of Public Prosperity*, 38.

14. "Notes," *TP*, 1 April 1885, 46; The article includes comment on the fact that Moravian missionaries were coming to Australia to engage in mission to Indigenous Australians, but that Australian Baptists were focused on mission in East Bengal. Jensz, *German Moravian Missionaries*, 227.

15. Piggin and Linder, *Fountain of Public Prosperity*, 553; O'Brien, *God's Willing Workers*, 129.

16. Davies, *Story of an Earnest Life*; Walker, "Earnest Life."

17. "Death of an Early Colonist," *Adelaide Observer* (Adelaide), 25 October 1884, 32.

Missions occurred, in part, because Baptists, together with other Evangelicals, sought to address the poor treatment of First Nations people and an Evangelical response was to convert unbelievers.[18] In 1926 many Baptists hoped that the newly formed Australian Baptist Home Mission would instigate work with First Nations people. However it was not until 1946 that Australian Baptist mission to First Nations people commenced under the auspices of the BUA.[19] However before 1945 more than forty Baptist women were engaged as missionaries to First Nations people mainly through the Aboriginal Inland Mission (AIM) and the United Aborigines [sic]Mission (UAM), which were the two largest organizations that undertook mission to First Nations people in the twentieth century.[20]

AIM and UAM originated from evangelistic work that was undertaken in the 1890s by Baptist and Congregational Petersham CE societies, who regularly went to La Perouse to conduct services with First Nations people. The work was relatively ad hoc in the 1890s, with some missions formed in communities in NSW. Among those involved was Baptist woman Margaret Long, who went to live and work at La Perouse. In 1899 the NSW Aborigines' [sic] Mission was established and brought together these various missions: "Its supreme object [was] the carrying of the Gospel of the Lord Jesus Christ to the Aborigines [sic] scattered throughout New South Wales."[21]

Margaret Long resigned from this mission in 1905 and formed AIM with a committee located in Singleton. The work at La Perouse became part of the Australian Aboriginal Mission, which became UAM in 1929. During the first half of the twentieth century AIM and UAM expanded to other locations around Australia. Both were interdenominational faith missions—workers were not paid a wage but relied on "the unsolicited freewill offerings of the Lord's people given in answer to prayer."[22] In 1945 throughout Australia AIM had around 130 workers and UAM had 90 workers, and both organizations had an extensive support network.[23] Although AIM and UAM had missions throughout Australia, a majority of missionary women in the two organizations were recruited from NSW.[24] Australian Baptist women

18. Mrs A.M. [Margaret] Small, "Retirement of Mrs. Retta Long," *Our AIM* (Sydney), 17 December 1953, 1.

19. Cupit et al., *From Five Barley Loaves*, 481.

20. Harris, *One Blood*, 555.

21. "New South Wales Aborigines' [sic] Mission: Its Aims and Objects," *New South Wales Aborigines'* [sic] *Advocate*, 23 July 1901, 1.

22. *Our AIM*, 19 November 1945, 1.

23. Retta Long, "Fortieth Annual Report of the Aborigines [sic] Inland Mission of Australia," *Our AIM*, 19 November 1945, 3.

24. Hilton, "ABW Database."

working in missions for First Nations people undertook a variety of tasks depending on the location and purpose of the mission. In many ways the work was like overseas mission work as it included evangelism, preaching, establishing congregations, teaching, managing orphanages, and providing medical assistance.

Margaret Long was an important figure in mission to First Nations people during this period because of her role in founding and sustaining AIM. She was born in 1878 in Sydney and in 1906 married Leonard Long, who joined her as a co-director of AIM in 1907.[25] Margaret Long influenced the direction of AIM through her role as editor of the organization's paper, *Our AIM*, from 1907 until 1953.[26] Four of Margaret and Leonard Long's five children became AIM workers. Their youngest child, the Rev. Edgerton Long, was also an ordained Baptist minister. Margaret Long and her family were members of various Baptist congregations, although AIM was interdenominational.[27]

Other Australian Baptist mission work to First Nations people existed but was spasmodic and localized. Some Baptist congregations situated in regional areas or areas with a large population of First Nations people undertook or supported local mission work. For example in the early 1930s Gladys Tompkins, who worked for AIM at Tarbulan, northern NSW, was regularly assisted by Lismore Baptist, located 100km away.[28] Such ongoing support was vital for faith missions, and Gladys Tomkins wrote: "God has, as ever, been faithful to His word, and every need—temporal, spiritual and physical—has been abundantly supplied."[29] Successive Baptist ministers at Murgon, Queensland, 270km north-west of Brisbane, regularly visited First Nations people at Cherbourg. From 1936 to 1938 Winifred Barnard worked with her husband, the Rev. Clement Barnard, in Murgon and she described how they held services and organized Sunday Schools in First Nations communities.[30] At times state Baptist Unions aided missions to First Nations people.[31] In 1898 the Baptist Union of WA appointed Ada Kennedy to work

25. "Second Annual Convention: Annual Business Meeting," *Our AIM*, October 1907, 3; "A Missionary Pioneer Passes," *TAB*, 31 October 1956, 8.

26. Small, "Retirement of Mrs. Retta Long," *Our AIM*, 17 December 1953, 1.

27. Edgerton Long, Eulogy for Olive Grace Collins, NSWBA. The four children who were AIM missionaries were Retta Collins, Arnold Long, Olive Long, and the Rev. Edgerton Long.

28. "Debit Turned to Credit: Baptist," *Northern Star*, 15 September 1934, 7.

29. G. [Gladys] Tomkins, "New South Wales: Tabulam," *Our AIM*, 23 December 1932, 8.

30. "Queensland Baptist Women," *TAB*, 1 November 1938, 9.

31. Gomm, *Blazing the Western Trails*, 78–79.

with the Noongar people, as "overseer of the work among black women and children."³² In 1927 the Bwgcolman people worshiping on Palm Island requested affiliation with the Baptist Union of Queensland. The AIM worker, Baptist Kathleen Simmons, believed that the congregation was best fitted to the Baptist denomination and the Union accepted Palm Island Baptist as an outpost of Townsville Baptist.³³ These missionaries to First Nations people undertook their tasks in difficult circumstances, with inadequate funding and support.

Australian mission to First Nations people had significant organizational challenges to overcome. Ongoing mission to First Nations people throughout Australia was at the behest of different state government policies, which often changed, usually at the expense of the First Nations people and the missions. The health requirements for acceptance as a missionary within Australia were not as rigorous as those applied for overseas mission organizations, and consequently some women who were not accepted for overseas mission then undertook mission to First Nations people.³⁴ Such examples included Ellen Sutton, who was rejected for service in 1901 for the Victorian Baptist Foreign Mission because of her health, but then worked as a missionary in remote Australia, albeit for a short period.³⁵ The poor health of mission workers and short periods of time in the community meant that many Baptist missionary women did not develop close and long-term relationships with First Nations people, nor did they exhibit a deep understanding of community needs or cultural mores and realities.

In retrospect, many mission policies and activities undertaken by the mission workers to First Nations people were inappropriate when judged through a twenty-first-century lens. Australian Government policies reflected widespread assumptions in Australian society that First Nations culture was inferior—a "half-civilised mode of living"—and that evangelistic work was the answer to their plight.³⁶ Essentially such sentiments continued throughout the first half of the twentieth century, such that in 1945 two UAM workers wrote: "The Gospel is the only power to save and uplift the

---

32. "West Australian Baptist Union: Half-Yearly Meetings, 26th May, 1898," *TSB*, 4 August 1898, 175.

33. Simmons, "Random Reflections from Queensland," *TAB*, 16 October 1928, 7; Piggin and Linder, *Attending to the National Soul*, 164.

34. O'Brien, *God's Willing Workers*, 129.

35. "Baptist Union: Annual Session," *Age*, 21 November 1901, 8; "Mission," *Bendigo Advertiser* (Bendigo, Victoria), 21 July 1909, 6.

36. "New South Wales Aborigines' [sic] Mission," *New South Wales Aborigines' [sic] Advocate*, 23 July 1901, 1.

Aborigines [sic] and make them worth-while citizens of Australia."[37] Yet most of the missionary women were indefatigable workers, committed to helping First Nations people, albeit with a focus on evangelism and conversion to Christianity. They were assisted by supporters and Christian First Nations people. In 1945 Margaret Long wrote: "By [God's] grace we have continued in the place where His faithfulness, His mercy, His deliverance, His provision, His empowering meets our helplessness."[38] Ultimately she and the other missionaries to First Nations people did not have sufficient government assistance or community support. Nor did many of the missionaries have the cultural understanding necessary to undertake effective missionary work to First Nations people. Australian Baptist women placed themselves into situations over which they had little control or power.

The history of mission to First Nations is fraught with contradictions and controversies. Stuart Piggin and Robert Linder observe that missionaries advocated for First Nations people on some issues, such as land acquisitions, and yet complied with governments on issues regarding assimilation.[39] Certainly, policies on assimilation resulted in significant harm to First Nations people including the loss of family units, language, and cultural understanding.[40] Government policies allowed for First Nations people to be placed in "homes," particularly children who had one First Nations parent—usually their mother—and one non-Indigenous parent. The homes, therefore, were not orphanages, and the children are now referred to as being part of the "Stolen Generations."[41]

In NSW the Bomaderry Home for Aboriginal Children was the only home established for First Nations people by Christian missionaries, and the key organizer was Baptist Eleanor Barron.[42] In 1908 she established the home while working for the UAM in Parramatta, where many children were deemed homeless, when they were not. She secured donations and ongoing funding for a Home in Nowra. Over the following four years Eleanor Barron expanded the premises, before resigning to marry in 1912.[43]

---

37. Marion and Harry E. Green, "The Old Order Changeth," *United Aborigines'* [sic] *Messenger* (Melbourne), 1 November 1945, 7.

38. Long, "Fortieth Annual Report of the Aborigines [sic] Inland Mission of Australia," *Our AIM*, 19 November 1945, 3.

39. Piggin and Linder, *Attending to the National Soul*, 163.

40. AIATSIS, "Stolen Generations." The article is based on information contained in the *Bringing Them Home Report*.

41. AIATSIS, "Stolen Generations."

42. NSW Government, "Bomaderry Aboriginal Children's Home."

43. "Early History of Bomaderry Home," *Shoalhaven Telegraph* (Nowra, NSW), 3 October 1928, 8. The home is mentioned in the *Bringing Them Home Report* because

Historian John Harris outlines the failures of missions, characterising them as being paternalistic, lacking good governance, with inappropriate policies and procedures, and not valuing and protecting First Nations culture. Yet Harris recognizes that often missionaries were the only people advocating for First Nations people.[44] Undoubtedly Australian Baptist women contributed to the loss of family networks and culture of some First Nations people; but most women were driven by a strong missionary zeal and tried to assist First Nations people to the best of their ability and knowledge. Potentially their actions were better than indifference, although of course this does not justify the harm that First Nations people were subjected to by the actions of non-Indigenous Australians.

SUPPORT OF NON-DENOMINATIONAL MISSIONS

While many Australian women volunteered in some way to support the Australian Baptist overseas mission organizations, some Australian Baptist women were involved in the support of non-denominational mission organizations. Some former missionary women remained connected to their non-Baptist mission organizations, while being a part of the Australian Baptist denomination. For example, Ella Davies regularly spoke at mission events within and outside the Baptist denomination and used her platform as a former CIM worker to discuss other religious work, such as revivals.[45]

Many women were connected to other mission organizations because of involvement with family members and friends. For instance, in 1892 in Victoria Ann Bird was the president of the Australasian CIM women's auxiliary and her husband, the Rev. Alfred Bird, was the first Secretary of the Australasian CIM.[46] In the 1890s in NSW Anne Palmer was a member of the "Ladies' Committee" of the NSW Bush Missionary Society, which had been formed by her husband Joseph Palmer. The organization operated within the Congregational denomination and it created and supported Sunday Schools in regional NSW. Anne and Joseph Palmer were members of Bathurst Street Baptist, and other women from that congregation were on the Committee such as Helen Harry and Mary Wells.[47] From 1905 to around 1930 several Baptist congregations in NSW supported AIM. In 1929

First Nations children who had been taken from their families went there.

44. Harris, *One Blood*, 137.

45. "Missionary Union: Presbyterian Women's Conference," *Telegraph* (Brisbane), 27 September 1932, 15.

46. "China Inland Missions: Australasian Branch," *Argus*, 7 June 1893, 7.

47. "Bush Missionary Society," *SMH*, 20 May 1896, 7.

one third of AIM prayer meetings in NSW were held in Baptist premises, and AIM's national Women's Auxiliary met in Bathurst Street Baptist.[48] It is not surprising that women wanted to support non-denominational missions—as evidenced throughout this book. While women and Baptist women's mission committees supported Australian Baptist mission, many also donated funds to other mission organizations. Australian Baptist women's commitment to different mission organizations reiterates the importance of mission.

SOCIAL REFORM THROUGH THE WOMAN'S CHRISTIAN TEMPERANCE UNION (WCTU)

Many Australian Baptist women sought to advance various social reforms with respect to alcohol restrictions, gambling controls, prison conditions, and suffrage. This work occurred within religious organizations, and usually these organizations sought reform in a specific area—at least initially.[49] To 1945 the most common social reform sought by Baptist women was temperance, or abstinence from alcoholic drinks. Temperance organizations welcomed women's attendance at meetings but rarely allowed women to be on the executive or to speak at meetings, and thus there are few records that document women's participation in temperance organizations, apart from the WCTU.

Many Australian Baptists sought temperance in society—temperance was viewed as an admirable trait of an Australian Baptist. In 1894 one Baptist columnist wrote that 87 percent of Baptist ministers did not drink any alcohol, and ministers often preached about temperance. Denominational papers devoted space to articles advocating temperance, including regular columns with updates on temperance activities. While Baptist men are known to have been involved in temperance activities, denominational papers appear more likely to reference temperance activities undertaken by Australian women than men. There were few references to other Australian temperance meetings apart from the WCTU.[50]

Originating in the USA in the 1870s, the WCTU was primarily a women's temperance organization to address the harmful influence of alcohol and drugs in people's lives, and enabled women to undertake activities supporting temperance and "do collectively what they were unable to do as

---

48. "Prayer Meetings," *Our AIM*, 20 December 1929, 14.

49. O'Brien, *God's Willing Workers*, 65.

50. "The Temperance World," *TP*, 16 August 1894, 247. For example, the Norwood WCTU visited public houses to denounce drinking alcohol.

individuals."[51] In addition the WCTU sought "equality of status between the sexes" through womanhood suffrage, and supported other reforms such as equal guardianship of children and equal pay.[52] From the 1890s until the mid-twentieth century the WCTU was one of the largest and most active women's organizations in Australia.[53] In the early 1880s local WCTU groups were formed throughout Australia and during the 1880s and early 1890s state unions were established. In 1891 the Australian WCTU was formed.[54] Some of the earliest WCTU meetings were chaired by men, such as the first annual meeting of the NSW WCTU in 1883.[55] However by the turn of the twentieth century all meetings were chaired and managed by women.[56] Most speakers were women, although some men, including Baptists, addressed meetings.[57]

The WCTU expanded to include other social reforms, initially women's suffrage, and Baptist women continued to be involved in this enlarged scope of activities.[58] Manley concludes that Australian Baptist women were "well represented" in the WCTU, and there are many examples of Baptist women's participation.[59]

Through the WCTU, Baptist women were actively engaged in an international organization.[60] The WCTU's motto adopted in 1897, "For God, Home and Humanity," connected temperance to Christian beliefs, family life, and individual well-being.[61] The WCTU stressed that alcohol abuse was anti-Christian: "Where the drink traffic triumphs Christ is dethroned,"

51. McCorkindale, *Pioneer Pathways*, x.
52. *Torch-Bearers*, 29.
53. O'Brien, *God's Willing Workers*, 65.
54. Pargeter, *For God, Home and Humanity*, 1.
55. "The Woman's Christian Temperance Union," *SMH*, 5 September 1883, 5. The meeting was chaired by Wesleyan Dr Benjamin Fawcett.
56. See, for example, *Woman's Christian Temperance Union of Australasia*; "WCTU," *Cumberland Argus and Fruitgrowers Advocate* (Parramatta, NSW), 8 August 1903, 6; "Women's [sic] Christian Temperance Union," *TSB*, 10 July 1906, 171.
57. See, for example, "Woman's Christian Temperance Union of New South Wales," *Daily Telegraph* (Sydney), 21 September 1891, 2; "The Churches," *SMH*, 17 February 1906, 11; "Woman's Christian Temperance Union: Twenty-Third Annual Convention," *TWA*, 20 August 1914, 5. Baptist minister spoke at these events along with other women.
58. Bebbington, *Baptists Through the Centuries*, 168; Manley, *From Woolloomooloo*, 1:445; Treloar, *Disruption of Evangelicalism*, 4, 56.
59. Manley, *From Woolloomooloo*, 2:445. For Baptist women identified as members of the WCTU see Hilton, "ABW Database."
60. Treloar, *Disruption of Evangelicalism*, 4, 56.
61. Pargeter, *For God, Home and Humanity*, 3.

wrote Margaret McLean in 1893.[62] Women in the WCTU viewed alcohol as a major cause of the disintegration of the family and two of the ways they sought improvements to family life was to argue for early closing of public houses—to restrict the time that men spent drinking—and conduct mother's meetings to support and educate socially disadvantaged women.[63] In addition they linked alcohol abuse with other social problems such as ill-health, crime, domestic violence, and poverty, and they sought to "remove the stumbling-blocks out of the way of our weaker brethren and sisters."[64] Baptist women were associated with the WCTU without being thought of as "unwomanly."[65]

The WCTU was part of several successful reforms such as suffrage, age of consent to marriage, gambling controls, and improvement in prison conditions, but—somewhat ironically—never achieved widespread Australian national temperance. In part the WCTU survived because it embraced a broad range of social and moral issues, while remaining advocates for temperance. Initially the WCTU, in the pursuit of temperance, argued that women would vote for candidates who supported temperance, and it was a key organization in gaining the franchise for Australian women.[66] Indeed, the WCTU continued to advocate for women's franchise until 1908 when the Victorian government granted most women the vote, the last Australian state to do so. Once the vote was won for most women, the emphasis shifted to education of women to enable them to use their vote more effectively. In the 1890s the WCTU advocated for specific reforms such as gambling restrictions and for public houses to be closed on Sundays. They argued for the repeal of state Contagious Diseases Acts, which they believed were inequitable and disadvantageous to women. This law allowed police the discretion to detain women, but not men.[67] In the early twentieth century the WCTU stressed the need for "peace and arbitration," and advocated for the Commonwealth Maternity Allowance, which was introduced in 1912.[68] After the First World War the WCTU continued to promote temperance, women's equality, and advocated against public funding to support the

---

62. McLean, "President's Address," 11.
63. See, for example, McLean, *Womanhood Suffrage*; Zenobia [Rosetta Birks], "Liquor Licences and Women," *Register* (Adelaide), 20 February 1908, 6; *Torch-Bearers*, 59.
64. "Initiation Service," 10.
65. Mead, *Awakened Woman*, 24.
66. West, *Daughters of Freedom*, 159.
67. Pargeter, *For God, Home and Humanity*, 10, 17.
68. Pargeter, *For God, Home and Humanity*, 32, 45.

emerging wine industry.[69] In the mid-twentieth century the WCTU increasingly focused on social welfare, pacifism, equal rights for women in pay and family matters, and rights for First Nations women.[70] Thus from 1890 to 1945 Australian Baptist women in the WCTU were agitating in respect of a wide range of social and political issues.

Despite the significant evidence of Baptist women's membership in the WCTU, the total Baptist membership cannot be determined. Membership of WCTU was linked to local branches—as was membership of Baptist congregations—and few membership rolls are extant. Baptist women are visible in the WCTU where they hold executive positions in local branches, or the state or national WCTU, or if their membership is included in newspaper articles or other publications, including obituaries. Local branches of the WCTU met in a variety of places, including town halls, private residences, and church buildings. For instance, from about 1890 to 1940 the North Adelaide Branch of the WCTU met in North Adelaide Baptist hall.[71] Baptist facilities throughout Australia continued to be used for WCTU meetings in the early twentieth century.[72] Baptist venues were very likely used because Baptist women from these congregations were WCTU members. In addition women's groups in Baptist congregations regularly invited WCTU representatives to address meetings.[73]

Baptist women wrote articles for WCTU papers, and many others made speeches about, or represented, the WCTU. These women included: Eleanor Barber, Lilian Brown, Cecilia Downing, Emily Hone, Margaret McLean, and Emily Price, and their involvement in the WCTU from 1894 to 1907 illustrates the diversity of issues covered by the organization. Eleanor Barber was the Victorian superintendent of "health and narcotics," with the aim of teaching women, particularly young mothers from low socio-economic families, about hygiene standards in their homes and the need to reduce rates of smoking.[74] In 1895 Lilian Brown spoke about "The Awakened Woman" at the SA WCTU convention. Her speech, which was later printed, used Scripture to claim "that man and woman, husband and

---

69. Pargeter, *For God, Home and Humanity*, 61, 64.

70. Pargeter, *For God, Home and Humanity*, 76, 84.

71. "Current Talk," *Bunyip* (Gawler, SA), 15 December 1899, 3; "Petersburg WCTU," *Petersburg Times* (Petersburg, SA) 1899, 2; "WCTU Activities," *Advertiser* (Adelaide), 13 June 1940, 6.

72. "Woman's Christian Temperance Union of New South Wales: Local Unions' Directory," *AWRS*, 1 January 1932, 6.

73. See Hilton, "ABW Database." At least seventy Baptist women were active members of the WCTU.

74. Barber, "Health and Narcotics," 32.

wife, were intended to be essentially equal and relatively different."[75] Lilian Brown affirmed that "enlightened women" knew it was unreasonable for women to be restricted to home life, and remarked: "Why . . . if an intellectually accomplished man is not unmanly, is an intellectually accomplished woman unwomanly?"[76] In 1907 Cecilia Downing was the Victorian superintendent for encouraging congregations to use unfermented wine in communion, and she stressed that, "it is humane and Scriptural to use the pure unalcoholized juice of the grape when celebrating our Lord's death."[77] In the 1890s Emily Hone was the national superintendent for the flower mission of the SA WCTU, and she prepared a booklet on how to undertake the work. She wrote: "[Flowers] are fragrant in themselves, but each carries the added fragrance of a Gospel message in the form of a prettily printed text attached to it."[78] Also at this time Margaret McLean supervised "drawing room meetings" whereby WCTU members organized meetings of interested women in their homes with the aim of increasing membership of the WCTU.[79] In 1897 Emily Price from NSW was the national superintendent for "Sabbath observance" and she believed that there were two important aspects to keeping Sunday holy, contending:

> This question has for us as Christian temperance workers two aspects, a special and a general one. In its special aspects, that of the Sunday closing of public houses, its close relation to our work is obvious enough. But in its general aspect Sabbath observance might seem to be a purely religious matter, yet I think it is in many ways a question deeply interesting to all Christian women, and one in which we may exert a mighty influence.[80]

By this statement Emily Price demonstrated how women's Christian beliefs melded with the aims of the WCTU. These women's writings and actions show how Baptist women were actively engaged in politics and social reform within the WCTU.

Baptist women's involvement in the WCTU continued into the twentieth century, although fewer writings by women are extant. Such a reduction can partly be explained by the reduced interest in temperance reforms more generally, and the fact that alcohol consumption reduced because of the 1930s

75. Mead, *Awakened Woman*, 2.
76. Mead, *Awakened Woman*, 24.
77. Downing, "Unfermented Wine Department," 43.
78. Hone, "Flower Mission," 104.
79. McLean, "Drawingroom Meetings," 31.
80. Price, "Sabbath Observance," 102.

economic depression.[81] The WCTU was less likely to be the subject of articles in mainstream papers after 1930 compared to the early twentieth century.[82]

Throughout its history the WCTU was the focus of criticism from various sources, with some commentators stating the WCTU was too political or had a repressive approach.[83] At times leaders were mocked as "wowsers" in attempts to lessen the impact of the organization.[84] From a twenty-first-century perspective it is evident that the work of the WCTU was limited in its scope and effectiveness, particularly given that the WCTU's efforts to achieve suffrage did not include extending the franchise to First Nations women or men. Between 1931 and 1939 Elizabeth Rees, as editor of *The White Ribbon Signal*, discussed the inequity of First Nations people compared to non-Indigenous Australians, as did other members, but the WCTU only pursued the issue seriously after 1945.[85] While the WCTU appeared to focus on protecting the family unit rather than increasing the role of women in society, the WCTU provided opportunities for women that were not available in other organizations.[86] The work that Baptist women undertook as part of the WCTU was worthwhile and led to various reforms in Australian society, specifically women's suffrage. Importantly the WCTU provided women—not least Baptists—with a mechanism to be actively involved in social reform.

CASE STUDY: MARGARET MCLEAN AND ELIZABETH REES AND THE WCTU

This case study examines and compares the writings of two Baptist women who were significant in the Victorian WCTU. Margaret McLean and Elizabeth Rees shared a concern for disadvantaged women and children, particularly those whose household included an alcoholic man. There was a

81. Pargeter, *For God, Home and Humanity*, 59.

82. Confirmed by analysis of the frequency of the use of the term in the 1930s. See https://trove.nla.gov.au.

83. Woolcock, "The Minister and His Church in their Relation to Outside Organizations [sic]," *TP*, 1 November 1894, 332. See Spence, *Ever Yours*, 353; "Not a 'Horrid' man, but a 'Fresh' Feminine," *Truth* (Brisbane), 20 October 1918, 10; "Wowsers on the War-Path," *Call and WA Sportsman*, 24 October 1919, 9. The WCTU was criticised more in the United States than in Australia, partly because prohibition was achieved by the WCTU in some cities. See Postel, "Political Chaos and Unexpected Activism."

84. "Wowsers on the War-Path," *Call and WA Sportsman*, 24 October 1919, 9; Lake, "Women's and Gender History in Australia," 192.

85. Pargeter, *For God, Home and Humanity*, 101.

86. O'Brien, *God's Willing Workers*, 82–83.

twenty-year age difference between them, but their key published writings were around forty years apart. Their appointments on the executive committee of the Victorian WCTU overlapped and so they knew each other. Both women worked in the Baptist denomination and the WCTU; both women have entries in the *Australian Dictionary of Biography*; and although both women were Evangelicals, only Margaret McLean has been included in the *Australian Dictionary of Evangelical Biography*.[87]

Margaret McLean was born in 1845 in Scotland and came to Australia as a child with her parents, Agnes, née Russell, and Andrew Arnot. She trained in Melbourne as a teacher and married William McLean in 1869 in Melbourne. Margaret and William McLean had six daughters and four sons who survived infancy. It is likely that she inspired four of her daughters to lead active lives in the public and intermediate spheres: Hilda McLean and Alice Barber were ABFM workers in East Bengal, and Alice Barber was one of the pioneers of psychotherapy in Melbourne; Ethel McLean was a teacher; and Lucie McLean was a nurse. A keen supporter of the WCTU, in 1890 she presented the key address at the Victorian convention of WCTU, entitled "Womanhood suffrage."[88] In 1891, when 30,000 Victorian women signed the Women's Suffrage Petition that was presented to the Victorian State Government, "Mrs William McLean" (Margaret McLean) was the first signature on the petition.[89] She was President of the Victorian WCTU in 1892 and from 1889 to 1907, and she wrote papers and articles, including president's reports, which outlined her views of the work and progress of the WCTU.[90] Margaret McLean died in 1923 in Melbourne.

Elizabeth Rees was born in 1865 in London and came to Australia as a child with her parents, Margaret Johnston, née Kirkcaldy, and Thomas Johnston. She married Evan Rees in 1892 in Melbourne and they had five children. Elizabeth Rees joined the Victorian WCTU as a young married woman, became the secretary in 1913, and was president from 1933 to 1936. Most significantly she was the editor of the WCTU's national paper, *The Australian White Ribbon Signal*, from 1931 to 1939. In 1921 she had advocated for women to be appointed as justices in Victorian courts, and in 1927 she was one of the first seven Victorian women appointed, although she had no formal qualifications. Elizabeth Rees died in 1939 in Melbourne.[91]

87. See https://adb.anu.edu.au; Dickey, *Australian Dictionary of Evangelical Biography*.

88. McLean, *Womanhood Suffrage*; *More about Womanhood Suffrage*.

89. "Women's Suffrage Petition." Elizabeth Rees was twenty-six at the time the Petition was presented; she does not appear on the list of signatories.

90. See, for example, McLean, "President's Address," 11–16.

91. "Mrs. E. L. Rees," *Argus*, 22 March 1939, 12; "Letters," *Table Talk* (Melbourne),

As members of the WCTU, Margaret McLean and Elizabeth Rees held very similar views on several issues. Both women believed in the importance of temperance, on the basis that alcohol was "evil" and prohibition was required to create a Christian and moral society. Margaret McLean wrote: "We believe that the drink traffic deserves to be outlawed, and are prepared to help forward every measure that makes for its suppression."[92] Likewise Elizabeth Rees was "firmly convinced of the benefits of prohibition."[93] They also believed that Australia needed to do more to achieve full equity between men and women. Margaret McLean said: "I contend that even in professedly Christian countries the true position of women is not yet attained."[94] Both women attended world WCTU conferences. In 1900 Margaret McLean was the only Australian delegate to the Edinburgh World WCTU Conference, and she preached in St Giles Cathedral.[95] In 1928 Elizabeth Rees was part of the delegation of thirty-six Australian women who attended the World WCTU Conference held in Lausanne, Switzerland, and was one of the conference speakers.[96] In addition she was the only woman to address the 1928 Baptist World Congress held in Toronto, Canada.[97] She attended both events as part of a nine-month worldwide trip with her husband Evan Rees and youngest daughter Margaret Moyle.

Margaret McLean and Elizabeth Rees were committed Evangelical Baptist women. They were active in pursuing temperance as a religious issue, they used Scriptural references in their articles, and spoke about the importance of Christ as Saviour.[98] Articles by Margaret McLean and Elizabeth Rees differed with respect to issues of interest to the WCTU at the time they were writing. Margaret McLean's writings had a focus on increasing the membership of the WCTU and on suffrage. With respect to increasing membership, she wrote: "We need the rank and file quite as much as we need leaders, and we must increase our membership before we can greatly increase our usefulness."[99] Her writings advocated for women's right to vote, while carefully not being too aggressive or overstepping women's implicit boundaries. The statement "it is of the right to vote only that I wish to speak

---

14 February 1929, 62; Smart, "Rees, Elizabeth Laurie."
- 92. McLean, "Letter to the Editor," *TSB*, 17 July 1901, 168.
- 93. "Letters," *Table Talk*, 14 February 1929, 62.
- 94. McLean, *Womanhood Suffrage*, 3.
- 95. Hyslop, "McLean, Margaret."
- 96. "Letters," *Table Talk*, 14 February 1929, 62.
- 97. "'Baptist Pentecost Is Here': First News from Toronto," *TAB*, 31 July 1928, 2.
- 98. Rees, "Eastertide: 'He Is Risen,'" *AWRS*, 1 March 1932, 43.
- 99. McLean, "President's Address," 14.

at present" implies there is more that she wanted to speak about.[100] Often she put the burden of proof onto those against women's suffrage to argue the case for prohibiting women's vote, stressing: "We women should not plead for [suffrage], . . . our opponents should show valid reasons why it has not been granted to us."[101] She took a pragmatic and conciliatory approach, emphasizing that women's suffrage would help men achieve temperance, stating: "We are not clamorous, but do not think that . . . we are careless about [the vote]. The women of this country are uniting to help your societies, and the churches also, in fighting the battle against evil. Give us the weapon you find so needful."[102] She was a forceful person. In 1901 Margaret McLean's husband resigned from his positions in the Victorian Baptist Union because he was unhappy with the choice of Union President. The day after he submitted his resignation *The Argus* reported that "Mr McLean had, in deference to the wishes of his wife and to the request of the assembly, consented to withdraw his resignation."[103]

While Margaret McLean's writing focused on women's suffrage, Elizabeth Rees's writings covered a broader range of issues given that women's suffrage had been implemented throughout Australia before her active involvement in WCTU commenced. However in 1921 she did express disappointment when women did not vote in a liquor licence poll.[104] She believed the WCTU had educated women to vote against liquor licences, and to support candidates who advocated for temperance.[105] Elizabeth Rees addressed the injustices suffered by First Nations people.[106] In 1938 she wrote an editorial about the celebration of 150 years of British occupation in Australia and how First Nations people labeled the day as "A day of mourning," concluding that: "We, as individuals, and as WCT Unions, can use our influence so that opportunities are given to the [A]boriginal women . . . so that they may be the torch bearers of their people . . . Every woman will hinder by her apathy, or help by her interest. Will you help or hinder?"[107] She was editor of the WCTU's national paper during the inter-war years and

100. McLean, *Womanhood Suffrage*, 2.
101. McLean, *More about Womanhood Suffrage*, 2.
102. McLean, *More about Womanhood Suffrage*, 8.
103. "Baptist Union," *Argus*, 22 November 1901, 8.
104. "Women's [sic] Christian Temperance Union," *Reporter* (Box Hill, Victoria), 5 August 1921, 2. Voting was not compulsory until 1924. The poll resulted in the withdrawal of liquor licences in the seat of Boroondara, Melbourne, but the turnout had been low.
105. McCorkindale, *Pioneer Pathways*, 81.
106. Smart, "Rees, Elizabeth Laurie."
107. Rees, "Bargains," *AWRS*, 1 March 1938, 44.

the 1930s economic depression, and she wrote articles addressing peace and inequality. Her daughter Margaret Moyle described her as "a peace-loving woman."[108] She believed that social reform led to productive growth of the Australian nation and religious life.[109]

Comparisons between Margaret McLean and Elizabeth Rees highlight how the WCTU changed its emphasis over time. Essentially Margaret McLean's articles were focused on achieving temperance through suffrage. Elizabeth Rees had more scope—more civic capacity—to express her opinions about a range of issues. Both women believed in the ability of the WCTU to achieve change in social reform, and their individual work was significant.

Margaret McLean and Elizabeth Rees demonstrated how some Baptist women engaged in pan-evangelical work while retaining an Australian Baptist identity. Both women were proud of being Australian. In 1900—before Federation—Margaret McLean wrote: "Personally I always was glad that my parents settled in Victoria, but I'm more glad to be an Australian."[110] Similarly in 1929 Elizabeth Rees was concerned that Australia did not have a good reputation in the UK.[111] Both women, despite the significant time they spent in work for the WCTU, were involved in their Baptist congregations as Sunday School teachers, along with other Baptist denominational work.[112] There is no evidence that either woman worked outside the denomination other than for the WCTU.

SOCIAL WELFARE

Many Australians faced poverty, destitution, and other related social inequity, particularly during the two depressions of the 1890s and 1930s, and consequently philanthropic Australians established and maintained social welfare services to address these issues. City mission organizations were created to address people's practical needs and many Baptist women worked for these organizations.[113] Undoubtedly the Baptist emphasis on evangelistic activities limited social welfare activities within the denomination, and

---

108. Margaret Moyle, "To the Members of the WCTU," *AWRS*, 1 May 1939, 92.
109. Wilkin, "Victorian Baptist Union," *TAB*, 14 June 1927, 12.
110. McLean, "Colonial President's Greetings," 37.
111. "An Observant Woman's Travels," *Age*, 24 January 1929, 11.
112. "The Late Mrs. William McLean," *TAB*, 27 February 1923, 4; Wilkin, *Baptists in Victoria*, 159.
113. "Wanted," *TAB*, 27 May 1924, 4. The Sydney City Mission advertised vacant nursing positions in *TAB*.

as a result most of the social welfare work undertaken by Baptist women occurred outside the Baptist denomination. Yet for some women, social welfare was viewed as "the union of faith and works."[114]

Australian Baptist women worked in a range of these social welfare activities including providing food and clothing for those in poverty, visiting men and women in gaol, teaching life skills to young mothers, and providing free kindergartens for disadvantaged children.[115] Not only was there a wide range of work undertaken, but some of the work was very localized and existed only for a short period. In Queensland, for instance, Edith Kerr wanted to become a CIM worker but instead worked as a Chinese teacher, followed by employment within the Methodist denomination in Brisbane undertaking social welfare activities. She resigned at the age of thirty-two when she "eventually married" a Baptist minister.[116] Other women were engaged with organizations that evolved over the twentieth century. In NSW Louisa Ardill worked in the Christian Sydney Rescue Work Society established by her husband George Ardill. Louisa Ardill was co-editor of the society's paper, *The Rescue*, and was integral in establishing the Home of Hope Hospital, which became the South Sydney Women's Hospital.[117] In Queensland several Baptist women, including Bertha Knight and Hepzibah Mirfin, were involved with the Brisbane Benevolent Society, which originated as a branch of the WCTU but in 1900 changed its name and focus to providing practical help to those in need.[118] Some Baptist women started their own social welfare work. In the Victorian town of Sale, Alice Skeel, for instance, donated land and funding for residential units for the elderly, and she successfully advocated for ongoing city council funding. She realized the need for an aged care facility partly because she operated a boarding house.[119] Social welfare activities show the adaptability of Baptist women in Australia, because women undertook activities that enabled them to express their faith in a way that was meaningful to them.

Various Baptist women were also involved in the YWCA as committee members, volunteers, or paid workers. The YWCA was formed in England to support young women in various ways, from creating hostels to prayer groups. In the 1880s women established YWCAs in Sydney, Melbourne, and

114. "In Memoriam: Mrs. T. Mirfin," *TAB*, 23 July 1935, 3.

115. Treloar, *Disruption of Evangelicalism*, 4, 477.

116. "Was Methodist Pioneer Sister," *Telegraph*, 25 November 1942, 4. She was a Baptist minister's wife for much longer than she was a Methodist worker. Perhaps this article title reflects that being a deaconess was unusual.

117. Radi, "Ardill, George Edward."

118. "Valley Benevolence," *Telegraph* (Brisbane), 9 February 1901, 14.

119. "Obituary: Alice Skeels," *Gippsland Times* (Sale), 20 October 1961, 3.

Adelaide. As in England the specific aims of these groups varied depending on the needs of each community. In 1882 Baptist woman Sarah Booth became the first—unpaid—General Secretary of YWCA in Victoria, a position she held for twenty-eight years. The Victorian YWCA was formed to assist women "less fortunate in life."[120] The SA YWCA had a similar focus, and in the early twentieth century Baptists Rosetta Birks, Helen Goode, Lucy Lavis, and Catherine Neill each served as President, and Annie Green and Dorothy Kentish worked full-time for the organization.[121] Annie Green's death notice stated that "She gave her life to 'the poorest, the lowliest, the lost.'"[122] In 1907 a national YWCA was formed to coordinate the different work being undertaken by local branches.[123] While the main activity was social welfare, the members hoped that "souls [were] won for Christ" through the work.[124] Sentiments such as these suggest that the women believed their social welfare work was also evangelistic in some respects.

The work of Margaret Bean—"Sister Grace"—was independent but for many years took place in Baptist facilities. In 1903 Margaret Bean arrived in Australia with her son, the Rev. Albert Bean. She lived with him until his marriage in 1907, at which point she commenced her own mission with poor people in Melbourne. She continued this volunteer work for nineteen years until she retired in 1926 at the age of seventy-five. Her work was initially based at the Gospel Hall Mission that had been established by Collins Street Baptist. In 1912 she moved to Albert Street Baptist, before her work became part of the Melbourne City Mission in 1920.[125] Margaret Bean was assisted by many Baptist women, particularly those from Collins Street Baptist. Her journal of the work contains numerous facts and observations. The front and back pages record exact numbers of activities she undertook, including meetings attended and visits to private homes, hospitals, and public houses. The journal listed instances when she helped men and women with their physical needs—food, clothing, and shelter—and stated her beliefs that God provided spiritual care. Of one alcoholic woman, she wrote "I . . . trust Him to keep her from sin and failure," and of another woman, "I wish she would

120. Booth, *Dinna Forget*, 17; "Young Women's Christian Association," *Leader* (Melbourne), 8 October 1910, 47.

121. Manley, *From Woolloomooloo*, 1:303.

122. Miss M. [May] Shorney, "Tribute to Miss Annie Green," *News* (Adelaide), 15 April 1936, 8.

123. "Young Women's Christian Association," *Leader* (Melbourne), 14 September 1907, 46.

124. "Young Women's Christian Association," *Christian Colonist* (Adelaide), 12 February 1886, 3.

125. Newnham, "Sister Grace's Mission," 37–38.

take my advice and have the Life."[126] Margaret Bean had a reputation for being difficult at times and after being called "exacting" wrote: "They don't relish their work being criticised."[127] She committed all her finances towards her work.[128]

Some social welfare was undertaken in association with the Baptist denomination, with women active in the work. In Victoria women worked in the Gospel Hall Mission and managed the Bouverie Street Kindergarten.[129] In SA women provided much of the paid and unpaid work required to maintain the Flinders Street Baptist missions established for the disadvantaged in Adelaide, called the West End Mission and the Halifax Street Mission.[130] Several women in SA supported the Morialta Protestant Children's Home, and the Baptist Women's League undertook other social welfare activities.[131] In Tasmania Mary Lamb ministered within Launceston Baptist and she also worked to support people living in poverty. She made about seven different visits to poor people every day, held a soup kitchen every Friday night, and arranged mothers' groups during the week. From 1912 the work was based in Inveresk, then the poorest area of Launceston, and Mary Lamb moved into the area to be closer to those she assisted. When the 1918 influenza pandemic was rampant in Launceston Mary Lamb helped poor families stricken with influenza who were unable to obtain hospital care, until late in 1919 when she contracted influenza and died.[132] In numerous Baptist congregations other women undertook social welfare activities such as sewing groups which distributed clothing to poor women outside the denomination, either freely or at a reduced cost.[133]

Social welfare activities had an additional impact on women, because as organizations were created and various activities supported, some women obtained unpaid or paid employment. As an example, from 1914 to 1932 the superintendent of the West End Mission in Adelaide was Robert Lavis, but his role was to oversee the direction and management of the mission. From 1916 women were employed to work in the mission, but many tasks were undertaken by women who volunteered at the mission, including Lucy

---

126. Margaret F. Bean, "A Record of the Work of 'Sister Grace' at Gospel Hall," 105, 110, BUVA. She underlined "trust Him."

127. Margaret F. Bean, "A Record of the Work of 'Sister Grace' at Gospel Hall," 111, BUVA.

128. Newnham, "Sister Grace's Mission," 42.

129. *Victorian Baptist Women's Association*.

130. "Death of Mr. R. J. Lavis," *Chronicle* (Adelaide) 1941, 18.

131. Wilcox, *Baptist Women's League*, 13, 17, 19.

132. "Launceston Tabernacle," *TAB*, 18 February 1919, 7.

133. Ladies Sewing Guild Glen Osmond MM, SABA.

Lavis, the wife of Robert Lavis.[134] Her obituary in *The Australian Baptist* stressed that "she was a real helpmate."[135] Yet Lucy Lavis was more than a "helpmate." Indeed, Robert Lavis's obituary in the *Chronicle*, a mainstream newspaper, observed that he conducted the mission work "with Mrs Lavis."[136] Arguably it was the work of Lucy Lavis—along with other women volunteers and workers—that developed the mission, rather than the superintendency of Robert Lavis. Robert Lavis had a full-time job outside the denomination and was unable to devote the time to this mission that his wife did. One conclusion about this situation is that, while Baptist women acted, men were credited with the achievements.[137]

The level of Baptist women's involvement in social welfare across Australian states was somewhat reflective of diverse theological views. Different theological views held by Baptists about the relative importance of personal salvation and implications of the social gospel impacted the interplay between social services originating or undertaken within or outside the denomination.[138] Of the four largest states it appears that Baptists in NSW and Queensland were less likely to initiate social welfare activities in the denomination compared to SA and Victoria.[139] Indeed in 1930 the Victorian Baptist Women's Association made a conscious decision to change their aims to acknowledge that "the association was striving to assist in the work of its own church and social work outside its own denomination."[140]

The level of social welfare activities by Baptist women changed over time and location. In the period prior to 1880 there are some examples of social welfare activities, such as in 1870 when Mary Holden advocated for, and partly funded, a public school in Norwood SA.[141] From about 1880 to 1945 there was a relatively constant level of social welfare activities undertaken by Baptist women in SA and Victoria, both within and outside the denomination. Conversely Baptist women in NSW and Queensland undertaking social welfare activities almost invariably did so outside the

---

134. "Flinders Street, Adelaide," *TAB*, 4 January 1916, 12.

135. "The Late Mrs. R. J. Lavis," *TAB*, 21 April 1936, 2.

136. "Death of Mr. R. J. Lavis," *Chronicle* 1941, 18.

137. This type of situation was common. See "South Australian Baptist Union Annual Assembly," *TAB*, 6 October 1936, 9.

138. Manley, *From Woolloomooloo*, 1:359.

139. See, for example, Grange Baptist Church Ladies' Guild MM, SABA; Flinders Street Women's Guild MM, SABA. Tasmania and WA have been excluded from analysis because of the small number of Baptists.

140. "Woman's Interests," *Age*, 23 October 1930, 11.

141. "News of the Churches: Laying Foundation Stone of the Norwood Public School," *TP*, December 1870, 141.

Women's Social Work and Activities Outside the Denomination

denomination. Perhaps they would have preferred to have worked within the denomination had that been an option. The actions of the Ladies' Aid Society at Hurlstone Park hint at this possibility. In late 1929 the Society, through the President Winifred Smith, had ongoing discussions with the Sydney City Mission, and assisted them in various ways in "supplying Xmas [sic] cheer to needy ones."[142] The women did not have the funds or the volunteers to deliver assistance themselves, and the NSW denomination did not have a suitable vehicle for such assistance. Indeed relatively fewer women in NSW and Queensland were engaged in social welfare activities in the 1920s and 1930s compared to other periods, which is somewhat surprising given the significance of the 1930s economic depression.[143] One possibility is that social welfare activities at this time were impacted by fundamentalist views which were becoming a feature in NSW and Queensland and tended to prioritize evangelism. Or perhaps women from NSW and Queensland turned to more evangelistic activities *because* of the depression and a general lack of funding.

Many women who undertook social welfare activities outside the denomination were also involved in activities within the denomination. For example, in Victoria Margaret Jenkin was involved in the Melbourne City Mission and was an active member of Brunswick Baptist and the Victorian Baptist Women's Missionary Union. As her obituarist stated: "Her loyalty as a Baptist did not prevent her keen interest in the whole work of God within and without all denominations."[144] Other Australian Baptist women may have chosen to undertake social welfare within or outside the denomination but did not have the opportunity due to the absence of necessary support and infrastructure. Margaret Bean was only able to structure her work in the way she did because the Baptist congregations at Collins Street and Albert Street owned appropriate facilities. While there are many factors that led to an increase in social welfare activities undertaken by Australian Baptists after 1945, particularly homes for the elderly, a major reason may have been the good examples set by these Baptist women forerunners.[145]

---

142. HPBLASM, NSWBA.
143. Manley, *From Woolloomooloo*, 1:359–62.
144. "Passing of Mrs. M. Jenkin," *TAB*, 31 October 1939, 5.
145. Piggin and Linder, *Fountain of Public Prosperity*, 436.

WOMEN IN PAID EMPLOYMENT OUTSIDE THE RELIGIOUS SPHERE

From the late nineteenth century several Australian Baptist women took advantage of increasing opportunities for further education or pursued various professional pathways.[146] To 1945 at least 100 Baptist women were trained nurses, over fifty were employed as teachers, and ten were doctors, indeed nearly forty Baptist women are known to have completed university education.[147] Yet it is difficult to draw firm conclusions about these women's motivations or the connection of their vocation to their Baptist faith.[148]

Women who were trained for a specific occupation often used these skills in denominational activities. A small number of women were able to donate money to the denomination because of their successful businesses.[149] Doctors Gertrude Mead and Eleanor Varley used their knowledge and status within the denomination to argue for medical mission and aged care facilities respectively.[150] Ministers' wives used skills obtained prior to their marriages in their lives as ministers' wives.[151] Sarah Sharp was the principal of Goulburn Primary School in NSW before her marriage to the Rev. Stephen Sharp. Her obituary declared that "teaching was her vocation rather than a profession ... The same qualities which made for success in her secular calling were in evidence in all she put her hand to in the various churches with which she was associated, both before and since her marriage."[152] Similarly Frances Aldridge was a nurse prior to her marriage, and nursing skills were useful for a minister's wife, and later for her role as a paid deaconess in the Brisbane Tabernacle.[153] Thus in many cases a woman's vocation had a direct impact on her work within the denomination.

Australian Baptists—women and men—rarely engaged with issues pertaining to low paid women's work, such as piece-workers, factory workers, shop assistants, or domestic service.[154] With respect to domestic service,

146. Mackinnon, *New Women*, 19.
147. Hilton, "ABW Database."
148. Sheard and Lee, *Women to the Front*, 1; Hilton, "ABW Database."
149. "Mrs. Rebecca Bullock," *Wellington Times* (Wellington, NSW), 12 May 1941, 2; "The Late Mrs Oliver," *TAB*, 6 December 1921, 8.
150. Mead, "Medical Missions," *WA Baptist*, 15 April 1907, 75; Potter, "Baptist Union of Victoria," *TAB*, 23 May 1944, 4.
151. See, for example, Simpson, "The Late Mrs. W. Gilmour: A Triumphant Passing," *TAB*, 14 June 1932, 9; "Was Methodist Pioneer Sister," *Telegraph*, 25 November 1942, 2.
152. "In Memoriam: Mrs Stephen Sharp," *TAB*, 31 August 1926, 4.
153. Parker, *Women Who Made a Difference*, 37.
154. Grimshaw et al., *Creating a Nation*, 200–201.

some Baptist women who wanted to undertake significant denominational or other religious work could only do so if they employed other women to do typical home duties. That is, wealthy women relied on other women, who were usually poorer women with less power, to fulfil their own calling. In 1907 Rosetta Birks argued that women domestics needed better protections to make the occupation more appealing. This was not a desire to empower working-class women domestics: Rosetta Birks wanted to increase the number of women attracted to working as domestics, to enable middle-class and wealthy women—who used domestics—to be more active in society.[155] Effectively middle-class and wealthy women acted against the interests of poor and working-class women. Obviously most men relied on women—with less public power—to support them to achieve their goals, an issue that is rarely discussed with respect to men's achievements. One cannot be critical of these women, unless one is critical of men in their actions, or inactions, in a societal structure that expected women to work for lower wages than men.[156] Yet it is important to acknowledge the significance of wealth and power inherent in some of the work undertaken by women. In this sense class was clearly a factor in what it meant to be an Australian Baptist woman.

INTERNATIONAL WOMEN TRAVELERS

International travel was a relatively common occurrence for Australian Baptists, even for women who were not excessively wealthy. Of course, a significant number of women traveled when migrating to Australia.[157] Angela Woollacott estimates that from 1880 to 1900 around ten thousand Australian women each year traveled to the UK—the "old country"—and that women were more likely to travel to the UK than men.[158] Often Australian Baptist women specifically referred to their travel experiences as strengthening their faith, rather than as a recreational activity.[159] Missionary women

155. Zenobia [Rosetta Birks], "Dearth of Domestic Servants," *Register* (Adelaide), 22 February 1907, 9.

156. Grimshaw et al., *Creating a Nation*, 200–201; Chilton, *Agents of Empire*, 157–59; Lack and Fahey, "Industrialist, the Trade Unionist and the Judge," 1, 16. There is significant scholarship on this issue, particularly about systematic court rulings that established different pay rates for men and women.

157. Hilton, "ABW Database."

158. Woollacott, *To Try Her Fortune in London*, 5.

159. See, for example, "Missionary News: Farewell to Miss Tranter and Mrs Bean," *TSB*, 15 October 1907, 247; "Welcomes and Farewells: Coronation Tour: Baptist Women's Association," *Age*, 25 February 1937, 13.

traveled to missions, and other women traveled for their work, especially those who enlisted for service during the two world wars.[160] Women visited family and friends.[161]

Baptist women traveled internationally as representatives of Australian Baptists or Australian women's organizations.[162] For World WCTU Conventions: Louisa Ardill attended in 1897; Eleanor Barber and Margaret McLean in 1900; Martha Thomson in 1906; and in 1928 at least four Australian Baptist women attended the World WCTU Convention in Lausanne.[163] In 1937 over fifty Australian Baptists traveled to London for the coronation of King George VI and Queen Elizabeth, and over half were women.[164] The Australian Baptist missions in East Bengal were visited by family members of mission workers including: Lilian Brown in 1897, who visited her brother; Linda Glasson in 1920, who visited her sister Ethel Masters; Eva McLean in 1925, who visited her sisters Alice Barber and Hilda McLean; and Amelia Harris in 1929, who visited her sister Florence Harris. Mission enthusiasts also visited, such as Irene Good in 1927, and Marion White in 1928.[165] In 1907 Annie Bean said that visiting the mission fields fulfilled "the dream of many years."[166]

Women travelers viewed themselves as active rather than passive participants in their travel. In 1924 Ella Shepard wrote of the ways in which she absorbed herself into the culture of women in East Bengal.[167] The feedback from women visiting the missions reinforced the view that Australian Baptist women needed to assist East Bengali women.[168] Of the travel in 1937

160. See "Missionary News," *TSB*, 15 October 1907, 247; Tranter, *Diary*; "Western Australia," *TAB*, 4 February 1919, 4.

161. "Farewell to Miss Sharp," *TAB*, 18 August 1931, 11.

162. See, for example, "Baptist Union: Farewell to Rev. A.S. and Mrs Wilson," *TWA*, 11 June 1901, 6; Lilian S. Mead, "Convention Impressions: 'Frisco, 1897," *TGL*, 1 September 1897, 16.

163. "A White Ribbon Tourist: Return of Mrs. Ardill: The World's WCTU Convention," *Daily Telegraph* (Sydney), 13 December 1898, 5; Mrs W. [Margaret] McLean, "World's Woman's Christian Temperance Union," *TSB*, 16 August 1900, 185; "Women's [sic] Christian Temperance Union," *TSB*, 10 July 1906, 171; "WCTU," *Observer* (Adelaide), 13 October 1928, 61.

164. W. G. [William] Pope, "Coronation Party," *TAB*, 1 September 1936, 3.

165. "Personal," *TWA*, 20 November 1920, 8; "Social," *OB*, January 1926, 4; "Home Notes," *OIF*, 6 December 1929, 7. S. Irene Good, "A Glimpse," *OB*, September 1927, 4; "Welcome Meeting," *OB*, January 1929, 4.

166. "Missionary News: Farewell to Miss Tranter and Mrs Bean," *TSB*, 15 October 1907, 247.

167. Miss W. [Ella] Shepard, "Christmas Day in India," *TAB*, 12 February 1924, 11.

168. See, for example, Shepard, "Christmas Day in India," *TAB*, 12 February 1924,

to the Coronation Mary Pope indicated that she "did not regard the trip merely as a pleasure trip . . . but intended to find out what was being done by the Baptist women's organizations overseas, and would return able to give those who had stayed at home something of their experiences."[169] There are many examples of women sharing their international travel experiences with others, particularly in Baptist women's meetings.[170] As Isabella Miles indicated, women wanted to impart experiences that were "worthy of note for . . . fellow women workers in Australia."[171]

The focus on women travelers has significance with respect to the connection of women to a place.[172] Perhaps women's identity as an Australian Baptist was easier to comprehend through a wider world view, which required travel, or at the very least, an understanding of places beyond one's local community.[173]

IN TIMES OF "CRISIS"[174]

Australian Baptist women were adversely impacted by Australian and world events, specifically wars, the depressions of the 1890s and the 1930s, and the 1918 influenza pandemic. Some chose to alleviate the suffering of others during these times, as demonstrated in the discussion earlier regarding social welfare. In times of crisis—with resulting shortages of men to undertake leadership or ministry roles, or money to pay salaries—the small Baptist denomination relied on women to support Baptist work and to react to the needs of others.

During the period from 1879 to 1945 the most disruptive events in Australian Baptist women's lives were wars: the Anglo-South African War, the First World War, and the Second World War. Many Baptist women spoke and wrote about the importance of peace, particularly prior to and after the First World War. Notwithstanding Baptists' commitment to peace, overall most Australian Baptists supported the justification for engagement

---

11; S. Irene Goode, "A Glimpse," *OB*, September 1927, 4.

169. "Welcomes and Farewells," *Age*, 25 February 1937, 13.

170. See, for example, "Fairfield," *TQB*, 1 March 1923, 14; "Visits From Our Girls in the Services," *Rising Tide*, April 1943, 4.

171. Miles, "Among Scottish Baptist Women," *TAB*, 2 April 1918, 161.

172. Friedman, *Mappings*, 151. Susan Friedman writes of identity being "based on travel, change, and disruption."

173. See, for example, Durbin, "An Endeavourer in Paris," *TRC*, 1 September 1937, 47.

174. Pargeter, *For God, Home and Humanity*, 59.

in these wars.[175] During wartime women were committed to ensuring that Australian life continued as normally as possible. Many women supported those who enlisted and were serving overseas and wanted them to maintain a connection to Australia.[176]

During the First World War Marian Tranter wrote a poem titled "Dear mother hands":

> The hands that rocked the cradles of men so true and brave,
> Who fight with our great Allies: Their nation's life to save . . .
> And now those hands are busied in knitting day by day,
> Or words of love are writing: To those so far away.[177]

These sentiments were true of many Baptist women. Women were involved in various organizations, particularly the Red Cross, and many Baptist women's groups joined the "war effort," which included raising money and making clothes.[178] In a letter to Mary Raws, her son Alec Raws on the front-line mentioned his "wonderful hand-made socks."[179] Helen Harry, the minister's wife at Perth Central Baptist, wrote weekly to each person from the congregation who had enlisted.[180] During the First World War the Australian Red Cross and St John Ambulance established Voluntary Aid Detachments to assist men returning to civilian life from military service, with women delivering the service, including many Baptist women. Some Voluntary Aid Detachments regenerated in the Baptist denomination during the Second World War.[181]

Australian Baptist women were personally impacted by the death of family members in war. Nurse Hilda Williams appears to have been the only Australian Baptist woman who died in consequence of service. Her death occurred at the Woodman's Point Quarantine Station WA, as she nursed soldiers who had returned to Australia with the 1918 influenza.[182] Hilda Williams's mother, Louisa Williams, also suffered the death of her son,

---

175. Manley, *From Woolloomooloo*, 2:407; Badger, *Duty, Sacrifice and Honour*, 4, 17.

176. McKernan, *Australians at Home*, 65–66.

177. Tranter, *Call of the Bush*, 19.

178. Badger, *Duty, Sacrifice and Honour*, 81, 91.

179. Young and Gammage, *Hail and Farewell*, 121.

180. Crofts, Letter; Manley, *From Woolloomooloo*, 2:418. Seventy-two men and one woman connected to Helen Harry's congregation enlisted.

181. "Australian Women's Register"; Women's Auxiliaries [NSW], *Annual Reports and Balance Sheets 1947–48*. In NSW the Voluntary Aid Detachment was considered a woman's organization.

182. The 1918 influenza is also called the Spanish Flu or the H1N1 Virus. See "Western Australia," *TAB*, 4 February 1919, 4.

Arthur Williams. Mary Pflaum, Mary Raws and Matilda Wilkins each suffered the death of two sons in the First World War.[183] Lennon Raws, the surviving son of Mary Raws, wrote that: "Father . . . occasionally would break down. Mother had to keep calm to help him, but we sorrowed even more for her than for him because she could not find relief in tears."[184] In 1934 Mary Raws's obituary observed that "she suffered the great trial of her life—the loss of two sons in the world war—with exemplary Christian fortitude."[185]

Several Baptist women were active participants in war zones through enlisting in the Australian Imperial Force (AIF), or as volunteers, although one cannot determine whether these women's Baptist commitment was a major factor in their decisions. At least twenty-five Baptist women enlisted as nurses in the First World War. Elsie Cumming's diary illuminates the advantages of service, such as the ability to travel and to undertake tasks that were not possible for a nurse to undertake in Australian hospitals.[186]

Doctors Laura Hope and Katie Ardill-Brice, who, because they were women, were not able to enlist in the AIF as doctors, volunteered for service. They traveled overseas and worked alongside men who were able to use relevant skills as enlisted members of the AIF.[187] Alice Barber returned to Melbourne from mission work in East Bengal to work in the Melbourne Women's Hospital, which had vacant positions due to enlistment of male doctors.[188] Cousins Elsie Patterson and Evelyn Wilson, who had graduated from the University of Sydney with a degree now known as physiotherapy, undertook work in the rehabilitation of soldiers.[189] At least three Baptist women suffered permanent injury because of their war service. Elsie Deakin, Dora Froome, and Rose Taylor found it difficult to continue their work as nurses once repatriated to Australia due to injury or illness.[190] Isabella Miles's elder son died in the First World War and she died in England between the wars—her husband, the Rev. Frederick Miles, said her death was due to her intensive work during the war, "the result of war work."[191]

183. See the stories in Badger, *Duty, Sacrifice and Honour*.
184. Young and Gammage, *Hail and Farewell*, 172.
185. "The Late Mrs. J. G. Raws," *TAB*, 18 September 1934, 4.
186. Tranter, *Diary*, 106.
187. Sheard and Lee, *Women to the Front*, 2, 64, 158.
188. "Home Notes: The Late Dr. Alice Barber," *OIF*, 6 June 1949, 5.
189. Driver and Colegrove, *For God, King and Country*, 235.
190. "The Late Mrs. Froome," *Daily News* (Perth), 8 June 1928, 8. Dora Froome died in 1918 age forty-three. Rose Taylor died in 1927 age fifty-four.
191. National Archives of Australia, Frederick James Miles. Letter from Frederick Miles to the Deputy Assistant Adjutant General dated 17 October 1947. Frederick Miles was an army chaplain in both world wars. Their younger son died in the Second

The end of the First World War was celebrated throughout Australia; but a resumption of normal life was delayed due to the 1918 influenza pandemic. Schools and businesses closed, and worship services and religious activities such as women's meetings were cancelled.[192] Baptist women volunteered to assist in treating those with the influenza. In Sydney, Florence Yule cared for influenza patients in her home.[193] Several Australian Baptist women died in the influenza pandemic including Mary Lamb in Launceston, Tasmania; and Anna White in Sydney.[194] Others suffered personal loss: In June 1919 in Rockhampton, Queensland, Marion Scott gave birth to her second child, and her husband, sister, and father died of influenza.[195]

During the Second World War many Australian Baptist women, as in the First World War, suffered the loss of close family members and friends. Two of Annie Yorkston's three sons were killed in March 1945.[196] Many women made themselves available to undertake tasks where there were not sufficient men available, which included executive positions and pastoral work.[197] Adelaide Bamford referred to the war in many of her columns.[198] She was concerned that Australians were "indifferent" to the possibility of invasion, but that it was "the critical hour for our land and ourselves." She implored her readers to pray and to "enlist others into the [prayer] army."[199]

Women who enlisted in the Second World War undertook a wider range of roles than in the First World War, and many completed their service in Australia. After initial reluctance to enlist women the Australian Government created organizations specifically to harness the workforce of young women, and 36,264 women enlisted. The largest of these organizations was the Australian Women's Army Service (AWAS), which had a contingent of over 24,000 women.[200] Several Baptist women are known to have joined the AWAS. Ellen Grace from Hurlstone Park, NSW, was a code breaker in Brisbane.[201] Dulcie Welch, from Queensland, worked on

---

World War.

192. For example: HPBLASM, NSWBA; Pargeter, *For God, Home and Humanity*, 59.

193. H. O. S., "New South Wales: Carlton," *TAB*, 3 June 1919, 10.

194. "Tasmania," *TAB*, 30 September 1919, 10; "Death of Mrs. William White," *TAB*, 1 July 1919, 3.

195. "Queensland: Rockhampton," *TAB*, 1 July 1919, 10.

196. "New South Wales: Annie Estill Yorkston," *TAB*, 26 June 1963, 14.

197. See Grange Baptist Ladies' Guild Annual Report, 4 February 1942, SABA.

198. Bamford, "OWTA: One Critical Hour," *TAB*, 17 March 1942.

199. Bamford, "OWTA: One Critical Hour," *TAB*, 17 March 1942, 5.

200. Ollif, *Women in Khaki*.

201. National Archives of Australia, Grace, Ellen Joyce.

a farm in regional NSW. She wrote a poem titled "Cast Thy Bread upon the waters," which implied that she saw her war work as being part of her Christian service, and it included the lines: "Thou know'st not what shall be: The outcome of thy service, accomplished faithfully."[202] Lorna Ollif was a member of Collins Street Baptist, and rose to the rank of Sergeant in the AWAS before her discharge at the end of the war. In 1981 she published a book about the AWAS called *Women in Khaki*.[203] She indicated that when she was discharged—"a somewhat bewildered free woman after the rather hectic three years of [her] service with the AWAS"—she was relieved that decisions about her life would be made on her own terms.[204]

Other Baptist women worked in various positions supporting the war effort, although most congregations did not detail women's activities. During the Second World War thousands of Australian women worked in ammunition factories or, for example, in the assembly plants for the seven-hundred Beaufort Bombers built in Australia.[205] Presumably some of these women were Baptists. Women undertook other positions that men had vacated, such as Phyllis Brunton who drove a truck for bakers Gartrell White—owned by a Baptist family—in Sydney, but then relinquished the work at the end of the war.[206] In Canberra Myrtle Wain worked in the Cabinet Office and her sister Gladys Joyce was the personal secretary of Prime Minister John Curtin, and recalled him saying to her "I will need all your prayers, Gladys, taking this job."[207]

The two world wars often impacted women over generations. Victorian Elsie Fraser was born two weeks after her father left for service in the First World War and he was killed before she was a year old. Her brother and her fiancé enlisted for service in the Second World War and both were killed in action. She joined the Red Cross in England as a hospital visitor and after the war she became a social worker.[208] Mary Dorman's husband was an army chaplain in both world wars. Other women had a husband who enlisted in the First World War and a son in the Second World War.[209]

202. Dulcie Welch, "Cast Thy Bread Upon the Waters," *Rising Tide*, August 1942, 2; "Visits from Our Girls in the Services," *Rising Tide*, April 1943, 4.

203. Ollif, *Women in Khaki*. Lorna Ollif was the first Secretary of the NSW Baptist Historical Association.

204. Ollif, *Women in Khaki*, 290–91.

205. "Australian War Memorial." There were 8,500 people employed in the Beaufort Bomber assembly plants and one-third were women.

206. Stanhope, *Seek Those Things*, 60.

207. Day, *John Curtin*, 414.

208. Wood, *Names to Lives*.

209. Hilton, "ABW Database."

Lorna Ollif wrote an eloquent summary of women in the Second World War that applied to any period of crisis:

> The women of Australia could be assured they had brought enthusiasm, optimism, and extraordinary capacity in varied contributions to the national effort, whether in the home, in the factories, in the auxiliary and enlisted services, or in volunteer work groups; they bore their full share of the burden of war work, as befitted those who were approximately half the Australian population . . . No matter what their designation, at heart they were women.[210]

CONCLUSION

This chapter has highlighted the wide range of social reform and social welfare activities that Baptist women participated in, ranging from large international organizations through to small-scale activities organized by local groups or individuals. Women undertook mission to First Nations people throughout Australia, in many cases with AIM. This mission work was fraught with problems, many of which have been highlighted in more recent years by the 1997 *Bringing them Home Report*.[211] Yet Baptist missionary women were committed to improving the lives of First Nations people and they undertook work that they believed was suitable.

Most Australian Baptist women undertaking activities outside the denomination continued to be a part of the Baptist denomination. While their roles outside the denomination were expansive, with opportunities for leadership, their roles within the denomination fitted within the bounds of expected behaviour. Their Baptist identity was important enough that they did not seek leadership within denominational structures. As their work in social reform and welfare was outside the denomination, they have not left a mark on the historical legacy of Australian Baptists.

There appear to be differences among the states regarding whether social reform and welfare activities were accepted as pressing concerns of evangelical Baptists. Accordingly some such activities, particularly in SA and Victoria, occurred within the Australian Baptist denomination, whereas most of this work, particularly in NSW and Queensland, occurred outside the denomination. Some of these responses were possibly linked to different interpretations of theology. From the early twentieth century Baptists

---

210. Ollif, *Women in Khaki*, 293.
211. AHRC, *National Inquiry into the Separation*.

Women's Social Work and Activities Outside the Denomination

in NSW and Queensland, for instance, were more fundamentalist in their views than other states, which may have impacted their views on undertaking social welfare. Yet overall Australian Baptist women's participation in social reform and welfare activities seems somewhat at odds with the embedded belief that Baptist adherents had a greater focus on evangelism than social reform or welfare.[212]

Did Australian Baptist women undertake social welfare and social reform because of their Baptist beliefs? Absolutely! Involvement in social reform and welfare was a consequence of their evangelical beliefs. The evidence points to a strong evangelical commitment of women to both care for people's physical needs and to seek to convert them to Christianity.[213] The extent to which Baptist women consciously sought to balance their evangelistic endeavors with social reform and welfare activities cannot be determined.

The Australian Baptist women discussed in this chapter reacted to circumstances around them, whether working to alleviate poverty and suffering through the provision of social services or working to minimize the impact of war and other calamitous events. Doubtless these women were the inspiration for later generations of Australian Baptist women who continued to be involved in Australian society in the latter half of the twentieth century in aged care, health services, education, mission, and further legal reform.

---

212. Manley, *From Woolloomooloo*, 1:359.
213. Piggin and Linder, *Attending to the National Soul*, 13.

7

Conclusion

WHAT IT MEANT TO BE AN AUSTRALIAN BAPTIST WOMAN

IN 1890 MARGARET MCLEAN pondered the nature of a woman's sphere. In a speech to the WCTU she acknowledged the prevailing view of the scope of women's sphere in the home, but suggested their lives would be enhanced if they expanded beyond their traditional roles:

> But we are met at the very onset with the supposed unanswerable objection about "woman's sphere." What is woman's sphere? . . . woman would find the monotonous drudgery of her life brightened by the thought that her interests were not confined to the narrow limits of her own home, and many an aimless life would receive a new stimulus to devoted effort for the good of others.[1]

To 1945, as this book has demonstrated, most Australian Baptists believed that it was appropriate for women to be involved in religious activities as part of the intermediate sphere. Australian Baptist women willingly undertook such work supporting Baptist congregations, the Baptist denomination, and other Australian religious endeavors. Women were crucial to the development of Baptist interests, most obviously through the work of women's groups, mission activity, other evangelistic efforts, and social reform and social welfare activities, although Baptists missed the opportunity to fully engage talented women in ministry.

These findings reveal three further themes regarding Australian Baptist women to 1945: the first relating to *identity*; the second to *roles and*

---

1. McLean, *Womanhood Suffrage*, 3, 6. The speech was later reprinted.

ministries within and outside the denomination; and the third to *institutional structures of the Baptist denomination*.

IDENTITY

Beliefs and practices of Australian Baptist women reflected evangelical and Baptist distinctives, including a desire for social welfare and social reform as part of an evangelical "dynamic altruism."[2] Christian beliefs were part of a living faith, including rituals and personal actions in the home and outside the home in small groups or in worship services. Spiritual practices were focused on praying, studying of the Bible, and singing. Women's spiritual practices were particularly expressed through Christian activities in the Baptist denomination, and sometimes beyond it.

Women lived in a patriarchal Australian society, and there were significant barriers that prevented them from participating fully in civil society. Australian society and the Baptist denomination largely viewed women as workers and "influencers" in their homes. Despite the extension of some legal, social, and economic rights to women, all members of Australian society were not treated equally.

Australian Baptists accepted and expected women to undertake various types of work in the intermediate sphere of the Baptist denomination. Some women pushed the boundaries of the intermediate sphere into other areas, particularly social reform and welfare activities that occurred outside the denomination, and some Baptist women participated in the public sphere. The expression of women's evangelical Baptist beliefs, especially in advocacy of temperance and their avoidance of "worldly" activities, led to adverse stereotypes of Baptist women—as naysayers, pious, or wowsers.[3] On the whole women appeared unconcerned about such stereotypes. Analysis of women's writings has indicated that women frequently clarified their identity as Australian Baptist women, by stating their connection to the denomination through baptism, membership, or family relationships.

Many single women worked within the denomination, although singleness was counter to cultural expectations. Australian women who were unmarried in this period were often pitied and described as "old maids" or by other derogatory expressions.[4] Yet Baptist single women were over-represented among the paid and volunteer workers in the Australian denomination, being particularly dominant among home and overseas mission

2. Piggin and Linder, *Attending to the National Soul*, 13.

3. "Wowsers on the War-Path," *Call and WA Sportsman*, 24 October 1919, 9; "Wit and Humour in the Assembly," *TSB*, 21 November 1912, 763.

4. "The Story of the Unmarried," *TSB*, 12 April 1900, 96.

workers. They were able to undertake paid work because they were single: Only one married woman—Catherine Phillips—is known to have been in paid employment in the Baptist denomination prior to 1945, and that was probably because her husband, a former Baptist minister, was unable to work. Most women embraced their roles within the family and attributes of wife and mother—"a woman's truest and greatest sphere."[5]

Mission was important to Australian Baptist women because it was a mechanism for the extension of the Kingdom of God, which was a key aspiration of Baptist women. Women's missionary zeal became part of their identity and directed their actions and ways of living in the world. Many Baptist women sought and found their own agency, or a sense of purpose and control of their activities, through overseas mission, local mission, or the support of mission. Women undertook leadership roles to fulfil their missionary zeal despite the denomination's implicit restriction on the roles of women in leadership. Australian Baptist women's religious identity led them to choose to be actively involved in activities within the intermediate sphere of Baptist congregations and the Australian denomination. For most, being an Australian Baptist woman to 1945 meant an active commitment to mission to build the Kingdom of God throughout Australia and the world.

ROLES, WORK, AND MINISTRIES

Baptist work required women's support through volunteer roles in congregations and denominational structures, given its small size and lack of financial stability. Women also chose to be part of interdenominational religious organizations, particularly CE and the WCTU.

Most women were active solely within their congregations, which suggests women felt their Baptist commitment was fulfilled within the congregational setting.[6] Women undertook roles that the congregation believed women could and should undertake, such as fundraising and supporting functions of the congregation, particularly teaching Sunday School and working to enhance worship services through cleaning the building, arranging flowers, and music. Women's groups were established within Baptist congregations and they provided the mechanisms by which women could undertake what was implicitly women's work. In addition most women's groups allowed for women to socialize and develop their biblical and spiritual knowledge with other women from their congregation. An examination of women's groups in North Adelaide Baptist, Jireh Baptist (Brisbane),

5. Tinsley, "The Late Mrs Complin," *TAB*, 27 May 1924, 3.
6. Hilton, "ABW Database."

and Hurlstone Park Baptist (Sydney) confirmed the inherent variety of aims and activities in women's groups, including fundraising, pastoral support, and a means for women to connect and cooperate with one another. The minister's wife was usually prominent within Baptist congregations, and most ministers' wives appear to have embraced their "designated" role and undertook tasks such as visiting adherents or chairing women's groups.

The most prominent women in the denomination were the one hundred women who worked for the Australian Baptist missions in East Bengal. Australian Baptist women volunteered for mission work to fulfill their evangelical missionary zeal and "calling" to mission. At least another one hundred and fifty women worked for other non-denominational overseas mission organizations. Missionary women's writings indicated the importance of the expansion of the Kingdom of God, and many women used this theme to elucidate their missionary work. These women undertook roles that were considered essential by Baptists and other Protestant Christians, especially as teachers, preachers, and evangelists. Yet the contradictions in the lives of missionary women cannot be overlooked. While missionary women were engaged in greater numbers than men, compared to men they had less autonomy in activities, their work was not considered as important, and generally they were paid less. They were also undertaking a role that existed in part because of the complex intersection of mission and colonialism whereby western culture and Christianity was often considered superior to the local culture.[7]

Twenty different Baptist women's denominational groups were formed at state and national levels, which allowed women to unite in fellowship and to work in areas of shared interest, notably the support of foreign and home mission. These groups allowed for women to be involved in larger Baptist projects in Australia. Baptist women worked or volunteered in social welfare projects in religious organizations outside the denomination, such as city missions. Women also joined the WCTU to effect social reform, including women's suffrage, temperance, gambling controls, and legal equality for women. Women's participation in largely autonomous state and national women's organizations within and outside the Baptist denomination gave them a level of control over the tasks undertaken and provided some opportunities for leadership and evangelistic roles. Women's involvement in social activities, alongside their work in social reform through the WCTU, shows that Baptist women were concerned about social inequality and poverty.

About two hundred Australian Baptist women gave extant religious speeches or published religious writings, which reveal their evangelical faith. Most of the women writers during the period were missionary women writing about their mission work, and they reveal the importance of the

---

7. Gladwin, "Mission and Colonialism," 282.

concept of the Kingdom of God alongside other conventional evangelical and Baptist themes. Margaret McLean and Elizabeth Rees, who wrote in the WCTU papers, applied their beliefs to social reform issues, particularly temperance. Lily Higlett's private notebook is a key document for understanding why women's state organizations were important, and reveals considered thoughts on the importance of mission, prayer, and active service. The writings of Florence Benskin and Adelaide Bamford were regular features in Baptist papers and provided insights on numerous issues, such as views on specific Bible passages, mission support, and women's meetings.

This book has thrown new light on women's leadership roles within the denomination and women's religious organizations outside the denomination. However the numbers so far documented are quite small: just over two hundred and fifty Baptist women have been identified as overseas missionaries; around two hundred Baptist women are known to have made public speeches or were published writers; and just under one hundred women are known to have preached, worked as evangelists, or undertaken mission work in Australia. Women showed leadership in their roles within state and national Baptist women's organizations. Thus, excluding ministers' wives, to 1945 there were fewer than six hundred Australian Baptist women who undertook leadership roles in the Baptist denomination or outside religious organizations, out of the approximately one hundred thousand women who identified as Baptists in Australia to 1945.[8] Obviously, when examining the context of leadership within the denomination, there were more men than women in leadership roles because all ministers were men. Yet, given societal and religious restrictions on women's activities, their roles in the leadership of the denomination were significant and more extensive than has hitherto been recognized. Such findings challenge the narrative that women did not hold leadership positions that had an impact on the activities and achievements of the Australian Baptist denomination.

In most states women's overall participation was relatively similar, although there were some differences among Australian states with respect to women's roles, ministries, and opportunities for leadership. There were proportionately fewer leadership opportunities for women in Queensland and Tasmania compared to SA, Victoria, and NSW.[9] WA women appear to have experienced the most opportunities in relative terms, which may have reflected the small size, the geographic isolation, and later development of the denomination in WA.

Across Australia more women worked in religious organizations outside the denomination than within the denomination, although this was

---

8. ABS, "Historical Censuses." This is an estimate of the total number of women.
9. See Hilton, "ABW Database."

largely driven by women working in other overseas missionary organizations. Over time the roles, work, and ministry of Baptist women changed slightly. To the 1880s their roles were almost entirely limited to their local congregations. From the 1880s to the 1910s women remained active in their congregations but were also active in a variety of roles across Christian organizations. After the First World War their roles became more likely to be within the denomination, rather than in outside organizations. There are various reasons for this. Involvement in CE and the WCTU, which had been so important in the late nineteenth and early twentieth centuries, was less of a feature at the state level for women after the First World War. Baptist women's organizations were at their zenith in the late 1930s and early 1940s.

The average Baptist woman did not have the opportunity to undertake an overtly obvious ministry in the denomination or Australian religious life. She worked in her home, often as a wife and mother. She undertook ostensibly small and unsung tasks within her congregation, maybe volunteered at local missions, provided food and clothing to those in need, or raised funds to be used in overseas and local missions. Hence, these women performed largely unacknowledged work, which does nothing to diminish their Baptist commitment or their essential role in developing and maintaining the Australian Baptist denomination.

Some Baptist Women—including the author—in Canberra Baptist Church, 2025, aged between 3 and 101. Continuing to maintain the Australian Baptist denomination. The stained-glass window in the background is dedicated to the memory of Elsie May Joyce and five of her descendants over three generations are in the photo. There are also the descendants of at least eight Baptist ministers' wives, along with friends and relatives of missionaries and other prominent Australian Baptists. Photograph by John Clark; used with permission.

WOMEN AND BAPTIST INSTITUTIONAL STRUCTURES

Did Australian Baptist institutional and denominational structures hinder women from undertaking some activities, leading to talented women leaving the Baptist denomination to fulfil their calling? The answer is complicated by the juxtaposition of Australia's patriarchal society and the Baptist denomination. As already observed, Australian society had explicit and implicit boundaries on roles women were able to undertake. Many in the Baptist denomination also held views restricting women's leadership roles, which were often based on biblical interpretations that restricted women's roles in the church. Overall the structure of Australian society and the Baptist denomination meant that men undertook most of the paid and public work in the denomination in their roles as Baptist ministers. There were few paid or unpaid leadership roles available to women within the general structure of the denomination, although women created significant parallel organizations, giving them opportunities for leadership. If the Baptist denomination had been equally supportive of men and women, some women may have sought ordination to work as a Baptist minister, as illustrated through the situation in Victoria where women could theoretically be ordained from 1928. That is, women themselves were part of a patriarchal society with its implicit expectations, and it is likely that few would have been impelled to seek ordination had it been an option. The book cannot categorically state that any women left the Baptist denomination permanently to fulfil their calling as preachers, evangelists, or ministers. Thus it is difficult to directly link the structure of the denomination to women's withdrawal from it.

The denomination permitted only males to be ministers and was not large enough to engage many women in other leadership roles—certainly not all the women who volunteered for overseas mission service. Baptist women's missionary zeal and a desire to serve to expand the Kingdom of God led one hundred women to fulfill their calling as overseas missionary women within the denomination, and they were essential to Australian Baptist mission work. Yet many more women fulfilled their calling through missionary work *outside* the denomination. Nearly two hundred women worked outside the denomination in overseas mission organizations or as missionaries in First Nations communities. The denomination could not have supported this number of additional mission workers. Many other women fulfilled their calling through a variety of pan-evangelical activities in social reform and welfare, especially in the WCTU and in CE unions. Again, such work could not have been supported by the denomination and in any case, few Baptists explicitly stated that all Christian work should be only denominational in scope and nature.[10] Many of the women who worked outside the denomination, in paid or unpaid roles, remained connected to the Baptist denomination, but some of their talents were exercised outside the denomination. In doing so they sometimes refocused the interests and financial support of many Baptists to areas outside the denomination. Such action reflects wider evangelical commitments and identity which, for some women, was more important than a Baptist identity.

Australian Baptist historians have debated the reasons why the denomination did not grow in Australia at the rate that it did in the USA, and often point to the denomination's refusal to accept state aid.[11] No historians, however, have specifically considered the role of women in the growth of the denomination. Many Australian evangelical Baptist women sought practical ways to demonstrate their faith and beliefs. When women were sidelined in evangelistic activities in the development of the Baptist denomination they channelled their collective energy into activities that were not focused on growing the denomination. In 1893 Lilian Brown wrote that the CE motto called members "to be subjects of His Kingdom."[12] Similarly in 1894 Margaret McLean expressed the same sentiment when she wrote of the WCTU: "All our work must be for His honour and the extension of His kingdom."[13] Thus their work had a wider pan-evangelical focus, which they saw as extending the Kingdom of God and the wider church, not simply the denomination.

SEIZING OPPORTUNITIES

Despite some constraints on opportunities, women ministered within the Australian Baptist denomination to 1945 more than most historians have realized, or even deemed significant to examine. Baptist histories have focused more on buildings and male ministers than on women's work to build relationships and establish communities. Women's state and national organizations within the Baptist denomination created a "parallel church" that gave autonomy to women's activities but also led to them being overlooked in Australian Baptist historiography. Women were forgotten participants in the history of the denomination and certainly later historians

---

10. See, for example, Goodman, "Denominational Efficiency," *TAB*, 25 April 1933, 1–2.

11. See, for example, Manley, *From Woolloomooloo*, 1:19; Petras, "Across the Frontier," 7.

12. Lilian S. Mead, "For Christ and the Church," *TGL*, 1 September 1893, 3.

13. McLean, "President's Address," 12.

have perpetuated the assumption that women were not influential, or that their roles were non-essential. Specifically, Baptist overseas mission provided profound opportunities for women, yet their achievements have been overshadowed by the work of men. Hence this book has enabled Baptist women's roles, missions, and ministries to be elucidated and revises the existing historiography—although there is much more that could be written.

In 1982 Australian commentator Dale Spender wrote a book contending that women had been removed from literary and historical records, and this had led to women not having their own "intellectual heritage."[14] Likewise twenty-first-century Baptist women cannot build on an unknown intellectual heritage, where Baptist women's writings, and other achievements, are not sought, identified, acknowledged, or included in the analysis of Baptist writings in Australia. Future Baptist histories need to include the full range and value of activities undertaken by women alongside other work that has usually taken precedence. The significant roles and writings of women in Baptist history should not be contained in an appendix, footnote, or as a separate theme.

Melody Maxwell has written of the "winding and widening path" of Baptist women in the USA in the twentieth century.[15] The concept of the "winding" path is applicable to the work of Baptist women in Australia, whose roles and ministries traversed and enriched the denomination to 1945. Opportunities for women, albeit limited, existed within congregations, the broader denomination, and within agencies such as the WCTU and CE in Australia. There were opportunities for women to serve as missionaries—indeed to be its pioneers—in Australian Baptist overseas missions, and their work was essential. In the early twentieth century women's opportunities for service expanded in some directions. As in the USA, the "widened" path was not fully evident until after the Second World War.

In January 1946, Mary Pope's hopeful message, published in *The Australian Baptist*, alongside other Baptist "leaders," expressed sentiments regarding the capability of women to minister to the Baptist denomination in the years beyond 1945:

> May 1946 prove a year when we as women will truly "launch out into the deep." Women's sphere and influence in all the world has increased . . . New associations, new demands, new responsibilities, new ideas, new and strange experiences have been theirs but all these have fitted women for better service . . . The world has a plan for a new world, and women are going to help in it. But

---

14. Spender, *Women of Ideas*, 21.
15. Maxwell, "Winding and Widening Path."

how essential it is, to have good women—Christian women—women filled with the love of Christ and an ardent desire to win the world for Him. Our denomination faces great tasks—women are urgently needed, for upon women's endeavours, enterprise, and fidelity; success may largely depend. Will you seriously and prayerfully seek to know in what way God wants you to use your gifts, your education, your strength, your life?[16]

By establishing a baseline for Australian Baptist women's history to 1945, this book has shown how women within the denomination fulfilled key facets of their evangelical and Baptist identities, through work in Baptist congregations, in Baptist organizations, as Baptist missionaries, in Australian religious life, and indeed, in civil and national life. The book has in this way identified and stressed the extent to which Baptist women were "writing with their lives" Australian Baptist history and seizing opportunities.[17]

---

16. Mary Pope, "Words of Inspiration for 1946 from Baptist Leaders," *TAB*, 8 January 1946, 1.

17. Mrs A. E. [Ruth] Smith, Women Through the Ages, BUVA.

APPENDIX

Some Australian Baptist Women

This appendix lists 398 women mentioned or referenced in the book. They are representatives of the more than 2,500 women contained in the Australian Baptist Women Database.

Surname, first name (birth surname)	Born	Place	Died	Place	Brief note on role/s
[Unknown] "Cousin Flora"	-	unknown	-	unknown	Writer
[Unknown] "Cousin Joyce"	-	unknown	-	unknown	Writer
[Unknown] "Felicity"	-	unknown	-	unknown	Writer
[Unknown surname], Mary	-	unknown	-	unknown	Member
Abbott, Anna (Pfunder)	1888	Queensland (Qld)	-	unknown	Minister's wife
Abbott, Mary	1879	Qld	1956	Brisbane, Qld	Paid Deaconess, PIVM Missionary
Alcorn, Agnes (Trudinger)	1920	Melut, Africa—on mission	2020	New Zealand (NZ)	ABFM missionary, writer
Aldridge, Frances (France)	1891	Shropshire, England	1983	Qld	Minister's wife, paid Deaconess

Surname, first name (birth surname)	Born	Place	Died	Place	Brief note on role/s
Allanby, Kate	1871	Melbourne	1931	Mayurbhanj, India—on mission	ABFM missionary, established Mayurbhanj Mission
Allanby, Mary (Brady)	1848	Ireland	1916	Brisbane	Mayurbhanj Mission support
Allen, Jean	-	unknown	-	unknown	Paid deaconess
Ambrose, Ethel	1874	South Australia (SA)	1934	Poona, India—on mission	Missionary with PIVM (Doctor)
Ambrose, Lily	1873	Mannum, SA	1966	Glen Osmond, SA	Missionary with PIVM
Archer, Ada	1862	SA	1924	Adelaide	ABFM missionary
Ardill-Brice, Katie (married to Charles Brice)	1887	Sydney, New South Wales (NSW)	1955	Sydney	Doctor, volunteered for service in WWI
Ardill, Lily (Southwell)	1872	United Kingdom (UK)	1958	Petersham, Sydney	Mission support, CE
Ardill, Louisa (Wales)	1853	England	1920	Sydney	Social welfare, evangelist, WCTU
Armstrong, Evelyn (Davis)	1882	Narrandera, NSW	1968	Canberra, ACT	Treasurer in congregation
Arnold, Ellen	1858	Aston, Warwickshire, England	1931	Faridpur, East Bengal, India—on mission	ABFM missionary
Ashworth, Margaret (Tomlinson)	1882	Lancashire, England	1913	NSW	Minister's wife, other missionary, Sunday School teacher (SST)
Baeyertz, Emelia (Aronson)	1842	Bangor, Wales	1926	London, England	Evangelist, writer, preached
Bailey, Charlotte (Salmon)	1863	Quebec, Canada	-	unknown	Other missionary, minister's wife, preached
Baker, Elizabeth (Bessie)	1853	Strathalbyn, SA	1917	Temora, NSW	SST

Some Australian Baptist Women

Surname, first name (birth surname)	Born	Place	Died	Place	Brief note on role/s
Baldwin, Effie (Steed)	1896	NZ	1987	Qld	ABFM missionary
Bamford, Adelaide (Dunkley)	1895	NSW	1969	Sydney	Writer, preached
Barber, Alice (McLean)	1884	Melbourne, Victoria (Vic)	1949	Melbourne	ABFM missionary (Doctor)
Barber, Eleanor (Napier)	1848	Essendon, Melbourne	1902	Warrnumbool, Vic	WCTU, writer
Barker, Florence	1861	SA	1951	Mount Barker, SA	Mission support, WCTU, executive positions in congregation and SA, organist
Barker, Sophia (Whitbread)	1823	Bedfordshire, England	1909	Mount Barker, SA	WCTU, Philanthropy
Barnard, Winifred (Cunningham)	1908	Qld	1996	USA	ABFM missionary
Barron, Eleanor (Thompson)	1882	NSW	1953	Nowra, NSW	UAM Missionary
Barry, Annie (Bacon)	1864	NZ	1946	Sydney	ABFM missionary
Batey, Mary (Hopkins)	1882	Wallsend, NSW	1966	Kurri Kurri, NSW	Secretary and Treasurer of congregation
Bean, Annie (Dougal)	1879	Edinburgh, Scotland	1951	Canterbury, Melbourne	Minister's wife
Bean, Margaret (Baillie)	1854	Edinburgh, Scotland	1940	Glen Iris, Melbourne	City mission worker, writer
Beattie, Dorcas (Parham, then Sharp)	1862	Evanston, SA	1941	SA	WCTU
Beeston, Agnes (Brown)	1901	Glasgow, Scotland	1999	Brookfield, Qld	ABWF
Bennell, Edna (Gregson)	1915	St Leonards, Sydney	1962	Adelaide	Minister's wife, Established kindergarten

Surname, first name (birth surname)	Born	Place	Died	Place	Brief note on role/s
Benskin, Emily (Lord)	1874	Hammersmith, London, England	1953	Bath, Somerset, England	Minister's wife, writer, home mission
Bird, Ann (Burge)	1844	London, England	-	unknown	Mission support for CIM
Birks, Rosetta (Thomas)	1856	Glenelg, SA	1911	SA	WCTU, writer
Booth, Sarah	1845	Nottingham, England	1928	St Kilda, Melbourne	YWCA, WCTU, writer, SST
Boreham, Stella (Cottee)	1877	Epping	1963	Kew, Melbourne	Minister's wife
Bowering, Beryl (married to Lorraine Barber)	1909	Norwood, Adelaide	1996	SA	SGMU, missionary with London Missionary Society (Doctor)
Bowie, Mary (Grey)	1903	Balaklava, SA	1990	Strathfield, Sydney	WCTU, Volunteer tutor at Morling College
Brainwood, Hazel (Thornton)	1903	Chatswood, Sydney	1999	Sutherland, Sydney	Treasurer of congregation
Brasnett, Emily (Smith)	1861	Bexley Heath, Kent, England	1936	Sydney	Member
Brice, Bessie	1895	SA	1949	Adelaide	CE, SGMU
Brindley, Ruby	1896	Vic	1975	Richmond, Vic	ABFM missionary
Brown, Fanny (Ardill)	1860	Parramatta, NSW	1944	Auburn, Sydney	Speaker, writer
Brown, Grace	1880	Western Australia (WA)	1962	Adelaide	ABFM missionary, supported by family
Brown, Lilian (Mead)	1865	Adelaide	1936	England	WCTU, CE, writer
Brown, Marie (Smith)	1838	UK	1924	SA	WCTU, mission support
Brunton, Phyllis (Irving)	1921	Hurstville, Sydney	1992	Australia	Member
Buckingham, Hannah	1861	Maitland, NSW	1918	Sydney	Home mission

Surname, first name (birth surname)	Born	Place	Died	Place	Brief note on role/s
Bullock, Rebecca (Hubbard)	1864	Rylestone, Sydney	1944	Gladesville, Sydney	Philanthropy
Burgess, Mabel	-	unknown	-	unknown	SGMU, missionary other
Butters, Ethel (Hiron)	1880	Melbourne	1966	Qld	Paid deaconess, preached
Carthew, Louise (Genat)	1881	Boort, Vic	1977	McLeod, Vic	CE, SST
Chambers, Emily	1868	Vic	1931	Vic	ABFM missionary
Chapman, Elizabeth	1869	UK	-	unknown	CIM missionary
Chapman, Sarah Ann (Bradshaw)	1831	Sheffield, England	1902	Melbourne	Minister's wife
Church, Isabel (Higlett)	1911	Grafton, NSW	1954	Sydney	Daughter of Lily Higlett
Churchward Kelly, Stella	1885	Norwood, Adelaide	1968	Bright, Vic	CE, ABFM missionary
Churchward, Verna (also Salter)	1886	Norwood, Adelaide	1979	Kew, Vic	ABFM missionary
Clark, Mahala (Beaumont)	1839	Colchester, England	1927	Sheffield, Tasmania (Tas)	Member
Coates, Rhoda (Peate)	1830	England	1916	Adelaide	Home mission
Collins, Gladys	1887	Birmingham, England	-	unknown	CE, ABFM missionary
Collins, Retta	1908	NSW	1998	Concord, NSW	AIM missionary
Cooper, Bertha (Bostock)	1854	Adelaide	1933	Adelaide	Deaconess
Cooper, Gladys	1887	SA	1962	SA	SGMU, mission support
Cordiner, Ellen May (Howden)	1861	Scotland	1937	Adelaide	Minister's wife, WCTU, public speaker, writer, preached

Surname, first name (birth surname)	Born	Place	Died	Place	Brief note on role/s
Cousin, Helen	1884	Vic	1961	Ashfield, NSW	ABFM missionary, mission support
Cousin, Margaret (Nicol)	1880	Petersham, Sydney	1973	Burwood, NSW	Organist, mission support
Crofts, Gwenyth (Harry)	1897	Darlinghurst, Sydney	1960	Perth, WA	CE, ABFM missionary
Crofts, Mary (Bray)	1858	London, England	1940	Perth	Deaconess
Cronou, Ethel (Cross)	1884	Sydney	1963	Burwood, Vic	Minister's wife, paid deaconess
Cross, Vera (Bavinton)	1897	Scrubby Creek, Vic	1978	Macleod, Vic	ABFM missionary, minister's wife
Crump, Clara May	1885	Footscray, Melbourne	1970	Kew, Melbounre, Vic	Worked for ABFM in Melbourne, mission support
Cumming, Elsie (Tranter)	1886	Geelong, Vic	1968	Tas	Nurse, enlisted in WWI
Davey, Susan (Morton)	1876	Staffordshire, England	1962	Ashfield, NSW	Writer, home mission
Davies, Eliza (Arbuckle)	1819	Scotland	1888	Kentucky, USA	Writer
Davies, Ella (Godbold)	1877	Surrey, England	1962	Qld	CIM missionary, WCTU, mission support, minister's wife
Davis, Ada	-	unknown	-	unknown	CE
Deakin, Elsie	1881	Emerald Hill, Vic	1969	Elsternwick, Vic	Nurse, enlisted in WWI
Dixon, Mary Janie (Bell)	1885	Qld	1953	Maryborough, Qld	SST, WCTU
Dixson, Emma (Shaw)	1844	NSW	1922	Sydney	Philanthropy, home mission
Dixson, Helen (Craig)	1810	Edinburgh, Scotland	1894	Ashfield, Sydney	Philanthropy

Surname, first name (birth surname)	Born	Place	Died	Place	Brief note on role/s
Dobie, Janet (McFadzean)	1878	Scotland	1922	Scotland	Member
Doery, Ada	1866	Vic	1925	Owara, NZ	ABFM missionary
Dorman, Mary (Freeman)	1884	Port Melbourne	1968	Fitzroy, Vic	Minister's wife, WCTU
Dorse, Edith (Marsh)	1869	Dungog, NSW	1945	Dungog, NSW	Deacon and Secretary in congregation
Doust, Irene	1897	NSW	1983	NSW	Volunteer tutor at Morling College
Dovey, Elizabeth (Witsed)	1858	England	1945	Sydney	Home mission, WCTU, writer
Downes, Marion	1864	Melbourne	1926	Vic	Writer
Downing, Cecilia (Hopkins)	1858	London, England	1952	Ivanhoe, Melbourne	Minister's wife (husband left ministry), WCTU, home mission, ABWF
Doyle, Marion (Bell)	1863	Bega, NSW	1908	Sydney	Writer, speaker
Driver, Annie (Newcombe)	1862	Vic	1942	NZ	ABFM missionary, other missionary, writer, mission training
Drummond, Heather	1902	NSW	1986	Roseville, Sydney	Volunteer tutor at Morling College (BSc)
Dunkley, Jessie	1869	Balmain, Sydney	1949	Hurlstone Park, Sydney	Minister's wife
Ellem, Janet	1892	Grafton, NSW	1933	Solomon Islands—on mission	Solomon Islands missionary, home mission, CE
Ellis, Ethel (Whittle)	1875	SA	1949	Adelaide	Deaconess
Embery, Ethel (Potter)	1876	Geelong, Vic	1963	Vic	CIM missionary

Surname, first name (birth surname)	Born	Place	Died	Place	Brief note on role/s
Embery, Winifred	1909	Tenqyuch, China	1996	Australia	CIM missionary
English, Florence	-	unknown	2007	unknown	ABFM missionary
Eustace, Elizabeth (Downes)	1852	Guildford, Surrey, England	1927	Qld	Minister's wife, preached
Evans, Elsie Winifred	1884	Gloucestershire, England	1979	Lismore, NSW	BZM missionary
Evans, Ethel Mary	1878	Gloucestershire, England	1962	Lismore, NSW	BZM missionary
Evans, Matilda (Congreve)	1827	Peckham, Surrey	1886	Adelaide	Minister's wife, writer, deaconess
Field, Rebecca (Chivers)	1854	Trowbridge, Wiltshire, England	1922	Sydney	SST
Fildes, Grace (Rogers)	1895	Albany, WA	1978	Katanning, WA	Treasurer of congregation
Findlay, Margaret	1890	Ararat, Vic	1958	Macleod, Melbourne	ABFM missionary, mission support
Finlayson, Helen (Harvey)	1811	Midlothian, Scotland	1884	Mitcham, Adelaide	"First Baptist people" in SA
Fleming, Lorna (MacColl)	1907	Melbourne	1986	Canterbury, Melbourne	CIM missionary
Foucar, Mary (Pigott)	1873	Colombo, Sri Lanka / India—on mission	1921	Colombo, Sri Lanka / India—on mission	CE, other missionary, paid deaconess
Fraser, Elsie	1916	Clifton Hill, Melbourne	1992	England	Volunteered for service in WWII
Fraser, Jane (Ikin)	1830	Liverpool, Sydney	1917	Haberfield, Sydney	Member
Froome, Dora (Deacon)	1885	England	1928	Perth	Nurse, enlisted in WWI
Fry, Hannah (Robins)	1824	Gloucestershire, England	1902	Adelaide	WCTU, writer

Surname, first name (birth surname)	Born	Place	Died	Place	Brief note on role/s
Fuller, Marion	1856	Vic	1897	Mymensingh, East Bengal / India—on mission	ABFM missionary
Fuller, Myra (Norman)	1891	Redfern, Sydney	1966	NSW	Member
Garland, Annie	1861	Newland, Vic	1929	China—on mission	CIM missionary, developed a Chinese Braille method
Garland, Susie	1870	Vic	1930	China—on mission	SST, CIM missionary, developed a Chinese Braille method
Garrett, Alice (McNair)	1856	Bellarine, Vic	1944	Adelaide	Deaconess
Gibbs, Harriet (Cox) (also Hill)	1821	Avening, Cloucestershire, England	1881	Lambton, NSW	Member
Gibson, Mary (Blackler)	1811	Ferrers, Devon, England	1903	Perth, Tas	SST, philanthropy, home mission
Gilbert, Jeanie (Davie)	1942	Greenock, Scotland	1910	Adelaide	Deaconess
Gilbert, Marie	1856	NZ	1926	Calcutta, India—on missioon field	ABFM missionary and independent worker
Gillings, Harriet (Jones)	1828	London, England	1890	Geelong, Vic	Minister's wife, writer
Gilmour, Annie (Welbourn)	1865	Mitcham, SA	1932	Perth	SST, minister's wife
Gladwin, Ruth	-	unknown	-	unknown	Volunteer tutor at Morling College
Glasson, Linda (Addison)	1893	Wilunga, SA	1972	Norwood, Adelaide	Member
Glassop, Matilda (Pontifex)	1852	Sydney	1949	Melbourne	SST, minister's wife, organist, CE

Surname, first name (birth surname)	Born	Place	Died	Place	Brief note on role/s
Good, Irene	1889	Carlton, Melbourne	1977	Macleod, Melbourne	Mission support
Goode, Helen (Smith) (also Lloyd)	1852	Greenhill, Burnside, SA	1936	Adelaide	Deaconess, philanthropist
Goode, Mary (Good)	1829	Bockleton, Worcestershire, England	1889	Adelaide	Writer
Gooden, Elizabeth (Jones)	1907	Rose Park, Adelaide	1971	Glen Osmond, Adelaide	SGMU
Goodman, Ruth (Arblaster)	1886	Eaglehawk, Bendigo, Vic	1970	Burwood, Sydney	Mission support, WCTU
Gowans, Margaret (Bell)	1885	Christchurch, NZ	1955	SA	Mission in Bolivia, minister's wife
Grace, Daisy (Boyden)	1894	Vic	1991	NSW	ABFM missionary
Grace, Ellen	1923	Ashfield, NSW	-	-	WWII Enlisted AWAS
Green, Annie	1858	Vic	1936	Adelaide	Evangelist, preacher, city mission
Greening, Bessie (Ellis)	1860	Devon, England	1947	Sydney	Deaconess, philanthropy
Griffiths, Emily [unknown marital status]	-	unknown	-	unknown	Mission support
Grimes, Annie Laura	1871	Melbourne	1950	Qld	SGMU, philanthropy
Grimes, Louise	1907	Qld	1990	Qld	Mission support, philanthropy
Grimes, Mary (Dawson)	1878	England	1953	Qld	Other missionary
Gunn, Jeannie (Taylor)	1870	Carlton, Melbourne	1961	Hawthorn, Melbourne	Fiction writer
Hale, Edna	1909	Petersham, Sydney	1975	NSW	ABFM missionary

Surname, first name (birth surname)	Born	Place	Died	Place	Brief note on role/s
Hale, Ellen (Boundy)	1864	North Adelaide	1949	SA	Deaconess
Hale, Nancy (Wadey)	1900	NSW	1966	SA	Deaconess
Hall, Caroline (Brown)	1871	England	1956	SA	ABFM missionary, mission support, WCTU
Hall, Edith (Elyea)	1892	unknown	1963	Woronora River, NSW	Minister's wife, preached
Hancey, Jessie (Burnell)	1863	SA	1948	Mt Lawley, Perth	Wrote music and poetry
Hann, Sarah (Staple)	1841	England	1915	Perth	Mission support
Harlen, Sarah (Warren)	1828	Eynsford, Kent, England	1892	Melbourne	Writer
Harris, Bertha	1886	Sydney	1969	Mildura, Vic	ABFM missionary
Harris, Ellen	1868	Birmingham, England	1946	Fremantle, WA	Evangelist, preached
Harris, Florence	1894	Ashfield, NSW	1972	Sydney	CE, ABFM missionary
Harris, Mary	1885	Balmain, Sydney	-	unknown	Member
Harris, Ruth (Pearson)	1858	Geelong, Vic	1944	Melbourne	Minister's wife
Harrison, Maria (Wilkins)	1861	Derbyshire, England	1950	Adelaide	WCTU, home mission
Harrison, Martha (Kelly)	1863	Bradford, England	1944	Marrickville, Sydney	Minister's wife, WCTU, preached
Harrison, Sarah (Phelan) (also Isaac)	1860	Amherst, Vic	1947	Melbourne	Minister's wife (in two marriages)
Harry, Helen (Hibberd)	1866	Sydney	1945	NZ	Minister's wife, CE
Harry, Jean	1906	Vic	1979	NZ	ABFM missionary
Hawkyard, Alice (Callister)	1892	Vic	1956	Melbourne	ABFM missionary

Surname, first name (birth surname)	Born	Place	Died	Place	Brief note on role/s
Hayden, (Unknown first name)	-	unknown	-	unknown	Volunteer tutor at Morling College
Hendry, Marjorie (Holland)	1901	Perth	1991	Perth	Minister's wife, WCTU, preached, CE
Hercus, Margaret (Macky)	1886	Auckland, NZ	1966	St Leonards, Sydney	Other missionary, minister's wife, SGMU
Hibberd, Isabel (Dixson)	1845	Sydney	1920	Sydney	Minister's wife, mission support
Hickson, Grace	1884	Essex, England	1980	Qld	BZM missionary
Higlett, Lily (Low)	1880	Qld	1943	NSW	Minister's wife, WCTU, mission support
Hill, Elfrida	1893	SA	1973	Adelaide	CE, ABFM missionary, writer
Hinton, Louisa (Simpson)	1874	NZ	1950	Malvern, Vic	PIVM missionary, writer, minister's wife
Hodgson, Florence (Hartley)	-	unknown	-	unknown	Minister's wife, preached
Hodgson, Nola (Hodgkinson)	1919	Maryborough, Qld	-	unknown	CE, ABFM missionary
Hogan, Florence	1905	Chewton, Vic	2000	Vic	Ministry, paid mission worker
Hogben, Janet	1887	Norwood, Adelaide	1953	Adelaide	ABFM missionary
Holden, Mary (Phillips)	1839	Kingston, Ontario, Canada	1914	Kensington Park, SA	Social welfare, philanthropy, deaconess
Hone, Emily (Sandland)	1844	Loppington, Shropshire, England	1914	North Adelaide	Minister's wife (husband left ministry), WCTU, CE
Hope, Laura (Fowler)	1870	SA	1952	SA	Independent doctor and missionary in East Bengal

Surname, first name (birth surname)	Born	Place	Died	Place	Brief note on role/s
Horsfall, Vera	1896	Dunolly, Vic	1982	Kerang, Vic	Writer, musician
Horwood, Florence	1915	Adelaide	1998	SA	ABFM missionary, SGMU
Howard, Daisy	1915	Adelaide	1986	SA	ABFM missionary
Howard, Thelma (Tulk)	1909	Ballina, NSW	-	Qld	Minister's wife, SST, CE
Hutson, A	-	unknown	-	unknown	CE
Ingram, May (Malyon)	1877	Sunderland, Durham, England	1950	Qld	Member
Ingram, Winifred	-	unknown	-	unknown	Writer
Janes, Isabella Adey	1872	Williamstown, Vic	1937	Cheltenham, Vic	Preached
Jarrett, Bertha	1873	NSW	1964	Windsor, NSW	Paid deaconess, WCTU
Jenkin, Margaret (Hudson)	1845	Yorkshire, England	1939	Melbourne	Mission support, WCTU, Benevolent Society
Joyce, Gladys	1917	Fitzroy North, Melbourne	2009	Canberra, ACT	Worked for John Curtin, PM, in WWII
Kekwick, Adelaide (Owens)	1842	Fremantle, WA	1907	Adelaide	Deaconess
Kennedy, Ada (Greenslade)	1869	Melbourne	1950	Perth	Minister's wife, evangelist, preached
Kennett, Annie (Daniell)	1863	Tea Tree Gully, SA	1926	Hindmarsh, SA	SST, deaconess
Kentish, Dorothy	1896	Clare, SA	1925	Adelaide	SST, YWCA
Kerr, Edith (Barnes)	1877		1942	Qld	Methodist paid deaconess, minister's wife
Kiddell, Agnes (Pearce)	1863	SA	1960	Tonbridge, Kent, England	ABFM missionary
King, Ada (Blackwell)	1858	Prahran, Vic	1920	Perth	Mission support

Surname, first name (birth surname)	Born	Place	Died	Place	Brief note on role/s
King, Edith	1881	Vic	1921	Perth	ABFM missionary
Knight, Bertha (Collings)	1847	Kent, England	1929	Qld	WCTU, Benevolent Society
Koehncke, Eleanor	1863	SA	1924	SA	Paid mission worker in Adelaide
Krueger, Johanna (Lobegeier)	1854	Germany	1900	Qld	Minister's wife
Lamb, Minnie	1867	Vic	1939	Vic	ABFM missionary, CE
Lamb, Susan Mary	1860	Launceston, Tas	1919	Launceston, Tas	Paid Baptist ministry, social welfare
Lane, L. Alice	1871	Sydney	1953	Ashfield, Sydney	Member
Lanyon, Emily [unknown birth surname]	1854	Devon, England	1944	Sydney	Member
Lavis, Lucy (Cooper)	1863	Adelaide	1936	Norwood, Adelaide	SST, home mission
Lawton, Ruth (Hall)	1856	Warwickshire, England	1954	Qld	State women's organisations
Leeder, Hermine (te Kloot) (also Black)	1886	Liverpool, Sydney	1948	NSW	Minister's wife (in two marriages)
Lewis, Gladys (Scowen)	1900	Leyton, Essex, England	1985	Kew, Melbourne	Speaker, minister's wife
Liddy, Sarah May	1884	Lilydale, Vic	1908	China—on mission	CIM missionary
Lister, Elizabeth (Chappel)	1831	England	1906	St Kilda, Melbourne	Member
Lloyd, Lorna (Dunkley)	1911	Longford, Tas	2003	Qld	Writer
Long, Margaret (Dixon)	1878	Ultimo, Sydney	1956	Normanhurst, Sydney	CE, AIM missionary
Long, Olive	1915	NSW	-	unknown	AIM missionary

Surname, first name (birth surname)	Born	Place	Died	Place	Brief note on role/s
Low, Fredrike (Hafner)	1858	Ludwigsburg, Baden-Wurttemberg, Germany	1935	Melbourne	Member
Lowe, Elsa	1914	NSW	1966	NSW	Volunteer tutor at Morling College
Lucas, Annie (Farmilo)	1875	unknown	1948	NZ	ABFM missionary
Lumb, Harriett [unknown birth surname]	1855	Reigate, Surrey, England	1926	Ashfield, Sydney	Home mission
Mackay, Enid (Elphinston)	1908	Leichhardt, Sydney	1972	Gosford, NSW	CE, writer
Malyon, Esther	1886	London, England	1974	Qld	CE
Marsh, Edna	-	unknown	-	unknown	CE, Secretary of WA mission organisation
Martin, Elsie	1891	Qld	-	unknown	CE
Martin, Hannah (Barber)	1829	UK	1905	Vic	Minister's wife, mission support
Mason, Elizabeth	1859	SA	1919	Adelaide	Deaconess
Masters, Ethel (Addison)	1888	Willunga, SA	1950	Flinders, SA	ABFM missionary
McCullough, Eva (Richardson)	1860	Tas	1925	Mount Barker, SA	Minister's wife
McGregor, Lorna	1902	Alexandra, Vic	1987	Newtown, Vic	ABFM missionary
McKie, Marion (Chapman)	1874	Adelaide	1969	Adelaide	CIM missionary
McLaren, Joanna (unknown birth surname)	1842	unknown	1924	Adelaide	Deaconess
McLean, Ethel	1873	Melbourne	1940	Melbourne	Teacher
McLean, Eva	1886	Vic	1968	Vic	Member

Surname, first name (birth surname)	Born	Place	Died	Place	Brief note on role/s
McLean, Hilda	1878	Vic	1938	Died at sea (newspaper) On way back from India—on missioon field	ABFM missionary
McLean, Lucie	1877	Melbourne	1945	Melbourne	Nurse
McLean, Margaret (Arnot)	1845	Scotland	1923	Melbourne	WCTU
Mead, Alice (Pappin)	1861	Crawford, SA	1935	Adelaide	ABFM missionary
Mead, Ann (Staple)	1839	England	1874	Adelaide	Minister's wife
Mead, Dorothy	1899	East Bengal, India—on mission	1988	Adelaide	CE, SGMU, Writer
Mead, Gertrude	1867	Adelaide	1919	Adelaide	SST, CE, Doctor
Mead, Marjory	1903	Faridpur, East Bengal, India—on mission	1973	Adelaide	SGMU, deaconess, writer
Meares, Ina (Trudinger)	1905	SA	1993	Adelaide	ABFM missionary
Mellor, Emma (Adams)	1867	Upper Sturt, SA	1957	SA	Member
Mellor, Jane (Neill)	1841	Adelaide	1934	Adelaide	Deaconess
Mellor, Jessie (Thomson)	1894	Adelaide	1991	Adelaide	Deaconess
Middleton, Elizabeth (London)	1844	London, England	1931	Sydney	SST, minister's wife
Middleton, Jane (Wilson)	1871	Nairne, SA	1949	Claremont, Perth	Member
Mildwaters, Elizabeth (Lewis)	1845	England	1889	Grey, SA	Member
Miles, Isabella [unknown birth surname]	1865	unknown	1937	London, England	Minister's wife, SST

Surname, first name (birth surname)	Born	Place	Died	Place	Brief note on role/s
Mirfin, Hepzibah (Chambers)	1855	Gravesend, Kent, England	1935	Melbourne	SST, State women's organisations, Benevolent Society, WCTU
Moody, Mary (Packer)	1842	SA	1924	Adelaide	Deaconess
Morling, Annie (Hillman)	1859	Brighton, Suxxex, England	1935	Burwood, Sydney	Minister's wife
Morphett, Minnie	1888	Morphett Vale, SA	1937	Adelaide	ABFM missionary
Moyle, Margaret (Rees)	1897	Melbourne	1964	Kew, Melbourne	WCTU
Mungomery, Ruth	1899	Granville, Sydney	1934	Manly, Sydney	Mission support
Mursell, Jeannie (Lockhart)	1862	Liverpool, Lancashire, England	1945	Melbourne	Minister's wife, state women's organisations
Nall, Annie (Swadling)	1874	NSW	1967	St Leonards, Sydney	ABFM missionary, minister's wife, CE, mission support
Neill, Catherine (Neill)	1851	Scotland	1924	North Adelaide	Deaconess, YWCA
Nelson, May (Dribden)	1881	unknown	1931	unknown	Minister's wife
Neville, Ruth (Wilkin)	1860	England	1910	Vic	ABFM missionary
Newcombe, Ethel (Forrester)	1874	Warnambool, Vic	1971	Box Hill, Melbourne	ABFM Missionary
Nicholls, Halley (White)	1910	Qld	2007	Vic	Treasurer of congregation, minister's wife
Oliver, Annie (Wilkinson)	1851	Talywain, Wales	1921	Melbourne	SST, Philanthropy
Ollif, Lorna (Box)	1913	Vic	2004	Sydney	WWII Enlisted AWAS, writer

Surname, first name (birth surname)	Born	Place	Died	Place	Brief note on role/s
Palmer, Anne (Smith)	1848	Rose Bay, Sydney	1932	Longueville, Sydney	Mission support, NSW Bush Missionary Society
Palmer, Ethel	1877	Glebe, Sydney	1956	Longueville, Sydney	Member
Paqualin, Louisa Ann	1841	Middlesex, England	1888	Adelaide	SST, preached
Parker, Thora (Jenkins)	1911	Taranake, NZ	1994	Blue Mountains, NSW	Minister's wife, preached
Patterson, Elsie	1883	Melbourne	1947	Sydney	Physiotherapist, volunteered for service in WWI
Penno, Edith (Norton)	1872	Adelaide	1939	Adelaide	SST, deaconess
Perrin, Kath	abt 1901	unknown	-	unknown	ABFM missionary, worked for YMCA during WWII
Pflaum, Mary (Criel)	1859	Fifth Creek, SA	1926	Birdwood, SA	State women's organisations
Phelps, Rachael (Adkin) (also Deacon)	1803	Bury, St Edmunds, Suffolk, England	1887	Walloon, Qld	Minister's wife, philanthropy
Phillips, Catherine (Read) (also Liddy)	1863	Dunolly, Vic	1929	Petersham, Sydney	Minister's wife (in two marriages), paid deaconess
Pigott, Ellen (Giles)	1839	Leeds, Yorkshire, England	1925	Burwood, Sydney	CE, BMS missionary, minister's wife
Pike, Louisa (Boulter)	1880	Ballarat, Vic	1954	Melbourne	CIM missionary, midwife
Playford, Mary Jane (Kinsman)	1834	Cornwell	1928	Kent Town, SA	Member
Plested, Martha	1854	England	1922	Sydney	ABFM missionary
Pocknall, Emily	1884	Molong, NSW	1924	Sydney	Paid deaconess

Surname, first name (birth surname)	Born	Place	Died	Place	Brief note on role/s
Pope, Mary (Lord)	1894	Mitta, Vic	1983	Canterbury, Melbourne	ABFM missionary, minister's wife, home mission
Price, Emily	1860	England	1932	NSW	SST, WCTU, NSW home mission
Proctor, Catherine (McFaddyen)	1850	Scotland	1897	Sea Lake, Vic	SST
Randall, Eliza	-	unknown	1902	Adelaide	Member
Raws, Mary Jane (Lennon)	1853	Moscombe, Lancashire, England	1934	Adelaide	Minister's wife
Redman, Jess	1909	Norwood, Adelaide	1992	SA	ABFM missionary, writer
Redshaw, Lillian (Brittain)	1886	Mt Egerton, Ballarat, Vic	1979	Perth	Minister's wife, preached
Rees, Elizabeth (Johnston)	1865	London, England (childhood in Wales)	1939	Melbourne	WCTU, writer
Reeves, Ada [unknown birth surname]	-	unknown	1942	Casino, NSW	Member
Reid, Elizabeth (Pitty)	1823	Ashwell, Hertfordshire, England	1897	Sydney	Mission support
Rogers, Doris (Prest)	1900	Ballarat East, Vic	1995	Melbourne	ABFM missionary
Rose, Elizabeth (Martin)	1858	Braintree, Essex, England	1931	Lakemba, Sydney	Member
Scott, Marion (Dawbarn)	1886	Rockhampton, Qld	1979	Rockhampton, Qld	Member
Selby, Grace (Allanby)	1879	Melbourne	1964	Balwyn, Melbourne	Mayurbhanj Mission support
Seymour, Iris	1862	India—on mission	1937	Belgrave, Vic	CE, ABFM missionary

Surname, first name (birth surname)	Born	Place	Died	Place	Brief note on role/s
Sharp, Sarah (Hanna)	1872	Bathurst, NSW	1926	Burwood, Sydney	Teacher, minister's wife, SST
Shaw, Mary [unknown birth surname]	1820	unknown	1881	Adelaide	Secretary of Flinders St Dorcas Society
Shepard, Ella	1908	unknown	-	unknown	Member
Shepard, Ellen (Herbert)	1874	Eaglehawk, Bendigo, Vic	1952	Preston, Melbourne	Executive Board ABFM
Shoults, Mary (Monro)	1884	unknown	1952	Padstow, NSW	Treasurer of congregation
Simmons, Kathleen	1914	Scone, NSW	1996	Cairns, Qld	AIM missionary
Simpson, Edith (no further information known)	-	unknown	-	unknown	Member, writer
Skeels, Alice	1883	Sale, Vic	1961	Sale, Vic	Evangelist, paid ministry, WCTU
Slinn, Lillias (McLeod)	1882	NSW	1970	Blackheath, NSW	Writer, mission support
Small, Florence (Hudson)	1902	Annandale, Sydney	1992	NSW	Volunteer tutor at Morling College
Smith, [unknown first name]	-	unknown	-	unknown	In establishment of Blackhealth
Smith, Alice	-	unknown	-	unknown	Volunteer tutor at Morling College
Smith, Augusta (Wearing)	1823	Edmonton, Middlesex, England	1907	Adelaide	Deaconess
Smith, Elsie May (Tudball)	1889	Glebe, Sydney	1941	Melbourne	CE
Smith, Emily Elizabeth	1889	Horsham, Vic	1964	Melbourne	Worked to establish Greenslopes Baptist, Qld

Surname, first name (birth surname)	Born	Place	Died	Place	Brief note on role/s
Smith, Ruth (Loft)	1907	Newport, Vic	1993	Melbourne	ABFM missionary, mission support, ABWF
Smith, Winifred (Filby)	1900	unknown	-	unknown	Minister's wife, mission support
Sorrell, Isabella Peterie	1845	Middlesex, England	1911	North Adelaide	Deaconess
Soundy, Lily	1872	England	1964	Tas	ABFM missionary
Speck, Margaret (Sinclair)	1910	Birkenhead, SA	2004	unknown	Paid worker in SA
Spurr, Ethel (Thompson)	1880	UK	1968	UK	CE, minister's wife, established health centres, WCTU
Stafford, Stella (Harris)	1888	Clifton Hill, Vic	1969	Eltham, Vic	Writer
Stark, Ella (Duncan)	1913	Maylands, WA	1996	Melbourne	Minister's wife, preached
Stark, Eva (Richards)	1857	England	1945	Marrickville, Sydney	Minister's wife, preached, paid Deaconess
Steed, Emma (Moulding)	1857	England	1935	North Sydney	Minister's wife, correspondent
Steel, Caroline (Jones)	1901	Sydney	-	unknown	CE
Steel, Victoria (Alves)	1885	Brunswick, Melbourne	1966	Brighton, Melbourne	Mission support
Stephen, Mabel (Duthie)	1872	Edinburgh, Scotland	1943	Parkside, Adelaide	Mission support
Stribling, Myrtle (Rogerson)	-	unknown	1988	SA	Ministry, minister's wife
Sturgess, Adeline	1911	Ashfield, Sydney	1976	Sydney	SGMU, writer
Sturgess, Elizabeth (Farquhar)	1887	Balmain, Sydney	1952	Sydney	Mission support, writer
Summers, Anne (Hearne)	1867	Adelaide	1957	Adelaide	CE, ABFM missionary

Surname, first name (birth surname)	Born	Place	Died	Place	Brief note on role/s
Sutton, Ellen (Gresswell)	1874	NZ	1953	Kensington, Melbourne	Missionary in Aust
Sutton, Elsie (Luke)	1871	Hawthorn, Melbourne	1951	Vic	ABFM missionary, mission support
Swan, Christina (Mackay)	1812	Scotland	1888	Brisbane	Home mission
Tapson, Ada	-	SA	1952	Adelaide	Paid mission worker
Tayler, Phoebe Hill	1840	Wales	1913	White Hills, Vic	Minister's wife
Taylor, Anna (Lush)	1838	Yoevil, Somerset, England	1895	Hawthorn, Vic	Member
Taylor, Grace	1854	NSW	1930	Sydney	Mission support
Taylor, Margaret (Morgan)	1827	UK	1909	Sydney	Mission support
Taylor, Rose	1873	Yorkshire, England	1927	Sydney	Nurse, enlisted in WWI
Telfer, Caroline (Masters)	1842	Tiffield, Northamptonshire, England	1929	SA	Writer
Thomas, Minnie (Janes)	1874	Williamstown, Melbourne	1933	Geelong, Vic	Preached, evangelist
Thompson, Lucie (Kealley)	1862	Angaston, SA	1951	Adelaide	ABFM missionary
Thomson, Grace	1881	Adelaide	1969	Adelaide	ABFM missionary
Thomson, Martha (Brake)	1852	Cavendish, Vic	1932	Hamilton, Vic	WCTU
Tinsley, Mildred (White)	1883	Redfern, Sydney	1969	NSW	Minister's wife, CE
Tomkins, Gladys	1895	Bournemouth, Hampshire, England	1947	Sydney	AIM missionary
Tomkinson, Freda (Eipper)	1887	Scone, NSW	-	unknown	CIM missionary, preached
Tranter, A. Marion	1874	Yarpturk, Vic	1935	Balwyn, Melbourne	SST, writer

Surname, first name (birth surname)	Born	Place	Died	Place	Brief note on role/s
Trestrail, Ellen (Trenwith)	1844	unknown	1921	Melbourne	Philanthropy
Trudinger, Gertrude	1870	Yorkshire, England	1945	Heathpool, SA	CIM missionary
Tuck, Bertha	1868	Gilbert, SA	1933	Norwood, Adelaide	ABFM missionary, writer
Tyas, Rosa Ann (Bradshaw)	1866	St Peters, Sydney	1944	Eastwood, Sydney	Member
Vandeau, Lillian (Dowling)	1864	Tas	1949	Tas	ABFM support, Secretary of Tas Mission Organisation
Varley, Eleanor	1899	Vic	1945	Melbourne	Missionary in Sudan (Doctor)
Varley, Ethel	1900	Kew, Vic	1966	Jos, Nigeria, Africa—on mission	Missionary in Sudan
Venn, Esma (Durbin)	1911	Newcastle, NSW	1971	Ulverstone, Tas	CE, AIM missionary
Vernon, Margaret	-	unknown	-	unknown	Evangelist
Wain, Myrtle (Joyce)	1923	Melbourne	2012	Melbourne	Worked in Cabinet Office during WWII
Waldock, Charlotte (Godfrey)	1870	Bathurst, NSW	1946	Sydney	Minister's wife, WCTU, home mission
Walker, Eleanor	-	unknown	-	unknown	Missionary in ABFM and other organisations
Walters, Eliza (Rollo)	1843	Sydney	1914	Tamworth, NSW	SST
Walton, Hannah (Taylor)	1853	Tansley, Derbyshire, England	1916	Homebush, Sydney	Minister's wife
Ware, Mary (Brooks)	1798	England	1858	Hobart, Tas	Early Tasmanian Baptist
Warner, Elsa (Smith)	1907	Caulfield, Vic	2000	Vic	Member, ABWF
Warner, Jessie	1872	unknown	-	unknown	CIM missionary

Surname, first name (birth surname)	Born	Place	Died	Place	Brief note on role/s
Warren, Charlotte (Soltau)	1850	St Thomas, Devon, England	1916	Hove, Sussex, England	Operated mission training school
Warren, Mary Ann (Goddard)	1801	Kent, England	1887	Melbourne	Mission training
Watson, Elsie (May)	1903	Bendigo, Vic	2008	Vic	ABFM missionary, writer
Watson, Mary Ann (Smith)	1853	Geelong, Vic	1926	Geelong, Vic	Deaconess, WCTU
Webb, Eliza (Marsh)	1854	Frant, Sussex, England	1940	Manley, Qld	Member
Webb, Janet (Underwood)	1843	Flinders, SA	1918	Geelong, Vic	Minister's wife
Welch, Dulcie	1925	Melbourne	-	unknown	WWII Enlisted AWAS, writer
Wells, Mary	1862	Sydney	1952	Northbridge, Sydney	SST and Superintendent
Whale, Sarah (Latchford)	1842	England	1933	Yeerongpilly, Qld	Minister's wife
Whalley, Elizabeth (Harris)	1858	Geelong, Vic	1929	Balwyn, Melbourne	Preached
Wheeler, Amelia (England)	1847	St Marylebone, Middlesex, England	1932	Heidelberg, Melbourne	Poet, organist
Whitbourn, Christina	1876	Caramut, Vic	1948	Heidelberg, Melbourne	Minister's wife
White, Anna (King)	1855	Essex, England	1919	Stanmore, Sydney	CE, philanthropist
White, Annie	1880	NSW	1913	NSW	SST
White, Isabella (Geggie)	1876	Northumberland, England	1927	Sydney	Speaker
White, Lillian (Wenban)	1888	Orange, NSW	1973	St Leonards, Sydney	CE, ABFM missionary
White, Marion (Holmes)	1886	Clarence Town, NSW	1975	Sydney	Writer
Whittle, Annie (Harry)	1886	Kooringa, SA	1955	SA	Deaconess
Whittle, Julia (Kutcher)	1854	Adelaide	1932	SA	Deaconess

Surname, first name (birth surname)	Born	Place	Died	Place	Brief note on role/s
Wilcox, Edith (Blackham)	1887	Burra, SA	1975	SA	Home mission, writer, preached
Wilkins, Lillian (Williams)	1886	Sydney	-	unknown	Paid deaconesses
Wilkins, Matilda (Bready)	1846	Ireland	1921	Melbourne	Mission support, WCTU
Wilkins, Rebecca Charlotte	1872	Melbourne	1960	Sydney	Mission support, SGMU
Wilkins, Ruth	1872	Adelaide	1949	Melbourne	Philanthropy
Williams, Constance	1877	Vic	1963	Vic	CE, ABFM missionary, writer, mission support
Williams, Elizabeth	1869	Vic	1955	Vic	BMS missionary
Williams, Hilda	1892	Vic	1919	Woodman's Point Quarantine Station, WA	Nurse, volunteered in WWI
Williams, Louisa (Waters)	1868	Ballarat, Vic	1947	Nedlands, Perth	Member
Wilson, Blanche (Mead)	1870	Adelaide	1961	Adelaide	Minister's wife, WCTU, mission support
Wilson, Evelyn	1884	Qld	1986	Melbourne	Physiotherapist, volunteered in WWI
Wood, Elizabeth (Childs)	1853	England	1927	Perth, Tas	Minister's wife
Woodall, Doris (Lewis)	1908	Northcote, Melbourne	1979	East Melbourne	Member
Wooster Greaves, Lilian	1869	Ballarat, Vic	1956	Perth	Poet, botanist
Yarrow, Mary (Tupling)	1872	Qld	1947	Petersham, Sydney	CE
Yorkston, Annie (Bailey)	1892	NZ	1963	Mosman, Sydney	CIM missionary
Yule, Florence	1895	Waterloo, Sydney	1923	Sydney	Social welfare

Bibliography

NEWSPAPERS

Adelaide Observer (Adelaide)
The Advertiser (Adelaide)
Advocate (Burnie, Tasmania)
The Age (Melbourne)
The Argus (Melbourne)
The Australian Aborigines Advocate (Sydney)
The Australian Baptist (Sydney)
The Australian Star (Sydney)
The Australian White Ribbon Signal (Melbourne)
The Ballarat Star (Ballarat, Victoria)
The Banner of Truth (Sydney)
The Baptist (Sydney)
The Baptist Record (Adelaide)
The Baptist Woman (Melbourne)
Barrier Miner (Broken Hill, NSW)
Bendigo Advertiser (Bendigo, Victoria)
The Bendigo Independent (Bendigo, Victoria)
The Biz (Fairfield, NSW)
Box Hill Reporter (Box Hill, Victoria)
The Brisbane Courier (Brisbane)
Bunyip (Gawler, SA)
Call and WA Sportsman (Perth)
China's Millions (Melbourne)
Christian Colonist (Adelaide)
Chronicle (Adelaide)
Colonial Times (Hobart)
Courier (Hobart)
The Courier Mail (Brisbane)
The Cumberland Argus and Fruitgrowers Advocate (Parramatta, NSW)
Currency Lad (Sydney)
Daily Mercury (Mackay, Queensland)
The Daily News (Perth)
Daily Standard (Brisbane)

Daily Telegraph (Launceston, Tasmania)
The Daily Telegraph (Sydney)
Evening Journal (Adelaide)
Evening News (Rockhampton, Queensland)
Examiner (Launceston, Tasmania)
The Express and Telegraph (Adelaide)
Geelong Advertiser (Geelong, Victoria)
Gippsland Times (Sale, Victoria)
Glenelg Guardian (Glenelg, SA)
The Golden Link (Melbourne)
Goulburn Evening Penny Post (Goulburn, NSW),
Gympie Times and Mary River Mining Gazette (Gympie, Queensland)
The Herald (Melbourne)
Kyneton Observer (Kyneton, Victoria)
Leader (Melbourne)
Maryborough Chronicle, Wide Bay and Burnett Advertiser (Maryborough, Queensland)
Morning Bulletin (Rockhampton, Qld)
Mount Alexander Mail (Castlemaine, Victoria)
The Mount Barker Courier and Onkaparinga and Gumeracha Advertiser (Mount Barker, SA)
News (Adelaide)
Newcastle Morning Herald and Miners' Advocate (Newcastle, NSW)
Northern Star (Lismore, NSW)
Observer (Adelaide)
Otago Witness (Dunedin, NZ)
Our AIM (Sydney)
Our Bond (Calcutta, India)
Our Indian Field (Sydney)
Petersburg Times (Petersburg, SA)
Port Piri Recorder and North Western Mail (Port Piri, SA)
Queensland Times (Ipswich, Queensland)
Saturday Mail (Adelaide)
The Sentinel (Sydney)
Shepparton Advertiser (Shepparton, Victoria)
The Shoalhaven Telegraph (Nowra, NSW)
The South Australian Advertiser (Adelaide)
South Australian Register (Adelaide)
The Southern Baptist (Melbourne)
The Sydney Mail and NSW Advertiser (Sydney)
The Sydney Morning Herald (Sydney)
Table Talk (Melbourne)
The Maitland Daily Mercury (Newcastle, NSW)
The Mercury (Hobart)
The New South Wales Aborigines' Advocate (Leichhardt, NSW)
The North Western Advocate and the Emu Bay Times (Burnie, Tasmania)
The Queensland Baptist (Brisbane)
The Queensland Freeman (Brisbane)
The Register (Adelaide)

Bibliography 273

The Reporter (Box Hill, Victoria)
The Rising Tide (Stanmore, NSW)
The Roll Call (Sydney)
The Telegraph (Brisbane),
Timaru Herald (Timaru, NZ)
Truth (Brisbane)
Truth and Progress (Adelaide)
The United Aborigines' Messenger (Melbourne)
Vision (Sydney)
The Victorian Baptist (Melbourne)
The Victorian Baptist Witness (Melbourne)
The W. A. Baptist (Perth)
Watchman (Sydney)
Wellington Times (Wellington, NSW)
The West Australian (Perth)
West Coast Sentinel (Streaky Bay, SA)
Western Mail (Perth)
Whyalla News (Whyalla, SA)
World (Hobart)

ARCHIVES

Angus Library and Baptist Archives, Regent's Park College, Oxford.
Australian Capital Territory Heritage Library, Canberra.
Baptist Association of New South Wales Archives, Morling College, Sydney.
Baptist Mission Australia Archives, Moore Potter House, Melbourne.
Baptist Union of Queensland Archives, Queensland Baptists' Centre, Gaythorne, Brisbane.
Baptist Union of Victoria Archives, Camberwell, Melbourne, Victoria.
Baptist Union of Western Australia Archives, Perth, Western Australia.
National Archives of Australia, Canberra.
South Australia State Library, Adelaide.
State Library of New South Wales, Sydney.
University of Tasmania, Hobart.

PRIMARY SOURCES

Australian Baptist Foreign Mission (ABFM). *Annals of Victory: The Annual Report of the Australian Baptist Foreign Mission Incorporated*. Sydney: Australian Baptist, 1940.

———. *Extending the Kingdom in Bengal Being the Annual Report of the Australian Baptist Foreign Mission: 1925*. Sydney: Australian Baptist, 1926.

———. *Facts from the Front Line!: Annual Report of the Australian Baptist Foreign Mission Incorporated*. Sydney: Australian Baptist, 1939.

———. *Forward Area: Report of the Australian Baptist Foreign Mission for 1945*. Sydney: Australian Baptist, 1945.

Australian Baptist Foreign Mission Victorian Committee (ABFMVC). *The Story of a Year's Work in Preaching, Teaching, and Distribution the Gospel in the Districts of Mymensingh, Tangail and Biri-Siri, Eastern Bengal, India.* [Melbourne]: N.p., 1913.

Australian Electoral Roll. Subdivision of Emerald Hill, Division of Melbourne Ports. Melbourne: N.p., 1919.

Baeyertz, Mrs [Emilia]. "Six New Addresses." Perth: City Printing, 1904. http://nla.gov.au/nla.obj-52821324.

Bamford, Adelaide. *Hills of Home.* Sydney: Christian, 1950.

———. *The Sunlit Road.* Glebe, NSW: Australian Baptist, 1945.

The Baptist Hymnal. London: East Marlborough, 1879.

The Baptist Union of Great Britain and Ireland (BUGBI). *The Baptist Handbook for 1927.* London: Baptist Union, 1927.

Baptist Union of New South Wales (BUNSW). *Annual Report.* Sydney: Baptist Union of New South Wales, 1944–1945.

———. *The Baptist Yearbook.* Sydney: Baptist Union of New South Wales, 1923.

———. *The Baptist Yearbook.* Sydney: Baptist Union of New South Wales, 1951.

———. *The New South Wales Baptist Year Book and Handbook: 1906–7.* Sydney: Packer, 1906.

The Baptist Union of Queensland (BUQ). *Year Book 1934.* Brisbane: W. R. Smith & Peterson, 1934.

———. *Year Book 1940: Reports, Balance Sheets, Statistics, 1939–1940.* Brisbane: W. R. Smith & Paterson, 1940.

———. *Year Book 1943.* Brisbane: W. R. Smith & Paterson: 1943.

Baptist Union of Victoria. *Victorian Baptist Union Yearbook.* Camberwell, Victoria: N.p., 1892.

Baptist Women's Training Sisterhood Committee. *The Grey Veil.* London: Kingsgate, [1936].

Barber, Eleanor. "Health and Narcotics." In *Ninth Annual Report of the Woman's Christian Temperance Union of Victoria*, 31–32. Melbourne: Woman's Christian Temperance Union, 1897.

Bean, Margaret F. *Studies in Romans.* London: N.p., [1903].

Beaver, Pierce. "Pioneer Single Women Missionaries." *Missionary Research Library Occasional Bulletin* 4.12 (1953) 1–7.

Booth, Sarah C. *Dinna Forget: Stories from Real Life.* Melbourne: George Robertson, 1907.

Boreham, F. W. *My Pilgrimage: An Autobiography.* London: Epworth, 1940.

[Bowering, Beryl]. "'Lydia' The Purple Seller." Pamphlet. N.p., [1940]

Brown, Lilian. Letter to Gertrude Mead. 13 October 1909. Adelaide. Private collection held by Ros Gooden.

Bush, Henry, and Walter J. E. Kerrison. *First Fifty Years: The Story of Christian Endeavour Under the Southern Cross.* Sydney: National Christian Endeavour Union of Australian and New Zealand, 1938.

Cable, Mildred. "The Missionary in Relation to God, Her Field, and Herself." Pamphlet. N.p., [1946].

Carey, Samuel P. "What Baptists Stand For." In *Baptists and Baptism*, edited by William Holdsworth et al., 4–7. [Melbourne]: Literature Committee of the Baptist Union of Victoria, [1912].

Centenary: 1848–1948. North Adelaide: North Adelaide Baptist Church, 1948.

Clark, Francis Edward. *The Christian Endeavor Manual.* Boston: United Society of Christian Endeavor, 1903.
Clifford, Mrs. H. Rowntree [Harriett]. "The Baptist Deaconess." *Baptist Times,* 31 October 1935. Reprint.
Collins, Gladys E. *Christ's Ambassador, India's Friend.* Melbourne: Australian Baptist Foreign Mission, 1949.
The "Coming-of-Age" of the Baptist Women's League: 1908–1929. London: Baptist Women's League, 1929.
Crofts, Gwenyth. Autograph Book, 1910–1919. Private collection held by Joyce Family.
———. *Bengali Brownies.* Sydney: Australian Baptist Foreign Mission, 1926.
———. *Glimpses into the Life of a Missionary Wife in the Wilds of East Bengal.* N.p., [1946]. Private collection held by Joyce family.
———, ed. *Our Bond Jubilee Edition.* Calcutta: Australian Baptist Foreign Mission, 1932.
Crofts, Wilfred. Letter to Alice Crofts. 22 November 1917. Private collection held by Joyce Family.
———. [Reflections on Alice Crofts]. N.p., 1940. Private collection held by Joyce Family.
Davies, Eliza. *The Story of an Earnest Life: A Woman's Adventures in Australia and in Two Voyages around the World.* Cincinnati: Central Book Concern, 1881.
Downes, Marion. *Swayed by the Storm: A Story of Australia Today.* Melbourne: Thomas C. Lothian, 1911.
Downing, Cecilia. "Unfermented Wine Department." In *20th Annual Report of the Woman's Christian Temperance Union of Victoria,* 43. Melbourne: Woman's Christian Temperance Union, 1907.
Driver, Mrs H. H. [Annie]. *Missionary Memories.* Dunedin, New Zealand: Driver, 1930.
Embery, Winifred. *Those That Endure: A True Story.* Melbourne: China Inland Mission, [1945].
Franc, Maud Jeanne [Matilda Evans]. *Beatrice Melton's Discipline.* London: Sampson Low, Marston, Searle & Rivington, 1880.
Fry, Hannah. *Poems.* Adelaide: Shawyer, 1900.
Furreedpore [Sic] Mission: Report: 1918–1919. Adelaide: N.p., 1919.
G., G. B. *Kate Allanby of Mayurbhanj.* Brisbane: Gillies, 1933.
George, F. [Flora] S. "Sister Dora." *That They Which See Not Might See.* Adelaide: Thomas, 1923.
Gomm, Leslie J. *Blazing the Western Trails: The Story of William Kennedy: Pioneer and Pathfinder.* Sydney: Packer, 1935.
———. *Soul of the Society: Thoughts About the C. E. Consecration Meeting.* Melbourne: National Christian Endeavour Union of Australia, [1942].
Greaves, Lilian Wooster. *The Road to Glory: A Patriotic Souvenir from Western Australia.* Perth: ST Upham, 1915.
———. *The Two Doves and Other Poems.* Perth: Upham & Williams, 1906.
Gunn, Mrs Aeneas [Jeannie]. *We of the Never Never.* 2008 ed. North Sydney: Random, 1908.
Handbook of the Baptist Union of Victoria, 1925. Sydney: Australian Baptist, 1925.
Harris, Bertha. *Mymensingh Mission School: The Trumpet of the Jubilee, 1888–1938.* Mymensingh, East Bengal: Australian Baptist Foreign Mission, [1938].
Harry, Helen. Letter to Gwenyth Crofts. 1930. Private Collection held by Joyce Family.

Hedger, Violet. "Some Experiences of a Woman Minister." *Baptist Quarterly* 10.5 (1941) 243–53. https://doi.org/10.1080/0005576X.1941.11750566.

Henderson, Nola. Letter to Gladys Heather. 25 November 1945. Private Collection held by Bergersen Family.

Hinton, Mrs W. H. [Louisa]. *Ethel Ambrose: Pioneer Medical Missionary.* London: Marshall, Morgan and Scott, 1937.

Holdsworth, William, et al. *Baptists and Baptism.* [Melbourne]: Literature Committee of the Baptist Union of Victoria, [1912].

Hone, Emily. "Flower Mission." In *Woman's Christian Temperance Union of Australasia: Minutes of the Third Triennial Convention*, 102–5. Adelaide: Woman's Christian Temperance Union, 1897.

Hughes, H. Escourt. *Our First Hundred Years: The Baptist Church of South Australia.* Adelaide: South Australian Baptist Union, 1937.

"Initiation Service of the Woman's Christian Temperance Union of Victoria." In *Sixth Annual Records and Methods of Work Done by the Woman's Christian Temperance Union of Victoria During the Year 1893*, 10. Melbourne: Spectator, 1894.

Kemp, Emily Georgiana. *"There Followed Him Women": Pages from the Life of the Women's Missionary Association of the Baptist Missionary Society, 1867 to 1927.* London: Baptist Missionary Society, [1927].

Labourers Together with God: A Record of Achievement for Twelve Months to June 30th, 1934. Sydney: Australian Baptist, 1934.

Lewis, Mrs J. Arthur [Gladys]. *He Talked with a Woman.* Sydney: N.p., [1937].

McCorkindale, Isabel. *Pioneer Pathways: Sixty Years of Citizenship: 1887–1947.* Melbourne: Woman's Christian Temperance Union, 1948.

———, ed. *Torch-Bearers: The Woman's Christian Temperance Union of South Australia, 1886–1948.* Adelaide: Woman's Christian Temperance Union of South Australia, 1949.

McLean, Margaret. "Colonial President's Greetings." In *Thirteenth Annual Report of the Woman's Christian Temperance Union of Victoria*, 37–39. Melbourne: Woman's Christian Temperance Union, 1900.

———. "Drawingroom Meetings." In *Ninth Annual Report of the Woman's Christian Temperance Union of Victoria*, 31. Melbourne: Woman's Christian Temperance Union, 1897.

———. *More About Womanhood Suffrage: A Paper Read by Mrs. Wm. Mclean at the Annual Conference of the Victorian Alliance on 25th August 1891.* Melbourne: N.p., 1891.

———. "President's Address." In *Sixth Annual Records and Methods of Work Done by the Woman's Christian Temperance Union of Victoria During the Year 1893*, 11–16. Melbourne: Spectator, 1894.

———. *Womanhood Suffrage: A Paper Read by Mrs. Mclean at the Annual Convention of the Woman's Christian Temperance Union of Victoria.* Melbourne: Woman's Christian Temperance Union, 1890.

Mead, Lilian S. *The Awakened Woman: Paper Read at Seventh Annual Convention of Woman's Christian Temperance Union of South Australia.* Adelaide: Hussey and Gillingham, 1895.

Mead, Lilian Staple [Mrs Crosbie Brown]. *A Brother's Need.* London: S. W. Partridge, [1903].

Mitchell, Donovan F. *Ellen Arnold: Pioneer and Pathfinder*. Adelaide: South Australian Baptist Union Foreign Missionary, [1932].

Montgomery, Helen Barrett. *Western Women in Eastern Lands: An Outline Study of Fifty Years of Woman's Work in Foreign Mission*. New York: Macmillan, 1911.

"New South Wales Aborigines' Mission: Its Aims and Objects." *The New South Wales Aborigines' Advocate: A Monthly Record of Missionary Work Amongst the Aborigines* [sic], 23 July 1901, 1.

North Adelaide Baptist Church: Manual, 1905. North Adelaide: North Adelaide Baptist Church, 1905.

One Hundred Years of Christian Worship in Kenton Valley: Ænon Chapel, 1849–1949. Kenton Valley, Australia: Kenton Valley Baptist Church, 1949. https://nla.gov.au/nla.obj-52849772/view?partId=nla.obj-101343475.

Order of Baptist Deaconesses and Women's Training College. London: Baptist Union of Great Britain and Ireland, [1941].

Packer, J. A., ed. *First Australasian Baptist Congress, Sydney, September 22–28, 1908: Official Volume of Proceedings*. Sydney: Congress, 1908.

Parliament of Victoria. "Women's Suffrage Petition Search." https://www.parliament.vic.gov.au/about/history-and-heritage/people-who-shaped-parliament/women-suffrage-search.

Price, Emily. "Sabbath Observance." In *Woman's Christian Temperance Union of Australasia: Minutes of the Third Triennial Convention*, 101–2. Adelaide: Woman's Christian Temperance Union, 1897.

Petersham Baptist Church: Fortieth Anniversary, 1882–1922. Sydney: Australian Baptist, 1922.

"Reports for 1896." In *Baptist Union of Victoria Handbook for 1897*. Melbourne: Baptist Union of Victoria, 1897.

Rowland, E. C. *A Century of the English Church in NSW*. Sydney: Angus and Robertson, 1948.

Souvenir of the Second Australasian Baptist Congress: Melbourne, March 29th to April 5th, 1911. Melbourne: E. H. Jenkin & Co, 1911.

Spence, Catherine Helen. *Ever Yours, C.H. Spence: Catherine Helen Spence's an Autobiography (1825–1910), Diary (1894) and Some Correspondence (1894–1910)*. Edited by Susan Magarey et al. Kent Town, SA: Wakefield, 2005.

Spurgeon, Charles H. *The Interpreter, or, Scripture for Family Worship*. London: Passmore and Alabaster, 1874.

Stafford, Mrs James [Stella]. *The Best for All: Stories for Young and Old*. Melbourne: Arbuckle, Waddell, 1944.

———. *The Path of Life*. 4th ed. Melbourne: Spectator, 1942.

Stanmore Baptist Church Year Book: 1911–1912. Sydney: Stanmore Baptist Church, [1912].

Stanmore Baptist Sunday School: Officers, Teacher and Helpers Installation Service, 1927. Sydney: N.p., 1927.

Telfer, Caroline. *Occasional Verses*. Adelaide: Hunkin, Ellis, and King, n.d.

Tranter, A. Marian. *The Call of the Bush and Other Poems*. N.p., 1919.

Tranter, Elsie. *In All Those Lines: The Diary of Sister Elsie Tranter, 1916–1919*. Edited by J. M. Gillings and J. Richards. Launceston: J. M Gillings and J. Richards, 2008.

Varley, Henry. *Henry Varley's Life-Story*. London: Alfred Holness, 1916.

Victorian Baptist Women's Association. "There Came Women Ministering." *Victorian Baptist Witness* (Melbourne), 5 November 1949, 6–7.
The Victorian Baptist Women's Association: 1924 to 1944. [Melbourne]: Victorian Baptist Women's Association, 1945.
Watt, Margaret H. *The History of the Parson's Wife*. 6th ed. London: Faber and Faber, 1946.
Whitley, William Thomas. *A History of British Baptists*. London: C. Griffin, 1923.
Wilcox, Edith K. *The Baptist Women's League, South Australia, 1924–1945: Twenty-One Years' Record of Happiness, Love, Service*. Adelaide: Baptist Women's League, 1945.
———. "Concerning Deaconesses." Paper Read at Half-Yearly Meetings of the SABU. 17 March 1936. Private collection held by Rosalind Gooden, Adelaide.
———. *A Rainbow of Hope: Three Address by Edith K. Wilcox, "A Founder of the Home."* Adelaide: South Australian Baptist Homes for Aged, 1999.
———. *South Australia Baptist Women's League: Past History and Future Aims*. Adelaide: South Australian Baptist Union, 1958.
Wilkin, F. J. [Frederick]. *Baptists in Victoria: Our First Century, 1838–1938*. East Melbourne: Baptist Union of Victoria, 1939.
Williams, Constance. *A Land of Promise*. Melbourne: G. A. Green, 1912.
Woman's Christian Temperance Union of Australasia. Adelaide: Women's Christian Temperance Union of Australasia, 1900.
Woman's Christian Temperance Union of Australasia: Minutes of the Third Triennial Convention. Adelaide: Woman's Christian Temperance Union, 1897.
Women's Auxiliaries [NSW]. *Annual Reports and Balance Sheets 1947–48*. Sydney: N.p., [1948].
Women's Foreign Missionary Societies of the Presbyterian Church (WFMSPC). *Woman's Work for Woman in Our Mission Field*. New York: N.p., 1886–1890.
Zenana Missionary Society, Church of England (ZMS). *India's Women*. London: N.p., 1881–1895.

SECONDARY SOURCES

Abjorensen, Norman, and James C. Docherty. *Historical Dictionary of Australia*. Lanham, MD: Rowman and Littlefield, 2015.
"Air Force Chaplain Makes History." Baptist Churches SA&NT, 6 March 2025. https://bcsant.org.au/news/air-force-chaplain-makes-history.
Arthur, Paul Longley, ed. *Migrant Nation: Australian Culture, Society and Identity*. London: Anthem, 2017. https://www.cambridge.org/core/books/migrant-nation/35B2EABCB2A38F74DAEEE51051AB7BE2.
Australian Bureau of Statistics (ABS). "Historical Censuses: 1901–1991." https://www.abs.gov.au.
Australian Human Rights Commission (AHRC). *National Inquiry into the Separation of Aboriginal and Torres Strait Islander Children from Their Families (Australia). Bringing Them Home: Report of the National Inquiry into the Separation of Aboriginal and Torres Strait Islander Children from Their Families*. Sydney: Human Rights and Equal Opportunity Commission, 1997.

Australian Institute of Aboriginal and Torres Strait Islander Studies (AIATSIS). "Stolen Generations." 2018. https://aiatsis.gov.au/research/finding-your-family/before-you-start/stolen-generations.

Australian Public Service Commission (APSC). "Aboriginal and Torres Strait Islander Peoples." Australian Government Style Manual, 7 March 2025. https://www.stylemanual.gov.au/accessible-and-inclusive-content/inclusive-language/aboriginal-and-torres-strait-islander-peoples.

Aylward, Julie. "The Order of Baptist Deaconesses." Baptists Together, 2019. https://www.baptist.org.uk/Groups/320354/Deaconesses.aspx.

Badger, Lorraine, ed. *Duty, Sacrifice and Honour: South Australian Baptists and World War I.* Adelaide: South Australia Baptist History Group, 2015.

Baldwin, Effie. Letter to Roy Henson. 8 September 1980. Private collection held by Rebecca Hilton.

Ball, Gerald. "Patterns of Presentation: The Australian Baptist Mission's Search for Method in Bengal." *The Baptist Recorder: Journal of the Baptist Historical Society of New South Wales* 3.87 (1987) 3–5.

Ball, Leslie. *Grow the Vision: The Sesqui-Centennial History of the City Tabernacle Baptist Church: 1855–2005.* Brisbane: City Tabernacle Baptist Church, 2005.

Baptist Missionary Society (BMS) World Mission. "Women in Mission." 2021. https://bmsworldmission.org/women-in-mission.

Barr, Beth Allison. *Becoming the Pastor's Wife: How Marriage Replaced Ordination as a Woman's Path to Ministry.* Ada, MI: Brazos, 2025.

———. *The Making of Biblical Womanhood: How the Subjugation of Women Became Gospel Truth.* Grand Rapids: Brazos, 2021.

Bebbington, David W. *Baptists Through the Centuries: A History of a Global People.* 2nd ed. Waco, TX: Baylor University Press, 2018.

———. *Evangelicalism in Modern Britain: A History from the 1730s to the 1980s.* London: Unwin Hyman, 1989.

———. "Introduction: Baptists and the Kingdom of God." In *Baptists and the Kingdom of God: Global Perspectives*, edited by T. Laine Scales and João B. Chaves, 1–14. Waco, TX: Baylor University Press, 2023.

Bhattacharya, Kahlia. "Zenana Missions and Christian Missionaries: Some Reflections of the 'White Woman's Burden' and Imperialism in the Nineteenth Century Bengal." *Exploring History* 7.1 (2015) 1–17.

Breward, Ian. *A History of the Churches in Australasia.* Edited by Henry Chadwick and Owen Chadwick. Oxford History of the Christian Church. Oxford: Oxford University Press, 2001.

Brookes, Stephanie. *Politics, Media and Campaign Language: Australia's Identity Anxiety.* London: Anthem, 2017. https://www.cambridge.org/core/books/politics-media-and-campaign-language/1DE5860631AAF7C77541E603764C5521.

Burn, Kerrie L. "The Australian Baptist Heritage Collection: Management of a Geographically Distributed Special Collection." Master's thesis, Melbourne College of Divinity, 2007.

Calvert, John David. "Douglas Pike (1908–1974): South Australian and Australian Historian." Master's thesis, University of Adelaide, 2008.

Carey, Jane. "National Woman's Christian Temperance Union of Australia." Encyclopedia of Women and Leadership in Twentieth-Century Australia, 2014. http://www.womenaustralia.info/leaders/biogs/WLE0774b.htm.

Chambers, Murray. *Centenary of Christian Endeavour in Australia*. N.p.: Australian Christian Endeavour Union, 1983.

Champness, Beryl. *The Servant Ministry: The Methodist Deaconess Order in Victoria and Tasmania*. Melbourne: Uniting Church, 1996.

Chapman, Mark, et al., eds. *The Oxford Handbook of Anglican Studies*. Oxford: Oxford University Press, 2015.

Chilton, Lisa. *Agents of Empire: British Female Migration to Canada and Australia, 1860–1930*. Toronto: University of Toronto Press, 2007. http://ebookcentral.proquest.com/lib/csuau/detail.action?docID=4672409.

Clack, W. S., ed. *We Will Go: The History of Seventy Years Training Men and Women for World Missionary Ministry*. Melbourne: Bible College of Victoria, 1990.

Clarke, Lyn. *Making a Difference: The Legends and Landmarks of Baptcare*. Melbourne: Melbourne Books, 2016.

Coe, Barbara. "So Much More than Pouring the Tea: Mary Louisa Bowie Née Grey (1903–1990)." Speech given to the Baptist Historical Society of NSW and ACT, 2022.

Condie, Pam. "The Views of Queensland Baptists Regarding the Ordination of Women." Doctor of Ministry diss., Australian College of Theology, 2020.

Crabb, Gordon D. *Mount Cooper Baptist Circuit: 1912–1981*. Adelaide: South Australian Baptist Union, 2020.

Croson, Rachel, et al. "Groups Work for Women: Gender and Group Identity in Social Dilemmas." *Negotiation Journal* 24.4 (2008) 411–27. https://doi.org/10.1111/j.1571-9979.2008.00195.x.

Cross, F. L., and Elizabeth A. Livingstone, eds. *The Oxford Dictionary of the Christian Church*. 3rd rev. ed. Oxford: Oxford University Press, 2013.

Cupit, Tony, et al., eds. *From Five Barley Loaves: Australian Baptists in Global Mission, 1864–2010*. Melbourne: Morning Star, 2012.

Davie, Martin, et al., eds. *New Dictionary of Theology: Historical and Systematic*. 2nd ed. Downers Grove, IL: IVP Academic, 2016.

Day, David. *John Curtin: A Life*. Pymble, NSW: HarperCollins, 1999.

Dempsey, Kenneth. *The Fate of Ministers' Wives: A Study of Subordination and Incorporation*. La Trobe Sociology Papers 15. Melbourne: Department of Sociology La Trobe University, 1985.

Department of Education, Training and Youth Affairs (DETYA), Australia. *Higher Education Students Time Series Tables 2000: Selected Higher Education Statistics*. Canberra: Commonwealth of Australia, 2001.

Dickey, Brian, ed. *The Australian Dictionary of Evangelical Biography*. Sydney: Evangelical History Association, 1994.

Doulman, Jane, and David Lee. *Every Assistance and Protection: A History of the Australian Passport*. Sydney: Federation: 2008.

Driver, David, and Hope Colegrove. *For God, King and Country: The Life Stories of the World War I Servicemen and Women of the City Tabernacle Baptist Church, Brisbane*. Brisbane: City Tabernacle Baptist Church, 2018.

Durso, Pam. "Baptist Women Ministers: A Bit of History for an Ordination Service." Baptist Women in Ministry, 14 December 2010. https://bwim.info/baptist-women-ministers-a-bit-of-history-for-an-ordination-service-by-pam-durso.

Dutta, Sutapa. *British Women Missionaries in Bengal, 1793–1861*. London: Anthem, 2017. https://www.cambridge.org/core/books/british-women-missionaries-in-bengal-17931861/71B9450D62064A9157F8B3BE949E01EB.

Dzubinski, Leanne M., and Anneke H. Stasson. *Women in the Mission of the Church: Their Opportunities and Obstacles Throughout Christian History*. Grand Rapids: Baker Academic, 2021.

Eldridge, Victor J. *For the Highest: A History of Morling College*. Macquarie Park, NSW: Greenwood, 2015.

Evans, Robert. *Emilia Baeyertz Evangelist*. Hazelbrook, NSW: Research in Evangelical Revivals, 2007.

Finnis, H. J. "Evans, Matilda Jane (1827–1886)." In *1851–1890: D–J*, edited by Douglas Pike. Vol. 4 of *Australian Dictionary of Biography*. Melbourne: Melbourne University Press, 1972. http://adb.anu.edu.au/biography/evans-matilda-jane-3487.

Flowers, Elizabeth H. *Into the Pulpit: Southern Baptist Women and Power Since World War II*. Chapel Hill: University of North Carolina Press, 2012.

Footscray Baptist Church, Paisley Street: 75th Anniversary Souvenir. Footscray, Victoria: Footscray Baptist Church, 1958.

Franklin, James. "Women in the Australian Church." Australian Catholic Historical Society. https://australiancatholichistoricalsociety.com.au/history-resources/women-in-the-australian-church.

Friedman, Susan Stanford. *Mappings: Feminism and the Cultural Geographies of Encounter*. Core Textbook ed. Princeton, NJ: Princeton University Press, 1998. doi: 10.1515/9781400822577.

Gladwin, Michael. "Mission and Colonialism." In *The Oxford Handbook of Nineteenth-Century Christian Thought*, edited by Joel Rasmussen et al., 282–304. Oxford: Oxford University Press, 2019.

Godden, Judith. "Containment and Control: Presbyterian Women and the Missionary Impulse in New South Wales, 1891–1914." *Women's History Review* 6.1 (1997) 75–93. https://doi.org/https://doi.org/10.1080/09612029700200137.

Gooden, Rosalind M. "'Mothers in the Lord': Australasian Baptist Women Missionaries at the Intersection of Cultural Contexts 1882–1931." PhD diss., Tabor College of Higher Education, 2016.

———. "'We Trust Them to Establish the Work': Significant Roles for Early Australian Baptist Women in Overseas Mission, 1864–1913." In *This Gospel Shall Be Preached: Essays on the Australian Contribution to World Mission*, edited by Mark Hutchinson and Geoffrey R. Treloar, 126–46. Sydney: Centre for the Study of Australian Christianity, 1998.

Gouldbourne, Ruth. "Baptists, Women, and Ministry." *Feminist Theology* 22 (2017) 59–68. doi: 10.1177/0966735017714392.

Green, Jay D. "Whither the Conference on Faith and History? The Politics of Evangelical Identity and the Spiritual Vision of History." *Fides et Historia; Terre Haute* 49.1 (2017) 1–10.

Grimshaw, Patricia, et al. *Creating a Nation*. Ringwood, Victoria: McPhee Gribble, 1994.

Habermas, Jürgen. "Further Reflections on the Public Sphere." In *Habermas and the Public Sphere*, edited by Craig Calhoun, 421–61. Cambridge: MIT Press, 1996.

Hagemann, Karen, and Sonya Michel. "Civil Society." In *The Oxford Encyclopedia of Women in World History*, edited by Bonnie G. Smith. Oxford: Oxford University Press, 2008. https://www.oxfordreference.com/view/10.1093/acref/9780195148909.001.0001/acref-9780195148909-e-184.

Ham, Janice M. *A History: The Australian Baptist Women's Fellowship: 1935–1951*. Camberwell: Victorian Baptist Historical Society, 1985.

Harris, John. *One Blood: 200 Years of Aboriginal Encounter with Christianity: A Story of Hope*. Sutherland, NSW: Albatross, 1990.

Harris, Jose. "Civil Society in British History: Ideas, Identities, Institutions." In *Civil Society in British History Ideas, Identities, Institutions*, edited by Jose Harris, 13–37. Oxford: Oxford University Press, 2005.

Harris, Stephen. *Stroud District Baptist Church: The First Hundred Years*. Macquarie Park, NSW: Baptist Historical Society of NSW, 2013.

Hayward, Bess. "Baptist Deaconesses in New South Wales and the Australian Capital Territory." *The Baptist Recorder* 97 (2007) 1–8.

Hayward, Victor E. W. "The Gathered Community." *Baptist Quarterly* 23.5 (1970) 195–200.

Helm, John. *The Baptists of Burnside: Knightsbridge Baptist Church 1884–1984*. Adelaide, SA: Hyde Park, [1984].

Helyar, Geoffrey. *A Voice in the City: Perth Baptist Church: 1895–1995*. Perth: Perth Baptist Church, 1995.

Henderson, Anne. *Mary Mackillop's Sisters: A Life Unveiled*. Sydney: Harper Collins, 2010.

Henson, Roy. "Florence Susannah Harris, 1981." Unpublished. Private Collection held by Rebecca Hilton.

Hilliard, David. "Methodism in South Australia: 1855–1902." In *Methodism in Australia*, edited by Glen O'Brien and Hilary Carey, 91–109. Farnham, Surrey: Ashgate, 2015.

Hilton, Rebecca. "Australian Baptist Women as Public Intellectuals: 1890–1918." *Lucas: An Evangelical History* 3.1 (2023) 121–40.

———. "Australian Baptist Women Database: 1830–1945." 2025.

———. "Evangelical Deaconess Orders in Australia: 1890–1950: A 'Decent Mess.'" *Lucas: An Evangelical History* 3.3 (2024) 153–65.

———. "Women in the Australian Baptist Denomination in Peace and War, 1920–1945." *Religions* 15.9 (2024) 1037. doi: 10.3390/rel15091037.

Hughes, R. W. [Bill]. *The Centenary of the City Tabernacle Baptist Church Organ, Brisbane, 1914–2015*. Brisbane: City Tabernacle Baptist Church, 2015.

———. *The History of the Queensland Baptist Senior Girls' Missionary Union [SGMU]: 1924–1991*. Brisbane: Baptist Union of Queensland Archives, 2012.

Hutchinson, Mark, and John Wolffe. *A Short History of Global Evangelicalism*. New York: Cambridge University Press, 2012.

Hyslop, Anthea. "Mclean, Margaret (1845–1923)." In *1891–1939: Lat–Ner*, edited by Bede Nairn and Geoffrey Serle. Vol. 10 of *Australian Dictionary of Biography*. Melbourne: Melbourne University Press, 1986. http://adb.anu.edu.au/biography/mclean-margaret-7414/text12897.

Jensz, Felicity. *German Moravian Missionaries in the British Colony of Victoria, Australia, 1848–1908*. Boston: Brill, 2010.

Kelshaw, Carolyn. *Baptistcare: 75 Years of Caring: 75 Stories That Shaped Us; Because We Care*. Edited by Kathryn Tafra. Preston, Victoria: Bounce, 2019.

King, Michael. *Tread Softly: For You Tread on My Life*. Auckland: Cape Catley, 2001.

Kingslover, Barbara. *The Poisonwood Bible: A Novel*. New York: HarperFlamingo, 1998.

Kingston, Beverley. "Faith and Fetes: Women and the History of the Churches in Australia." In *Women, Faith and Fetes: Essays in the History of Women in the Church in Australia*, edited by Sabine Willis, 20–27. Melbourne: Dove Communications; Australian Council of Churches, NSW, Commission on Status of Women, 1977.

Klapdor, Michael, et al. "Australian Citizenship: A Chronology of Major Developments in Policy and Law." Parliamentary Library, Parliament of Australia, 11 September 2009. https://parlinfo.aph.gov.au/parlInfo/download/library/prspub/5252442/upload_binary/5252442.pdf.

Lack, John, and Charles Fahey. "The Industrialist, the Trade Unionist and the Judge: The Harvester Judgement of 1907 Revisited." *Victorian Historical Journal* 79.1 (2008) 3–18.

Lake, Marilyn. "Women's and Gender History in Australia: A Transformative Practice." *Journal of Women's History* 25.4 (2013) 190–211. doi: 10.1353/jowh.2013.0043.

Leonard, Bill. *Baptists in America*. New York: Columbia University Press, 2005.

Lienemann-Perrin, Christine, et al., eds. *Putting Names with Faces: Women's Impact in Mission History*. Nashville: Abingdon, 2012.

Loane, Marcus L. *The Story of the China Inland Mission in Australia and New Zealand: 1890–964*. Sydney: Halstead, 1965.

Macdonald, Stella Mary Churchward. *My First Ten Years: Spent Mostly in India*. Brighton, Victoria: N.p., [1995].

Mackinnon, Alison. *The New Women: Adelaide's Early Women Graduates*. Netley, SA: Wakefield, 1986.

Manley, Ken. *From Woolloomooloo to "Eternity": A History of Australian Baptists*. 2 vols. Milton Keynes, UK: Paternoster, 2006.

———. "'Our Own Church in Our Own Land': The Shaping of Baptist Identity in Australia." In *Baptist Identities: International Studies from the Seventeenth to the Twentieth Century: Studies in Baptist History and Thought*, edited by Ian M. Randall et al., 275–98. Milton Keynes, UK: Paternoster, 2006.

———. "Shaping the Australian Baptist Movement." Paper presented at BWA Congress, Melbourne, 2000.

———. "'Swayed by Life's Storms': Marion Downes (1864–1926). Australian Baptist Poet and Novelist." In *Baptists and Gender*, edited by M. Maxwell and T. L. Scales, 270–82. Macon, GA: Mercer University Press, 2023.

Maughan, Steven S. *Mighty England Do Good: Culture, Faith, Empire, and World in the Foreign Missions of the Church of England, 1850–915*. Edited by R. E. Frykenberg and Brian Stanley. Studies in the History of Christian Missions. Grand Rapids: Eerdmans, 2014.

Maxwell, Joan L. *Triumphant Through Trials: True Life Story of Thelma Howard*. Toowoomba, Queensland: J. L. Maxwell, 1996.

Maxwell, Melody, ed. *Reclaiming Voices: Women's Contributions to Baptist History*. Basel, Switzerland: MDPI, 2024. doi: 10.3390/books978-73-7258-2643-8.

———. "A Winding and Widening Path: American Women's Roles in Twentieth-Century Baptist Life." *Baptist History and Heritage* 53.2 (2018) 8–22.

McGrath, Alister. *Christianity: An Introduction*. 3rd ed. London: Wiley, 2017.

McKernan, Michael. *Australians at Home: World War I*. Scorseby, Victoria: Five Mile, 2014.

Mead, Marjory. *God Building: Flinders Street Baptist Church: Adelaide: 1861–1961*. Adelaide: Flinders Street Baptist Church, 1961.

Merrilees, Bill, et al. "Volunteer Retention Motives and Determinants Across the Volunteer Lifecycle." *Journal of Nonprofit and Public Sector Marketing* 32.1 (2020) 25–46. doi: 10.1080/10495142.2019.1689220.

Mitcham Baptist Church: A Brief History of One Hundred Years' Work for God. Adelaide, SA: Hyde Park, [1958].

Mitchell, Doris M. *Working Together: The Story of the Women's Auxiliary to the Australian Board of Missions, 1910–985*. Parramatta, NSW: Macarthur, 1985.

Monk, Anne. "Stained Glass Windows at NABC." North Adelaide: North Adelaide Baptist, 2022.

Moore, Ray. *An Ordinary Church in the Country: The Centenary History of the Traralgon and District Baptist Church: 1903–2003*. [Traralgon, Victoria]: Kyeema, 2011.

Moore, Richard K. *"All Western Australia Is My Parish": A Centenary History of the Baptist Denomination in Western Australia, 1895–1995*. [Perth]: Baptist Historical Society of Western Australia, 1996.

Moxey, Nicky, and Linda Devereux, eds. *Exploring Boarding School Challenges for Women and Third Culture Kids*. London: Routledge, 2025.

Murphy, Edwina, and David Starling, ed. *The Gender Conversation: Evangelical Perspectives on Gender, Scripture, and the Christian Life*. Macquarie Park: Morling, 2016.

Neill, Stephen. *A History of Christian Missions*. Harmondsworth, Middlesex: Penguin, 1964.

Newnham, Lindsay. "Sister Grace's Mission." *Our Yesterdays: The Victorian Baptist Historical Society* 12 (2004) 34–43.

New South Wales (NSW) Government. "Bomaderry Aboriginal Children's Home." 2011. https://www.hms.heritage.nsw.gov.au/App/Item/ViewItem?itemId=5061330.

North Adelaide Baptist Church: Tynte Street, North Adelaide: 150th Anniversary: 1848–1998: Souvenir Program, May 1998. North Adelaide: North Adelaide Baptist Church, 1998.

O'Brien, Anne. "Australian Methodist Women." In *Methodism in Australia*, edited by Glen O'Brien and Hilary Carey, 211–24. Farnham, Surrey: Ashgate, 2015.

———. *God's Willing Workers: Women and Religion in Australia*. Sydney: University of New South Wales, 2005.

———. "Historical Overview Spirituality and Work Sydney Women, 1920–1960." *Australian Historical Studies* 33.120 (2008) 373–88.

O'Brien, Glen, and Hilary Carey, eds. *Methodism in Australia*. Farnham, Surrey: Ashgate, 2015.

Ollif, Lorna. *Women in Khaki*. [Sydney]: Ollif, 1981.

Olsen, Roger E. *How to Be Evangelical without Being Conservative*. Grand Rapids: Zondervan, 2008.

O'Neill, Sally. "Gunn, Jeannie (1870–961)." In *1891–1939: Gil-Las*, edited by Bede Nairn and Geoffrey Serle. Vol. 9 of *Australian Dictionary of Biography*. Melbourne: Melbourne University Press, 1983. http://adb.anu.edu.au/biography/gunn-jeannie-6506.

Otzen, Roslyn. "Calling the Roll: What We Can Learn from the Membership Roll of the Collins Street Baptist Church." *Our Yesterdays: The Victorian Baptist Historical Society* 27 (2019) 39–57.

———. *Whitley: The Baptist College of Victoria, 1891–1991*. South Yarra, Victoria: Hyland, 1991.

Pargeter, Judith. *"For God, Home and Humanity": National Woman's Christian Temperance Union of Australia: Centenary History: 1891–1991*. Geelong, Victoria: National Woman's Christian Temperance Union of Australia, 1995.

Parker, David, ed. *Pressing on with the Gospel: The Story of Baptists in Queensland 1855–2005*. Brisbane: Baptist Historical Society of Queensland, 2005.

———. *"A True Pastor": The Life and Ministry of William Higlett*. Brisbane: Baptist Historical Society of Queensland, 2002.

———, ed. *Women Who Made a Difference—Celebrating the Contribution of 24 Queensland Baptist Women to Church, Community and Mission*. Brisbane: Baptist Heritage Queensland, 2009.

Peterborough Baptist Centenary: 1880–980: Souvenir Programme. Peterborough: Peterborough Baptist, 1980.

Petras, Michael John. "Across the Frontier and Around the Fringe: Baptist Growth in America and in Australia." PhD diss., Macquarie University, 2017. http://hdl.handle.net/1959.14/1262068.

Piggin, Stuart, and Robert D. Linder. *Attending to the National Soul: Evangelical Christians in Australian History 1914–2014*. Edited by Sean Scalmer. Australian History. Clayton, Victoria: Monash University Publishing, 2020.

———. *The Fountain of Public Prosperity: Evangelical Christians in Australian History 1740–914*. Clayton, Victoria: Monash University Publishing, 2018.

Pitman, Julia. "The Green and Gold Cookery Book: Women, Faith, Fetes, Food and Popular Culture." *Journal of the Historical Society of South Australia* 35 (2007) 64–80.

———. *"Our Principle of Sex Equality": The Ordination of Women in the Congregational Church in Australia, 1927–1977*. North Melbourne: Australian Scholarly, 2016.

Porterfield, Amanda, ed. *Modern Christianity to 1900*. People's History of Christianity 6. Minneapolis: Fortress, 2007.

Postel, Charles, "Political Chaos and Unexpected Activism of the Post-Civil War Era." Literary Hub, 14 July 2019. https://lithub.com/the-political-chaos-and-unexpected-activism-of-the-post-civil-war-era.

Prior, Alan C. *Some Fell on Good Ground: A History of the Beginnings and Development of the Baptist Church in New South Wales, Australia, 1831–1965*. Sydney: The Baptist Union of New South Wales, 1966.

Radi, Heather. "Ardill, George Edward (1857–1945)." In *1891–1939: A–Ch*, edited by Bede Nairn and Geoffrey Serle. Vol. 7 of *Australian Dictionary of Biography*. Melbourne: Melbourne University Press, 1979. http://adb.anu.edu.au/biography/ardill-george-edward-5048/text8413.

Randall, Ian. *What a Friend We Have in Jesus: The Evangelical Tradition*. Edited by Philip Sheldrake. Traditions of Christian Spirituality. Maryknoll, NY: Orbis, 2005.

Redman, Jess. *The Light Shines On: A Story of One Hundred Years of Australian Baptist Missionary Work*. Hawthorn, Victoria: Australian Baptist Missionary Society, 1982.

Richardson, Shelley. *Family Experiments: Middle-Class, Professional Families in Australia and New Zealand c. 1880–920*. Canberra: Australian National University Press, 2016.

Robert, Dana Lee. *American Women in Mission: A Social History of Their Thought and Practice*. Macon, GA: Mercer University Press, 1996.

———. *Christian Mission: How Christianity Became a World Religion*. Chichester, West Sussex: Wiley-Blackwell, 2009.

———, ed. *Gospel Bearers, Gender Barriers: Missionary Women in the Twentieth Century*. Maryknoll, NY: Orbis, 2002.

Rogers, Doris. Letter to Roy Henson. 25 May 1980. Private Collection held by Rebecca Hilton.

Rogers, E. Ron. *George Henry Morling: "Our Beloved Principal." A Definitive Biography*. Macquarie Park, NSW: Greenwood, 2014.

Rowston, Laurence F. *Baptists in Van Dieman's Land*. Hobart: Baptist Union of Australia, 1985.

———. *Baptists in Van Diemen's Land. Part 2: The Story of the Launceston Particular Baptist Chapel, York Street 1840–916*. Longford, Tasmania: Baptist Union of Tasmania, 2020.

———. "Spurgeon's Men: The Resurgence of Baptist Belief and Practice in Tasmania 1869–1884." Master's thesis, University of Tasmania, 2011.

Rubio, Julie Hanlon. *Family Ethics: Practices for Christians*. Washington, DC: Georgetown University Press, 2010.

Secomb, Robin. "Borne in Empire: Issues of Gender, Ethnicity and Power Behind Laura Fowler Hope's Journey to Kalimpong." *Outskirts: Feminisms Along the Edge* 7 (2000). https://www.outskirts.arts.uwa.edu.au/volumes/volume-7/secomb.

The Senior Girls' Missionary Union of NSW (SGMUNSW). *Reunion Dinner: Souvenir Programme*. Sydney: N.p., 1967.

Seton, Rosemary. *Western Daughters in Eastern Lands: British Missionary Women in Asia*. Santa Barbara, CA: Praeger, 2013.

Sheard, Heather, and Ruth Lee. *Women to the Front: The Extraordinary Australian Women Doctors of the Great War*. North Sydney: Penguin, 2019.

Sheldrake, Philip. *Spirituality: A Brief History*. 2nd ed. Oxford: Wiley-Blackwell, 2013.

Smart, Judith. "Rees, Elizabeth Laurie (Bessie) (1865–1939)." In *1580–1980: A–Z*, edited by Christopher Cunneen et al. *Australian Dictionary of Biography* Supplement. Melbourne: Melbourne University Press, 2005. http://adb.anu.edu.au/biography/rees-elizabeth-laurie-bessie-13167/text23831.

Souter, Zachary Aaron. "Place and Pedagogy: Sunday School in the Eighteenth and Nineteenth Centuries." PhD diss., Southern Baptist Theological Seminary, 2023.

Spender, Dale. *Women of Ideas and What Men Have Done to Them*. Melbourne: Routledge & Kegan Paul, 1982.

Stanhope, John M. *Seek Those Things Which Are Above: A History of the Auburn Baptist Church to 2002*. Lismore, NSW: Auburn Baptist Church, 2005.

Stanley, Brian. *The History of the Baptist Missionary Society: 1792–1992*. Edinburgh: T&T Clark, 1992.

Starling, Ian. *They Went Before Us*. Sydney: Ian Starling, 2015.

Starr, Barry. "My Words on 180 Years of CBC [Central Baptist Church, Sydney]." *iCentral Corner* 4 (2016) 5–6.

Stone, Lawrence. "Prosopography." *Daedalus* 100.1 (1971) 46–79.

Taylor, Howard, and Geraldine Taylor. *Hudson Taylor and the China Inland Mission.* 1918. Reprint, London: China Inland Mission, 1958.
These Fifty Years: Being a Brief Summary of God's Many Mercies to Mortdale Baptist Church, Issued on the Occasion of the Golden Jubilee. Sydney: N.p., 1955.
This Corner: Stories of Newstead Baptist Church, 1936-1996. Launceston, Tasmania: Regal, 1996.
Thompson, P. E. "Baptist Theology." In *New Dictionary of Theology: Historical and Systematic,* edited by Martin Davie et al., 101. 2nd ed. Downers Grove, IL: IVP Academic, 2016.
"Through These Years": Golden Jubilee: The Story of the Hurlstone Park Baptist Church: 1913-1963. Sydney: Hurlstone Park Baptist Church, 1963.
Toit, Megan du. "Gender: Counter-Cultural Practice? Cultural Construct? New Creation?" In *The Gender Conversation: Evangelical Perspectives on Gender, Scripture, and the Christian Life,* edited by Edwina Murphy and David Starling, 161–70. Macquarie Park: Morling, 2016.
Treloar, Geoffrey R. *The Disruption of Evangelicalism: The Age of Torrey, Mott, Mcpherson and Hammond.* History of Evangelicalism 4. Downers Grove, IL: IVP Academic, 2017.
Trigg, Jean, and Majorie Robertson. "History of Mount Barker." 1950. *LocalWiki,* 2014. https://localwiki.org/adelaide-hills/History_of_Mount_Barker.
Tyler, Jim, and Helen Tyler. *Mount Barker Baptist Church: "The Lessons for Today."* Adelaide: South Australia Baptist Historical Society, 1985.
Walker, Deaville F. *William Carey: Missionary Pioneer and Statesman.* Chicago: Moody, 1960.
Walker, John. "The Baptists in South Australia, Circa 1900 to 1939." PhD diss., Adelaide College of Divinity, 2006.
———. "'An Earnest Life': The South Australian Years of Eliza Davies, Member of Adelaide's First Baptist Church." Speech to SA Baptist History Group, 10 November 2023.
Watkin-Smith, Hubert. *Baptists in the Cradle City: The Story of Parramatta Baptist Church: 1838-1986.* Sydney: Baptist Historical Society of New South Wales, 1986.
Watts, Michael R. *The Dissenters.* Vols. 1, 3. Oxford: Oxford University Press, 1995, 2015. doi: 10.1093/acprof:oso/9780198229681.001.0001; 10.1093/acprof:o so/9780198229698.001.0001.
Webb, Ken. *"Illoura": The Beginning.* [Adelaide]: N.p., 1999.
Webb, Val. *Why We're Equal: Introducing Feminist Theology.* St. Louis, MO: Chalice, 1999.
West, Janet. *Daughters of Freedom: A History of Women in the Australian Church.* Sutherland, Australia: Albatross, 1997.
White, John E. *A Fellowship of Service: A History of the Baptist Union of Queensland 1877-1977.* Brisbane: Baptist Union of Queensland, 1977.
Wilson, Linda. *Constrained by Zeal: Female Spirituality Amongst Nonconformists 1825–75.* Carlisle, Cumbria: Paternoster, 2000.
Wood, Janine. *Names to Lives: The Canterbury Baptist Church Honour Roll Board.* Canterbury, Victoria: Canterbury Baptist Church, 2016.
Woollacott, Angela. *To Try Her Fortune in London: Australian Women, Colonialism, and Modernity.* New York: Oxford University Press, 2001.

Young, Len. *Greenslopes Baptist Church: Centenary Celebration Service*. Brisbane: Greenslopes Baptist, 2020.

Young, Margaret, and Bill Gammage, eds. *Hail and Farewell: Letters from Two Brothers Killed in France in 1916: Alec and Goldy Raws*. Kenthurst, NSW: Kangaroo, 1995.

Index

People; Baptist Congregations; and Baptist and other significant Organizations

[Unknown surname], Mary, 24, 245
Abbott, Anna (Pfunder), 133, 245
Abbott, Hedley Rev., 133
Abbott, Mary, 92–93, 168, 245
Abermain Baptist, NSW, 40–41
Aborigines [sic] Inland Mission, 169, 181, 204–9, 232
Albert Park Baptist, Melbourne, 39
Alberton Baptist, SA, 93n
Alcorn, Agnes (Trudinger), 77–78, 245
Aldridge, Frances (France), 59, 168, 224, 245
Aldridge, Frank, Rev., 168
Allanby, Kate, 76–77, 80n, 85, 88, 95, 246
Allanby, Mary (Brady), 77, 246
Allen, Jean, 166, 168, 246
Ambrose, Ethel Dr, 61, 64, 76, 77n, 85n, 88, 90, 246
Ambrose, Lily, 76, 88, 246
Anderson, Rufus, 103
Archer, Ada, 97n, 246
Ardill, George, 219
Ardill, Lily (Southwell), 183, 246
Ardill, Louisa (Wales), 177, 219, 226, 246
Ardill-Brice, Katie Dr, 229, 246
Ariah Park, NSW, 171
Armstrong, Evelyn (Davis), 40, 246
Arnold, Ellen, 8, 65–66, 67, 68, 72, 79, 86, 87n, 91, 94, 97, 101–2, 113, 121, 124, 246

Arnot, Agnes (Russell), 215
Arnot, Andrew, 215
Ashburton Baptist, Victoria, 44
Ashworth, Margaret (Tomlinson), 4, 189, 246
Auburn Baptist, NSW, 35–36, 45
Australian Baptist Foreign Mission (ABFM), 13n, 16, 17, 53, 60–69, 71–75, 76–82, 84–97, 99–106, 107–10, 115–17, 126, 131–32, 133n, 136, 140, 141, 142, 146, 161, 174, 180, 182, 188, 201, 202, 215, 237
Australian Baptist Women's Board (ABWB), 119, 141, 146–50
Australian Baptist women's organizations, NSW, 94, 118–19, 120–23, 129, 130–31, 133, 141–46
Australian Baptist women's organizations, Queensland, 50, 52, 54, 118–19, 126, 131–33, 150
Australian Baptist women's organizations, SA, 7, 55, 118–19, 121, 124, 127–28, 139, 150n, 151, 152, 170, 174n, 195, 196, 221
Australian Baptist women's organizations, Tasmania, 118–19, 124–25, 130
Australian Baptist women's organizations, Victoria, 118–20, 123–24, 128–29, 138, 151–52

Australian Baptist women's organizations, WA, 118–19, 125–26
Australian Imperial Force (AIF), 229
Australian Women's Army Service, 230–31

Baeyertz, Emelia (Aronson), 176, 177, 246
Bailey, Charlotte (Salmon), 95, 246
Baker, Elizabeth (Bessie), 26, 246
Baldwin, Effie (Steed), 78n, 102, 109, 247
Ballarat Baptist, Victoria, 202n
Bamford, Adelaide (Dunkley), 40n, 139n, 140n, 154, 160–61, 172, 178, 187–88, 190, 191n, 194–98, 230, 238, 247
Baptist Evangelist Society (NSW), 120
Baptist Mission Australia, 16, 66n
Baptist Missionary Society (UK) (BMS), 66–67, 69–72, 75, 76n, 85, 92, 114
Baptist Union of Australia (BUA), 12, 16, 146, 147–49, 174, 204
Baptist Union of New South Wales, 12, 16, 24, 121, 122–23, 137, 162, 166, 186
Baptist Union of Queensland, 12, 24, 126, 132, 150, 206
Baptist Union of South Australia, 12, 16, 42, 54, 121, 128, 139, 171, 176
Baptist Union of Tasmania, 12, 124, 130, 134
Baptist Union of Victoria, 12, 26, 39, 129, 138, 151, 159, 176, 217
Baptist Union of Western Australia, 12, 175, 205
Baptist Zenana Mission (UK), 70–71, 114, 119–20
Barber, Alice (McLean), 87–88, 109, 131, 173, 215, 226, 229, 247
Barber, Eleanor (Napier), 212, 226, 247
Barker, Florence, 32, 247
Barker, Sophia (Whitbread), 31–32, 247
Barker, William, 32
Barnard, Clement Rev., 205
Barnard, Winifred (Cunningham), 205, 247
Barraport Baptist, Victoria, 180–81

Barrett Montgomery, Helen, 70
Barron, Eleanor (Thompson), 207, 247
Barry, Annie (Bacon), 102, 109, 247
Barton, Helen (Robertson), 172
Barton, William, 195n
Batey, Mary (Hopkins), 40, 247
Bathurst Street Baptist, Sydney, 24, 28, 34, 36, 38, 42, 208–9
Bean, Albert Rev., 220
Bean, Annie (Dougal) 226, 247
Bean, Margaret (Baillie), 7n, 8, 169, 200, 220–21, 223, 247
Beattie, Dorcas (Parham, then Sharp), 44, 247
Beeston, Agnes (Brown), 149, 247
Bell, William Rev., 132
Bendigo Baptist, Victoria, 191
Bennell, Edna (Gregson), 21, 247
Benskin, Emily (Lord), 7, 11n, 13n, 19, 20n, 55n, 127–28, 187, 194–98, 238, 248
Benskin, Frederick Rev., 127
Bird, Alfred, 208
Bird, Ann (Burge), 208, 248
Birks, Rosetta (Thomas), 23, 211n, 220, 225, 248
Bomaderry Home for Aboriginal Children, 207
Booth, Evangeline, 197
Booth, Sarah, 27, 200n, 220, 248
Boreham, Frank Rev., 7, 23, 268n
Boreham, Stella (Cottee), 23, 248
Bowering, Beryl, 76, 85, 88, 135, 248
Bowie, Mary (Grey), 162, 248
Brainwood, Hazel (Thornton), 41, 248
Brasnett, Emily (Smith), 48, 248
Breenan, M.A. Dr, 157
Brice, Bessie, 133, 248
Brindley, Ruby, 131–32, 248
British and Foreign Bible Society, 5
Broken Hill Baptist, NSW, 44
Brown, Fanny (Ardill), 186, 193, 248
Brown, Grace, 89, 94, 125, 134, 181, 248
Brown, Lilian (Mead), 90n, 104, 178, 179, 183, 184, 189, 192, 212–13, 226, 241, 248
Brown, Marie (Smith), 125, 248
Brunton, Phyllis (Irving), 231, 248

Buckingham, Hannah (Gellalty), 48, 248
Bullock, Rebecca (Hubbard), 32, 249
Burgess, Mabel, 137, 249
Butters, Ethel (Hiron), 167–68, 249

Cable, Mildred, 106
Cardwell, Bernice, 142
Carey, William, 66–67, 79, 129n, 187n
Carlton Baptist, Sydney, 53
Carthew, Louise (Genat), 180–81, 249
Casino Baptist, NSW, 21
Castlemaine Baptist, Victoria, 45
Chambers, Emily, 61, 249
Chapman, Elizabeth, 78, 249
Chapman, Samuel Rev., 57, 191
Chapman, Sarah Ann (Bradshaw), 21, 57, 249
China Inland Mission, 44, 61, 67, 69, 75, 77, 78, 81–82, 85, 86, 88, 89, 90, 91, 104, 109, 117, 208, 219
Christian Endeavor, 5, 11, 14, 18, 21, 23, 34, 38, 79, 99, 113, 149, 169, 170, 179–84, 185, 193, 198, 204, 236, 240, 242
Church, Isabel (Higlett), 133, 142, 143, 144, 249
Churchward Kelly, Stella, 56, 79, 85, 87n, 88n, 93, 94, 97–99, 109, 130, 173, 249
Churchward Kelly, Thomas Rev., 56, 75, 97, 99, 130
Churchward, Verna (also Slater), 75, 249
Clark, Francis Rev., 179, 183
Clark, Henry Rev., 27
Clark, Mahala (Beaumont), 184, 249
Clayfield Baptist, Queensland, 43
Clifford, Harriett (birth surname unknown), 167
Clifton Hill Baptist, Victoria, 202n
Coates, Rhoda (Peate), 21, 249
Coburg Baptist, Victoria, 41
Collins Street Baptist, Melbourne, 21, 34, 46, 57, 85, 152, 191, 220, 223, 231
Collins, Gladys, 56n, 64, 85, 249
Collins, Retta (Long), 29n, 205n, 249
Cook, Rose Terry, 25

Cooper, Bertha (Bostock), 51, 249
Cooper, Gladys, 148, 249
Cordiner, Ellen May (Howden), 4, 189, 249
Cousin Flora, 189, 245
Cousin Joyce, 189–90, 245
Cousin, Helen, 64, 67, 95, 96, 97, 102n, 143n, 146, 250
Cousin, Margaret (Nicol), 36, 250
Crofts, Gwenyth (Harry), 8n, 23n, 62, 65n, 79, 85, 86, 90–91, 93, 103, 106n, 107–9, 250
Crofts, Mary (Bray), 22, 250
Crofts, Wilfred Rev., 62, 94
Cronou, Ethel (Cross), 59, 250
Crosby, Fanny 197
Cross, Vera (Bavinton), 96, 250
Crump, Clara, 31, 161, 250
Cumming, Elsie (Tranter), 23, 229, 250

Davey, Susan (Morton), 53, 92n, 93n, 94, 143, 178, 189, 250
Davies, Eliza (Arbuckle), 203, 250
Davies, Ella (Godbold), 56–57, 77, 86, 109, 208, 250
Davis, Ada, 21, 250
Davis, Addie Rev. 157–58
Deakin, Elsie, 229, 250
Deane, John Rev., 146
Devonport Baptist, 130
Dixon, Mary Janie (Bell), 160, 250
Dixson, Emma (Shaw), 32, 120–21, 166, 250
Dixson, Helen (Craig), 30, 250
Dixson, Hugh, 30
Dobbinson, Richard Rev., 159
Dobie, Janet (McFadzean), 22, 251
Doery, Ada, 64, 78, 251
Doery, George Rev., 39
Dorcas Society/ies, 45–46, 51
Dorman, Mary (Freeman), 231, 251
Dorse, Edith (Marsh), 40, 251
Doust, Irene, 162, 251
Dovey, Elizabeth (Witsed), 146, 178, 193, 197, 251
Downes, Marion, xi, 26, 191–92, 193n, 251

Index

Downing, Cecilia (Hopkins), 29, 37, 44n, 58, 147–48, 163, 178, 186, 212–13, 251
Doyle, Marion (Bell), 185, 251
Driver, Annie (Newcombe), 82, 85, 102, 251
Driver, Harry Rev., 82
Drummond, Heather, 162, 251
Dulwich Hill Baptist, Sydney, 50, 53
Dunkley, Frederick Rev., 190, 194
Dunkley, Jessie (Chidley), 194, 251

Eden Valley Baptist, SA, 45
Ellem, Janet, 77, 90, 251
Ellis, Ethel (Whittle), 52, 251
Embery, Ethel (Potter), 77, 81–82n, 251
Embery, Winifred, 77, 85, 252
English, Florence, 134–35, 252
Eustace, Arthur Rev. 176
Eustace, Elizabeth (Downes), 176–77, 252
Evans, Elsie, 71, 252
Evans, Ephraim Rev., 191
Evans, Ethel, 71, 252
Evans, Matilda (Congreve), 52, 59, 184, 191–92, 252

"Felicity," 190, 245
Field, Rebecca (Chivers), 8, 252
Fildes, Grace (Rogers), 41, 252
Findlay, Margaret, 131, 135, 252
Finlayson, Helen (Harvey), 33, 76, 203, 252
Finlayson, William, 33, 76, 203
Fitzroy Baptist, Melbourne, 39
Fleming, Lorna (MacColl), 78, 252
Flinders Street Baptist, Adelaide, 5, 14, 38, 39, 42, 46, 127, 180, 194, 221
Foucar, Mary (Pigott), 127, 183, 252
Fowler, James, 30n
Franc, Maud Jeanne, see Evans, Matilda (Congreve)
Francis, Laura, 165
Fraser, Elsie 231, 252
Fraser, Jane (Ikin), 35, 252
Freeth, Florence, 173
Froome, Dora (Deacon), 229, 252
Fry, Hannah (Robins), 72–73, 191, 252

Fuller, Marion, 74, 123, 253
Fuller, Myra (Norman), 29, 41, 253

Garland, Annie, 88, 253
Garland, Susie, 88, 253
Garrett, Alice (McNair), 49, 253
Gates, Edith Rev., 156
Gibbs, Harriet (Cox), 34, 253
Gibson, Mary (Blackler), 30, 31, 124, 253
Gibson, William, 31
Gilbert, Jeanie (Davie), 51, 253
Gilbert, Marie, 67, 72, 74, 79–80, 253
Gillings, Harriet (Jones), 34–35, 185–86, 253
Gilmour, Annie (Welbourn), 1, 253
Gladwin, Ruth, 162, 253
Glasson, Linda (Addison), 226, 253
Glassop, Matilda (Pontifex), 34, 253
Glen Osmond Baptist, SA, 47, 49
Goldsack, William Rev., 64n
Gomm, Leslie Rev., 197n
Good, Irene, 226–27, 254
Goode, Helen (Smith), 32, 51–52, 59, 220, 254
Goode, Mary (Good), 184, 254
Gooden, Elizabeth (Jones), 135, 254
Goodman, Ruth (Arblaster), 136, 254
Goodwood Baptist, SA, 47
Gould, George Pearce Dr, 156–57
Goulburn Baptist, NSW, 40
Gowans, Margaret (Bell), 136, 254
Grace, Allan Rev., 94
Grace, Daisy (Boyden), 88n, 99n, 254
Grace, Ellen, 230, 254
Grange Baptist, SA, 49
Green, Annie, 176–77, 220, 254
Greening, Bessie (Ellis), 32, 254
Greenslopes Baptist, Queensland, 37, 169
Greenwood, James, 25–26
Griffith Baptist, NSW, 37
Griffiths, Emily, 189n, 254
Grimes, Annie Laura, 32, 136, 254
Grimes, Louise, 132, 254
Grimes, Mary (Dawson), 72n, 85, 254
Gunn, Aeneas, 192
Gunn, Jeannie (Taylor), 192, 254

Index

Haberfield Baptist, Sydney 53, 143
Hale, Edna, 68n, 91, 142, 254
Hale, Ellen (Boundy), 52, 255
Hale, Nancy (Wadey), 52, 255
Hall, Caroline (Brown), 125–26, 255
Hall, Edith (Elyea), 173, 255
Hampson, Margaret (Spencer), 172
Hancey, Jessie (Burnell), 197, 255
Hann, Sarah (Staple), 126, 255
Harlen, Sarah (Warren), 189, 255
Harris, Bertha, 64, 85, 100, 109n, 188, 255
Harris, Edward Rev., 30, 188
Harris, Ellen, 175–76, 255
Harris, Florence, 64, 80, 90, 92, 94, 95–96, 97n, 103, 134n, 255
Harris, Mary Amelia, 226, 255
Harris, Ruth (Pearson), 188, 255
Harrison, Maria (Wilkins), 127, 255
Harrison, Martha (Kelly), 21, 255
Harrison, Sarah (Phelan), 59, 255
Harry, Frederick Rev., 26
Harry, Helen (Hibberd), 25n, 182–83, 189, 208, 228, 255
Harry, Jean, 78, 80, 84n, 86, 255
Hawkyard, Alice (Callister), 89n, 255
Hayden, (Unknown first name), 162, 256
Haynes, Karen Rev., 155
Hedger, Violet Rev., 156–57
Hendry, Marjorie (Holland), 183, 256
Henson, Roy Rev., 96
Hercus, Margaret (Macky), 133, 256
Hibberd, Isabel (Dixson), 122, 256
Hickson, Grace, 71, 256
Higlett, Lily (Low), 21, 53, 84n, 113, 133, 136, 142–46, 178, 238, 256
Higlett, William Rev., 142, 143, 144, 146
Hill, Elfrida, 85, 256
Hinton, Louisa (Simpson), 8n, 64, 77, 85, 90n, 256
Hobart Baptist, Tasmania, 23–24, 45
Hodgson, Florence (Hartley), 256
Hodgson, Nola (Hodgkinson), 85, 256
Hogan, Florence, 128, 171, 172, 256
Hogben, Janet, 80, 87, 256
Holden, Mary (Phillips), 222, 256
Hone, Emily (Sandland), 58, 155, 193, 212–13, 256

Hone, Frank Dr, 42
Hope, Laura Dr (Fowler), 88, 229, 256
Hornsby Baptist, Sydney, 40, 92
Horsfall, Vera, 19, 257
Horwood, Florence, 134, 257
Howard, Alan Rev., 58
Howard, Daisy, 61, 257
Howard, Thelma (Tulk), 55, 58, 181, 257
Hughes, H. Escourt Rev., 11, 151, 175
Hughes, Hugh, 163, 165
Hurlstone Park Baptist, Sydney, 36, 43, 50–54, 135, 223, 230, 236–37
Hurst, William Rev., 160
Hutson, A, 183, 257

Ingram, May (Malyon), 28, 257
Ingram, Richard, 28
Ingram, Winifred, 38, 257
Ings, Robert Rev., 8

Jaggers, Lawrence Rev., 21
Janes, Isabella Adey, 156, 176, 257
Jarrett, Bertha, 166–67, 197, 257
Jenkin, Edmund, 174
Jenkin, Margaret (Hudson), 223, 257
Jireh Baptist, Brisbane, 50–54, 236–37
Johnston, Margaret (Kirkcaldy) 215
Johnston, Thomas, 215
Joyce, Elsie (Spicer), 239
Joyce, Gladys, 231, 257

Keik, Winifred Rev., 158
Kekwick, Adelaide (Owens), 51, 257
Keller, Helen, 197
Kemp, Georgiana, 71, 81
Kennedy, Ada (Greenslade), 56, 58, 176, 178, 205–6, 257
Kennedy, William Rev., 58
Kennett, Annie (Daniell), 49, 257
Kentish, Dorothy, 220, 257
Kenton Baptist, SA, 40
Kerr, Edith (Barnes), 219, 257
Kiddell, Agnes (Pearce), 74, 85, 95, 257
King, Ada (Blackwell), 126, 257
King, Edith, 64, 83, 86, 94, 97–99, 125–26, 258
Knight, Bertha (Collings), 219, 258
Knightsbridge Baptist, SA, 5, 41

Koehncke, Eleanor, 170, 180, 258
Kruegar, Carl Rev., 24
Krueger, Johanna (Lobegeier), 24, 258

Lake, Serena (Thorne), 178
Lamb, Minnie, 64, 68, 258
Lamb, Susan Mary, 170, 221, 230, 258
Lambton Baptist, NSW, 34
Lane, L. Alice, 4, 258
Lanyon, Emily (unknown birth surname), 26, 258
Launceston (York St) Baptist, Tasmania, 39–40, 162, 170, 221, 230
Lavis, Lucy (Cooper), 220, 221–22, 258
Lavis, Robert, 221–22
Lawton, James, 133
Lawton, Ruth (Hall), 132–33, 258
Leeder, Hermine (te Kloot), 59, 258
Lewis, Gladys (Scowen), 42, 187, 258
Lewis, Marianne (Gould), 70, 120
Liddy, Sarah May, 90, 258
Lismore Baptist, NSW, 44, 206
Lister, Elizabeth (Chappel), 6, 258
Living-Taylor, John Rev., 156
Living-Taylor, Maria Rev., 156
Lloyd, Lorna (Dunkley), 190, 258
Long, Arnold, 205n
Long, Edgerton Rev., 205
Long, Leonard, 205
Long, Margaret (Dixon), 181, 202, 204–5, 207, 258
Long, Olive, 205n, 258
Low, Fredrike (Hafner), 143, 259
Low, John, 143
Lowe, Elsa, 162, 259
Lucas, Annie (Farmilo), 68, 81–82n, 259
Lumb, Harriett (unknown birth surname), 48, 259

Mackay, Enid (Elphinston), 35, 259
Mallee District Baptist, Victoria, 39
Malyon, Esther, 181–82, 183, 259
Marsh, Edna, 116, 259
Marshman, Hannah, 69–70
Marshman, Joshua, 69
Martin, Elsie, 181–82, 259
Martin, Hannah (Barber), 46, 119–20, 123–24, 259

Martin, James Rev., 46
Martin, John Rev., 131
Maryborough Baptist, Queensland, 160
Mason, Elizabeth, 51, 259
Masters, Ethel (Addison), 226, 259
McCullough, Eva (Richardson), 57, 259
McDowell, Ruth (Nesbit), 177
McGregor, Lorna, 64, 77, 86, 259
McKaeg, John Rev., 32
McKie, Marion (Chapman), 89, 259
McLaren, Joanna (unknown birth surname), 51, 259
McLean, Ethel, 215, 259
McLean, Eva, 226, 259
McLean, Hilda, 79, 80, 86, 91, 97, 215, 226, 260
McLean, Lucie, 215, 260
McLean, Margaret (Arnot), 178, 202, 210–11, 212, 213, 214–18, 226, 234, 238, 241, 260
McLean, William, 215
Mead, Alice (Pappin), 8n, 23n, 77, 93, 108, 109, 260
Mead, Ann (Staple), 184, 260
Mead, Cecil Dr, 125–26, 180
Mead, Dorothy, 108, 133, 260
Mead, Gertrude Dr, 174n, 224, 260
Mead, Marjory, 42n, 260
Mead, Silas Rev., 47, 125, 180
Meares, Ina (Trudinger), 78, 260
Mellor, Emma (Adams), 260
Mellor, Jane (Neill), 51, 260
Mellor, Jessie (Thomson), 37, 260
Middleton, Elizabeth (London), 55, 260
Middleton, Jane (Wilson), 180, 260
Mildwaters, Elizabeth (Lewis), 29–30, 260
Miles, Frederick Rev., 56, 229
Miles, Isabella (unknown birth surname), 56, 140n, 151, 185n, 227, 229, 260
Mimosa Baptist, NSW, 171
Mirfin, Hepzibah (Chambers), 52, 219, 261
Moody, Mary (Packer), 51, 261
Morling, Annie (Hillman), 20, 261
Morling, George Rev., 30, 162n
Morphett Vale Baptist, SA, 45

Index

Morphett, Minnie, 95–96, 261
Mortdale Baptist, Sydney, 41
Mott, John, 79
Mount Barker Baptist, SA, 40
Mount Cooper Circuit, see Port Kenny Baptist, SA
Moyle, Margaret (Rees), 216, 218, 261
Mungomery, Ruth, 133, 134, 261
Murgon Baptist, Queensland, 205
Murwillumbah, NSW, 58
Mursell, James Rev., 126
Mursell, Jeannie (Lockhart), 43, 126, 261
Munroe, Marita Rev. Dr, 155
Meyers, Frederick, 163

Nall, Annie (Swadling), 136, 261
Neill, Catherine (Neill), 51, 220, 261
Nelson, May (Dribden), 59, 261
Neville, Ruth (Wilkin), 123, 261
New Zealand Baptist Missionary Society, 73, 75
Newcombe, Ethel (Forrester), 68, 261
Newmarket Baptist, Melbourne, 39
Nicholls, Halley (White), 40, 261
North Adelaide Baptist, SA, 25, 37, 50–54, 212, 236–37
Norwood Baptist, Adelaide, 14, 21, 41, 48
Norwood, Frederick Rev., 37

Oliver, Annie (Wilkinson), 32, 261
Ollif, Lorna (Box), 24, 230–31, 232, 261

Palm Island Baptist, Queensland, 206
Palmer, Anne (Smith), 208, 262
Palmer, Ethel, 43, 262
Palmer, Joseph, 208
Paqualin, Louisa, 200n, 262
Parker, Thora (Jenkins), 94–95, 173, 262
Partridge, Sybil, 197
Parramatta Baptist, Sydney
Patterson, Elsie, 229
Pennant Hills Baptist, Sydney, 29, 41
Penno, Edith (Norton), 28, 262
Perrin, Kath, 64, 96–97, 262
Perth Central Baptist, 181, 228
Petersham Baptist, Sydney, 43, 96
Pflaum, Mary (Criel), 229, 262

Phelps, Rachael (Adkin), 32, 262
Phillips, Catherine (Read), 59, 166, 236, 262
Pigott, Ellen (Giles), 70, 262
Piggot, Henry Rev., 70
Pike, Douglas, 91
Pike, Louisa (Boulter), 88, 91, 109, 262
Playford, Mary Jane (Kinsman), 7, 262
Plested, Martha, 91, 97, 150n, 262
Pocknall, Emily, 167, 169, 262
Pocknall, Irene, 179
Poona and Indian Village Mission, 61, 69, 75–76, 77, 85, 88, 92–93, 168
Pope, Mary (Lord) 96, 138–39, 193, 226–27, 242–43, 263
Port Kenny Baptist, SA, 128, 171
Port Pirie Baptist, SA, 38
Press, Margaret, 31
Price, Emily, 29, 53, 202, 212–13, 263
Proctor, Catherine (McFaddyen), 22, 263

Randall, Eliza, 184, 263
Raws, Alec, 228
Raws, Mary Jane (Lennon), 228–29, 263
Redland Bay Baptist, Queensland, 40
Redman, Jess, 65, 76n, 79–80, 84n, 85, 86n, 87n, 88n, 90, 100n, 126n, 263
Redshaw, Lillian (Brittain), 173, 263
Rees, Elizabeth (Johnston), 147, 238, 214–18, 238, 263
Rees, Evan, 215
Reeve, Charles Rev., 75
Reeves, Ada (unknown birth surname), 21, 263
Reid, Elizabeth (Pitty), 81–82n, 122, 263
Ringwood Baptist, Victoria, 173
Robinson, Henry Wheeler Dr, 157
Rogers, Doris (Prest), 96, 263
Rooke, Deborah Dr, 157
Rose, Katherine, 156
Rose, Elizabeth (Martin), 48, 263

Sale, Elizabeth (Geale), 70
Sandringham Baptist, Victoria, 173
Scott, Marion (Dawbarn), 230, 263
Selby, Grace (Allanby), 77, 263

Senior Girls' Missionary Union (state and national), 119, 129–37, 140–41, 146, 148–49, 153
Seymour, Iris, 80, 102, 263
Sharp, Sarah (Hanna), 7, 40, 224, 264
Shaw, Mary (unknown birth surname), 46, 264
Shepard, Ella, 226, 264
Shepard, Ellen (Herbert), 116, 264
Shipton, Anna, 61n
Shoults, Mary (Monro), 40, 264
Simmons, Kathleen, 206, 264
Simpson, Edith (unknown birth surname), 1, 264
Sims, Florence, 161–62
Skeels, Alice, 170, 171–72, 219, 264
Slinn, Lillias (McLeod), 167, 264
Small, Florence (Hudson), 162, 264
Smith, (unknown first name), 40, 264
Smith, Alice, 192, 264
Smith, Augusta (Wearing), 52, 264
Smith, Elsie (Tudball), 264
Smith, Emily, 37, 169, 172, 243n, 264
Smith, Ruth (Loft), 19, 149, 265
Smith, Winifred (Filby), 223, 265
Sorrell, Isabella, 52, 265
Soundy, Lily, 81–82n, 83, 265
Southwark Baptist, SA, 42, 177
Speck, Margaret (Sinclair), 128, 170, 182, 265
Spence, Catherine, 158
Spurr, Ethel (Thompson), 23, 265
Spurr, Frederic Rev., 23, 30
Stafford, Stella (Harris), 23, 188, 265
Stanmore Baptist, Sydney, 38, 48, 77, 162, 166–67
Stark, Ella (Duncan), 173, 265
Stark, Eva (Richards) 167, 265
Steed, Emma (Moulding), 139, 265
Steel, Caroline (Jones), 181, 265
Steel, Percy, 129
Steel, Victoria (Alves), 129, 265
Stephen, Mabel (Duthie), 117, 265
Stratton, Grace, 197
Stribling, Myrtle (Rogerson), 128, 171–72, 265
Stroud Baptist, NSW, 40
Stuckley, Julia, 182

Sturgess, Adeline, 137, 265
Sturgess, Elizabeth (Farquhar), 189, 265
Sudan Inland Mission, 88
Sudan United Mission, 78
Summers, Anne (Hearne), 180, 265
Summers, Arthur Rev., 105
Sutton, Ellen (Gresswell), 206, 266
Sutton, Elsie (Luke), 96, 266
Swan, Christina (Mackay), 22, 34, 266
Swan, James, 34

Tapson, Ada, 180, 266
Tayler, Phoebe (Jones), 58, 266
Tayler, William Rev. 58
Taylor, Anna (Lush), 192, 266
Taylor, Grace, 44n, 113, 122, 189n, 266
Taylor, Hudson, 75
Taylor, Margaret (Morgan), 122, 266
Taylor, Rose, 229, 266
Taylor, Thomas, 192
Telfer, Caroline (Masters), 191, 266
Temora Baptist, NSW, 171
Thomas, Minnie (Janes), 176, 266
Thompson, Lucie (Kealley), 83, 109, 174n, 266
Thomson, Grace, 80, 109, 134, 266
Thomson, Martha (Brake), 226, 266
Tinsley, Mildred (White), 48, 183, 266
Tomkins, Gladys, 205, 266
Tomkinson, Freda (Eipper), 43, 266
Townsend, Ethel, 56
Townsville Baptist, Queensland, 206
Tranter, A. Marion, 2, 43, 191, 228, 266
Traralgon Baptist, Victoria, 40, 171
Trestrail, Ellen (Trenwith), 32, 267
Trudinger, Gertrude, 78, 267
Tuck, Bertha, 60, 64, 68, 97, 174n, 180, 267
Tyas, Rosa Ann (Bradshaw), 48, 267

United Aborigines [sic] Mission, 204, 206–7

Vandeau, Lillian (Dowling), 74, 83, 116, 124–25, 267
Varley, Eleanor, Dr, 88, 138, 224, 267
Varley, Ethel, 88, 267
Venn, Esma (Durbin), 23, 181, 267

Index

Venn, Henry, 103
Vernon, Margaret, 156, 169, 170, 177, 267

Wain, Myrtle (Joyce), 231, 267
Waldock, Arthur Rev., 26
Waldock, Charlotte (Godfrey), 137, 267
Walker, Eleanor, 74–75, 267
Walters, Eliza (Rollo), 28–29, 267
Walton, Hannah (Taylor), 21, 267
Ware, Mary (Brooks), 32–33, 267
Warne, Harriett, 172
Warner, Elsa (Smith), 149, 267
Warner, Jessie, 67, 81–82n, 267
Warracknabeal Baptist, Victoria, 171
Warren, Charlotte (Soltau), 81, 83, 268
Warren, Mary Ann (Goddard), 189, 268
Warren, William Dr, 81
Warwick Baptist, Queensland, 55
Watson, Elsie (May), 79, 268
Watson, Mary (Smith), 49, 268
Webb, Allan Rev., 30, 123–24
Webb, Eliza (Marsh), 35, 268
Webb, Janet (Underwood), 189, 268
Welch, Dulcie, 197, 230–31, 268
Wellington Baptist, NSW, 154, 167
Wells, Mary, 38, 208, 268
West Melbourne Baptist, Victoria, 47
Whale, Sarah (Latchford), 21, 268
Whale, William, 105
Whalley, Elizabeth (Harris), 188, 268
Wharf Street Baptist, Brisbane, 24, 44, 50, 180
Wheeler, Amelia (England), 184, 268
Whitbourn, Christina, 31n, 57, 268
White, Anna (King), 48, 181, 182–83, 230, 268
White, Annie, 43, 268
White, Isabella (Geggie), 53, 268
White, Lillian (Wenban), 93, 268
White, Marion (Holmes), 133n, 187, 226, 268
White, Victor Rev., 93, 94

Whittle, Annie (Harry), 49, 52, 268
Whittle, Julia (Kutcher), 51, 52, 268
Whyalla Baptist, SA, 170–71
Wilcox, Edith (Blackham), 23n, 44n, 46n, 55n, 57, 127n, 128, 133, 137, 139, 147n, 151n, 152, 158n, 163, 170n, 173n, 178, 195n, 221n, 269
Wilkin, Frederick Rev., 10, 65n
Wilkins, Lillian (Williams), 167, 269
Wilkins, Matilda (Bready), 229, 269
Wilkins, Rebecca Charlotte, 132, 269
Wilkins, Ruth, 138, 269
Williams, Arthur, 228–29
Williams, Constance, 64, 85, 102, 269
Williams, Elizabeth, 71, 76n, 92, 269
Williams, Hilda, 228, 269
Williams, Louisa (Waters), 228–29, 269
Wilson, Blanche (Mead), 126, 180, 181, 183, 269
Wilson, Evelyn, 229, 269
Woman's Christian Temperance Union (WCTU), 14, 18, 23, 31, 127, 169, 177, 178, 185, 193, 201, 202, 209–18, 219, 226, 234, 236, 237, 238, 239, 240, 241, 242
Women's Auxiliary of the Baptist Union of East Bengal, 100
Wood, Elizabeth (Childs), 6, 56, 269
Wood, Harry Rev., 56
Woodall, Doris (Lewis), 44, 269
Wooster Greaves, Lilian, 191, 193, 197, 269

Yarrow, Mary (Tupling), 48, 269
Yorkston, Annie (Bailey), 230, 269
Young Men's Christian Association (YMCA), 96
Young Men's Missionary League (NSW), 140–41
Young Women's Christian Association (YWCA), 5, 201, 219–20
Yule, Florence, 230, 269